Economic Growth and Environmental Regulation

T0300155

This volume assembles a group of eminent scholars to look at the problem of growth and environment from the perspective of environmental regulation. The questions addressed are: How does economic growth interact with regulation, and what are the best approaches to regulation in use today?

The context for the volume is the current situation in China, where twenty years of rapid growth have created a situation in which there are both demands for environmental regulation and needs for choosing a future development path. The advent of "A Macro-Environmental Strategy" for China presents an opportunity to ask how and why China should introduce regulation into its management of its development. The volume includes contributions from leading Chinese experts and established environmental economists from other countries, including Timo Goeschl, Ben Groom and Andreas Kontoleon.

The volume looks at both the demand side of environmental regulation and the supply side. The demand side of regulatory intervention examines how regulation operates to supplement existing resource-allocation mechanisms, via effective demand aggregation and implementation mechanisms. The supply side of regulation examines how regulation operates to guide industrial growth down particular pathways, in the pursuit of managed development. Both sides of environmental regulation involve the important issue of implementation and enforcement.

This volume will be of most value to academics and scholars of environmental economics, growth economics, the Chinese economy and policy-makers of environmental regulations.

Tun Lin is a Natural Resources Economist at the Asian Development Bank, focusing on issues dealing with China's growth and development. He took his PhD at Cambridge University, focusing on issues dealing with environmental regulation and enforcement. **Timothy Swanson** is Chair of Law and Economics at University College London. He has worked on issues dealing with regulation and growth in China for more than fifteen years, and has examined issues dealing with regulation across many industries and many parts of the world.

Routledge explorations in environmental economics
Edited by Nick Hanley
University of Stirling, UK

Economic Growth and Environmental Regulation

The People's Republic of China's path to a brighter future

Edited by Tun Lin and Timothy Swanson

Routledge
Taylor & Francis Group

LONDON AND NEW YORK

First published 2010
by Routledge
2 Park Square, Milton Park, Abingdon, Oxon OX14 4RN

Simultaneously published in the USA and Canada
by Routledge
711 Third Avenue, New York, NY 10017

Routledge is an imprint of the Taylor & Francis Group, an informa business

© 2010 Tun Lin and Timothy Swanson
Typeset in Times by Wearset Ltd, Boldon, Tyne and Wear

6 ADB Avenue, Mandaluyong City
1550 Metro Manila, Philippines
Tel: +63 2 632 4444
Fax: +63 2 636 2444
www.adb.org

British Library Cataloguing in Publication Data
A catalogue record for this book is available from the British Library

Library of Congress Cataloging in Publication Data
Economic growth and environmental regulation: China's path to a brighter future/[edited by] Timothy Swanson and Tun Lin.
p. cm. – (Routledge explorations in environmental economics; 20)
1. Environmental policy–China. 2. Economic development–Environmental aspects–China. 3. China–Economic policy. I. Swanson, Timothy M. II. Lin, Tun.
HC430.E5E34 2009
333.70951–dc22   2009014545

ISBN10: 0-415-55127-7 (hbk)
ISBN10: 0-203-86872-2 (ebk)

ISBN13: 978-0-415-55127-4 (hbk)
ISBN13: 978-0-203-86872-0 (ebk)
ISBN13: 978-0-415-53984-5 (pbk)

Contents

Figures

Tables

Contributors

Shuming An is a lecturer in the Environmental School of Renmin University.

Keyong Dong is a professor and the dean of the Public Administration School of Renmin University.

Jixi Gao is a director of the Institute of Environment Ecology within the Chinese Research Academy of Environmental Sciences. He specializes in ecosystem management and sustainable development in the PRC.

Timo Goeschl holds the Chair in Environmental Economics at Heidelberg University. He has published numerous articles on issues dealing with environmental regulation, crime, sanctions and enforcement.

Ben Groom is a lecturer in economics at the University of London, School of Oriental and African Studies. He specializes in the economics of managing water resources in developing countries, and has undertaken substantial work on the management of water in the PRC and in Africa.

Yongwei Han is a researcher at the Institute of Environment Ecology within the Chinese Research Academy of Environmental Sciences.

Jiming Hao is a member of the Chinese Academy of Engineering and the dean of the Institute of Environmental Science and Engineering at Tsinghua University. He received his PhD in Environmental Engineering from the University of Cincinnati in 1984. His research interests include air pollution control, regional and global environmental issues, and sustainable development.

Yi Jiang is an economist at the Asian Development Bank (ADB). His research interests include public economics, environmental economics and development economics. He earned his PhD in Economics from the University of Maryland, College Park.

Andreas Kontoleon is a lecturer in economics at the University of Cambridge, Department of Land Economy. He specializes in the economics of environmental policy, with special emphasis on biological and wildlife resources. He is an expert on the management of wildlife and ecosystems in the PRC, having commenced work on the panda reserves more than ten years ago.

Shaun Larcom is a research student at the Faculty of Law and Department of Economics, University College London.

Wenzhao Li is a professor in the Public Administration School of Renmin University.

Tun Lin is a natural resources economist at the ADB, specializing on issues dealing with the PRC's growth and development. He took his PhD at Cambridge University, focusing on issues relating to environmental regulation and enforcement.

Zhong Ma is a professor and vice-dean of the Environmental School of Renmin University.

Wei Meng is a professor, doctoral advisor and the dean of the Chinese Research Academy of Environmental Sciences. He specializes in environmental watershed management and long-term stratagem for environmental management in the PRC.

Xiaofei Pei is an associate director at the Political Economy Research Centre within the PRC's Ministry of Environmental Protection. He is responsible for developing the Centre's approach to growth and development in environmental regulation.

James Salzman is a professor of law and of environmental policy at Duke Law School. He has worked previously in London and at the Organization for Economic Co-operation and Development, and is a specialist on the issues dealing with best practices in environmental policy and regulation across the world.

Timothy Swanson holds the Chair in Law and Economics at University College London. He has worked on issues dealing with regulation and growth in the PRC for more than 15 years, and has examined issues dealing with regulation across many industries and many parts of the world.

Haakon Vennemo is a director of ECON, Norway, and has long been involved in developing air management and control practices in the PRC. His experiences with environmental management in the PRC date back nearly 15 years and he is involved in aiding the PRC's policy-makers and practitioners in many investigations.

Shuxiao Wang is an associate professor at the Institute of Environmental Science and Enginnering at Tsinghua University.

Beidou Xi is a professor and vice-director of the Laboratory of the Water Environmental System Engineering within the Chinese Research Academy of Environmental Sciences. He is proficient in water resources management and environmental system engineering.

Guang Xia is a director of the Political Economy Research Centre within the PRC's Ministry of Environmental Protection. He is an expert on the regulation of environment in the PRC, and on the country's economic growth and development.

Xiaoming Yang is a researcher at the Political Economy Research Centre within the Ministry of Environmental Protection.

Juzhong Zhuang is an assistant chief economist at the ADB. His recent research works cover issues related to economic growth, income distribution and the economics of climate change. He obtained his PhD in economics from Manchester University.

Foreword

The 30 years of remarkable economic growth in the People's Republic of China (PRC) have spawned growing demands for a better environment. This has driven policy makers to design a national development path that not only protects the environment, but also reverses environmental degradation while maintaining strong economic growth.

While the PRC's economy grew faster than those of the rest of the world, the country became more polluted, less ecologically diverse and more environmentally vulnerable. Prevalent water and air pollution, water scarcity, land degradation and climate change are among the growing and diverse environmental challenges currently faced by the PRC.

Recognizing the shortcomings of the previous economic growth-oriented development strategies, the PRC government has adopted a new focus for its national strategic plans. The eleventh Five-Year Plan (FYP), for 2006–10, described how the PRC government intends to address its development problems by achieving a better balance between economic growth and environmental protection. Various indicators of progress were identified in the eleventh FYP, each with qualitative and quantitative targets to be achieved by 2010. These included, for example, reducing pollution by 10 percent and energy intensity by 20 percent. In the forthcoming twelfth FYP, the PRC government will need to recognize that, to manage scarce natural resources and protect the country's environment more effectively, it will have to establish supporting regulations aimed at promoting environmentally sustainable development as well as inclusive growth.

In response to the rapid economic growth in the PRC and elsewhere in the Asia-Pacific region, as well as to the significant shifts in the development, aid and financial landscape, the Asian Development Bank (ADB) has adopted a new long-term strategic framework – *Strategy 2020: The Long-Term Strategic Framework of the Asian Development Bank (2008–2020)*. Strategy 2020 reaffirms the ADB's vision of "an Asia and Pacific free of poverty" and its mission "to help its developing member countries improve their living conditions and quality of life." Environmental sustainability is one of the crosscutting themes of Strategy 2020, along with a developmental agenda for inclusive economic growth and regional integration.

To contribute to the PRC's quest for sustainable development characterized by a balance of economic growth, environmental protection and energy conservation, the ADB in November 2007 approved the technical assistance for the PRC on the *National Strategies for Environmental Management and Energy Conservation.* This publication presents the outcome of the study conducted under the technical assistance project. A group of eminent scholars were invited to examine the role of environmental regulation in solving the problems of rapidly developing economies, with a special emphasis on the PRC. Specifically, this publication presents the analyses gathered from international experiences and the lessons learned from developed countries regarding (i) the balancing of economic growth and environmental protection; (ii) environmental management of air, water, and ecosystems; and (iii) environmental policies and institutions. The purpose is to shed light on how the PRC could strengthen its institutional capacity, legal framework, and market mechanism for environmental protection. There are also specific recommendations on environmental management for the PRC government to consider.

This publication has been greatly facilitated by the support of the Ministry of Environmental Protection of the PRC, and should prove useful to researchers and policy makers in the PRC, as well as in other developing countries. We hope you will find that it provides a fresh look at familiar issues – and sheds new light on the way forward.

Klaus Gerhaeusser
Director General, East Asia Department
Asian Development Bank

Preface

Tun Lin and Timothy Swanson

This volume assembles works of a group of eminent scholars to look at the problem of growth and environment from the perspective of environmental regulation. The questions addressed are: how does economic growth interact with regulation, and what are the best approaches to regulation in use today?

The context for the volume is the current situation in the PRC, where 30 years of rapid growth have created a situation in which there are both demands for environmental regulation and the need to choose a future development path. The advent of "A Macro-Environmental Strategy" for the PRC presents an opportunity to ask how and why the country should introduce regulation into the management of its development.

The volume looks at both the demand side of environmental regulation and the supply side. The demand side of regulatory intervention examines how regulation operates to supplement existing resource allocation mechanisms, via effective demand aggregation and implementation mechanisms. The supply side of regulation examines how regulation operates to guide industrial growth down particular pathways, in the pursuit of managed development. Both sides of the environmental regulation involve the important issues of implementation and enforcement.

The volume consists of four parts. Part I examines the general questions of growth and regulation and introduces the case study of the PRC and its issues of environmental degradation. Part II examines the PRC's experiences with growth and environmental regulation, setting the scene in the sectors of air, water, and ecosystems. Part III sets out the relationships between growth and regulation, giving international "best practices" in various sectors concerned with environmental regulation and management. Part IV examines the institutional environment in the PRC, looking at both its current institutional context and also the sorts of reforms that are suggested for moving toward the international "best practices" in environmental regulation.

Overall, the volume is an attempt to examine the role of environmental regulation as a means for solving existing problems and creating better futures in rapidly developing economies.

We would like to thank the Asian Development Bank for its sponsorship of this work, and the Ministry of Environmental Protection, PRC, for hosting the workshops and the program. We need to thank Liu Xiaoying for her contribution in organizing the workshops and aiding communications, especially in the final weeks. Shaun Larcom and Nick Swanson provided research assistance to the project. The Routledge staff provided competent and professional support through the editorial process. Finally, we are all grateful for the assistance, support and oversight provided by many ADB colleagues in the undertaking of the project, especially Trisa Camacho, Joy Quitazol-Gonzalez, Kunhamboo Kannan and Qingfeng Zhang.

1 Economic growth and environmental regulation in the People's Republic of China

Introduction to the volume

Tun Lin and Timothy Swanson

An overview of the People's Republic of China's growth and environmental quality

The transformation of the People's Republic of China (PRC) over the last 30 years from a closed agricultural economy to what it is today – i.e. the world's third largest economy, after the United States and Japan – has not only materially enriched the country's population to varying degrees, but has also brought about environmental degradation. The environmental challenges confronting the PRC are diverse and growing, and include the following:

1 land degradation;
2 water scarcity and pollution;
3 air pollution;
4 inadequate urban environmental infrastructure;
5 contamination of the rural environment;
6 increasing frequency and intensity of environmental accidents;
7 loss of biodiversity; and
8 global climate change.[1]

The PRC has recognized this legacy of resource depletion and environmental degradation, and is increasingly determined to develop a strategy for addressing these problems. Its initial efforts have focused on cataloguing the range and causes of these problems.

Soil erosion, desertification, deforestation and salinization are among the many manifestations of land degradation in the PRC. More than one-third of the country's land area today, or roughly 3.56 million square kilometers (km²), is eroded, while the desertified area has now reached 2.64 million km² or 27 percent of the national territory. This translates to a desertification rate of more than double that of the period between the 1950s and 2000. Desertification has adversely affected the lives of nearly 400 million people and has brought about an annual direct economic loss of RMB54 billion.[2]

The northern PRC, where 40 percent of the country's total population and 60 percent of the nation's farmlands are found, experiences the most severe water

Table 1.1 Water quality of seven major rivers[3]

Name of river	Water quality level		
	I–III (%)	*IV–V (%)*	*V– (%)*
Yangtze	72.1	18.3	9.6
Yellow	36.4	34.1	29.5
Pearl	78.8	15.1	6.1
Songhua	21.9	53.7	24.4
Huai	19.8	47.6	32.6
Hai	25.4	17.9	56.7
Liao	32.4	29.7	37.9
Overall	**41.8**	**30.3**	**27.9**

Source: State Environmental Protection Agency (SEPA). 2004. *State of the Environment Report.*

scarcity and pollution, having only 20 percent of the PRC's water resources. Of the ten water-short provinces, eight are found in the northern region. About 60 percent of the PRC's 669 cities are experiencing water shortages and about 360 million out of the 800 million farmers do not have access to safe drinking water. The PRC's precious water resources are plagued by pollution. Of the state-monitored bodies of water, only eight out of 28 large lakes meet the level II water quality standard, while 59 percent of the rivers have water quality below level III (see Table 1.1).[4] Meanwhile, 76 out of the 118 large cities in the PRC are experiencing serious ground water pollution.

Hazardous air quality characterizes the areas where almost 70 percent of the total urban population (more than 360 million) lives (see Figure 1.1). Motor vehicles have been found to be the number one source of air pollutants in many large cities, overtaking both industrial and residential sources. Urban areas are mainly polluted by fine particulates, while 218 out of the 530 monitored cities have acid rain precipitation with an annual pH value of 5.6, way below the neutral pH value of seven. Meanwhile, acid deposition caused by sulfur dioxide (SO_2) emissions is prevalent.[5]

The volume of sewage now produced by the PRC's cities, amounting to 36 billion cubic meters annually, has exceeded that from industrial sources since 1999, and has been growing at a yearly rate of 7.7 percent. In 2005, the capacity of secondary sewage treatment facilities is only 37 percent of this volume, while the actual quantity treated was even lower due to inadequate operation of treatment plants and sewage collection systems. Centralized sewage treatment in the 669 cities of the PRC is at 52 percent, with 264 cities having no sewage treatment facilities at all. The main source of chemical oxygen demand (COD) has become urban sewage, overtaking industrial sources. In fact, the PRC has just become the number one generator of municipal solid wastes, surpassing the United States. A large proportion of the municipal solid wastes is not adequately disposed of, with a disposal rate of about 37.19 percent and zero sanitary disposal in 130 cities of the PRC, causing direct or secondary water and land pollution.[6]

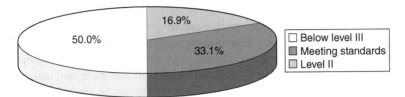

Figure 1.1 Percentages of urban population exposed to different air quality (2004) (source: Asian Development Bank (ADB) 2007. Country Environmental Analysis for the People's Republic of China).

The incongruous situation deriving from the inadequacy of PRC's farmlands for its population has led to the over-exploitation of its farmlands beyond their optimal limit. The PRC's farmland area is just 7 percent of the world's total, contrasted with its 20 percent share of the world's total population. In order to maintain production and to feed the population, the average fertilizer application rate in the PRC, even on areas unsuitable to agriculture, is about double the average rate in developed countries. About 1.3 million tons of pesticides are applied annually, two-thirds of which have been estimated to end up in bodies of water, soil and agricultural products, seriously threatening public health. The contamination of 10 percent of the PRC's farmlands by intensive agriculture has resulted in annual grain losses of 12 million tons or an annual direct economic loss of RMB20 billion. More than eight billion tons of sewage and 120 million tons of garbage, mostly untreated, are produced in the rural areas. Meanwhile, intensive animal production units generate wastes that have become the top source of COD, exceeding the combined amount from industrial wastewater and urban sewage. Severity in both frequency and intensity has been noted in the occurrence of environmental accidents, which numbered 67 in 2004 and 76 in 2005. Loss of biodiversity has been noted over the years due to the destruction of large areas of natural forests, grasslands, wetlands and other natural habitats. Population growth and rural urban expansion, among others, have led to wild animals losing their habitats and being in danger of extinction.[7]

Carbon emissions from both agricultural and industrial sectors also represent a significant problem for the PRC. Apart from being a major global source of greenhouse gas emissions, the PRC is also under serious threat from global climate change. It is seen as a potential threat to the distribution of water across the country, leading to exacerbation of the water shortages and pollution in the northern PRC, an increase in flooding incidents in the southern PRC, and the inundation of the PRC's coastal areas. It is also expected that cropping patterns will be affected, while it is seen that grain production will be reduced by as much as 10 percent. Biodiversity will be reduced, while grassland desertification will intensify; and morbidity and mortality from infectious diseases will increase.[8]

Against this backdrop, the PRC is currently in the process of developing a long-term strategy running through to 2050 for the better management of the country's main environmental concerns. The PRC has assembled many of its best experts in the field of environmental management and institutional change in order to try to see how the choices taken today might help to produce a better set of economic and environmental outcomes for the future.

This volume summarizes the approach that has been taken to try to develop this pathway into the PRC's future. The volume consists of four parts, and makes use of the inputs of both the Chinese and international experts on environmental management and institutional change.

First, a pathway into the future is built upon a fundamental understanding of the various relationships between growth and environment. It is especially built upon the understanding of how environmental regulation is able to manage this relationship. The first part of the volume turns to a discussion of these important ideas, laying down the basic relationships between economic growth and environmental degradation and the ways regulation manages this relationship. This part of the volume provides the necessary background information in addressing the various environmental concerns and issues facing the PRC through a discussion of the country's economic development phases, current state and trend of environmental problems, control and management, and history and status of institutional development for environmental management.

Meanwhile, the second part of the volume goes into the problems of the PRC's environment in regard to three distinct sectors: air, water, and ecology. Each of these chapters provides a more detailed understanding of how the PRC's growth and development have impacted the country's environment. The sector analyses give an indication of the causes of the sectoral problems related to economic growth and often recommend goals and targets for air and water pollution control and ecosystem management in the PRC as well as the strategies, policies and specific measures to achieve these targets.

The third part of the volume provides some lessons and case studies from other countries to aid the PRC in its development. These chapters which are presented on a sectoral basis delineate particular problems and solution concepts pursued in already-developed countries. The chapters thus give some indication on the "toolkit" available for environmental regulation, in respect to these sectoral problems. The international experiences in the management of air, water, and ecology give the Chinese experts some material to consider when selecting their own pathway.

The fourth part of the volume provides an explicit discussion of how institutional reforms in the PRC and elsewhere helps to link up environmental management and environmental regulation. It discusses the evidence on institutional reforms used in other countries to address similar problems in the PRC, and offers policy review and recommendations to develop the position, authority and capability of the PRC's national environmental protection agency. These chapters establish the PRC's institutional environment's need for reform and how other countries facing the same need have responded to the challenge. The volume concludes with a discussion on the importance of governance and institution building in the PRC, as the means for building a path to a brighter future.

All these parts of the volume combined are intended to assist in the mapping of that pathway for the PRC, setting off from its recent past of rapid development and environmental change toward a future entirely of its own choice. The message of the volume is simply that environmental regulation is the mechanism that enables that choice to be made, and institutional reform is the method by which that choice can be implemented.

Economic growth and environmental regulation: the PRC's experience and its pathway

Part I of the volume maps out the fundamental principles linking economic growth and the environment. Chapter 2 maps out the seemingly inevitable degradation that has occurred during the PRC's phase of rapid growth and development. It summarizes the state of existing problems and proposals for how to deal with them. Then the role of environmental regulation is introduced, in such a way that it is able to guide development in various directions and toward different goals. Chapter 3 looks at the relationship between environmental decline and the growth in the demand for regulation. This chapter indicates that economic growth need not necessarily lead to environmental decline; in fact, the experiences of developed countries indicate that environmental regulation is usually successful at halting degradation without halting economic development. How is this possible? Chapter 4 argues that environmental regulation is the mechanism by which economic growth is initially geared toward the production of mixed goods (both economic and environmental goods) and then toward the direction of technological and structural change in the economy. Environmental regulation plays a fundamental role in shaping economies and their development in the long run.

The PRC's development and its environmental degradation

Chapter 2 is an overview of the manner in which the PRC's economic and regulatory development has evolved over the past 30 years. This chapter chronicles many of the development gains and the environmental costs attendant upon the PRC's long-run economic growth. Xia *et al.* classify the economic development phases into four main periods. The period from 1978 to 1984 witnessed the birth of environmental problems in the *rural reform phase*. In this phase, the PRC experienced the period of opening up and of economic construction and reform, characterized by rural reform and agricultural development. Due to the large number of randomly scattered township enterprises with unsound product structure, laggard technical equipment and poor management – and also because of the intensive consumption of resources and energy, and the lack of corresponding pollution prevention measures – pollution damage became prominent and hard to prevent. Pollution became widespread, from hotspots to the whole region, spanning both urban and rural areas. During this period, environmental protection work lagged far behind economic development.

The period from 1985 to 1992 saw the emergence of environmental problems in the *light industry development phase*. In this phase, economic development in the PRC featured the rapid development of light industry, mainly light and textile industries, to meet the population's demand for food, clothing and other consumables. Symptoms of economic overheating had become quite evident such that some areas and departments blindly adopted inefficient, resource- and energy-intensive, and heavy-polluting projects such as small-scale paper mills, electroplating, and coking and smelting plants. Deforestation and over-exploitation of natural resources became common, accelerating environmental quality deterioration even further. Urban air pollution was considerably severe. Water quality suffered even more. The aggregate untreated industrial residues and urban domestic wastes became the second largest source of pollution. Eco-system deterioration was not avoided either.

The period from 1993 to 1999 experienced increasingly serious environmental problems in the *preliminary heavy chemical industry phase*. This phase witnessed the acceleration of the PRC's industrialization and urbanization. The proportion of the heavy industry in the industrial structure significantly exceeded that of the light industry. The period was marked by the continuous geographic expansion of environmental pollution from urban centers to rural areas, and the expansion of ecological deterioration due to the energy-intensive economic growth and backward technology and management which resulted in pollution and destruction outpacing treatment. Environmental pollution and ecological damage not only impeded the economic development of certain regions but also caused harm to the public's health.[9]

The period from 2000 to the present has been characterized by an intense out-burst of environmental problems in the form of a *heavy chemical industry phase*. This phase ushered in the era of heavy chemical industry in the PRC. This phase also witnessed accelerated urbanization as well as the fastest and longest-lasting economic growth. The significant increase in coal consumption directly resulted in high emissions of main pollutants, while SO_2 and COD emissions also posted sharp increases. The limited area of arable land and the consequent high reliance on the use of pesticides and fertilizers for increased food production have led to the prominence of non-point source pollution in agriculture. A severe outbreak of malignant water pollution accidents in several bodies of water brought serious harm to life and production.

Three recurring themes stand out on the fundamental causes of these environmental problems:

1   the constricting changes of natural and demographic conditions in the PRC;
2   the fast-paced economic growth; and
3   the still unsound environmental management, as a result of the first two points.

Xia *et al.* discuss how less than half of the actual total land area of the PRC (about 10,000,000 km², or equivalent to the area of the whole of America or the eastern part of the Ural Mountains in Europe) is suitable for human settlement and development, due to the poor natural conditions in the country. This has led to the overwhelming environmental pressure on unit area and to intense and heavy pollution. Meanwhile, the large population base and change of population structure have invariably led to the exploitation of the natural resources to meet the demands of survival and development, and thereby exerted tremendous pressure on the environment, leading to a shortage in various mineral and water resources. The strong demands on resources and energy by the urban population, driven by the accelerated urbanization, has hastened the development of heavy chemical industries.

The PRC's rapid economic growth over the past 30 years has not only dramatically enlarged the size of its economy, but has also brought about significant changes in the country's industrial structure, technology and energy consumption. Xia *et al.* find that steep economic growth, mainly brought about by huge investments in the manufacturing industry, has resulted in sharp increases in the production of industrial gas and solid wastes, while the change in industrial structure was accompanied by a change in pollutants consisting of the pollution created by the fast-growing heavy chemical industry. The rough growth mode – characterized by high input, high consumption, high emission, difficult circulation and low efficiency – has brought about excessive consumption of resources. There is also a perceived incompatibility between the PRC's industrial structure and the carrying capacity of its resources and environment due mainly to the failure to take into consideration the conditions of the resources and environment in industrial structure and layout. Excessive and arbitrary exploitation and utilization of water, soil and biological resources brought about uncertain factors which have potential adverse impacts on the material cycle, energy flow and information transmission of regional ecosystems that may lead to an incomplete and uncoordinated ecological process. The significant increase in energy consumption over the last 20 years is particularly of concern. Xia *et al.* observe a significant increase in coal consumption, while desulfurization in power stations has brought about sharp emission increments. The high energy consumption due to economic growth also caused the increase of pollutant discharges and put pressure on the environment.

Last but not least, inadequate environmental management has also contributed to the PRC's environmental problems. Environmental management is inadequate at three major levels. At the legislation level, certain environmental laws or regulations are either missing, inconsistent or difficult to enforce. At the input level, inputs from government have not been sufficient while those from the private sector are limited due to the missing markets for certain environmental and ecological assets. Finally, at the management level, there is a serious lack of capacity in the institutional setup of the PRC's environmental management system, and a strategic and centralized ecological management system is also absent.

The amalgamation of these three factors (natural constraints, rapid economic growth and unsound environmental management) have combined to produce the current situation facing the PRC. The economy has generated tremendous growth and opportunity for the Chinese people, but it has also produced significant challenges and environmental problems. A review of the PRC's economic development and environmental degradation must be able to aid learning from the past which should in turn be used to arrive at an informed choice on the way forward.

Pathways into the future: Environmental Kuznets Curve

The relationship between growth and environment is an often-studied topic across many countries experiencing the consequences of rapid economic growth. The reason is that it is a common occurrence for economic growth to be initially associated with resource and environmental degradation, resulting in a need for increased environmental management. This need for management is prompted by an increased emphasis on environmental regulation, which in turn is stimulated by income growth. Looking across developed countries, it is straightforward to observe that this induced manner of environmental regulation has occurred in many places previously. The charting of this relationship between growth and environmental management is often referred to as the "Environmental Kuznets Curve" (EKC), where the basic variables of economic income are associated with environmental quality. In many already-developed countries and for several types of environmental emissions, it can be seen that the EKC takes the form of an inverted-U, demonstrating that increased growth induces environmental degradation in the initial phase and then environmental regulation subsequently.

Chapter 3 examines the relationship between economic growth and environmental sustainability in the PRC by empirically estimating the EKC models using provincial-level panel data from 1985 to 2005. The results show that there exists an inverted-U shape relationship as hypothesized by the EKC model between per capita income and per capita emissions (or discharges) in the cases of waste gas from fuel burning and wastewater, with a turning point at US$12,903 and US$3,226, respectively, in purchasing power parity (PPP) terms. This relationship, however, does not hold in the case of waste gas from production or solid waste. The estimation results from the model, allowing region-specific slope coefficients, show that the EKCs of the more developed coastal regions have a flatter rising portion with turning points occurring at a higher income level than those of the less developed central and western regions. Jiang *et al.* argue that this may reflect technology diffusion and institutional imitation across regions at different stages of development.

Jiang *et al.* emphasize the importance of distinguishing waste gas due to production from waste gas due to fuel burning, as the per capita emission of the former is showing no signs of letting up. Identifying the stricter air pollution policy on emissions from fuel burning than from production as one of the possible causes of this trend, Jiang *et al.* call for a more balanced policy between the two. Also finding that less developed regions have lower turning points (which implies that technology diffusion and institutional imitation play an important role as mechanisms to reduce emissions and improve environmental quality), Jiang *et al.* recommend the formulation of public policies which facilitate technology diffusion and transfer, knowledge-sharing on energy efficiency and emission abatement, and capacity building and institutional strengthening targeted at less developed regions.

In general, it is to be anticipated that economic growth will result in increased environmental degradation, at least initially. The crucial need is to have a well-focused governmental response to increased degradation in the form of targeted environmental regulation that reduces the growth-generated problems. The chapter by Jiang *et al.* demonstrates that the PRC is starting to respond to these problems in a systematic manner, and that further efforts at regulation, technological change and institutional reform will continue to bring about significant changes to the environmental impacts of development.

The relationship between economic growth and environmental regulation: three phases

Chapter 4 continues this theme, and takes into consideration the important role of environmental regulation in the future. This chapter also emphasizes the general relationship between economic growth and environmental regulation, as described in the previous chapter. Economic growth is often seen to create environmental degradation initially, and the response then is to undertake environmental management as a "clean-up" activity. In these early phases of development, the main role of environmental regulation is reactive: it deals with the problems of environmental quality after they have been generated by economic growth. This might be termed the phase of reactive environmental regulation.

The second phase of the growth and regulation relationship is less reactive but still not forward-looking. This phase focuses on the role of regulation in resource allocation. All economic growth must be spent on different forms of productive and consumptive activities. When there is no regulation in place, it is possible for some forms of activities (i.e. some types of private production activities) to appropriate all of society's resources which necessarily results in misallocation of resources, and which in turn tends to generate a demand for the creation of mechanisms that will enable the reallocation of resources toward other activities. For example, the appropriation of a river's water (quantity or quality) by some private industry might be sufficient to deny a wide range of other private and public uses (e.g. drinking, fishing, cleaning, swimming and recreation). There is little chance that the routing of resources simply toward those able to appropriate them first (and foremost) is going to put in place the socially correct balance of usage. The role of regulation, in this instance, is to ensure that there is some mechanism available for balancing the allocation of resources among the various uses. Therefore, the second phase of economic growth and environmental regulation emphasizes resource allocation and the role of regulation to create the essential mechanisms for achieving a balanced allocation of resources across all of their potential uses in society.

Finally, the most interesting phase of the relationship between economic growth and environmental regulation is the final phase, when governments begin to respond proactively to both processes. In the proactive phase, the government views economic growth and environmental regulation as a paired process and involving the management of the path of technological change so that both growth and environment are optimized. In this phase, the government comes to recognize that technological change can contribute to both the process of economic growth and the avoidance of environmental degradation, and so policy-making becomes focused on creating incentives for guiding specific forms of technological change. For example, many developed countries have adopted policies that provide incentives for the creation of energy-saving technologies by means of labeling, which reduces the amount of information required to ascertain the aggregate benefits of a given technology, thus rendering investments in energy-saving technologies more easily rewarded. Even more proactive is Denmark's investments in wind turbine technologies, based on the fundamental belief that long-run energy prices would reward such investments. In these cases, environmental regulation functions as a form of industrial policy leader and allows the regulator to place the state's industries at the forefront of change. This has been done most explicitly in Japan when it attempted to acquire patent-based advantages and privileges with respect to environmental frontier technologies such that patents acquired by it on specific environmental technologies (e.g. advances in automotive emissions and energy-saving technologies) have enabled it to acquire a share of the societal benefits or be a beneficiary whenever any other country adopts the environmental policies necessitating those technologies, as in those in automotive production.

The relationship between economic growth and environmental regulation has an interesting series of phases through the process of development. Initially, economic growth is often antithetical to environmental quality, and the role of regulation is reactive ("clean-up"). Later, the role of regulation becomes more contemporary, when the mechanisms to balance the allocation of resources are established. Finally, the role of regulation becomes proactive when the regulator itself becomes the guiding force of the economy toward the direction of combined economic and environment growth and development.

A long-term review of economic growth and environmental quality needs to see the movement of regulation through these phases of management, from reactive to proactive. The pathway toward a brighter future requires that the PRC's environmental regulation becomes increasingly effective, and even active, over the coming decades.

The PRC's environmental problems: a sectoral review

Part II summarizes the extent and nature of the environmental problems in the PRC that have developed along with the country's growth process over the past

30 years. We consider each of the primary environmental sectors in turn: air, water and ecosystems. The objective of this part of the volume is to provide further details about the problems and policies that have resulted in the environmental degradation during the PRC's period of economic growth. What is the nature of the environmental degradation in each of these sectors? And, why has the PRC's growth generated so many highly significant environmental problems?

The PRC's air sector problems and policies

Chapter 5 examines air pollution problems in the PRC. They find that within the last three decades, all types of air pollution problems occurred in the developed regions of the PRC. Regional air pollution complex, coal-combustion pollution, vehicle exhaust pollution, and pollution caused by multiple other pollutants were experienced in key local and regional clusters of the PRC. Regional air quality, in particular, exhibited a worsening trend with the frequent occurrence of toxic and hazardous photochemical smog, regional haze and acid deposition.

Particulate matter (PM_{10}) is the primary pollutant affecting urban air quality in most cities of the PRC. Generally speaking, PM_{10} and SO_2 concentrations in the cities of the PRC are about four to six times those in the developed countries, and nitrogen dioxide (NO_2) concentration is similar or a little higher than that in the developed countries. Meanwhile, during the period of 1993–2006, the areas with precipitation pH lower than five (also known as acid-rain areas) remained stable and made up 30–40 percent of the whole country. However, heavily polluted areas with precipitation pH lower than 4.5 increased. SO_2 and nitrogen oxides (NO_x) emitted into the atmosphere can be transformed through chemical reaction into sulphate and nitrate in particles, respectively, resulting in regional fine particulate ($PM_{2.5}$) pollution, which is one of the major factors responsible for regional haze. Haze is a common turbidity phenomenon characterized by large amounts of imperceptible dry dust particles that float in the air uniformly making the visibility lower than 10 km. The simulation of Congestion Mitigation and Air Quality (CMAQ) model, a regional air quality model developed by the US Environmental Protection Agency (EPA), indicated that large regions of the PRC were covered with high $PM_{2.5}$ concentrations, signifying that $PM_{2.5}$ pollution is also a severe regional environmental issue in the PRC. It has also been noted that photochemical smog and high-ozone concentrations frequently occur in Beijing, the Pearl River Delta and the Yangtze River Delta.

Looking into the future, Hao and Wang cite the 2007 edition of the International Energy Agency's *World Energy Outlook* which states that under both the baseline scenario (with improvement of energy efficiency) and policy scenario (with further improvement of energy efficiency and shift to clean energy), which estimated the total energy demand by 2030, coal is seen to remain as the dominant source of energy. Therefore, from now until 2030, the PRC is faced with the task of controlling air pollution from fossil-fuel consumption. Meanwhile, the future energy scenario estimated that under the current control policy, SO_2

emissions will rapidly increase after 2015 and reach 35 million tons by 2030. This signifies that efforts to strengthen pollution control policies should also consider other sectors beside the coal-fired power plants. On the other hand, the total NO_x emissions are estimated to exceed 30 million tons absent a national NO_x emission control program and if no measures are taken to stem this kind of pollution.

The PRC's water sector problems and policies

Chapter 6 discusses how the main river basins of the PRC have increasingly been threatened by complex water pollution problems and the over-exploitation of water resources, which have resulted in quality deterioration of both drinking and underground water, water ecosystem degradation and lake eutrophication. In the 1970s, among the 34 lakes surveyed, only 5 percent showed eutrophication problems. The percentage increased to 36 percent during 1986 and 1989, and further climbed to 75 percent in 2002. In 2005, out of the 28 lakes and reservoirs of national importance which are nationally monitored, only two reached water quality of Class 2, six had water quality standard of Class 3, three were rated Class 4, and five reached Class 5. The water quality of the other 12 lakes and reservoirs, or about 43 percent of the total, was below Class 5. Water pollution in the country has changed from simple industrial pollution to integrated complex pollution coming from the industry, agriculture and household sectors; and, it is increasingly characterized by compound pollution and high organic basin pollution load which greatly exceeds the ability for self-purification. The nationwide levels of COD, five-day biological oxygen demand (BOD5), ammonia nitrogen, total nitrogen, total phosphorus and escherichia coli have alarmingly exceeded the standard and tolerable amounts. Moreover, the influence of persistent organic pollutants (POPs) and endocrine disrupters (EDs) is becoming serious. From 2001 to 2004, nearly 4,000 pollution disasters have been recorded. In 2005, around half of the 693 pollution events were water pollution disasters, with total estimated annual economic losses of more than RMB240 billion, or about 3 percent of the country's gross domestic product (GDP). Serious water pollution has also affected rivers in the country resulting in water ecological degradation, water quality deterioration and water shortage.

Xi and Meng list six major deficiencies in the PRC's water environmental regulation and management. First, water environmental monitoring and enforcement are weak which has lowered the cost of pollution. Second, the integrated approaches using legislative, regulatory, market and technological measures are yet to be developed. Third, institutional and organizational complexities have prevented an integrated water management system which incorporates water supply, water quality, water ecological system and river-basin management. Fourth, from the technical perspective, the water environmental standard system is incomplete and lacks operability. Fifth, at the provincial and local levels, public investments for environment and the environmental infrastructure are inadequate. The decision-making procedures within the governments need to be improved to reduce incidents of interference by government officials in the enforcement of environmental laws and regulations. Sixth, the human resource system also has to be improved to align government officials' incentives with environmental protection rather than merely with economic growth.

The PRC's ecosystem problems and policies

Chapter 7 discusses the PRC's ecological problems, including complex ecosystem structure, uncoordinated ecological process and declining ecosystem functions. These ecological problems are reflected by vegetation degradation, land degradation, declining wetland function, threatened biodiversity and glacier retreat in the country. Gao and Han conclude that primary vegetation, such as forests and grasslands, have seriously deteriorated as a result of climate warming, rapid economic growth, rapid population increase and continuous urbanization. Consequently, forest vegetation functions have also been declining continuously. Land degradation in the PRC has also become increasingly prominent. There has been continuous increase and aggravation in land salinization, desertification, soil erosion and pollution, while the decrease in arable land area has been incessant. Apart from these, the PRC's wetland area is rapidly and sharply declining. With the reduction of wetlands in the PRC, wetland ecological functions have also decreased significantly, resulting in biodiversity reduction and ecological deterioration. It has also been observed that over the years, population growth and rural and urban expansion have destroyed large areas of natural forests, grasslands, wetlands and other natural habitats. Consequently, a large number of wild animals have lost their habitats and are in danger of extinction. Also, the past two to three decades have seen severe losses of glacier materials brought about by the climate warming and the environmentally damaging impacts of human activities. Apart from area reduction, some glaciers have also thinned.

The PRC's resource- and energy-intensive economic growth is one of the principal root causes of its ecological problems, as identified by Gao and Han. The over-usage and unreasonable exploitation of land resources resulting from rapid economic growth have led to unreasonable river-basin structures and severely imbalanced river-basin ecosystems. The other factors causing severe damages to the service functions of the natural ecosystems include: deforestation, steep slope cultivation in mountain areas, blind cultivated land reclamation from lakes, and occupation of flood-draining river beaches in plain areas. In some inland river basins, the over-exploitation of water and soil resources through human activities has led to the reduction of mountain vegetation, deterioration of the water condition in the middle and lower reaches, degradation of coastal natural oasis, staggered shrinking of transitional strips, and expansion of oasis desertification.

In terms of ecological preservation, Gao and Han further note that although it is observed that the influence of international conventions on the PRC's ecological and environmental protection has become increasingly apparent, there is deficiency in the country's capability to perform its undertakings under the conventions. The status, system and capacity of ecological environmental protection and management in the PRC are short of the requirements specified in the international conventions.

The three chapters combined provide greater depth and detail on the environmental degradation that has resulted during the PRC's 30 years of economic progress. The question addressed in the remainder of the volume is to what extent such environmental degradation is a part of economic progress.

Examples of environmental management: international experiences to inform the PRC's choices

In Part III of the volume, we have accumulated a set of case studies in order to demonstrate the manner in which other countries have managed to deal with the relationship between economic growth and environmental degradation. The studies pertain to the same three sectors that were examined by the Chinese scholars in the previous section, and they each elucidate two or three examples of institutions or policies that have been developed to address the sectoral problems. The focus of most of these studies is on the issue of environmental policy effectiveness, but they also demonstrate very innovative approaches to policy implementation. For example, we examine trading or market-based approaches to air, water and ecological management. But we also look for basic lessons on how regulation can be adopted, as well as how monitoring and enforcement might be implemented. The three chapters provide a large amount of sector-based experiences with the tools and techniques available for environmental management.

Air sector management: international experiences

The first international case study, in Chapter 8, examines various experiences of developed countries in the area of air quality management. This is an interesting analysis of the way the US and the EU approaches to air quality management have differed. For the most part, the United States has built its system on air quality management on particular emissions control programs, such as the sulfur oxides (SO_x) trading system. The EU, on the other hand, has managed emissions by focusing on the control of the aggregate level of industrial activity and formulation of energy conservation laws. Although the two approaches could not be more different, with that of the US based more on market-based instruments and that of the EU based more on technology and emission standards, the results are very similar. The air quality in both the EU and the United States has improved dramatically over the past two decades, and the emissions of particular pollutants have all been in decline. The important message from this particular sectoral study is that effective regulation can come in many different forms and packages.

The chapter examines three particular case studies, and often contrasts the approach taken in the United States with that of the EU. The first case study looks at the management of SO_2 emissions. In the EU, the management of SO_x was an important instance of regional and transboundary problem-solving. Since the problem of acid-rain deposition is derived as much from neighboring states' emissions as from a state's own emissions, regional (pan-European) cooperation is therefore required. Europe addressed this through a series of agreements that sets targets for reductions and establishes objectives for limiting depositions. To meet these agreed targets, the EU approved directives that required the adoption of specific forms of the "best available technology." Finally, much of the progress in emissions reduction in the EU was achieved by the adoption of general policies promoting energy conservation. By way of contrast, the objective of the US was reducing the emissions by half through the adoption of a cap and trade system. This system provided incentives for the creation of new technologies for emissions reduction and enabled flexibility in the way emissions reduction targets were achieved. The most notable thing about these two policies of the United States and the EU is that both were huge successes. The EU actually reduced emissions more substantially (to 1930 levels), while the United States achieved its target of a 50 percent reduction in emissions at lower than anticipated costs.

The next case study looks at the management of urban air pollutants in Europe (e.g. ozone, particulates, volatile organic compounds). The interesting lesson to be learned from this is that the general policies used to influence the attainment of SO_x targets were also the same policies responsible for the achievement of many of Europe's urban air quality targets. One of the primary contributors to the improvements in urban air quality was the huge progress made in terms of energy conservation which, in turn, was triggered by increasing fuel prices. The second main contributor was the imposition of mandatory technology standards on the main polluters (e.g. motor vehicles and large plants). The combination of market-based intervention at the primary level with command-and-control approach at the secondary level has, in general, served Europe well.

The final case study is on mercury emissions. This environmental problem is particularly difficult because the flow of emissions across boundaries is perceived to be highly intrusive. In this case, regional or international coordination is required, more than ever, in order to achieve outcomes. No one region is going to take action until it sees that its neighbors are ready to reciprocate. In this instance, the contrast between the European command-and-control approach and the US trading-based approach demonstrates the difficulty of combining flexibility with complexity. The European system is up and running, while the US system continues to be debated upon.

In summary, the international experiences with air sector management demonstrate that the problem of environmental management in this sector is one that combines transboundary cooperation problems with technology adoption problems. For purposes of reaching agreement across boundaries (and to ensure that the system is readily monitored and enforced), it is sometimes easiest to simply adopt prescribed solutions and to forsake some flexibility. If it is possible to focus on flexibility (market-based instruments) then the US experiences indicate that substantial cost savings might be acquired.

Water sector management: international experiences

Chapter 9, on international experiences in the water sector, reiterates many of the lessons learned in the air sector. With large water basins the environmental problems are nearly always transboundary and the problems are often as much about coordinated implementation as about management. Creating systems that are able to span boundaries and create incentives for water conservation are issues that have been the focus of environmental management across the world.

The first case study examines the Murray–Darling River Basin (MDRB) in southern Australia. This large water basin spans four large and economically diverse states in Australia, and there has long been a competition between sectors (agriculture, industry, drinking water) and between states over both the quantity and the quality of the water available. To address this situation, the MDRB Commission was established in 1994, and this inter-state Commission was given the responsibility for establishing a program capable of resolving this transboundary problem. The MDRB Commission operates under the requirement of securing unanimity from the member states, with the member states responsible for implementing any agreed upon joint program. In 1994, the Commission first acted to cap all extractions from the basin at 1993 levels. Since then the emphasis has been on:

1   encouraging the trading of extraction rights within the MDRB; and
2   addressing joint quality problems such as salinization.

The trading program has been reasonably successful at the intra-state level, but with only minor trades occurring to date across states. The lesson of the MDRB Commission is that it is crucial to establish governmental units at the water resource level, albeit inter-state cooperation can still be difficult to achieve under such frameworks.

The second case study examined in the water sector comes from Europe and relates to the level of international cooperation required to address the problems of pollution existing within the Rhine river basin. The Rhine is notable because it spans nine separate countries and supports 60 million people. In the recent past, it was a dumping ground for a large number of heavy industries, especially the chemical industry. The International Commission for the Protection of the Rhine (ICPR) was created in 1950 across these states in order to help aid the management of the basin. In 1976, the EU joined the ICPR. This initiated a long and ongoing process of river basin management, involving the sequential adoption of substance-based regimes. A separate protocol was agreed on the reduction of emissions of each of the various pollutants – first chloride and heavy metals, and then subsequently various other chemicals and pollutants. The series of disasters in the 1980s and 1990s prompted the drafting of the Rhine Action Plan (RAP), and true river basin management was adopted. After 1986, the member states coordinated their standards and their implementation programs to attain massive reductions (generally greater than 50 percent) of most chemical and other pollution levels in the Rhine. This river-basin management approach was then extended to all basins in the EU under the Water Framework Directive of 2000. The lesson to be learned from Europe is that provincial regulation must give way to water basin-based management for effective implementation and control of pollution. In the case of the Rhine river basin, the problems with unco-ordinated regulation had to reach disastrous levels before integrated management resulted.

The third case study examined in the water sector concerns the use of Total Maximum Daily Loads (TMDLs) in the US water management program. The 1972 Clean Water Act (CWA) in the United States requires the pursuit of uniform national water quality standards through the imposition of uniform tech-nology and control standards. This has been generally successful at reducing emissions by a significant extent in most parts of the United States. However, a back-up program in the CWA provided that implementing states might use TMDLs as a mechanism for meeting unattained targets. TMDLs are based on the idea of capping emissions in order to attain target standards. In the Long Island Sound (New York State), it was agreed that emissions of nitrogen would be capped at 1990 levels, and then subsequently a reduction of about 60 percent of nitrogen emissions was agreed within the watershed. Most of the emissions were to be reduced from point sources, and these were allocated permits to facil-itate trading. The overall goal was to aid in the attainment of water quality objec-tives (which have never been attained with respect to nitrogen) by means of encouraging innovative ways of limiting emissions.

In summary, the international experiences in water-sector management again emphasize the importance of transboundary management of environmental prob-lems. Water basins tend to span numerous jurisdictions by reason of their sheer scale and interconnectedness. When management is based on individual admin-istrations, incentives for improvements are nil; large amounts of cooperation and coordination are required to secure management and control. This highlights the importance of creating administrative units that have effective control over the water resource across many boundaries, and then to adopt monitoring and imple-mentation programs that are enforceable at the level of the watershed manage-ment unit. Finally, the case studies demonstrate that many of the standards are attainable with basic technology and controls, and that more complex regimes are seldom required in this context. What are usually deemed as necessary are cooperation, coordination and control across the resource's territory.

Ecosystem management: international experiences

Chapter 10, the third chapter on international experiences, focuses on ecosystem management. Here the long run of experience has definitely been command and control. For many decades, ecosystems have been conserved primarily through the land use planning process and the parks and protected areas programs. The former simply mandates a specific (conservation-oriented) land use for a given area – or, in other words, it restricts the sorts of development that are allowed to be undertaken in a given area. The problem with such a command-and-control approach is that they provide very little in the way of positive incentives; and, hence, developing societies are inclined to avoid or overcome them. For this reason, it may be important for a growing and developing country (such as the PRC) to consider other systems that provide more positive incentives for managing development pressures, rather than just negative ones. This chapter considers two such examples, both from the United States.

The first case study concerns the concept known as "payment for environmental services" (PES). Such schemes are based on the "beneficiary pays" principle, and attempt to create structures that will provide payments to those who choose to provide conservation services on their lands. A classic example of the PES scheme is the Hudson River watershed program, wherein urban residents pay for the conservation of lands upstream to provide freshwater to urban users. At the national level, the United States has adopted the Conservation Resource Program (CRP) which provides a systematic approach to paying for conservation services. Adopted in 1986, this program mandates that the US government will provide payments under long-term contracts for placing designated lands under specific management regimes. The CRP provides for individual landholders to "bid in" their lands to the program, specifying the sorts of habitats available and the types of services and conservation that would be provided under the contract. The landholders are also required to specify the price at which they are willing to offer the land/service package. The CRP then ranks the various bids, and offers contracts to landholders based on an evaluation of the combined bid price/package on offer. This enables the government to acquire the largest set of services possible for a given conservation budget, so long as the bids are provided on a reasonably competitive basis (which is always a problem).

The second case study concerns the concept known as "biodiversity offsets." These schemes are based on the "polluter pays" principle, and attempt to create structures whereby developers of land provide compensation for the developments they pursue. This was initiated within various voluntary and state-run programs, usually as a means by which developers provide some manner of compensating lands for habitats that were lost. In the United States, the scheme has been systematized to provide for wetland banking. This system was developed under the auspices of the 1972 Clean Water Act, which required developers to secure permits for any proposed developments within existing wetlands. The implementing body (the US Army Corps of Engineers) required all forms of mitigation first, but provided that unavoidable losses of wetlands must be compensated for by the establishment of wetland reserves. Since developers were not experts in the selection of comparable reserves, a commercial industry was tasked to develop and provide certifiably compensating wetlands. This industry establishes such reserves and holds them in "wetland banks," and they are made available for purchase by developers as compensation for their developments. These banks have grown tenfold over the past decade. In order to broaden the conservation options, some of these schemes have even developed the commodification of a broader class of "conservation credits" instead of just wetland properties. Such credits might then be banked for a broad range of conservation actions and activities (not just reserves), and they may be purchased by developers in amounts required by the Corps. This type of scheme is now in place in some states in the United States, such as the North Carolina Ecosystem Enhancement Program (NCEEP). It allows the government to bid for the supply of credits (and thus receive competitive supply of conservation efforts) and also to provide them to developers in response to existing growth and demand.

In summary, these international experiences with ecosystem conservation demonstrate that there are interesting options available for encouraging land use and development down certain pathways, rather than simply attempting to combat its encroachment. Programs that provide incentives for developers to invest in conservation efforts help developers to find ways to simultaneously attain both objectives: development and conservation. Programs that do this with auctions, banks and trading systems encourage the efficient supply of both development and conservation projects. The US experiences give an indication of some early attempts at developing these sorts of initiatives. The PRC could learn a lot from these programs about how growth and development might be channeled.

Environmental regulation and institutional development and reform

Part IV of the volume addresses the ways in which institutional development and reform in the PRC can help in the management of environmental problems. As was discussed previously, economic growth results in both environmental degradation and also in the demand for increasingly effective regulation and management. This is because societies clearly demand a balanced mix of goods, both public and private. The allocation of environmental resources to public uses – from drinking water to breathable air – requires management and regulation. The significance of these public goods highlights the importance of developing institutions capable of efficiently delivering them.

In this part, we examine how environmental regulation has evolved in the PRC, from the inception of the Ministry of Environmental Protection (MEP) as a small agency to its current status as a full ministry of the PRC government. We will see how its responsibilities have grown along with environmental regulations, and the fundamental nature of the problems that make it difficult for MEP to meet these responsibilities. In Chapter 12, we turn to examples of institutional evolution in other countries. What structures and what forms of government have been most capable of meeting the demands created by the onset of environmental degradation? Finally, we discuss the set of institutional reform issues most clearly required in the PRC. What do the problems and case studies we have examined in this volume suggest are the best ways forward in terms of institutional reform? Chapter 13 concludes with a list of "cross-cutting issues" important for leading the PRC to its path to a brighter future.

The PRC's institutional evolution

Chapter 11 discusses the history, status, lessons and challenges in the PRC's environmental management. It provides an overview of the evolution of environmental regulation in the PRC.

The environmental protection system in the PRC traces its roots to the 1971 stewardship of Premier Zhou Enlai, when the Environmental Protection Leading Group Office (EPLGO) was established under the State Planning Commission. This was the first time that environmental protection became an endeavor by the PRC's government. In 1974, the EPLGO was transferred to the State Construction Commission. In 1979, the promulgation of the Environmental Protection Law of the PRC, the first ever comprehensive environmental protection law in the country, paved the way for environmental protection management to be brought into the legal system. Within the 20-year period that followed, several laws, rules and regulations on environmental protection were passed and issued, bringing about the establishment of a basic environmental protection legal system in the PRC providing adequate legal and policy support for the implementation, enforcement and development of the national environmental protection agenda.

In 1982, the Environmental Protection Leading Group under the State Council was replaced by the State Environmental Protection Bureau (SEPB) which was placed under the Ministry of Urban and Rural Construction (MURC). In 1984, the State Council created the State Environmental Protection Commission which was attached to the MURC, and placed under the supervision and authority of the SEPB. In 1984, the State Environmental Protection Bureau was renamed the National Environmental Protection Agency (NEPA) but remained under the MURC. Thereafter, in 1988, the NEPA was detached from the MURC, and was elevated to the status of an independent agency under the State Council. In 1998, the NEPA was further elevated to the ministerial level as the State Environmental Protection Administration (SEPA), ushering in a budding stage in the PRC's environmental protection administration. Ten years later, in 2008, the MEP's establishment as an affiliate to the State Council launched a new era for the PRC's environmental protection. Fifteen departments were created under the MEP. The MEP is envisaged to play a more important role in the PRC's future environmental protection and development programs.

The state laws, State Council-issued ordinances, administrative regulations, state planning and state standards are the five legal components to the institutional establishment of the PRC's environmental protection administration. There are four levels in the legal governance of the PRC's environmental protection system, and these are the Constitution, the basic laws of environmental protection, specific environmental protection laws and provisions and stipulations in relation to environmental protection in other laws. The MEP and other local-level departments of the environmental protection administration are the principal bodies tasked with the PRC's environmental protection agenda. Other agencies involved are the comprehensive economic management organizations, such as the State Development and Planning Commission, the State Economic and Trade Commission, and the Ministry of Finance. Sectoral departments, such as the Ministries of Agriculture and Construction, also form part of the national environmental protection system. Completing the structure of the PRC's environmental protection system are the resource exploitation administrative departments, such as the Ministry of Water Resources, the State Forestry Administration and the Ministry of Land and Resources.

The unrelenting efforts of the PRC's government to strengthen environmental protection administration and institutions contributed to the significant progress and achievements of the country's environmental protection initiatives during the past 30 years. These efforts include the following:

1   inclusion in the national policies of environmental protection;
2   elevation of the responsibility mechanism on environmental protection to the level of the party leaders, and clarification of the responsibilities of the different levels of local government on environmental quality and protection;
3   establishment of the environmental protection legislative system, and provision of powerful legislative supports for the effective administration of environmental protection;
4   enhancement of judicial role to ensure adherence to national laws and guarantee fairness in the implementation of the policies on environmental protection;
5   formulation and promulgation of administrative and environmental management regulations, policies and actions;
6   gradual ascent of department levels in charge of environmental protection administration, and constant improvement of the management functions of these departments;
7   distribution among the different departments of the functions of environmental protection, with administrative supervision on pollution prevention and control assigned to the MEP and the function of environmental protection agencies given to the different levels of governments; and
8   constant adjustment of environmental protection strategies to keep up with the times.

Although the PRC's environmental institutions are capable of meeting the basic requirements of environmental protection and improvement, the lack of management instruments and the conflicts among departments prevent them from properly addressing new environmental problems and meeting the actual needs of environmental protection. For one, there is the observed lack of necessary and clear legislation to serve as basis for the institution of environmental protection administration. Also seen is the lack of management instrument needed for the integration of environmental protection work with social and economic development decision-making. As opposed to economic development, environmental protection has not been properly integrated with the comprehensive decision-making process. Another observation is the decline of the environmental protection coordination ability. In addition, the absence of a clear definition of the functions and jurisdiction of the environmental protection department and the natural resources management department makes unified supervision of ecological conservation impossible. There is also a perceived necessity for reforms in the regional and watershed management institutions. Finally, a serious lack of personnel and funds has adversely affected the PRC's environmental protection administration.

Environmental institutions: international experiences

Chapter 12 summarizes the development of environmental management institutions in developed countries. Goeschl breaks down the important ingredients of effective institutions as follows: institutionalization; horizontal relations; vertical relations; openness; and enforcement. We will consider each of these important issues in turn.

First, the issue of institutionalization within any state concerns the different roles for the different parts of the state. Most states find it essential to create roles for each branch of government – i.e. legislative, administrative and judicial. The legislative role is usually to set standards and establish targets, and this is fairly uniform. The role of public involvement in the legislative process can be crucial, as evidenced by the shift in environmental quality which occurred in Eastern Europe once the public became more actively engaged in the policy-making process. The relative roles of the administrative and judicial arms of government vary quite considerably. Some states such as Germany rely heavily on administrative control and agency intervention, while others such as the United States place much more reliance upon judicial control and intervention by individuals and others. The lesson here is that all branches of government are important for the institutionalization of environmental policy.

Second, the horizontal relations between governmental institutions are important for purposes of environmental management. Too often, environmental problems span sectors and territories that fall under the rubric of a specific branch of government. For this reason, it is crucial to develop inter-agency working parties that are able to address the issues in a coordinated and cooperative fashion. Germany provides a good example with an inter-ministerial commission that links the parts of all ministries that work on environmental protection.

Third, the vertical relations between governmental units require an equal amount of coordination. National levels of government may be the appropriate level at which to make standards, but it is still incumbent upon local or regional levels of government to monitor or enforce them. It is therefore critical that mechanisms are put in place by which the national level of government is able to effectively influence the choices of the local levels. In the United States, this is accomplished by means of the doctrine of federal pre-emption, whereby the federal government has the right to step in and substitute itself for the state administration if the latter is not being effective. Less comprehensively, it is also possible for the federal government in the United States to withhold federal monies (on wholly unrelated matters) if state-level implementation of environmental laws is not satisfactory. Together these rights of intervention result in the national and the local governments working closely together, even if the threats are not often carried out.

The next factor to consider in institution building is openness. This concerns the role of information in generating environmental implementation. It can be the case that simple transparency of operations is enough to result in environmental quality in many instances. Information can come either by push or by pull programs. The United States provides good examples of both. The US judiciary-based approach to enforcement relies heavily upon the information that exists at the local and individual level. This makes it possible for agencies to depend on the ground-level incentives of those most heavily impacted by environmental harms to report on and act upon them. This is information pulling environmental policy forwards. On the other hand, the United States also provides information to citizenry in order to push programs. An example of this is the Emergency Planning and Community Right-to-Know Act (EPCRA), which stipulates that local communities must be provided with information on any toxic releases occurring in their environment. The right to information is meant to push environmental policy and quality forwards. In both push and pull programs, the idea is that information can move policy and so environmental quality, and this sort of openness tends to be critical for institutionalizing environmental policy.

Finally, this section emphasizes the importance of rights in monitoring and enforcement. All effective environmental institutions bear the hallmarks of effective monitoring and clear-cut enforcement measures. This is usually accomplished by making it clear that rights to environmental standards exist, and also making it evident who the responsible parties are for enforcing these rights. There are three groups in which these rights might be invested: individuals, administrators or prosecutors (on behalf of the society). Individual citizens are often able to bring actions on some rights in the United States; whereas, in Europe, the rights are more often vested in regulators and administrators. In both jurisdictions, public prosecutors may be given rights to bring charges for specific acts of environmental pollution. In all cases, it is clear that expenditures on monitoring and enforcement result in much higher rates of return in terms of pollution abatement and incident avoidance.

In summary, Chapter 12 elucidates that there are important common ingredients to environmental institutions across all developed countries. These commonalities indicate that institutional effectiveness is not a happy accident. Effective institutions arise from ascertaining that all of the links within institutions are completed, and that all of the holes within monitoring and enforcement are addressed.

Environmental institution: cross-cutting issues in the PRC

Chapter 13 on cross-cutting issues re-emphasizes many of the points made in Chapters 11 and 12. Salzman looks at the set of sectoral reviews as well as the set of international experiences, and draws conclusions regarding the sorts of issues that arise consistently across sectors in the PRC and elsewhere. These are the cross-cutting issues regarding environmental governance raised by this long-run review. His conclusions are that the PRC needs to emphasize institutional development in many of the dimensions identified already in the other studies, namely: government coordination; enforcement; individual rights and participation; information and openness. We consider each of these here in turn.

The first point concerns the manner in which central and local authorities interrelate. This is crucial in the context of the PRC's environmental governance, as there are very different interests at stake at both levels. National-level governance wishes to establish standards in order to provide a reasonable balance of public and private goods in the process of development, while local-level governance is usually more focused on the competition with other local authorities for economic and industrial development. It is fundamental for national governance to be able to provide a level playing field across local units, by ensuring that basic environmental standards are met everywhere. This is apparent from the experiences with environmental governance in both the EU and the United States. These experiences point to the five important aspects regarding national and local governmental coordination:

1   uniform national standards;
2   shared authority in implementation;
3   secondary enforcement capabilities;
4   directed funding (from national to local authorities); and
5   conditional funding authority (of national over local authorities).

As mentioned previously, uniform national standards perform the crucial role of ensuring that there is no "race to the bottom" across local units of government. It is more important to create this competition in terms of implementation, by delegating authority to local authorities in choosing the mechanism for attaining environmental goals. This is done in both the United States and the EU, where the member states are given authority for selecting the means of attaining nationally-set environmental standards. A crucial feature of this delegated authority is that it is made conditional on the attainment of set goals. If implementation in any locality is deemed ineffective, then the national authorities have the authority to step in and undertake the implementation themselves. This implies the need for secondary enforcement, wherein some entity other than the local authority has the capacity to carry out the monitoring of local environmental quality. This secondary monitoring provides the check against local authorities' avoidance of national standards. It can be done by either providing authority for inspections by central authorities, or by giving rights to individuals to file complaints to central authorities or judicial officials. As long as some entities are given rights to secondary monitoring and enforcement, local officials have an incentive to attempt to implement the national standards. A final aspect of this coordinated governance scheme is the provision of some forms of incentives, other than penalties, for local authorities' compliance. This is provided in the United States by means of directed and conditional spending, in which central authorities are given control over funding to local authorities in order to provide a ready means of rewarding and penalizing implementation.

The importance of secondary enforcement is evident in many countries. Local authorities simply do not have the incentives to act in accordance with national standards in many contexts. For this reason, it can be important to provide some rights of access by local individuals to complain about local authorities to another agency. In the United States, this is accomplished by means of providing rights to individuals for citizen suits. These rights of action allow local individuals to complain to local courts about inaction by local authorities. If the court finds in favor of the local individual, it might then order the local authority to move toward compliance with national standards. In Sweden, the authority that individuals complain to is called the environmental ombudsman. The ombudsman is an independent government official authorized to decide on whether or not local authorities are in compliance with national standards. But compared to the local courts, the process of complaint to an ombudsman is much less formal. In this instance, the citizens are simply provided an independent official with whom to speak to in the event of dissatisfaction with local authorities.

An important aspect of governmental coordination is the provision of some means for securing information about both local industrial activities and local authorities' performance. The provision of various means by which information is automatically disseminated, together with the provision of mechanisms to ensure its reliability, is critical for the attainment of environmental standards. One important means for ensuring information sharing is to make the undertaking of economic activity conditional on the ongoing provision of information. This may be done, on a project by project basis, by requiring environmental impact assessments. Or it may be done by requiring information in exchange for permits for ongoing activities. In order to ensure accuracy of information, it is interesting to note that some governments rely upon the incentives of local communities to provide this. In the United States, so-called bucket brigades provide individual monitoring stations to households who then report directly to central authorities about any environmental incidents that are detected.

In sum, the review of the PRC's environmental governance indicates that there is a real need for coordination between national and local authorities in order to ensure that incentives for implementation, monitoring and enforcement are properly in place. All other countries have been faced with this dilemma in the course of developing their respective environmental strategies. The cross-cutting issues discussed above all point to the need to create a framework in which both local and central authorities (and local communities) share responsibility to ensure that monitoring and implementation will occur.

The PRC's path to a brighter future: recommendations

This final chapter (Chapter 14) of the volume describes the conclusions reached after considering the situation in which the PRC now finds itself. The PRC has benefited from two decades of unprecedented economic growth, but it is also faced with unprecedented environmental degradation. This collaborative study concludes that the combination of economic growth and environmental degradation creates substantial pressures for the development of regulatory institutions in the PRC. At this juncture in the PRC's development, these institutions need to become more capable at balancing social demands in order to implement desired social outcomes. It is no longer adequate for environmental management to simply focus on clean-up activities of the past.

This shift in emphasis will require that significant efforts be invested into institutional development in the PRC. The PRC's experiences as well as the experiences of other countries are both important for informing these developments. The PRC's experiences demonstrate the manner in which unbridled economic growth is able to target outcomes that result in significant environmental degradation. Other countries' experiences demonstrate that the same outcomes have been targeted there as well. The important message is that it is possible to alter institutions so that different outcomes are targeted.

Most developed countries have followed the same sort of development path – i.e. periods of substantial economic growth combined with significant amounts of environmental deterioration. It has happened in different places at different points in time, but the experience has been very much the same. This is because economic activities often make use of environmental resources (such as air, water, ecosystems) for production or for disposal of wastes, and expanded activities place increased pressures upon them. When environmental regulation does not exist, there is usually no other mechanism that effectively controls access to environmental resources. This absence of control encourages economic activities to over-exploit usage of these resources, resulting in predictable declines in the quantities and qualities of these resources.

Unregulated access allows environmental resources to be used on a first-come, first-served basis. This may provide incentives for firms and individuals to access them quickly and completely, but it is not a very rational basis for efficiently allocating them among competing uses. Economists advocate allocating resources to the uses that value them most highly, providing some resources to various uses in accordance with the value generated. Unregulated use of environmental resources usually results in unbalanced and excessive use. It becomes increasingly costly to society as all other uses are denied by reason of their prior appropriation by a few polluters. As other users becoming increasingly frustrated with their inability to use environmental resources (e.g. for breathing air or for drinking water), demands increase for the regulation of environmental resources. This demand for environmental regulation is specifically a demand for a more rational, balanced or "efficient" basis for allocating environmental resources among various competing uses.

Most developed countries have gone through this economic growth process and created systems for environmental regulation and management. It is seen in the usual pathway through the development process, whereby initial growth is often combined with environmental degradation but that later growth is combined with environmental improvement. Such paths are to be expected as the demand for a regulatory system arises in response to environmental regulation. The increasing need and demand for environmental regulation is now observed in the PRC, after 30 years of economic growth.

In setting up a regulatory system for environmental resources, it is important to provide a mechanism for recognizing public demands for such resources. Some measures for balancing public and private demands to determine a rational allocation should also be put in place. Finally, it is critical to create a governance system capable of implementing and enforcing the environmental standards that result. We have seen in this volume how this process is occurring in the PRC, first with the creation of environmental standards and increasingly with the recognition that public participation and environmental governance are crucial to a successful regulatory system.

It is well known that growth can be slowed down by the introduction of regulation, but this misses the point that growth cannot be the sole objective of any society. There are many other forms of value provided by environmental resources, including health, stability, leisure, tradition and enjoyment. A balanced regulatory approach aims to maximize the total value from the use of environmental resources, and growth is one of those objectives. The approach also aims to lead economic growth in positive directions that are most compatible with environmental objectives. Economic growth and environmental regulation must go hand-in-hand in the long run. The development experiences of other countries demonstrate that this should be the case.

The situation in the PRC shares important, indeed fundamental, similarities with the environmental protection challenges faced by other countries. While these challenges are not identical, the strategies employed to address them provide useful lessons and experiences for the PRC officials to consider in drafting the country's long-term growth strategy.

The following chapters in this volume provide a careful assessment of the PRC's management of air pollution, water pollution, ecosystems and institutional governance. This overview allows us to summarize some of the findings about the sorts of institutional changes required in the PRC, highlighting four of the most important cross-cutting themes. The remainder of the volume fleshes out the nature of these proposed solutions.

Theme 1: coordination between central and local authorities

An issue that comes up in all the case studies is the relationship between local authorities and the central government. The MEP depends critically on local Environmental Protection Bureaus (EPBs) for effective implementation of national laws, meaningful enforcement of legal requirements and information on local problems. The local EPBs, in turn, rely on the MEP for technical expertise and standard setting. While both local and national authorities need each other, their relationship is complex.

While the details obviously differ, 40 years ago, the United States and the EU also faced a similar problem of central authority wanting stronger environmental protection resulting in occasional conflict with local authorities who are more closely committed to development. The evolution of environmental protection in both the United States and the EU has shown a similar transition to the current models of strong central authorities that set strict environmental requirements with generally effective compliance at the local level.

If one looks broadly across the history of the US and European environmental protections over the last 40 years and, in particular, the coordination between national and local authorities, five separate coordination strategies emerge. It is important to note that the MEP is relatively weak in two of the most important areas, namely secondary enforcement and conditional funding. The Macro-Environmental Policy will need to consider these explicitly.

At a minimum, coordinating environmental protection between national and local authorities requires a clear understanding of their respective rights and responsibilities. In both the United States and the European Union, consolidation of authority has been preceded by passage of national laws that supplant state environmental authority in place of a national, uniform program. While passage of laws alone is never enough to ensure effective implementation, it is, nevertheless, a necessary precondition. The PRC has done well in this regard.

In the transition from decentralized environmental protection to centralized protection, the primary responsibility has shifted from the provincial and state levels to the central ministries and agencies. Importantly, however, the transfer of power from local to central authorities is not absolute – i.e. local levels still retain significant authorities. This is true in the United States and the EU, where the most appropriate manner of sharing authority remains a contentious topic. In the PRC, too, significant authority is shared between the MEP and the local EPBs. How this relationship evolves in the coming decades will be a fundamental issue for the PRC's Macro-Environmental Strategy.

The role of enforcement, for example, should be delegated to local authorities in order to minimize the costs of enforcement (information, compliance, incentive compatibility). At the same time, the ultimate responsibility for enforcement still needs to be administered by the central authorities in order to facilitate coordination across local authorities. This highlights the importance of providing some incentive structure between the central level and the local authorities, in order to induce functional performance at the provincial and local levels. It also points to the importance of providing some manner of centralized appellate procedure (such as a judicial mechanism at the central level) to hear complaints on, and pronounce upon need for, harmonization of implementation procedures across regional and local authorities.

Secondary enforcement is an important strategy permitting central authorities to ensure adequate local implementation and enforcement of environmental laws. In some cases, the central authority retains the power to bring enforcement actions against the polluter or the local authority if the local enforcement is deemed to be inadequate. In other cases, local officials have primary responsibility for permitting certain actions and enforcing national laws, but complaints (say, in the form of lawsuits) may be brought against polluters or the government agencies by individuals.

As mentioned above, it is crucial that the central authorities have some means for creating incentives for enforcement by local authorities. But it could also be the case that weak performance by local environmental authorities sometimes stems from inadequacy of resources. Local authorities may want to enforce environmental laws, but they do not have enough funds to hire inspectors, analyze air samples from monitoring stations, or carry out enforcement activities. Having the necessary mechanisms for central authorities to channel these funds to the local authorities is important in linking the roles of local authorities to the responsibilities of central authorities.

A key strategy for effective coordination lies in *conditioning central funds* on local authorities meeting specific performance goals. This strategy is even more effective if the central authority is able to withhold funds that are not controlled by it, thus limiting the ability of *other* agencies to disburse funds to the local levels, and consequently raising the potential impact of the sanction considerably. In some cases, the central authority is given control over funds from *another* ministry, such as the Ministry of Transportation.

Theme 2: environmental enforcement

One of the themes addressed in every chapter of this volume is the importance of enforcement activities in attaining environmental standards. Two different types of concerns have been raised. First is the problem of *under-enforcement* – the concern that current penalties for pollution are too low to change behavior. Second is the problem of *misdirected enforcement* – the concern that there should be greater emphasis by government on the need to create incentives for compliance, not just sanctions to non-compliance.

Much of the problem of under-enforcement derives from the coordination problems between central and local authorities, as described above. Incentives at these different levels are so diverse; hence coordination between them is crucial. The need for supplemental monitoring mechanisms is another aspect of the problem. There is no group with greater motivation (or capability) for monitoring local environmental environments than the local communities. This underscores the importance of citizen engagement and information, the two themes considered next.

Another important aspect of enforcement concerns the type of mechanism that is used in regulation. Systems that rely too much on command and control often leave the regulator with few options other than to monitor and to sanction. The studies in this volume demonstrate that, although command and control is always a viable option, other more market-friendly institutions have the capacity to guide industries in the desired direction instead of simply imposing sanctions for non-compliance. For example, the SO_x regime in the United States provided for real-time monitoring on stacks and the requirement of permit purchases as a means of attaining environmental standards. Such a regime demonstrates that attainment is possible on a property rights basis rather than on a penalty basis. It provides incentives for compliance, rather than penalties for non-compliance.

Importantly, such a regime also creates incentives for innovation rather than evasion. In market-based regimes, industries are provided with a clear market signal and a technological route for meeting the requirements of the regime, by means of finding techniques and methods of production that require fewer permits. These types of incentive-based regimes help to turn environmental enforcement problems into environmental innovation solutions.

Theme 3: individual participation models

Many experts, both Chinese and international, emphasize the important roles that can be played by individuals and private environmental groups. There is currently a limited legal basis for public participation in environmental protection in the PRC compared to Organisation for Economic Co-operation and Development (OECD) countries. Both formal and informal participation by individuals and groups in environmental protection can increase the effectiveness of current efforts. The Ministry of Environmental Protection and the local Environmental Protection Bureaus have limited resources. Thus one model for citizen participation lies in partnership, i.e. by providing citizens and environmental groups opportunities to reinforce government protection efforts. This can be done in the fields of enforcement and compliance monitoring, among others. For example, in some parts of the United States, individual citizens are formed into "bucket brigades" and supply individual-based monitoring of local environmental conditions.

The second model for citizen participation lies in providing an avenue for citizens' voices to be heard. While this can also reinforce environmental protection efforts, the goal here is to create structures so citizens' voices can be heard in a constructive fashion. This could be done through greater use of environmental ombudsmen, such as those existing in some countries in Scandinavia.

In the United States, much of environmental enforcement and legal development occurs within the court system. There, the judiciary sees itself as arbitrating between the rights of citizens to a clean environment and the property rights of individuals and their development. In the first instance, environmental agencies provide the means by which the public and the private sector are able to be heard, but the courts remain an independent arbiter of most disputes regarding the environment. In this way, individuals are participating in the system both as monitors (of any activities violating local standards) and as enforcers (by filing complaints with officials).

Theme 4: information management

An environmental regulator needs accurate information to understand the nature of the problem and the consequences of potential responses. Likewise, the regulated community needs information to help them decide how best to comply with adopted rules. The public also needs information in order to feel adequately protected and to effectively participate in the regulatory regime. These challenges of information management are posed with special significance in the context of environmental law.

A key consideration of information management is whether, on balance, initiatives to collect information, provide access to information, or disseminate information actually improve agency actions or just hinder them. In theory, more (quality) information will improve decision-making. The challenge is that government resources are limited (as are private resources), and the time and money spent collecting, generating and sharing information would mean fewer resources and lesser time available for allocation to other worthy needs.

In sum, the problems of environmental management in the PRC are indicative of fundamental problems of institutional development. This has been the case with all countries that have gone through the same process in the past. It is especially a difficult predicament for the PRC because of the pace at which the problems have progressed, and the evident need for rapid institutional change to deal with these problems in the future.

In conclusion, the PRC is in a good position to make these choices and to implement these changes. It has 30 years of economic growth in hand, and it clearly recognizes the need for the institutional developments to address these problems. This is an opportunity, as much as it is an obstacle, for future development in the country. The PRC's long-term strategy needs to focus as much on the choice of its development institutions as on the choice of its environment regulation. The two will come together to shape the path toward the PRC's future.

Notes

1 Asian Development Bank (ADB). 2007. *Country Environmental Analysis for the People's Republic of China.*
2 Ibid.
3 State Environmental Protection Agency (SEPA). 2004. *State of the Environment Report.*
4 Asian Development Bank (ADB). 2007. *Country Environmental Analysis for the People's Republic of China.*
5 State Environmental Protection Agency (SEPA). 2004. *State of the Environment Report.*
6 Ibid.
7 Ibid.
8 Ibid.
9 Li Peng, "Implement Sustainable Development Strategy, Ensure the Realization of Environmental Protection Targets" – speech at the symposium of the Fourth National Environmental Protection Conference, see in the documentation of the Fourth National Environmental Protection Conference compiled by SEPA, Beijing: China Environment Science Press, 1996, p. 7.

Part I

Growth and environmental regulation

2 Economic growth and environmental protection in the People's Republic of China

Guang Xia, Xiaofei Pei and Xiaoming Yang

Introduction

The history of environmental protection is a history of addressing the relationship between economic development and environmental protection. During their century-long industrialization, most Western developed countries experienced a traditional economic growth characterized as "pollution first, treatment after," due mainly to the limited recognition of the importance of environmental protection and level of economic and technological advancement. While accumulating substantial wealth, these Western developed countries have also paid dearly in terms of environmental degradation. The government of the People's Republic of China (PRC) recognized relatively early the importance of appropriately addressing the relationship between economic development and environmental protection. On December 31, 1983, during the Second National Environmental Protection Conference, the State Council included environmental protection in the basic national policies. To achieve the unification of economic, social and ecological benefits, the Council emphasized the need for synchronized planning, implementation and development in economic construction, urban and rural construction, and environmental protection ("Three Synchronizations" and "Three Unifications"). The inclusion in the basic national policy defined the importance of environmental protection in the PRC's economic and social development. Being the PRC's first strategic guideline for environmental protection, "Three Synchronizations" and "Three Unifications" wields profound influence on the development of the environmental protection cause, and signifies that the country's environmental protection program has transformed from the initial phase of simple pollution treatment into a new phase of harmonious development of economy, society and environment.[1]

After the United Nations Environment and Development Conference in 1992, the PRC took the lead in proposing the "Ten Measures for Environment and Development," the first nation to propose the transformation of the traditional mode of development into the sustainable mode of development. The proposal is a testament to the strategic solution most suitable to the PRC's current situation, and it brought forth a new and crucial meaning to development – a sustainable progress with the confluence of environmental protection and economic growth.

This is the inspiration derived from the United Nations Environment and Development Conference, as well as the experience drawn from years of practice. If the traditional mode of resource- and energy-consuming economic growth is not transformed and the dependence on mere remedial measures continues, environmental problems will not be fundamentally resolved.

A strategy based on basic national policy and sustainable development is the most appropriate policy guide to harmonize economic development and environmental protection. The effective implementation of this strategy in the PRC would have spared the country from encountering serious environmental problems. However, instead of the ideal harmonization of economic development and environmental protection, the present situation – characterized by rapid modernization, intensive development activities, large-scale infrastructure construction, high consumption, and pollution-intensive industrial development – has taken precedence. And although environmental protection has been incorporated into the basic national policy, firm regulations can rarely be seen on human, financial and material resources configuration nor in cadres' performance examination, which are deemed as necessary guarantee measures for basic national policy. As a result, the intent and objectives of the national policy have not been put in place, and the rough style development mode of high resource consumption and high environmental pollution which is unsuitable to the PRC's national situation have not been eliminated. Economic development had indeed materially enriched the PRC's population, but it had also rendered the PRC's two decades of accelerated industrialization and urbanization fraught with so many environmental problems. Developed countries experienced similar environmental problems, but in gradual measures during their century-long industrialization which enabled them to address the problems in phases. Despite the examples provided by, and lessons learned from, the developed countries' industrialization experiences, the complexity and intensity of the environmental problems in the PRC made it impossible to veer away from the developed countries' "pollution first, treatment after" solution.

This chapter discusses the environmental costs of the economic growth in the PRC, renders an analysis of the causes of environmental problems related to economic growth, and proposes the route and policies that will enable the transformation of the relationship between economic growth and environmental protection from conflict to integration.

Economic development phases and environmental problems of the PRC

From 1949 when the PRC was founded, to 1978 when the country adopted reforms and opened up, the PRC undertook the "Great Leap Forward" and experienced "Cultural Revolution," which had caused fairly severe environmental pollution and ecological damage. However, due to the small production scale and the still big environmental capacity during that period, the conflict between economic construction and environmental protection was generally not apparent, and the environmental problems were only regional, and thus controllable, in scope. After the Third Plenary Session of the 11th National Congress of the Communist Party in 1978, the whole country began the hard work toward economic progress. Since all efforts were centered on economic construction, and various development projects were initiated all over the PRC, the economic growth accelerated sharply. The gross domestic product (GDP) in 1992 (RMB2,756.5 billion) alone exceeded the sum of the GDPs in the ten-year period of 1969 to 1978 (RMB2,700.9 billion).[2] With such rapid economic growth, the amount of pollutants discharges increased sharply, and the conflict between environmental protection and economic development became increasingly prominent.

Environmental problems are closely associated with industrialization progress. During the period of industrialization in the PRC, the economic growth experienced four phases:[3] Phase I (1978–84) – rural reform; Phase II (1985–92) – light industry development; Phase III (1993–9) – preliminary heavy chemical industry development; and Phase IV (2000 to present) – heavy chemical industry development (see Figure 2.1). Each of the phases of economic growth is characterized by distinct attributes and brings about different environmental problems.

Birth of environmental problems in the rural reform phase (1978–84)

In this phase, the PRC experienced the period of both opening up and economic construction and reform, characterized by rural reform and agricultural development. During this phase, the proportion of the primary industry in the GDP was

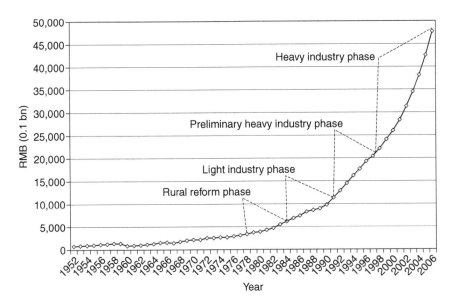

Figure 2.1 Four phases of GDP and economic growth.

higher than that of the tertiary industry (equal in 1985, 28.5 percent). It was after this phase that the first round of economic growth reached its peak. In 1984, both industrial and agricultural production values doubled those in 1978,[4] and township enterprises especially in the industrial sector experienced rapid growth. From 1978 to 1983, the total township industrial production value registered an annual growth rate of 14.5 percent.[5] Although this phase featured rural land reform, non-point source agricultural pollution was not severe due to the backward agricultural production and the then limited supply of production materials such as pesticides and fertilizers.

This phase also saw the formulation of a series of environmental protection guidelines, policies and measures. In particular, environmental protection was made part of the basic national policies during the Second National Environmental Protection Conference held by the State Council at the end of 1983. It was also during this Conference that synchronized planning, implementation and development and the unification of economic, social and ecological benefits were made requirements for economic construction, urban and rural construction, and environmental protection. This phase also witnessed the setting up of environmental protection institutions at the central and local levels, the intensification of environmental management in many regions and sectors, and the conduct of pollution investigation and treatment in key areas where certain effective achievements were made. However, due to the large number of randomly scattered township enterprises with unsound product structure, laggard technical equipment and poor management, and due to the intensive consumption of resources and energy and lack of the corresponding pollution prevention measures, pollution damage became even more prominent and harder to prevent. Pollution became widespread, from hotspots to the whole region, spanning both urban and rural areas. During this period, environmental protection work lagged far behind economic development.

Emergence of environmental problems in the light industry development phase (1985–92)

In this phase, economic development in the PRC featured the rapid development of light industry, mainly light and textile industries, to meet the population's demand for food, clothing and other consumption. By 1988, the symptoms of economic overheating had become quite evident such that some areas and departments blindly adopted inefficient, resource- and energy-intensive, and heavy polluting projects such as small-scale paper mills, electroplating and coking and smelting plants. Moreover, deforestation and overexploitation of natural resources became common, accelerating environmental quality deterioration even further. Urban air pollution was considerably severe. In concrete terms, the average annual total suspended particulates exceeded 800 micrograms per cubic meter ($\mu g/m^3$) in the PRC's northern urban area, and surpassed $1,000\,\mu g/m^3$ in some cities in the winter. Water quality suffered even more. The monitoring data on 532 rivers indicated that 436 had been polluted at different levels, and among the 15 major urban reaches of the seven large rivers, 13 had been severely polluted. In addition, the aggregate untreated industrial residues and urban domestic wastes amounted to 6.6 billion tons and spanned 536 square kilometers (km^2), becoming the second largest pollution source. Ecosystem deterioration was not avoided either. The stretch of land with soil and water loss had increased from 1.16 million km^2 in the early PRC to 1.50 million km^2.[6]

The abovementioned facts showed that the proposals of "Three Synchronizations" and "Three Unifications" by the State Council in 1983 were not effectively carried out. Thus, in order to resolve the increasingly prominent and serious environmental problems, the State Council convened the Third National Environmental Protection Conference in 1989, during which a proposal was made for the establishment of a new order for environmental protection work, improvement and rectification through the enhancement of system construction, comprehensive implementation of both the old and new eight environmental management systems,[7] and intensification of supervision and management. In 1990, the State Council promulgated the "Decisions on Further Strengthening Environmental Protection Work" and emphasized the importance of industrial pollution prevention and control through strict execution of environmental protection laws and regulations, legal implementation of effective measures such as the eight environmental management systems, and highlighting the application of environmental protection target responsibility system. These policies and measures were essential in the efforts to achieve by 1992 the specific environmental protection targets set by the Third National Environmental Protection Conference. And in fact, except for the control of the aggregate industrial wastewater discharges, other targets such as the control of (sulfur dioxide) SO_2 and smoke emissions and the comprehensive utilization of industrial solid wastes were mostly realized.

Increasingly serious environmental problems in the preliminary heavy chemical industry phase (1993–9)

This phase witnessed the acceleration of the PRC's industrialization and urbanization. During the period encompassed by the Ninth Five-Year Plan (FYP) (1996–2000), the GDP registered an average annual growth of 8.3 percent, which surpassed the target of 8 percent. In 1997, the strategic target of quadrupling the 1980 per capita GDP was realized three years ahead of schedule. Also in this phase, the proportion of the heavy industry in the industrial structure significantly exceeded that of the light industry. High growth industries included those of:

1 energy and raw materials such as oil and natural gas exploitation;
2 infrastructure and basic industries such as highways, ports and electricity; and
3 electrical products such as color televisions, refrigerators, washing machines and air-conditioning units.

Apart from meeting the demands of civil "convenience" and addressing the shortage in energy and raw materials, the accelerating urbanization drove the rapid development of these industries. In 1999 alone, the PRC's urbanization rate was at 30.9 percent, 1.7 times that in 1978.[8]

Environmental management in this phase faced even stronger challenges. In 1996, the State Council convened the Fourth National Environmental Protection Conference and made the important conclusion that environmental protection is in fact the way to protect productivity. After the conference, the State Council promulgated the "Decisions on Several Issues in Environmental Protection," which, in order to ensure the realization of the environmental protection targets of the Ninth FYP, called for the following:

1   adoption of definite targets and implementation of the governor responsibility system for environment quality;
2   emphasis on key tasks and focus on regional environmental problems;
3   control and prohibition of new pollution;
4   timely compliance with standards and acceleration of the treatment of old pollution;
5   adoption of effective measures forbidding the shift of pollution from solid waste;
6   preservation of ecological balance and protection and reasonable exploitation of natural resources;
7   improvement of economic instruments and feasible increase of environmental protection inputs;
8   intensification of the enforcement, supervision and monitoring of environmental protection policies;
9   active encouragement of research on environmental science and development of environmental protection industry; and
10   increase in publicity and improvement of the public's environmental awareness.

The main challenges in this period included the continuous geographic expansion of environmental pollution from urban centers to rural areas, and the expansion of ecological deterioration, by reason of the energy-intensive economic growth and backward technology and management, which resulted in pollution and destruction outpacing treatment. Within seven years, industrial wastewater discharges totaled 144.9 billion tons, industrial gas emissions aggregated to 77 trillion cubic meter (m^3), and the total industrial SO_2 emissions amounted to 98.18 million tons. Environmental pollution and ecological damage not only impeded the development of economy in certain regions but also harmed the public's health.[9]

Intense outburst of environmental problems in the heavy chemical industry phase – severe environmental situation (2000–present)

This phase ushered in the era of heavy chemical industry in the PRC. Industries such as electricity, steel, automobile, shipbuilding and the production and manufacture of mechanical equipment, chemicals, electronics and building materials became the main drivers of economic growth which leaned toward "large value consumption" in housing and travel. Beginning in 2003, the PRC underwent even more rapid economic growth at a rate exceeding 10 percent in five consecutive years. In 2007, the per capita GDP exceeded US$2,460, following the per capita GDP of US$1,100 in 2002, when it surpassed for the first time US$1,000. This phase also witnessed accelerated urbanization and the fastest and longest-lasting economic growth. In 2007, the rate of urbanization reached 44.9 percent, 8.8 percent higher than the 36.1 percent rate in 2000, registering an average annual increase of 1.3 percent in a span of seven years. The consumption of resources and energy also posted a significant increase. In particular, coal consumption rose from 1.376 billion tons in 2000 to 2.58 billion tons in 2007, an increase of nearly 87.5 percent which directly resulted in high emissions of main pollutants. SO_2 and chemical oxygen demand (COD) emissions in 2007 were 24.681 million tons and 13.818 million tons, respectively, with the SO_2 emissions increasing by 23.7 percent from those in 2000. With the limited area of arable land, the increase of food production still relied largely on the use of pesticides and fertilizers (see Figure 2.2), making the problem of non-point source pollution more prominent in agriculture. Meanwhile, the severe outbreak of malignant water pollution accidents in the Songhuajiang River, the Guangdong Beijiang River, the Hunan Xiangjiang River, Dianchi Lake and Taihu Lake brought serious harm to life and production.

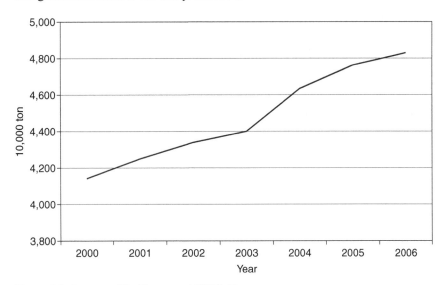

Figure 2.2 Amount of fertilizers used (2000–6).

During this phase, the State Council twice convened a national environmental protection conference. The Fifth National Environmental Protection Conference held in 2002 planned environmental protection work for the Tenth FYP (2001–5), recognizing that environmental protection is one of the important functions of the government. Notwithstanding, the targets for environmental protection of the Tenth FYP were not realized due to the irrational economic structure, rough mode of economic growth and ineffective enforcement, supervision and monitoring.[10] The data shows that between 2000 and 2005, SO_2 emissions increased by 27 percent while COD emissions decreased by only 2 percent, none of which are close to the control target of 10 percent reduction. Because of this, the State Council convened the Sixth National Environmental Protection Conference in April 2006, wherein Premier Wen Jiabao emphasized "synchronization" and "equal importance" of environmental protection and economic development, and directed the resolution of environmental problems through "comprehensive" measures. Environmental protection was then placed in a more strategic position. Energy-saving measures and emissions reduction were made the restrictive obligations in the Eleventh FYP, during which environmental protection responsibility was given particular emphasis and significance, bringing about new hope for the resolution of environmental problems in the PRC.

To sum up, environmental problems in the PRC are closely connected to the process of industrialization, which is characterized by the significant proportion of heavy chemical industry, continuous increase in energy and raw materials consumption, and the resulting excessive discharge of pollutants. On the other hand, while the demands for environmental protection policies in the different phases of economic development have been fairly high without exception, the implementation and enforcement of these policies have been very poor and ineffective, such that environmental deterioration and degradation occurred alongside economic growth in the PRC.

Analysis on causes of environmental problems related to economic growth

To some extent, development is very similar to the process of combustion. A country's resources are burned to generate GDP and the residue is pollution.[11] The causes and characteristics of environmental problems have been closely linked to the scale, speed and modes of economic growth, which interact in turn with the natural environment, population, industrialization, urbanization and energy demand, all together causing the severe environmental problems.

Limited area of land suitable for human settlement and development

Although the PRC's land area is nearly $10,000,000\,km^2$, which is similar to that of the whole of America or that part of Europe east of the Ural Mountains, the actual land area suitable for human settlement and development is less than half of the said total area, due to the poor natural conditions in the country. In fact, more than 90 percent of the Chinese population occupy an area less than one-third of the total area. The limited nature of the land area suitable for human settlement and development has led to the overwhelming environmental pressure on unit area and intense and heavy pollution. Worse, a series of objective factors unfavorable to environmental protection – such as uneven spatial and seasonal distribution of water resource, large sludge and sand content in rivers, shallow continental shelf along the coastline, poor diffusivity of pollutants, fragile ecological system – contributed to the hardship of environmental protection work.

Large population base and change of population structure

The large population of the PRC has been the perennial and fundamental cause of its environmental problems. Although the government adopted the family planning policy as early as the 1970s, the population still kept on increasing annually until it reached 1,321,290,000 in 2007. The huge population has exploited the natural resources to meet the demands of survival and development, and thereby exerted tremendous pressure on the environment, leading to a shortage in various mineral and water resources. The population structure has also changed significantly. The slow increase by 0.358 billion in the population from 1978 to 2007 was characterized by an urban population increase of 2.35 times, from 0.17 billion to 0.57 billion, and a rural population decrease by 7 percent, from 0.79 billion to 0.73 billion (see Figure 2.3).

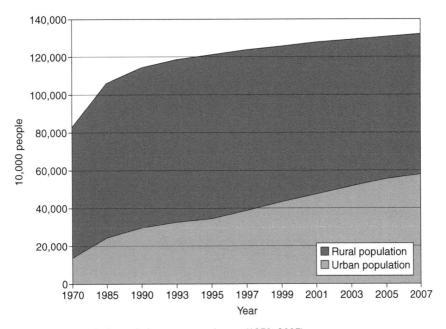

Figure 2.3 Trend of population structure change (1970–2007).

A change in population structure translates to a change in consumption structure, since the demand on resources and energy by urban people is much higher than that of rural people. The strong demand driven by the accelerated urbanization currently taking place in the PRC hastens the development of heavy chemical industries such as electricity, metallurgy, cement and building materials, petrochemical, transportation and coal, resulting in the large output of heavy chemical products and the rapid development of the heavy chemical industries (see Figure 2.4 and Figure 2.5).

Sharp increase of economic scale

The PRC's enormous economic growth in the past decades was mainly brought about by huge investments in the manufacturing industry. During the period

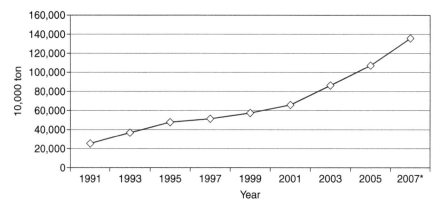

Figure 2.4 Cement production (1991–2007).

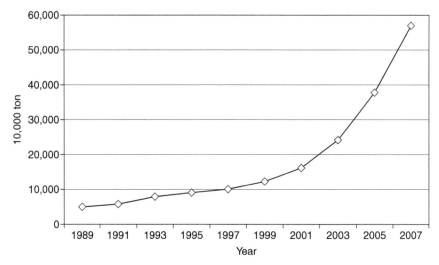

Figure 2.5 Finished steel production (1989–2007).

from 1998 to 2007, domestic industrial production increased sharply, especially during the heavy chemical industry phase after 2000. To be more precise, during the period covered by the Tenth FYP (2001–5), the annual average growth rate of industrial added value was 10.9 percent. Meanwhile, in 2007, the total added value reached RMB10,736.7 billion, 2.26 times that in 2002, with an annual growth rate exceeding 11 percent (Figure 2.6).

With the rapid growth of the economic aggregate, the production of industrial gas and solid wastes also increased sharply. From 2002 to 2007, when the

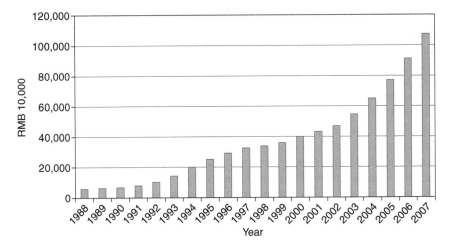

Figure 2.6 Domestic industrial production value (1988–2007).

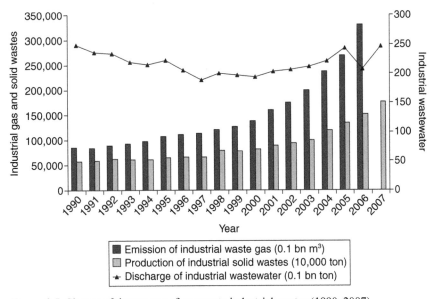

Figure 2.7 Change of three types of aggregate industrial wastes (1990–2007).

domestic industrial added value increased by 126 percent, industrial waste gas emissions and industrial solid wastes increased by 121 percent and 84 percent, respectively (Figure 2.7). Relevant research[12] showed that what most contributed to the growth of SO_2 during the period covered by the Tenth FYP is the expansion of economic scale, as is the case during the first two years of the Eleventh FYP.

Change in industrial structure

The industrial structure has undergone numerous changes during the rapid economic progress in the PRC. Although the proportion of the secondary industry remained stable as a dominant industry since 1978, a steady rise in the development of the tertiary industry and the fall of the proportion of the primary industry were observed (Figure 2.8).

The structure change was accompanied by a change in pollutants. During the Tenth FYP period, when the added value of the secondary industry, pulled by the high investments, grew fastest among the three industries, with an average annual growth rate of 10.9 percent, the pollution created by the fast-growing heavy chemical industry was prominent. For example, from 2000 to 2006, the total industrial products of black-metal melting and calendering increased by 437 percent (same-year price), while industrial gas emissions and industrial solid wastes increased by 245 percent and 141 percent, respectively (see Figure 2.9).

Rough growth mode

The rough growth mode of the PRC's economy has remained the same for a long period of time. In 2006, when the PRC's GDP exhibited a growth rate of 10.7 percent and accounted for 5.5 percent of the world's GDP (based on same-

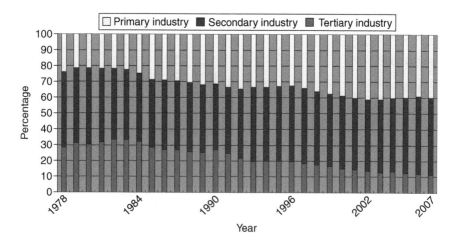

Figure 2.8 Configuration of the PRC's three industries (1978–2007).

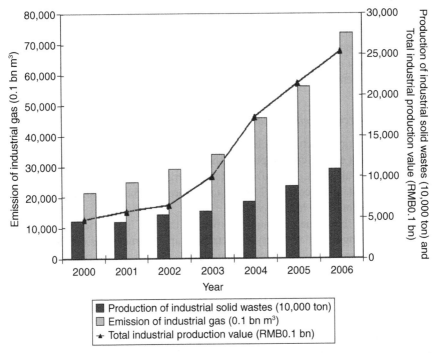

Figure 2.9 Total industrial products, waste gas emissions and solid waste production of black metal melting and calendering (2000–6).

year exchange rate), it consumed 2.46 billion tons of standard coal as energy (15 percent of the world coal consumption), 0.45 billion tons of steel (30 percent of the world steel consumption), 8.65 million tons of aluminum (25 percent of the world aluminum use), and 1.24 billion tons of cement (54 percent of world level).[13]

The excessive consumption of resources has been brought about by many reasons, among which were the phase and transfer factors and the country's still rough mode of economic growth. The PRC is in the historical phase of accelerated industrialization and urbanization which has been shown by international experiences to be the period of resource consumption growth. The process of economic globalization and the international industrial structure adjustment brought about the transfer to the PRC of some high consumption and resource-intensive industries, which significantly contributed to the country's already immense consumption of resources. What is significant to note is that the high resources consumption and the huge environmental pressure distinctly indicate that the PRC's rough mode of economic growth – characterized by high input, high consumption, high emission, difficult circulation and low efficiency – has not been transformed fundamentally. Compared to the advanced international consumption levels, the energy consumption of the PRC's large- and medium-scale steel enterprises is 15 percent higher, the coal consumption in the PRC's

48   *G. Xia* et al.

power stations is 20 percent higher, and the cement consumption is 23 percent higher.[14] If in the immediate future, the mode of economic growth in the PRC is not replaced and the high consumption of its resources is not reduced, the country's rapid economic growth will be short-lived. There is thus a necessity to transform, if not replace, the mode of economic growth in the PRC to pursue the road toward scientific development.

Significant increase in energy consumption

The PRC's energy structure has been coal-dominated for a long time. In Figure 2.10, the PRC's energy consumption is shown to have increased significantly in the recent two decades. In 2007, the total energy consumption reached 2.65 billion tons of standard coal, 1.13 billion tons more than that in 2002 and exceeding the increment of the last 20 years.

Figure 2.11 shows the continuous growth in the PRC's electricity consumption. Considering that the country's electricity supply structure is dominated by coal power, there was also a consequent significant increase in coal consumption. And although measures have been undertaken to improve the aggressive treatment of pollution caused by desulfurization in power stations, the environment is still under massive pressure due to the increasing energy consumption and emission increments.

The change in the public's consumption mode brought about an aggressive development in infrastructure construction and the transportation industry, and a significant increase in petrochemical energy consumption (see Figure 2.12).

The high energy consumption due to economic growth also caused the increase of pollutants discharges (see Figure 2.13), and put pressure on the environment.

To sum up, despite the existence of objective unfavorable factors, such as the shortage of natural conditions and the large population, the PRC's severe

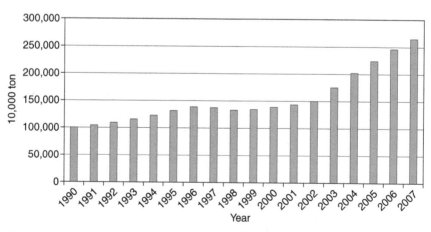

Figure 2.10 Total energy consumption (1990–2007).

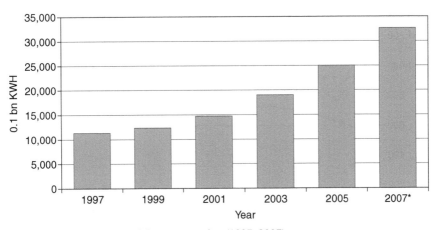

Figure 2.11 National electricity consumption (1997–2007).

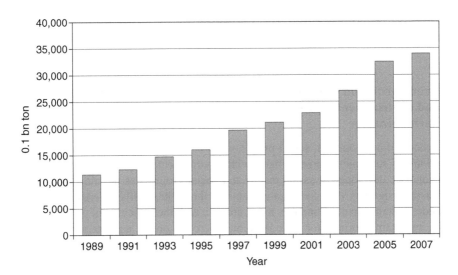

Figure 2.12 Total oil consumption (1989–2007).

environmental problems are directly attributable to the fast expansion of economic scale, heavy industrialization of the industrial structure, rough mode of economic growth, and the excessive coal-dominated energy consumption. Simply put, the incomplete decoupling between the environment and the economy, as well as the synchronized growth of the economy and most pollutants discharges, have resulted in the serious environmental problems the PRC is facing today.

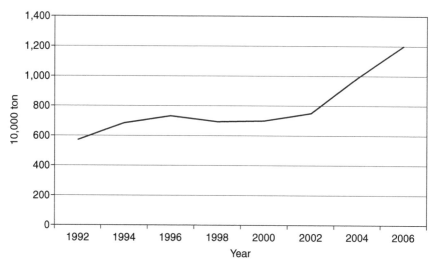

Figure 2.13 SO₂ emissions in electricity and heat generation and supply industry (1992–2006).

Transformation of the relationship between economic growth and environmental protection: from conflict to harmonization

Economic development, social progress and environmental protection are three pillars of sustainable development, with environmental protection as the basis, economic development as the means and social progress as the aim. This relationship signifies that coordination among these three pillars necessarily precedes sustainable development. In accordance with the basic rule of ecology, and as important premises for the continuous use of resources and energy to enable sustainable support of social development by the environment, the consumption rate of non-renewable resources and energy must be lower or equal to the rate of the development of renewable ones, so that resource and energy substitutes may be sustainably used, while pollutants discharge rate must be lower or equal to the rate of assimilation or self-cleaning of the natural environment. Just as Lester R. Brown said,

> The ecological theory is as one hundred percent correct as all aerodynamics. If a plane wants to take off, it must accord with the demand of thrust force and lift force theories. Similarly, if a kind of economy wants to progress continuously, it must follow the basic ecological theory; violation of these theories will surely result in the change from consolidation to decline, and will finally collapse just like the gone river. One or the other, and there is no third choice.[15]

The reason for the severe environmental problems of the PRC is the non-application of the foregoing ecological theories in environmental management such that the discharge of main pollutants exceeded the capacity of the environment, resulting in the trend of the deterioration of environmental quality. A positive development is the recent recognition by the government of this concern, for the resolution of which it proposed new measures. In December 2005, the State Council promulgated "Decisions on Implementing Scientific Development Outlook and Strengthening Environmental Protection" (hereafter referred to as the *Decision*) which is a programmatic document for implementing scientific development outlook, constructing a harmonious socialist society and guiding the harmonious development of the PRC's economy, society and environment. The highlight of the *Decision* is the proposal to coordinate economic and social development with environmental protection. Compared to the previous proposal for the coordination of these three endeavors where there was implied priority of economic growth over the two, environmental protection in the *Decision* has been put in the basic and strategic position, such that development of the economy is under the precondition of environmental protection. This is obviously a change in the central government's handling of the relationship of the three and a manifestation of the implementation of the scientific development outlook – the precondition for the historic transition of environmental protection.

During the Fourth National Environmental Protection Conference held in April 2006, Premier Wen Jiabao pointed out that to effectively carry out environmental protection work under the new situation, the key is to accelerate the realization of three transitions. First is the transition from the focus on economic growth over environmental protection to equal attention on both. This entails the adoption of environmental protection measures as the important means to adjust economic structure, change the economic growth mode and seek the development of environmental protection. Second is the transition from the situation where environmental protection lags behind economic development to the synchronized development of both environmental protection and economic development. There must be a change of the "pollution first and treatment after" or "damage alongside treatment" attitude. Third is the transition from the employment of administrative measures in solving environmental problems to the comprehensive exertion of legal, economic, technological and necessary administrative measures coupled with the conscious compliance with economic rules and natural laws and improvement of the level of environmental protection work. The proposal to undertake these three directive, strategic and historic transitions is indicative of the recognition of the reciprocal relationship between the PRC's economic development and environmental protection, a milestone in the PRC's history of environmental protection development.

To push forward the three transitions and effectively coordinate economic and social development with environmental protection, the following measures must be taken.

Promotion of the harmonious development of regional economy and environment

The eighth article of the *Decision* emphasized the promotion of harmonious development of regional economy and environment. Every region should determine its function orientation and development direction in accordance with its available resources, environmental capacity, ecological situation, population and the national development plan and industrial policies, and combine organically the regional economic plan and environmental protection targets. Regions with limited environmental capacity, insufficient supply of natural resources but comparatively advanced economy, in order to optimize development, should insist that priority be accorded environmental protection, strenuously develop new and responsive technologies, optimize industrial structure, accelerate the upgrading of industries and product, and take the lead in total emission reduction, production increase and pollution reduction. On the other hand, regions with certain environmental capacity, affluent resources and greater development potential, in pursuit of priority development, should accelerate infrastructure construction, scientifically utilize the environmental capacity, push forward industrialization and urbanization, and strictly control the total discharge of pollutants, thereby achieving production growth without pollution aggravation. With respect to protection areas, regions with fragile environment and key ecological functions, restrictive development under the premise of protection priority should be achieved through efforts to reasonably decide development direction, develop characteristic and dominant industries, ensure the rehabilitation and maintenance of ecological functions, and gradually restore the ecological balance. Finally, in nature reserves and regions with special environmental protection considerations, prohibitive development should be achieved through the legal implementation of protection measures, and strict prohibition of any development activities which violate regulations. Best efforts should be exerted to carry out ecological function regionalization work and determine the dominant functions of the different regions to allow the formation of a responsive and comprehensive development structure. There must also be compliance with national regulations and conduct of environmental impact assessment on various development and construction plans. Decisions with major influence on the environment should come after environmental impact argumentation.

A prime illustration of this endeavor is the regionalization or zoning of national major body function when, on October 11, 2006, the State Council general office released the "Notifications Concerning Conducting the Compilation Work for Regionalization of National Main Body Function" (hereafter referred to as the *Notifications)*. The *Notifications* emphasized that the regionalization of national main body function entails:

1   the planning as a whole of the PRC's future population distribution, economic arrangement, national land use and urbanization pattern taking into consideration the resource carrying capacity of the environment, existing development intensity and development potential;

2   division of the national land area into four types of main body functional regions for optimization development, priority development, restrictive development and prohibitive development;

3   adjustment and improvement of regional policies and performance assessment according to the orientation of main body function;

4   standardization of the spatial development system to form a reasonable spatial development structure; and

5   realization of the harmonious development of population, economy, resource environment, urban and rural areas and all regions.

On July 26, 2007, the State Council published the "Opinions about the Compilation of Regionalization of National Main Body Function" (hereafter referred to as the *Opinions)*, which defined three major tasks for compiling regionalization of national main body function:

1   analytical assessment;

2   determination of main body function regions; and

3   improvement of regional policies.

The *Opinions* directed that priority be accorded the implementation of the national main body function regionalization plan, realization of the orientation of main body function regions, and the adjustment and improvement of relevant policies in the areas of finance, investment, industry, land, population management, environmental protection, performance assessment and political performance examination. The *Opinions* proposed the formulation of regulations and policies for environmental protection using classification management based on the environmental carrying capacity of different main body function regions. More strict standards for pollutants discharge and environmental protection should be carried out in areas classified as optimization development regions, to reduce pollutants discharge significantly. Meanwhile, environmental carrying capacity should be maintained in areas classified under priority development regions, to increase production and reduce pollution. It is also proposed that environmental protection priority should be safeguarded in areas which belong to restrictive development regions, to ensure the rehabilitation and maintenance of ecological functions, while areas considered as prohibitive development regions must be strictly protected by law.

Another illustration is the rehabilitation of heavily polluted rivers, lakes and oceans. Most watersheds in the PRC are characterized by heavy pollutant discharges. Many rivers, lakes and oceans have been extremely polluted and the ecological system has been experiencing sharp deterioration. In 2007, the outbreak of blue-green algae in Taihu Lake watershed greatly damaged the drinking water safety of Wuxi residents, thereby arousing the public's interest. In response, the state's Ministry of Environmental Protection proposed the adoption of six measures to rehabilitate these rivers, lakes and oceans.

The first measure is the restriction of pollution access to the environment.

New types of pollution must be strictly controlled. And for the coming years, there must be disapproval of all projects that:

1   discharge heavy metals and organic pollutants that are hard to degrade, to rivers, lakes and oceans needing rehabilitation as defined by the state; and
2   discharge nitrogen and phosphorus to closed or semi-closed waters.

The second measure is the elimination of backward productivity, particularly in 12 heavily polluted and energy intensive industries along rivers, lakes and oceans needing rehabilitation as determined by the state, in accordance with the energy saving and emission reduction work plan and national industrial policies regulated by the State Council. Straw pulp and chemical pulp production equipment with limited production capacity should also be eliminated.

The third measure is the reinforcement of drinking-water sources protection. It is an essential goal in pollution prevention that safety of drinking water is guaranteed to the communities along rivers, lakes and oceans. There is also a need to stop illegal emission activities, strictly conduct supervision on projects affecting water safety and to establish water pollution warning mechanisms.

The fourth measure proposed is the enhancement of pollution sources treatment in key industries. All industries and enterprises should only be allowed to discharge pollutants which comply with pollution discharge standards. Industries and enterprises whose pollution discharges are unable to comply with the standards should stop production and conduct rectification. There should also be efforts to accelerate the establishment of scientific emission reduction indices and monitoring and examination systems. A mechanism to track and determine responsibility for heavy pollution must also be formulated.

The fifth measure is the acceleration of the construction of urban sewage treatment facilities. In pursuit of this, the following must be undertaken:

1   configuration work for sewage treatment plants;
2   enhancement of sewage treatment policies;
3   moderation of the sewage treatment charging standards; and
4   intensification of marketing efforts for sewage treatment equipment and operation.

The final and sixth measure is the reasonable development and use of water resources. In this way, there is a necessity to handle well the relationship between livelihood, production and ecological operation, pay equal attention to protection of surface water and ground water, and refrain from unsystematic development of ground water. It is also imperative to strengthen ecological protection and construction in water source conservation regions, and ensure the stable flow of water from the upper reaches.

Strenuous development of the circular economy

The ninth article of the *Decision* emphasized the need to strenuously develop circular economy. All regions and departments should make the development of circular economy the important guideline in the compilation of various development plans, formulate and implement the plan of circular economy promotion, push forward the formulation of policies, relevant standards and an assessment system promoting the development of circular economy, and intensify technological development and innovative system construction. Efforts should also be undertaken to design and reconstruct industrial products and zones according to the principle of "Reducing, Re-using and Resourcing" and pursuant to the demand of the environment. In the production link, focus should be on the institution of measures to strictly control the emission intensity admittance, encourage energy saving and consumption reduction, and carry out clean production and legally mandated auditing. Meanwhile, in the waste output link, it shall be necessary to strengthen pollution prevention and whole-process control, implement extended producer responsibility systems, reasonably extend the industry chain, and intensify the circular utilization of various wastes. In the consumption link, there must be active promotion of the environment-friendly consumption mode, implementation of environmental labeling, environmental certification and government green procurement systems, improvement of the system of renewable resources recycling, adoption of energy-saving measures, construction of green buildings and water-saving cities, endorsement of sewage recycling and waste treatment, and creation of ecological provinces, municipalities and counties, environmental protection cities, environment-friendly enterprises and green schools and communities.

There is now an unfolding circular economy in the PRC. Circular economy is a new economic development mode with higher ecological efficiency. It aims to implement reducing, resourcing and sound management and control on the resource flow in social production and reproduction activities. There must be control on the flow and efficiency of resources and energy in the production and consumption processes and a change from the traditional linear logistic mode (resource–product–waste) to the material circulation mode (resource–product–renewable resource) in accordance with the ideals of reducing, re-using and sound management of environmental resources and based on scientific technologies, policy measures and market mechanisms. In addition, it is imperative to sufficiently improve the ecological effectiveness of production and reproduction activities, obtain the optimum economic output and the minimum pollution emission with the least consumption of resources and energy, realize the unification of economic, environmental and social benefits, and establish the sustainable production and consumption mode (Ren Yong 2004).

The following are the targets and indices in the development of a circular economy in the PRC:

1 establishment of a fairly complete law and regulation system, policy support system, mechanism and technology innovation system and incentive and restrictive mechanism for developing circular economy by 2010;

2   significant improvement of the efficiency of resources utilization, reduction of final disposal of wastes, and establishment of a great number of typical enterprises meeting the requirements of circular economy development;

3   promotion of green consumption and improvement of renewable resources recycling system;

4   construction of a batch of resource-saving and environment-friendly cities and industrial and agricultural parks compliant with the requirements of circular economy development;

5   increase in the output GDP from the 15 kinds of important resources (e.g. energy, iron ores, non-ferrous metal and non-metal minerals) by 25 percent than that in 2003 on the basis of ton consumption;

6   reduction by 15 percent or more of the consumption of energy per RMB10,000 GDP;

7   improvement to 0.5 of the average coefficient of effective use of agricultural irrigation, and reduction of water consumption to $120\,m^3$ per RMB10,000 industrial added value;

8   improvement by 5 percent of both the total recycle rate of mineral resources and the comprehensive use rate of intergrown minerals, and increase of the comprehensive use rate of industrial solid waste by 60 percent at least;

9   restructure of the proportion of secondary copper, aluminum and lead in the production to reach 35 percent, 25 percent and 30 percent respectively, and improvement of the recycling rate of renewable resources by at least 65 percent; and

10 control of the stock and disposal of industrial solid wastes within 0.45 billion tons, and the growth rate of urban domestic wastes within 5 percent. (The State Council's "Opinions on Accelerating Development of Circular Economy," 2005).

In October 2005, after the approval by the State Council, the National Development and Reform Commission, State Environmental Protection Administration (now MEP), the Ministries of Science and Technology, Finance and Commerce, and the National Bureau of Statistics jointly published the "Notifications Concerning Organizing and Carrying Out Circular Economy Pilot Work (I)," which officially kicked off the national circular economy pilot work and determined the first batch of national circular economy pilot units (42 enterprises in seven key industries such as steel and non-ferrous metal and chemicals, 17 institutions in four key fields such as renewable resources recycling, 13 industrial parks in national and provincial development zones, heavy chemical industry clusters and agricultural demonstration areas, some resource cities and resource-scarce cities in ten provinces and municipalities in the east, middle, west and the north-east old industrial base) where pilot work will be undertaken to explore the mode of circular economy development in key industries such as steel, non-ferrous metal, chemical and building material, establish a batch of typical circular economy enterprises, improve the system of renewable resources recycling in key fields, establish resources recycling mechanisms, propose ideas for planning, constructing and reconstructing the industrial parks according to the circular economic mode in pilot development zones and industrial parks, establish a batch of circular economy industry demonstration parks, solicit ideas for developing circular economy in urban areas, and establish some circular economy development demonstration cities.

In December 2007, the six ministries and commissions jointly published again the "Notifications Concerning Organizing and Carrying Out Circular Economy Pilot Work (II)" and decided to conduct pilot work in 12 key industries such as steel, non-ferrous metal, coal and electricity, four key fields of renewable resources processing base, renewable metal recycling, discarded electronics, tires, batteries and package recycling, 20 industrial parks (heavy chemical industry clusters), five provinces and 12 cities.

On August 29, 2008, the Fourth Session of the 11th National People's Congress (NPC) Standing Committee approved the "Circular Economy Promotion Law," to be implemented beginning January 1, 2009. The Law formulated a series of systems promoting the development of circular economy, including a system for circular economy planning, a system for restriction of resources wasting and total control of pollutants discharges, a system for assessment and examination of circular economy, an extended producer responsibility system, and a system for particular supervision on high energy consumption and high water consumption enterprises. The issuance of this law will vigorously promote the PRC's development of circular economy, improve resources use rate, protect and improve the environment, and realize sustainable development.

Active development of environmental protection industry

The tenth article of the *Decision* emphasized the need to actively develop the environmental protection industry; accelerate the construction of industrial structure with the features of nationalization, standardization and modernization for the environmental protection industry; strengthen policy support and market supervision; abide by market economy rules; break up local and industrial protectionism; promote fair competition; encourage the social capitals to take part in the development of environmental protection industry; attach more importance to the development of important environmental protection technical facilities and basic equipment with independent intellectual property on the basis of independent research; develop and master, through introduction and absorption, core environmental protection technologies and key technologies; improve the environmental protection equipment and the manufacturing enterprises' capability for independent innovation; push forward the independent manufacture of major environmental protection technical equipment; foster a batch of advanced environmental protection enterprises with famous brands, high capability of core technology, big market share and more job opportunities; accelerate the development of environmental protection services; promote marketing of environmental consultation; and effectively make use of the intermediary organizations such as the industry association.

It has been noted that the PRC's environmental protection industry is the new economic growth point. In recent years, the PRC's environmental protection industry has experienced rapid development characterized by the quick expansion of the total industry scale, continuous expansion of the industry field, and advancement of the overall level of the operation quality and benefits. This development has played an important role in preventing environmental pollution, protecting natural resources, ameliorating the environment and maintaining sustainable social development. It has also become an important part of the national economic structure and provided strong material and technological guarantee for environmental management. According to preliminary estimates, in 2006, there were about 35,000 institutions nationwide, which were involved with the environmental protection industry. These institutions employed three million staff members and generated an annual production value of about RMB600 billion and profits of approximately RMB52 billion. During the Eleventh FYP period, the average annual growth rate of environmental protection industry is targeted to exceed 15 percent, while the annual production value is targeted to reach RMB1.1 trillion by the end of the said period. In the next 20 years, it is projected that the PRC's environmental protection industry will maintain its accelerated development, and the compound annual growth average of the total industry production value will reach 15–20 percent.[16]

Optimization of economic growth through environmental protection

Economic development is the most fundamental and important factor that impacts environmental protection. The PRC's previous economic development process had the feature of sacrificing environment for economic growth. Since the 1980s, many domestic and foreign research institutions and scholars have successively conducted estimation of the loss caused by some environmental pollution and ecological damage and they found that its proportion to GDP ranged from a maximum of 7.7 percent (World Bank 1997[17]) to a minimum of 2.1 percent (Dixon and Sherman 1990). According to the data released in 2006 by the former State Environmental Protection Administration and National Bureau of Statistics, the national economic loss caused by environmental pollution in 2004 was RMB511.8 billion, accounting for 3.05 percent of the GDP in the same year while the subjunctive treatment cost was RMB287.4 billion, accounting for 1.8 percent of the GDP of the same year. Four institutions and scholars estimated the loss caused by ecological damage to be 5.4–13 percent of the GDP of the same year.[18] These researches showed that the economic loss caused by environmental pollution and ecological damage to the PRC has been about 7–20 percent of the GDP. The different connotations, methods and bases adopted by these researches, coupled with the inadequate calculation and underestimation at different degrees, resulted in the difference in the calculation results, which suggests that the actual loss may be bigger than the figures presented. These data have clearly shown the severity of the PRC's environmental pollution and ecological damage, and the enormity of the economic loss they have caused. These considerations must not be ignored in economic and environmental decision-making.

It has indeed become obvious that the development mode which entails the sacrifice of the environment for economic growth has brought serious repercussions to the PRC, and is thus not a suitable development mode for long-term application. The appropriate response would be a change to the optimization of economic growth through environmental protection, and the adoption of environmental protection as a measure to ameliorate and promote economic growth, achieve the double objective of environmental protection and economic development, and establish a new relationship between environment and economy. Much like the effect of an examination to the student, environmental protection may bring strain or pressure to the economy, but it may also bring about better performance by the economy. This effect of the environmental protection on the economy has been observed after a certain phase in the PRC's economic development, a favorable development in the relationship between the PRC's environment and economy.

A prime illustration of efforts to achieve optimization of economic growth through environmental protection is in the area of the PRC's automobile industry where competitiveness and innovation have resulted from the imposition of strict environmental standards which did not at all impede development.

While the PRC was introducing foreign automobile production technologies in the initial stages of reform and opening up, the automobile emission standards were not as high as those of today. The exhaust purifier was left out in the exhaust treatment production line and in the automobile to reduce the cost, allowing the low-income segment of the population to afford cars and satisfy their desire for mobile life. The price was the aggravation of automobile exhaust pollution and the decrease of urban environmental quality, ushering in the phase when environment was sacrificed for economic growth. With the current significant increase of automobiles in the PRC, the urban atmosphere's environmental capacity has progressively become smaller, while the public's demand for environmental quality has become higher, for which reason the employment of the original development mode must be discontinued and the exhaust emission standards must be improved (Beijing implemented Euro-III Standard in 2005). The improvement of environmental protection standards has not only improved urban atmospheric environment, but also resulted in the large-scale reform in the automobile industry, with the backward and heavy pollution automobile production technologies having been phased out, and new and advanced technologies and techniques having been developed and applied. It has been proven that the strict environmental protection standards have not impeded the development of the automobile industry, but pushed forward technology innovation and improved market competitiveness when, in 2007, the PRC's automobile production reached 8,882,400, to become the third largest in the world, next only to the United States and Japan.

Similarly, energy saving and emission reduction measures resulted in the upgrade of the energy and emission intensive steel industry which is the pillar industry in the PRC's national economic development. The provisions for energy-saving efforts and emission reduction in the Eleventh FYP accelerated the elimination of backward productivity in the PRC's steel industry and began the optimization of the steel industry's structure and the improvement of its overall competitiveness.

Guided by industrial policies, particularly those set in the Eleventh FYP, the steel industry in the PRC is strengthening energy-saving and emission reduction efforts and implementing waste heat and waste energy recycling and major environmental protection projects. At present, the PRC has 50 coke dry quenching installations, 121 sets of $1,000\,m^3$-above blast furnaces which are equipped with residual pressure power generation installation, and ten sets of blast furnaces which have adopted combined cycle generation by using low heat-value gas. By the end of 2007, the energy consumption in the PRC's large and medium scale steel enterprises decreased by 2.32 percent of the previous year's 624.4 kilogram (kg) standard coal per ton of steel, which translates to savings of 17.65 million tons of standard coal. New water consumption was 5.64 ton/ton production of steel, a decrease of 16.24 percent which translates to savings of 0.35 billion tons of water. Total SO_2 emissions decreased by 0.4 percent, a reduction of 2,535 tons. These savings show the significant effects of circular economy in the PRC's steel industry, which realized total emission reduction despite increase in production. Additionally, in 2007, the world's first low-pollution, low-emission clean type C3000 COREX direct iron-making equipment was set up and put into production in Bao Steel, ushering in a new era of iron-making without agglomeration and coking. Works were also successively undertaken in a batch of major restructuring projects in numerous steel plants. The implementation of these restructuring projects has led to a significant escalation of overall industrial level, optimization of industrial structure and diminution of the gap with the world's advanced industrial level.

In conclusion, there must be a change in the relationship between the PRC's environment and economy from one of opposition and contradiction to one of coordination and integration in order to maintain sustainable economic growth and solve the increasingly severe environmental problems. There must also be efforts to promote the harmonious development of regional economy and the environment, develop circular economy and the environmental protection industry, and ensure the coordination between economic development and environmental protection through the improvement of environmental standards, intensification of energy-saving and emission reduction efforts, strict implementation of environmental laws and regulations, enhancement of industrial technologies and optimization of economic growth through environmental protection.

Policy recommendations

In order to transform the relationship between economic growth and environmental protection from opposition to integration, there must be two major adjustments at the national policy level. First, adjustment is in the aspect of economic growth which includes policy modification, change of the growth mode that is harmful to the environment, and realization of environment-friendly economic growth. Second, adjustment is in the aspect of environmental protection which includes the implementation of relevant and existing policies, restructuring and upgrading of economic structure, technology advancement in the field of economy, and optimization of the mode of economic growth.

In the field of economy, there is a need to adjust national policies according to the scientific development outlook. With respect to industrial policies, re-evaluation and formulation of the national major industrial distribution plan, especially the development arrangement of "double-high, one-resource" indus-tries[19] must be undertaken in accordance with the demand of the national main body function regionalization. There must also be:

1 strict implementation of the system of environmental impact assessment and responsibility tracking in the national industrial development plan;
2 strenuous development of circular economy and clean production, strict control of emission intensity admittance, advancement of energy saving and consumption reduction measures, and implementation of clean production and legally mandated auditing;
3 intensification of pollution prevention and whole-process control, imple-mentation of extended producer responsibility system, reasonable extension of the industrial chain, and reinforcement of the circular utilization of various wastes; and
4 formulation of a national strategy for low-carbon economic development, and assumption in the helm of the international renewable energy market.

With respect to consumption policies, the following are recommended:

1 active promotion of environment-friendly and ecology-civilized consump-tion mode and execution of whole-people environment-friendly and green consumption activities;
2 comprehensive conduct of environmental labeling, environmental certifica-tion, energy efficiency label certification, and water-saving product certification;
3 restriction of the consumption and export of one-time products, and devel-opment of the renewable resources recycling system;
4 promotion of energy-saving efforts and construction of green buildings; and
5 mandatory and comprehensive implementation of the government green procurement system.

With respect to financial policies, the following adjustments should be made:

1 reasonable demarcation of responsibilities and power in environmental pro-tection between the central government, the local governments and enter-prises, and implementation of the public financial system of government

("top-level financial control and top-level power") in environmental protection;

2   completion of the local governments' "211 environmental protection" financial budget items, integration and establishment of a national environmental protection special fund, and gradual increase of the public finance's proportion in environmental protection input;

3   formulation of an active national environmental protection policy of public investment and stabilization of the proportion of expenditure for environmental protection in long-term construction national bonds;

4   establishment of a double-linkage mechanism between environmental protection expenditure, and GDP and financial income growth while guaranteeing that the rate of increase of environmental protection public financial expenditure will be higher than the growth rate of GDP and financial income;

5   establishment of the system of environmental financial transfer payment with full consideration of the environmental factors, and increase in the financial expenditure of key ecological areas and development-forbidden regions;

6   establishment of a national environment compensation system, a withdrawal compensation mechanism for "double-high, one-resource" industries, acceleration of the construction of ecological compensation mechanism in western regions, upper and lower reaches of watersheds, important ecological function conservation areas, nature reserves, and development of drinking-water sources and mineral resources;

7   reform of the mechanism and policy with respect to the support of public finance to environmental infrastructure construction, and operation and improvement of the investment efficiency of environmental protection public utilities; and

8   comprehensive reform and integration into the environmental taxation system of all pollution-emission charging systems.

Pricing policies should include:

1   comprehensive implementation of environmental resources repayment-use system, and establishment of index repayment-distribution for major pollutants discharges and pricing system favorable to environmental protection and resource saving;

2   government pricing which considers the scarcity of resources and environmental costs, and guidance and supervision mechanisms over market-adjusted prices to favor environmental protection;

3   implementation of an electricity pricing policy beneficial to the development of renewable energy and wastes-burning power plants and a sum purchase policy for grid electricity generated by renewable energy power generation projects; and

4   exploration of major pollutants discharge trading system in pilot key areas and pollution industries.

Taxation policies should steadily accelerate the greening of taxation system; reform the existing taxation systems, such as resource tax and consumption tax; establish tax preference policy system for promoting resource saving and environmental protection; fully play the role of guiding and supporting environmental protection; accelerate the formulation and implementation of an independent environmental tax system; levy environmental tax on production and consumption activities causing environmental pollution and ecological damage; improve the PRC's image in environmental responsibility; and choose priority items in the independent environmental tax, such as pollution intensive and "double-high" enterprises, pollution products and projects which bring about ecological damage and carbon dioxide (CO_2) emissions.

Trading policies should formulate and promulgate the catalog of "double-high, one-resource" industries and products, adjust the resource environment deficit through the scientific use of export quota regulation and export tax rebate and tariff, actively promote green technology standards, environmental labeling, green packaging, green sanitation and quarantine and green subsidy systems in export-oriented industries, support sustainable development of export trade, establish environmental supervision system for overseas investment and assistance, improve overseas investment construction projects' corporate environmental responsibility and national image, establish environmental supervision system for foreign capital projects and import trade, improve imported wastes trading policy, and effectively prevent pollution "import" and environmental risk in wastes trading.

Financial policies should immediately establish the catalog of environmental protection credit guidance; regularly release the list of "double-high" industries and products; guide the banking industry to avoid credit risks; support development of environmental protection industry; direct state-owned commercial banks and development banks to consciously take the lead in implementing green credit and environmental risk checking system, and cease issuing credit to enterprises violating national industrial policies and environmental protection standards; accelerate the establishment of environmental pollution responsibility insurance system; implement environmental pollution responsibility mandatory insurance for key pollution industries and enterprises in environment sensitive regions; establish and consummate environmental auditing and supervision standards for listed companies; carry out environmental performance assessment and information disclosure systems for listed companies; and release environmental performance indices for the PRC's securities market.

Science and technology policies should reflect the state's priority support to the development and promotion of resource-saving and environment-friendly energy technologies; strengthen the construction of basic platform for environmental protection science and technologies; list as priority the major environmental protection scientific research projects into the national science and technology plan; conduct research on environmental protection strategies and standards, and environment and health issues; encourage research on pollution prevention; organize efforts to tackle key and difficult technologies such as sewage depth treatment, coal power station desulfurization and denitration, clean coal and automobile exhaust purification; and accelerate the application of high and new technologies in environmental protection.

Finally, in order to optimize growth through environmental protection, the following must be undertaken:

1   establishment of economic development criteria from the environmental protection perspective;
2   imposition of environmental rules, regulations and standards in economic activities;
3   integration of environmental protection standards into the whole process of production, circulation, distribution and consumption;
4   enhancement of the comprehensive environmental and economic decision-making mechanism;
5   intensification of environmental protection enforcement and management; and
6   formulation of incentive-based environmental protection policies.

Notes

1 Compiling Committee of "Twenty Years Environmental Protection Administration in China," *Twenty Years Environmental Protection Administration in China*, Beijing: China Environment Science Press, 1994, P22.
2 Calculation based on "expenditure method" (present value).
3 Wang Mengkui, "Important Issues in China's Long-and-Medium-Term Development 2006–2020," China Development Publishing House, 2005, Beijing.
4 Sustainable Development Research Group, CAS, "Report on China's Sustainable Development 2006," Science Publishing House, 2006, Beijing.
5 The industrial production value in 1978 and 1984 was RMB423.7 billion and RMB761.73 billion, respectively, and the agricultural production value was RMB111.75 billion and RMB218.165 billion, respectively.
6 Wang Jianmin and Wu Huanzhong, "Development of Township Enterprises and Environmental Pollution Prevention Measures in China," http://sq.smehen.gov.cn/ArtPaper/show.aspx?id=3126.
7 "Exploiting the Road of Environmental Protection with Chinese Characteristic" – work report by Mr Qu Geping in the Third National Environmental Protection Conference, see in the documentation of the Third National Environmental Protection Conference, pp. 25–6.
8 Denotes on the basis of implementing environmental impact assessment, "Three Synchronizations" and pollutant discharge charging systems, add another five new systems: environmental protection targets responsibility system; quantification examination of comprehensive urban environmental improvement; pollutant discharge licensing system; collective pollution control system; and pollution treatment with time limit.
9 Ren Yong and Chen Gang *et al.*, "Strategic Transition of Environment and Development in China," see in "China Council for International Cooperation on Environment and Development Annual Policy Report 2006," CCICED compiled, Beijing: China Environment Science Press, 2007, p. 3.
10 Li Peng, "Implement Sustainable Development Strategy, Ensure the Realization of Environmental Protection Targets" – speech at the symposium of the Fourth National

Environmental Protection Conference, see in the documentation of the Fourth National Environmental Protection Conference compiled by SEPA, Beijing: China Environment Science Press, 1996, p. 7.

11 "Completely carry out scientific development outlook, accelerate the construction of environment-friendly society" – State Council Premier Wen Jiabao's speech in the Sixth National Environmental Protection Conference, see in the documentation of the Sixth National Environmental Protection Conference compiled by SEPA, Beijing: China Environment Science Press, 2006, p. 3.

12 Zhou Shengxian, "Opportunities and Options – In-Depth Deliberation on the Event of Songhuajiang River," Beijing: Xinhua Publishing House, 2007, p. 66.

13 He Jianwu and Li Shantong, "Analysis on Environmental Impacts by Factors of Economic Growth in Recent Years," *Research Report*, Vol. 27, 2008 (Serial no. 3139).

14 Song Yangyan and Song Jiechen, "Be Aware of Four Kinds of Overdrafts in High Economic Growth," *China Economic Times*, January 25, 2008.

15 Ma Kai, "Transform Economic Growth Mode and Realize the Sound and Rapid Development" – speech at the PRC High-Level Forum 2007, http://zys.ndrc.gov.cn/wldzyjh/t20070319_121961.htm.

16 Written by Lester R. Brown, translated by Lin Zhixin and Ji Shouzhi *et al.*, "Ecological Economy", Beijing: Dongfang Publishing House, 2002, p. 83.

17 World Bank "Clear Water, Blue Skies: China's Environment in the New Century," Washington, DC: World Bank, 1997.

18 Huang Shengli, "Environmental Industry in Urgent Need of Fund Raising Channels," *China Economic Times*, September 11, 2008.

19 Guo Xiaomin, Wang Jinnan, Yu Fang and Jiang Hongqiang, "Research on Problems and Prospects for China's Economic Loss Caused by Environmental Pollution and Ecological Damage," online, available at: www.gdepb.gov.cn/hjgl/lsgdp/zjsd/200510/t20051011_3339.html. Denotes heavy pollution, high energy consumption and resource-oriented industries.

3 Environmental Kuznets Curves in the People's Republic of China

Turning points and regional differences

Yi Jiang, Tun Lin and Juzhong Zhuang

Introduction

Recent data show that, during the Tenth Five-Year Plan (FYP) of the People's Republic of China (PRC), reduction in its emissions or discharges fell short of the targets for a number of pollutants. In 2005, sulfur dioxide (SO_2) emissions increased by 27 percent from its 2000 level, totaling 25.5 million tons and exceeding the target by 7.5 million tons; and chemical oxygen demand (COD) emissions reached 14.13 million tons, 8 percent higher than the target. In contrast, the country's economic development indicators surpassed the goals. Gross domestic product (GDP) registered a 9.48 percent annual average growth during the Tenth FYP period.

The relationship between economic growth and environmental sustainability has been a subject of intensive discussions in recent years. The PRC's rapid pace of growth and its performance in mitigating environmental degradation inevitably attract attention. Would the country's environment continue to deteriorate or would it improve as its income level grows further? Given the country's significant regional differences in industrial structure, the level of urbanization, and the stage of development, does the relationship between the PRC's economic growth and level of pollutant emissions (or discharges) differ across regions? This chapter attempts to answer these questions by empirically estimating Environmental Kuznets Curves (EKC) models using the PRC provincial panel data.

The EKC model, one of the controversial topics in environmental economics in recent years, hypothesizes that the relationship between income and environmental quality which is often measured by the level of pollution is inverted-U shaped: at relatively low levels of income, pollution increases and the environment deteriorates with rising incomes; beyond some turning point, pollution declines and the environment improves with rising incomes. This relationship was first noted in a series of empirical studies in the early 1990s (Shafik and Bandyopadhay 1992; Panayotou 1993; Grossman and Krueger 1995; Selden and Song 1994). Subsequent empirical studies, however, showed that while the relationship holds in some cases, it cannot be generalized in many other cases.

Further, researchers and policy-makers are far from agreeing on the policy implications of the EKC model.

The EKC hypothesis has been tested in the case of the PRC by several authors. Groot *et al.* (2004) estimated EKCs for emissions or discharges of waste gas, wastewater and industrial solid wastes using the PRC provincial panel data from 1982–97. It is found that the emission–income relationship depends on the type of pollutants and how the dependent variable is constructed. The waste gas emission measured in levels is found to follow an inverted-U pattern, but waste gas emissions in per capita or per unit of output terms as well as the wastewater discharges do not. Liu *et al.* (2007) examined time-series concentration data of various water pollutants in Shenzhen, a fast developing southern city of the PRC, and found that production-induced pollutants, as opposed to consumption-induced pollutants, support the EKC hypothesis. Shen (2006) estimated a simultaneous three-equation model to address the endogeneity problem associated with per capita GDP and per capita pollution abatement expenses, and results show that EKC relationship holds for water pollutants but not for air pollutants. Auffhammer and Carson (2008) find the EKC relationship between (log) per capita waste gas emissions and (log) total GDP in a two-way fixed effects model specification.

This chapter differs from the existing EKC studies on the PRC in a number of aspects. First, the provincial-level panel data used in this chapter span from 1985 to 2005, the longest and most up-to-date compared to the existing studies. Second, the chapter puts greater emphasis on identifying turning points of the EKC which does not seem to have been adequately looked at.[1] Third, in light of the PRC's considerable and persistent regional disparity, this chapter explores the regional heterogeneity in EKC and its policy implications by estimating a model allowing for region-specific coefficients of the explanatory variables, per capita income, and its square. Fourth, to estimate the EKC, the chapter looks at four pollutants: waste gas from fuel burning; waste gas from production; wastewater; and solid waste. The separation of waste gas emissions due to fuel burning from those due to production is justified on the basis that industries largely producing the former are not necessarily the industries largely producing the latter, and vindicated by the estimation results.

Key findings of this chapter are as follows. First, it is found that an inverted-U shaped EKC exists for waste gas emissions from fuel burning and wastewater discharges at an acceptable level of statistical significance; such a relationship also exists for discharges of solid waste, but it is statistically insignificant; and a U-shaped relationship between per capita emission and income is found for waste gas from production. Second, the turning point of the EKC for waste gas emissions from fuel burning occurs at a higher income level than that for wastewater discharges. Third, in the EKC model allowing for regional heterogeneity, the poorer central and western regions appear to have turning points occurring at lower income levels than the coastal region, suggesting that technology diffusion and institution imitation among regions at different developmental stages may have played a part in shaping the relationship between economic growth and environmental sustainability.

The rest of this chapter is organized as follows. The second section simply summarizes the literature on EKC. The third section discusses methodology and data. The fourth section reports the results. Finally, the fifth section projects the status of the provinces by 2010 and 2015 and discusses policy implications.

The Environmental Kuznets Curve: a brief literature review[2]

The most common explanation for the EKC is that the income elasticity of demand for environmental quality is high, such that consumers who have achieved a high standard of living will increase their demand for environmental amenities. Not only are richer consumers more willing to pay for green products, they also ask for better institutions to protect the environment (e.g. Selden and Song 1994). Grossman and Krueger (1995) argue that economic growth affects environmental quality both negatively (through scale effects) and positively (through composition effects and technological effects). When an economy is in the early stage of development, increasing output requires more natural resources, and thus puts a heavier burden on the environment – this is the so-called scale effect. As the level of income grows, the economy shifts from being energy-intensive to knowledge- and technology-intensive in production – this is the composition effect. With economic growth also come cleaner production technology and more effective abatement procedures which improve the environment while maintaining high output – this is the technological effect. A turning point eventually occurs when the scale effect is outweighed by the composition and technological effects.

Several factors are considered important in determining the shape and turning point of the EKC. Among others, trade and investment across regions or nations are two of the most important forces (e.g. Bommer 1999; Harrison 1996; Wheeler 2000). Underdeveloped economies usually have comparative advantage in producing labor-intensive goods which are often more pollution-intensive. They also tend to have relatively loose environmental legislation and regulation, which may attract dirty industries from developed economies through trade and direct investment. By moving pollution from developed to the underdeveloped economies, trade and investment could result in an EKC characterized by the underdeveloped countries (regions) on the rising segment of the curve and the developed ones on the declining segment.

There are, however, researchers who argue against this line of reasoning on the basis that investment and trade could potentially facilitate diffusion of environment-friendly technology (e.g. Reppelin-Hill 1999). By gaining access to the advanced technologies that allow more energy-efficient production and effective pollution abatement, developing countries could in fact reach the turning point of an inverted-U shaped EKC at a lower income level, or even bypass certain portions of its rising part.

Enforcement of property rights and market rules, reduction in information asymmetry, formal regulation through the governments, and informal regulation pursued by civil communities and/or non-governmental organizations (NGOs) are effective in preventing environmental degradation (e.g. Lopez 1994; Vukina *et al.* 1999; Dasgupta *et al.* 2000; Pargal and Wheeler 1996). As these institutional setups often start in a weak position and tend to be enhanced with progress in economic development, they are also seen as underlying factors of the inverted-U shaped EKC. If the underdeveloped countries (regions) fail to catch up with the developed ones in establishing the institutions to protect the environment, they may experience a prolonged period of deteriorating environment as income grows.

Most empirical studies on EKC use cross-country data and, due to data limitation, focus largely on air and water pollutants. Both pollutant emissions (flows) and concentrations (stocks) have been used to measure the environmental quality. In general, it has been found that the EKC relationship is more likely to hold for certain pollutants, including SO_2, particulate matter (PM), nitrogen oxide (NO_x), but less likely for carbon dioxide (CO_2). Results are more mixed for water pollutants than for air pollutants. Evidence of EKC for some water quality indicators is weak or conflicting (e.g. Hettige *et al.* 2000; Shafik 1994). As far as the turning points are concerned, although wide variations are noted across studies even for the same pollutant, the majority falls within the per capita income range of US$5,000–US$8,000. Using a globally representative panel data set, Halkos (2003) found that the estimated turning point for SO_2 is US$5,648 for Organisation for Economic Co-operation and Development (OECD) sub-sample and US$3,401 for non-OECD sub-sample.

A relatively small number of studies make use of single-country data. Millimet *et al.* (2003) examined the relationship between air pollutants SO_2 and NO_x and per capita income using the US state-level panel data from 1900 to 1994. The turning point is found to be in the range of US$7,000–US$9,000 for SO_2 and US$8,000–US$12,000 for NO_x. List and Gallet (1999) used the same data set to estimate models allowing each state to have its own EKC. The results show considerable differences across states. The turning points vary from US$1,770 for Arizona to US$125,000 for Mississippi in the case of NO_x, and from US$2,989 for Rhode Island to US$69,047 for Texas in the case of SO_2. Vincent (1997), using a panel data set of Malaysian states, found that the EKC hypothesis does not hold in any of the six pollution–income relationships examined.

As mentioned in the previous section, several authors have tested the EKC hypothesis using the PRC provincial-level panel data, and found that it generally holds in the case of waste gas, but not in the case of wastewater. Given the important policy implications which may be drawn from such studies, there is a need for a more in-depth analysis, including estimating turning points and exploring cross-region heterogeneity which have not been adequately looked at, using more up-to-date data.

Methodology and data

To test the existence of the EKC in the PRC, we estimate the following model using provincial-level panel data:

$$E_{ikt} = \beta_{1k}Q_{it} + \beta_{2k}Q_{it}^2 + \alpha_{ik} + \mu_{ik} + \varepsilon_{ikt} \tag{1}$$

$i = 1, 2, \ldots, 31,^3$

$t = 1, 2, \ldots, 21$ or $1985, 1986, \ldots, 2005,$

where E_{ikt} is the per capita emission or discharge of waste k in province i at year t, Q_{ikt} and Q_{it}^2 are, respectively, the per capita GDP and its square term of province i at year t.[4] α_{ik} is a province-specific fixed effect that accounts for the time-invariant factors unique to each province (e.g. resource endowment), μ_{ik} is a time-specific fixed effect that captures common shocks to all the provinces in each year such as changes in environmental regulation, technological progress, or shift in preferences, and ε_{ikt} is the contemporaneous error term assumed to be stationary.

β_{1k} and β_{2k} are the slope coefficients that jointly define the relationship between per capita emissions (or discharges) of pollutant k and per capita GDP. Equation (1) provides a depiction of the emission–income relationship rather than a causal explanation of why the relationship is as such, as would be the case if variables which are potential determinants of income growth and environmental quality, such as industrial structure, urbanization, investment in environmental protection and regulatory intensity, are included on the right-hand side of the equation. The two coefficients therefore capture all the direct and indirect marginal impacts of economic development on environment as measured by the level of per capita emissions (or discharges) of a particular pollutant. An inverted-U relationship between pollution and income requires that $\beta_{1k} > 0$ and $\beta_{1k} < 0$. Note that, in Equation (1), β_{1k} and β_{1k} do not vary by province, implying an isomorphic EKC for all provinces.

The PRC's economic reform took an intended gradual approach. The focus of pro-development policies was first set in the coastal provinces, and later shifted to the central and western regions. One advantage of this approach is that the trial regions could accumulate development experiences and lessons, which the latecomers could learn at a much smaller cost. Meanwhile, industrial relocation could occur between the relatively developed regions and underdeveloped ones, during which the environment in the central and western regions could become vulnerable if more polluting industries move inland from the coastal region. From 1985 to 2005, the average per capita GDP for the coastal provinces increased from RMB3,733 to RMB23,476; for the central provinces from RMB1,933 to RMB10,513; and for the western provinces from RMB1,649 to RMB7,613.[5] The large disparity in growth suggests that there is considerable room for technology transfer, institution imitation, as well as industrial relocation across regions. One possible consequence is that the three regions form distinct relationships between income and pollution. Therefore, it is worth exploring whether and how the EKCs vary by region.

Following List and Gallet (1999), we estimate a model assuming region-specific slopes for per capita GDP and its square:

$$E_{ikt} = \sum_r (\beta_{1k}Q_{it} + \beta_{2rk}Q_{ik}^2) + \alpha_{ik} + \mu_{ik} + \varepsilon_{ikt} \qquad (2)$$

where r denotes the coastal, central or western region, to which province i belongs. In other words, each of the three regions is assumed to have distinct EKCs characterized by region-specific β_1 and β_2.

To implement above methodology, we compiled provincial-level panel data from the PRC's statistical yearbooks, covering the period 1985–2005. To the best knowledge of the authors, this is the longest and most up-to-date panel data among similar EKC studies in the PRC. For the dependent variable, we look at per capita emissions or discharges of four pollutants, namely: waste gas from fuel burning, waste gas from production, industrial wastewater and industrial solid waste. The dependent variable measures the quantity of emitted or discharged waste gas, wastewater or solid wastes in which the pollutants (e.g. SO_2, PM, COD) are contained. As the concentration of the pollutants in these waste emissions or discharges varies by sources, the damage to the environment caused by the same amount of waste emissions or discharges could differ.[6] For the explanatory variables, we use the per capita real GDP of each province, normalized to the 1998 level by applying province-specific deflators, and its square term.

We treat waste gas emissions due to production and those due to fuel burning separately because these are from two different industrial processes. Some industries, such as power, steam and hot water supply, produce waste gas emissions mainly from fuel burning, while some others, such as cement manufacturing, produce waste gas emissions largely from production. As the lifecycles of industries are correlated with economic developmental stages and evolve at unequal paces, waste gas emissions from different industrial sources may have different relationships with the level of economic development. To the extent that different industries may be subject to different regulatory regimes in environmental protection, differentiating waste gas emissions according to different sources helps to design more targeted environmental protection regulations.

Table 3.1 reports summary statistics of the variables used in estimation. For the PRC as a whole, the mean per capita GDP of 31 provinces during 1985–2005 was RMB6,581 measured at the 1998 price. The maximum per capita GDP was RMB58,014 recorded in Shanghai in 2005, while the minimum was RMB1,049 recorded in the western province of Guizhou in 1985. As far as per capita emissions is concerned, large gaps also exist between the means, minimums and maximums. Figure 3.1 presents a perspective on how the emission (or discharge) levels of the four pollutants change over time. Per capita waste gas emissions, especially those from production, increased sharply from 1985 to 2005, by 3.6

times. On the other hand, per capita wastewater discharges and solid waste decreased during the same period. In particular, the level of per capita solid wastes discharge fell by 90 percent from 1986 to 2005.

Table 3.1 also reports summary statistics of the concerned variables for the three regions: coastal, central, and western.[7] The coastal region of the PRC is more developed than the central and western regions. Over the 21-year period, average per capita GDP of the coastal provinces is 2.2 times that of the central provinces, and 2.7 times that of the western provinces. Moreover, the gap between the coastal provinces and the western provinces has further expanded to 3.1 times by 2005. Central provinces are slightly richer and have grown faster in recent years than the western provinces. Mean per capita emissions of waste gas and wastewater were higher in the coastal provinces than in other provinces, which is not the case with respect to the solid wastes discharge.

Results

Table 3.2 reports estimation results of Equation (1) for each of the four pollutants. For both per capita waste gas emission from fuel burning and wastewater discharges, β_1 is positive and β_2 is negative, both significant at 5 percent or 1 percent level, suggesting an inverted-U shaped EKC. For these two models, the adjusted R^2 reaches 0.85 and 0.91, respectively. In the case of per capita solid waste discharges, however, although β_1 and β_2 have the expected signs, they are statistically insignificant. The adjusted R^2 is as low as 0.55. In the case of per capita waste gas emission from production, β_1 and β_2 have the wrong signs. With β_1 being negative and β_2 positive, it suggests a U-shaped relationship between per capita waste gas emission from production and per capita GDP. To visually show the relationships, Figure 3.2 plots the estimated EKCs for waste gas emissions from fuel burning and wastewater discharges conditional on the province and time fixed effects, along with the actual observations.

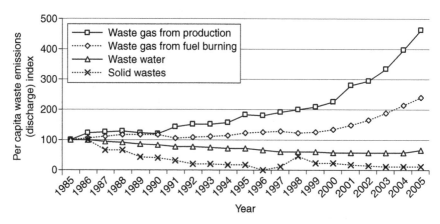

Figure 3.1 Per capita emissions (discharges) in the PRC (1985–2005).

Table 3.1 Summary statistics (1985–2005)

	Mean	Std. Dev.	Minimum	Maximum
Whole country				
GDP per capita (RMB 1998)	6,581.40	6,498.12	1,049.48	58,013.79
Per capita waste gas from production (m³)	4,630.87	4,540.62	0	38,679.67
Per capita waste gas from fuel burning (m³)	7,659.66	5,867.91	39.76	37,440.61
Per capita industrial wastewater discharge (ton)	20.38	15.39	0.316	123.22
Per capita industrial solid wastes discharge (ton)	0.046	0.069	0	0.544
Coastal provinces				
GDP per capita (RMB 1998)	10,274.79	8,747.85	1,413.41	58,013.79
Per capita waste gas from production (m³)	6,296.54	5,758.17	245.69	38,679.67
Per capita waste gas from fuel burning (m³)	9,780.39	6,615.23	876.66	37,440.61
Per capita industrial wastewater discharge (ton)	28.91	20.11	8.55	123.22
Per capita industrial solid wastes discharge (ton)	0.027	0.050	0	0.427
Central provinces				
GDP per capita (RMB 1998)	4,687.69	2,691.72	1,419.08	14,101.29
Per capita waste gas from production (m³)	3,546.44	2,968.10	928.83	20,714.24
Per capita waste gas from fuel burning (m³)	7,262.15	5,377.97	2,364.47	36,884.01
Per capita industrial wastewater discharge (ton)	17.43	7.59	8.82	61.09
Per capita industrial solid wastes discharge (ton)	0.049	0.085	3.14e-07	0.544
Western provinces				
GDP per capita (RMB 1998)	3,744.32	2,021.19	1,049.48	10,390.79
Per capita waste gas from production (m³)	3,535.52	3,188.00	0	20,462.93
Per capita waste gas from fuel burning (m³)	5,333.85	4,101.00	39.76	27,255.95
Per capita industrial wastewater discharge (ton)	12.37	5.78	0.316	35.91
Per capita industrial solid wastes discharge (ton)	0.068	0.066	0	0.368

Source: *China Statistical Yearbook* (1985–2005).

Table 3.2 also reports the level of per capita GDP at which the quadratic curve reaches a turning point, calculated as $-\beta_1/2\beta_2$. Conditional on the province and time fixed effects, per capita waste gas emissions from fuel burning starts to decline when per capita GDP reaches RMB44,280. This level of income at which the turning point is realized is relatively high compared to the mean per capita income of the sample. Only Shanghai reached per capita GDP of over RMB40,000 since 2002 (RMB41,510 in 2002; RMB46,354 in 2003; RMB52,521 in 2004; and RMB58,013 in 2005). In the case of per capita wastewater discharges, the income level at which the turning point occurs is much lower, at RMB11,146. Most coastal provinces, except Hainan and Guangxi, are on the right side of the turning point by the end of 2005; and four central provinces (Heilongjiang, Hubei, Inner Mongolia and Jilin) just reached this level recently (Heilongjiang in 2004 and the other three in 2005). Plotting per capita wastewater discharges against per capita income (see Figure 3.2) shows that the data points for Shanghai stand out far above the rest of the country. To evaluate the impact of Shanghai as an outlier in the case of wastewater discharges, we re-estimated Equation (1) without Shanghai. The turning point moves up to RMB17,916, and only eight coastal provinces have passed the threshold by 2005.[8] The turning point for solid wastes, at RMB20,888, is not statistically distinguishable from zero ($t=0.14$).

Table 3.3 presents estimation results for Equation (2) as well as the calculated turning points by region. Consistent with the isomorphic EKC model, waste gas emissions from fuel burning and wastewater emissions exhibit inverted-U shaped relationships with income, while waste gas from production displays a U-shaped relationship with income for all the three regions. The estimates for solid wastes are imprecise and thus not informative.

Table 3.2 Estimates of the coefficients and turning points of isomorphic EKC model

	Fuel waste gas	Prod. waste gas	Wastewater	Solid waste
GDP per capita	0.668***	−0.208**	7.33e-04**	1.27e-07
	(0.111)	(0.0931)	(3.13e-04)	(1.83e-06)
GDP per capita squared	−7.54e-06***	9.05e-06***	−3.28e-08***	−3.04e-12
	(1.47e-06)	(1.82e-06)	(5.63e-09)	(2.40e-11)
Turning point (1998 RMB)	44,280***	n/a	11,146***	20,888
	(3,142)		(3,129)	(152,596)
Time fixed effects	Yes	Yes	Yes	Yes
Province fixed effects	Yes	Yes	Yes	Yes
Obs.	630	627	634	543
Adjusted R^2	0.854	0.836	0.906	0.548

Notes
Robust standard errors in the parentheses.
*** indicates 1% statistical significance.
** indicates 5% statistical significance.

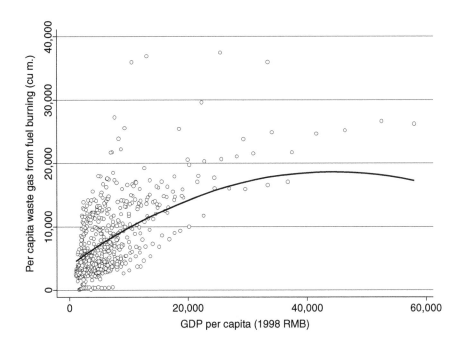

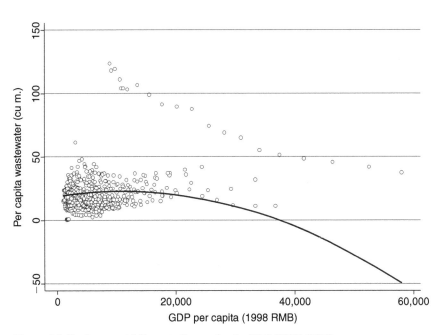

Figure 3.2 Environmental Kuznets Curves for the PRC (1985–2005).

Table 3.3 Estimates of the coefficients and turning points of heterogeneous EKC model

	Fuel waste gas	Prod. waste gas	Wastewater	Solid waste
Coastal provinces				
GDP per capita	0.761***	−0.258**	8.35e-04**	−3.32e-06*
	(0.140)	(0.112)	(3.95e-04)	(1.95e-06)
GDP per capita squared	−8.54e-06***	9.64e-06***	−3.61e-08***	2.92e-11
	(1.64e-06)	(2.00e-06)	(6.79e-09)	(2.43e-11)
Turning point (1998 RMB)	44,573***	n/a	11,580***	n/a
	(2,329)		(3,570)	
Central provinces				
GDP per capita	1.074*	−0.422	1.07e-03	−3.90e-06
	(0.568)	(0.363)	(8.13e-04)	(5.78e-06)
GDP per capita squared	−2.36e-05	1.57e-05	−1.53e-07***	−2.42e-10
	(5.17e-05)	(2.65e-05)	(4.46e-08)	(3.96e-10)
Turning point (1998 RMB)	22,769	n/a	3,504*	n/a
	(39,441)		(1,860)	
Western provinces				
GDP per capita	1.334**	−0.937*	3.06e-03**	−1.26e-05
	(0.617)	(0.508)	(1.29e-03)	(9.58e-06)
GDP per capita squared	−4.69e-05	7.75e-05*	−2.73e-07***	−3.09e-10
	(4.79e-05)	(4.61e-05)	(9.10e-08)	(8.38e-10)
Turning point (1998 RMB)	14,229	n/a	5,606***	n/a
	(9,041)		(1,103)	
F-tests for turning points				
Coastal = central	0.31	n/a	15.93	n/a
Central = western	0.05	n/a	3.60	n/a
Coastal = western	10.57	n/a	4.82	n/a
Time fixed effects	Yes	Yes	Yes	Yes
Province fixed effects	Yes	Yes	Yes	Yes
Obs.	630	627	634	543
Adjusted R²	0.854	0.836	0.916	0.559

Notes
Robust standard errors in the parentheses.
*** indicates 1% statistical significance.
** indicates 5% statistical significance.
* indicates 10% statistical significance.

An examination of the estimates across regions reveals that the part of the EKC curve on the left-hand side of the turning point is steepest for the western region and flattest for the coastal region (i.e. the absolute value of β_1 being the largest for the western region, followed by the central region, and then the coastal region). This suggests that per capita waste gas emissions from fuel burning and wastewater discharges have increased faster in the western and central regions than in the coastal regions at the initial stage of economic growth. Meanwhile, the central and western regions also have larger absolute value of β_2 than the coastal region does, which implies that the former have been more aggressive in correcting the "more developing, more polluting" pattern than the latter.

As a result of differences in both β_1 and β_2, the per capita GDP at which the turning point occurs is higher for the coastal region than for the western and central regions. For waste gas emission from fuel burning, the coastal region's turning point is at RMB44,573, compared to RMB22,769 for the central region, and RMB14,229 for the western region. Shanghai is the only municipality that is on the right of the turning point of waste gas from fuel burning. Concerning wastewater discharges, the coastal region's turning point is at RMB11,580, while those of the central and western regions are at RMB3,504 and RMB5,606, respectively. All coastal provinces (except Hainan and Guangxi), all central provinces, and all western provinces (except Guizhou) have entered the declining segment of the EKC curve. Due to the concern about Shanghai being an outlier, we re-estimated Equation (2) to exclude Shanghai.[9] The wastewater turning points increased to RMB19,626, RMB7,322 and RMB8,054 for the coastal, central and western regions, respectively. Under this scenario, six coastal provinces (Beijing, Guangdong, Jiangsu, Shanghai, Tianjin and Zhejiang), all central provinces and four western provinces (Chongqing, Qinghai, Sichuan and Xinjiang) have had per capita wastewater discharges decreasing with per capita GDP by 2005.

The bottom panel of Table 3.3 reports results of F-tests on the equality of income levels corresponding to the turning points between the three regions. The coastal region has significantly higher turning points for both waste gas from fuel burning and wastewater than the western region. The central region differs from the other two regions in turning points of wastewater discharges but not of waste gas from fuel burning, which is not surprising given the sizable standard errors of the estimates for the central region. These results imply that the isomorphic EKC model does not fully account for the heterogeneity in pollution-development patterns in the PRC.

Discussions and conclusions

This chapter estimated two EKC models using the PRC provincial-level panel data: one with isomorphic EKC for all provinces, and the other allowing the three regions – coastal, central and western – with substantially uneven economic development, to have region-specific EKCs. We found that an inverted-U shaped EKC holds for the PRC as a whole, and for each of the three regions in the cases of waste gas emissions from fuel burning and wastewater discharges. The relationship between per capita waste gas emissions from production and per capita income turns out to be U-shaped. The models fail to produce statistically significant results for solid wastes.

The chapter also found that the turning point of the EKC occurs at per capita GDP of RMB44,000 for waste gas emission from fuel burning and at RMB11,000 for wastewater discharges for the entire country, which correspond to US$12,903 and US$3,226, respectively, in purchasing power parity (PPP) terms.[10] The per capita incomes at which the turning points occur are comparable to the estimates yielded by many EKC studies using cross-country data (e.g. Halkos 2003).

The chapter further found that there are regional variations in the shape of the estimated EKCs. The EKCs of the more developed coastal region have flatter rising portions with turning points occurring at higher income levels compared to those of the less developed central and western regions. This may reflect technology diffusion and institution imitation through learning across regions at different stages of development, which may have enabled provinces in less developed regions to use cleaner technologies and institute better regulatory frameworks for environmental protection at a lower income level as opposed to their counterparts in more developed regions, even though the relocation of more polluting industries from developed regions to less developed ones could partly offset such impacts.

Based on the estimated turning points, we carry out a back-of-envelope exercise as follows. First, we use the average annual growth rate of per capita real GDP over the sample period (1985–2005) to project per capita GDP for each province for the future years. Second, using these projections and the estimated turning points of the EKCs for waste gas emission from fuel burning and wastewater discharges, we identify the provinces which will see their per capita emissions or discharges of these two types of waste declining by 2010 and 2015.[11] The results are presented in Table 3.4. By 2010, two more coastal provinces (Beijing and Tianjin) and one western province (Xinjiang) will join Shanghai on the right-hand side of the EKC for waste gas emissions from fuel burning, and four coastal provinces (Fujiang, Heibei, Liaoning and Shandong) and five western provinces (Gansu, Ningxia, Shaanxi, Tibet and Yunnan) will move to the right-hand side of the EKC for wastewater discharges. By 2015, an additional four coastal provinces, five central provinces and eight western provinces will pass their respective turning points of the EKCs for waste gas emissions from fuel burning. All provinces, except Guangxi, will pass the wastewater turning points as well. According to these projections, the central and western provinces will catch up with the coastal provinces faster in pollution reduction than in economic development, as a consequence of technology leapfrog and institution imitation for environmental protection.

Our results also indicate that it is important to distinguish waste gas due to production from waste gas due to fuel burning. Per capita emission of the former does not seem to show signs of slowing down. One of the possible causes of this could be that the PRC's current policy governing air pollution is stricter on emissions from fuel burning than from production. If this is the case, then a more balanced policy is called for.

The fact that the less developed regions have lower turning points implies that technology diffusion and institutional imitation play an important role as mechanisms to reduce emissions and improve environmental quality. In this regard, public policies which facilitate technology diffusion and transfer, knowledge sharing on energy efficiency and emission abatement, and capacity building and

Table 3.4 Projected provinces to pass the turning points of EKCs

	Coastal	Central	Western
Projected annual average growth rate of per capita GDP during 1985–2005 (%)			
Mean	10.2	9.0	8.1
Maximum	12.2	10.0	10.5
Minimum	8.1	7.8	9.6
Provinces that pass the turning points			
2005 — Fuel waste gas	Shanghai	None	None
2005 — Wastewater	Beijing Guangdong Jiangsu Shanghai Tianjin Zhejiang	All nine provinces	Chongqing Qinghai Sichuan Xinjiang
Projected in 2010 — Fuel waste gas	Beijing Shanghai Tianjin	None	Xinjiang
Projected in 2010 — Wastewater	All provinces except Guangxi and Hainan	All nine provinces	All provinces except Guizhou
Projected in 2015 — Fuel waste gas	Beijing Fujian Guangdong Jiangsu Shanghai Tianjin Zhejiang	Heilongjiang Hubei Inner Mongolia Jilin	All provinces except Guizhou
Projected in 2015 — Wastewater	All provinces except Guangxi	All nine provinces	All ten provinces

Note
The turning points are RMB44,573, RMB22,769 and RMB14,229 for waste gas from fuel burning for the coastal, central and western provinces, respectively; and RMB19,626, RMB7,322 and RMB8,054 for wastewater discharges for the three regions, respectively.

institutional strengthening targeted at less developed regions are recommended for the PRC to move forward. Moreover, the concerned government agencies at various levels should be encouraged to share successful regulatory experiences. NGOs also have an important role to play in disseminating good practices in environmental protection. It is encouraging to note that the Eleventh FYP starting in 2006 set the binding indicators in energy consumption, pollutant emissions and ecosystem protection, indicating enhanced government actions in combating environmental degradation in the PRC.

Table 3.A1 Region definition

Region	Coastal	Central	Western
Provinces (municipalities)	Beijing	Anhui	Chongqing
	Fujian	Heilongjiang	Gansu
	Guangdong	Henan	Guizhou
	Guangxi	Hubei	Ningxia
	Hainan	Hunan	Qinghai
	Heibei	Inner Mongolia	Shaanxi
	Jiangsu	Jiangxi	Sichuan
	Liaoning	Jilin	Tibet
	Shandong	Shanxi	Xinjiang
	Shanghai		Yunnan
	Tianjin		
	Zhejiang		

Notes

1 Shen (2006) finds that turning points for water pollutants vary between RMB8,257–17,516.
2 For a comprehensive survey of the empirical EKC literature, see Dinda (2004) and He (2007). Cavlovic *et al.* 2000 provide a meta-analysis of EKC.
3 Hainan province was separated from Guangdong province in 1988 and Chongqing municipality was separated from Sichuan province in 1997. Included in the data are 29 provinces and municipalities before 1988, 30 between 1988 and 1996 and 31 in 1997 and after. To account for the territorial changes, two dummies for post-1987 Guangdong and post-1996 Sichuan were added to the models.
4 The authors also tried cubic models. Similar as in the literature of List and Gallet (1999) and Cole and Elliott (2003), the authors found N-shaped curves for waste gas from fuel burning, wastewater and solid waste and an inverted-N curve for waste gas from production. The peak turning points for the N-curves are very close to those from quadratic models. The bottom turning points often fall far out of the sample.
5 The RMB (renminbi), or sometimes abbreviated as "CNY," is the currency of the PRC whose principal unit is the yuan. All the RMB numbers hereafter have been normalized to its 1998 value, unless otherwise indicated.
6 A more desirable measure is emissions of the pollutants. Unfortunately, such information is not consistently available in the statistical yearbooks.
7 See the Appendix at the end of this chapter for the list of provinces and municipalities belonging to each region.
8 Estimates are $\beta_1 = 1.06 \times 10^{-3}$ (3.35×10^{-4}), $\beta_1 = -2.96 \times 10^{-8}$ (9.59×10^{-9}), and the

adjusted R^2 is 0.786. The eight provinces (municipalities) are Beijing, Fujiang, Guangdong, Jiangsu, Liaoning, Shanghai, Tianjin and Zhejiang.

9 Estimation results are available from the authors upon request.

10 Applying World Bank International Comparison Program (ICP) 2005 results, US\$1 = RMB3.41.

11 This approach is meant to be illustrative rather than rigorous forecasting. The latter is technically difficult. For instance, the time fixed effects may not be stationary, which could lead to inaccurate prediction about timing. To be conservative, we use turning point estimates from sample excluding Shanghai for wastewater discharge in projection.

References

Auffhammer, Maximilian and Richard T. Carson. 2008. "Forecasting the Path of China's CO2 Emissions Using Province-level Information," *Journal of Environmental Economics and Management* 55, 229–47.

Bommer, R. 1999. "Environmental Policy and Industrial Competitiveness: The Pollution Haven Hypothesis Reconsidered," *Review of International Economics* 7(2), 342–55.

Cavlovic, T.A., K.H. Baker, R.P. Berrens and K. Gawande. 2000. "A Meta-analysis of Environmental Kuznets Curve Studies," *Agricultural and Resource Economics Review* 29(1), 32–42.

Cole, M.A. and R.J.R. Elliott. 2003. "Determining the Trade-environment Composition Effect: the Role of Capital, Labour and Environmental Regulations," *Journal of Environmental Economics and Management* 46(3), 363–83.

Dasgupta, S., H. Hettige and D. Wheeler. 2000. "What Improves Environmental Compliance? Evidence from Mexican Industry," *Journal of Environmental Economics and Management* 39, 39–66.

Dinda, Soumyananda. 2004. "Environmental Kuznets Curve Hypothesis: a Survey," *Ecological Economics* 49(4), 431–55.

Groot, Henril, L.F. Cees, A. Withagen and Mingliang Zhou. 2004. "Dynamics of China's Regional Development and Pollution: an Investigation into the Environmental Kuznets Curve," *Environment and Development Economics* 9, 507–37.

Grossman, Gene M. and Alan B. Krueger. 1995. "Economic Growth and the Environment," *Quarterly Journal of Economics* 110(2), 353–77.

Halkos, George E. 2003. "Environmental Kuznets Curve for Sulfur: Evidence using GMM Estimation and Random Coefficient Panel Data Models," *Environment and Development Economics* 8, 581–601.

Harrison, A. 1996. "Openness and Growth: a Time-series, Cross-country Analysis for Developing Countries," *Journal of Development Economics* 48, 419–47.

He, Jie. 2007. "Is the Environmental Kuznets Curve Hypothesis Valid for Developing Countries? A Survey," Working Paper 07–03, GREDI.

Hettige, H., M. Mani and D. Wheeler. 2000. "Industrial Pollution in Economic Development: the Environmental Kuznets Curve Revisited," *Journal of Development Economics* 62, 445–76.

List, John A. and Craig A. Gallet. 1999. "The Environmental Kuznets Curve: does One Size Fit All?" *Ecological Economics* 31, 409–23.

Liu, X., G.K. Heilig, J. Chen and M. Heino. 2007. "Interactions between Economic Growth and Environmental Quality in Shenzhen, China's First Special Economic Zone," *Ecological Economics* 62(3,4), 559–70.

Lopez, R. 1994. "The Environment as a Factor of Production: the Effects of Economic Growth and Trade Liberalization," *Journal of Environmental Economics and Management* 27, 163–84.

Millimet, Daniel L., John A. List and Thanasis Stengos. 2003. "The Environmental Kuznets Curve: Real Progress or Misspecified Models?" *Review of Economics and Statistics* 85(4), 1038–47.

Panayotou, Theodore. 1993. "Empirical Tests and Policy Analysis of Environmental Degradation at Different Stages of Economic Development," Working Paper WP238, Technology and Employment Program, Geneva: International Labor Office.

Pargal, S. and D. Wheeler. 1996. "Informal Regulation of Industrial Pollution in Developing Countries: Evidence from Indonesia," *Journal of Political Economy* 104(6), 1314–27.

Reppelin-Hill, V. 1999. "Trade and Environment: an Empirical Analysis of the Technology Effect in the Steel Industry," *Journal of Environmental Economics and Management* 38, 283–301.

Selden, T.M. and D. Song. 1994. "Environmental Quality and Development: is there a Kuznets Curve for Air Pollution Emissions?" *Journal of Environmental Economics and Management* 27(2), 147–62.

Shafik, N. 1994. "Economic Development and Environmental Quality: an Econometric Analysis," *Oxford Economic Papers* 46, 757–73.

Shafik, N. and S. Bandyopadhyay. 1992. "Economic Growth and Environmental Quality: Time Series and Cross-Country Evidence," World Bank Policy Research Working Paper, WPS904.

Shen, Junyi. 2006. "A Simultaneous Estimation of Environmental Kuznets Curve: Evidence from China," *China Economic Review* 17, 383–94.

Vincent, Jeffrey R. 1997. "Testing for Environmental Kuznets Curves within a Developing Country," *Environment and Development Economics* 2, 417–31.

Vukina, T., J.C. Beghin and E.G. Solakoglu. 1999. "Transition to Markets and the Environment: Effects of the Change in the Composition of Manufacturing Output," *Environment and Development Economics* 4(4), 582–98.

Wheeler, D. 2000. "Racing to the Bottom? Foreign Investment and Air Pollution in Developing Countries," World Bank Development Research Group Working Paper, No. 2524, Washington, DC.

4 Economic growth and environmental regulation

What is the role of regulation?

Timothy Swanson

Introduction: the role of regulation in the growth process

The People's Republic of China (PRC) has now been experiencing rapid growth for more than two decades. At the same time, its environment has experienced rapid degradation, in terms of air, water, ecosystems and all other resources imaginable. For this reason, it might seem that there is an obvious connection between economic growth and the environment – one in which growth continues to drive resource degradation. The object of this chapter is to investigate this relationship a bit more comprehensively in order to examine more generally how economic growth and economic regulation interact within economies.

What is the role of environmental regulation in respect to economic growth? This question has been debated since at least the time of the initial statement of the "Porter hypothesis" (Porter and van der Linde 1995 and 2005). In one respect, the simple Porter hypothesis posited the unlikely idea that more regulation might be good for an economy, by inducing innovation and encouraging growth and competitiveness. This seems unlikely in an economy such as the PRC after two decades experience of unregulated growth, where industries achieve increasing market shares by out-competing firms and industries in more regulated countries. The PRC needs to consider very carefully the ways in which environmental regulation might impact upon its nascent economy, both positively and negatively.

For this reason, this chapter will consider the question within the broader context of technological change. A more complex view of the Porter hypothesis would place it firmly within the boundaries of the literature on the economics of growth and technological change (Stoneman 1995). In this view, governments must intervene within economies in many ways in order to encourage innovation and growth (e.g. policies on intellectual property rights). Such intervention is important as a means for inducing innovation, and for directing the process. Then environmental regulation may be seen within this context as just one more instrument in society's toolkit of economy-directing interventions.

Intervention is critically important for these purposes. It has been known, since at least the time of the seminal work of Arrow (1962a and 1962b) and the structural work of Kamien and Schwartz (1982), that competitive firms and competitive markets need not produce the optimal amount of innovation and growth within an economy. Governments must intervene in industries in order to provide incentives for investment in research and development (R&D). This is because industries in competitive markets have few incentives to invest in technological change or even in product innovation, since any returns would be immediately competed away. This is one of the best-known examples of market failure in the context of competitive markets, and provides the rationale for various forms of interventions (Blair and Cotter 2005). So, some manner of intervention is required in order to encourage growth and technological change, at least at some point in the development process.

Of course, firms and industry off the technological frontier may be able to grow via "catching up" processes for a very long period of time. In the 1950s and 1960s, the governments of Japan and the Republic of Korea primarily sponsored domestic innovation and technological change by importing them (Teece 1981). These governments accomplished this via the requirement that foreign firms license technologies to domestic firms, in exchange for the opportunity to invest in domestic markets (Mowery 1995). In Japan, during this period, the Ministry of International Trade and Industry (MITI) was responsible for drawing up the terms for licensing technologies from foreign firms, in return for providing access to Japanese productive capacity and Japanese markets. For two or three decades of growth, the experiences of Japan and the Republic of Korea demonstrate that it is possible to rely upon the importation of technology, and upon imitation over innovation.

After a couple of decades, the growth and development of an economy must rely increasingly upon its own capacity for technological change and innovation. Again, this is borne out by the more recent experiences of Japan and the Republic of Korea. By the 1970s, Japan was one of the leading economies in the world in terms of R&D investment, and as the succeeding case studies illustrate, many of these investments were going into environment or energy-related industries. By 1987, Japan was the world leader in R&D per unit gross domestic product (GDP) at 2.8 percent, and the world leader in the proportion of income spent on energy-related R&D at 23 percent (Mowery 1995). In Japan, the transition from imitation to innovation was completed in a couple of decades.

Why did Japan undertake this shift in investment priorities? Experience tells us that the process of catching up (through imitation and investment) can last only for a limited time, and that as a country approaches the technological frontier, imitation-based growth must continue to fade away (Gomulka 1990). Then the country concerned needs to become more focused upon its own innate capacities for innovation, growth and development. This implies a shift in priorities away from imitation and toward policies focused on encouraging internal processes of innovation and technological change. As the PRC follows in the footprints of its Asian neighbors, it will come to recognize that it will soon enter this transition phase and begin to focus more on innovation and less on imitation. Policies will soon need to take a central role in guiding the growth and development process of the country.

To that end, environmental regulation plays an important and central role in guiding and encouraging R&D. It does so by providing incentives for particular pathways of technological change. Placing prices on scarce resources (such as energy, water or air) encourages firms and industries to invest in innovations that will conserve on these resources in order to minimize costs. These innovations then become important to the core competitiveness of the firms and industries, as they compete to provide innovations or to provide products that economize on scarce resources. So, environmental regulation is just one manner in which competitive firms and industries are provided direction on how and where to invest in potentially profitable innovation.

In this chapter, we set out a general framework for thinking about how environmental regulation might be conceived as a mechanism for directing innovation and potential growth, and we consider where this framework stands in relation to other ways of thinking about environmental regulation. In particular, we will explore the extent to which environmental regulation can drive economic growth, rather than the other way around.

In the following sections we examine this idea by first constructing a general framework and then considering the empirical evidence. Next, we examine a series of case studies that demonstrate different ways in which environmental regulation might be used to direct the growth process: technology diffusion; technology direction; and policy leadership.

The importance of environmental regulation in economic growth: a conceptual framework

This section provides an overview of the sections and case studies that follow in the chapter. The case studies in subsequent sections give examples of how states have intervened within the economy in order to guide technology and growth. In this section, we will create a framework within which we examine all of the various ways in which environmental regulation can impact upon the path of an economy. One of the main themes of this chapter is that environmental regulation is about choosing the way forward, both in terms of consumption choices and supply decisions.

The most basic view of environmental regulation sees it simply as a means of restricting industrial access to environmental resources (air, water, ecosystems) in order to provide some of these resources to other sectors of society. That is, the role of regulation here is to substitute the provision of public goods for further growth in private goods. For example, this might be the case if a particular forest was turned into a protected area, in order to provide natural habitat by the prevention of further logging. In this view, the sole impact of this sort of regulation in terms of economic growth is negative, although its impact on societal welfare or development may be very positive indeed. Social welfare is enhanced by meeting the public demand for all of those goods and services provided by the forest (watersheds, wildlife, biodiversity) other than those provided through logging.

However, even in this instance, it is important to recognize that environmental regulation may be seen as having a role in providing direction and incentives to the industrial part of the economy. Once it is recognized that logging activities entail these additional costs (watersheds, habitats, etc.), there are incentives for the industry to acquire the maximum amount of timber with the minimum amount of habitat disruption. Resources that were previously valueless are now recognized as costly. Investments are then made in finding techniques and approaches (in logging) that will consider the cost of these resources. Resources that were previously and needlessly wasted are now valued and considered. The imposition of a constraint generates incentives for thinking about solutions regarding these resources. This is the manner in which a simple and obvious restraint turns into a positive incentive for innovation.

In the remainder of this section, we demonstrate how environmental regulation performs this role, and how it can either add or subtract from economic growth, depending on how it is administered.

Views on environmental regulation – what impacts?

The views on environmental regulation, and its impacts on industry and the economy, are very diverse. Some view it as an expensive method for supplying environmental goods and services. Others view it as an essential means for harmonizing industries across the globe. We will place each of the views into a common framework, so that it is straightforward to analyze the differences between the viewpoints.

Consider Figure 4.1, a representation of the "Production Possibilities Frontier" (PPF) for a standard closed economy. It shows that the fundamental capital endowments of the society may be used to produce two sorts of goods – termed Good A and Good B. The fundamental difference between the two sorts of goods is that Good A uses a lot of environmental resources in its production (air, water, ecosystems), while Good B does not. We might think of Good A as being those goods and services deriving from traditional heavy industry (steel, chemicals, forestry or agriculture), and Good B as being those goods or services deriving from less environmentally intensive activities (financial services, retailing, light manufactures). The society concerned has a given endowment of physical capital (K), labor (L), and environmental resources (E) that are used in producing its entire national product. The same figure is generated again in Figures 4.2 through 4.4. The question that is addressed in each figure is: how does the introduction of environmental regulation impact upon the productive economy? That is, how does the PPF respond to environmental regulation? We will see below that there is a diverse set of answers to this enquiry.

Static view of environmental regulation

When there is no environmental regulation, the PPF will be represented by the heavy line in Figure 4.1. The absence of environmental regulation has the

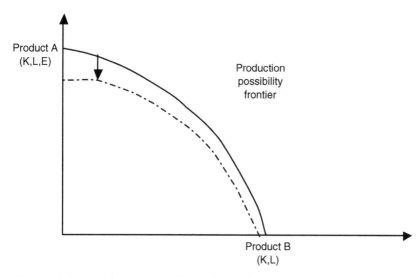

Figure 4.1 Impact of environmental regulation – static view.

implicit effect of pricing environmental resources at zero. Any firm or industry wishing to use the air or water for disposal of its waste products or for production of its goods and services may do so without restraint. This maintains the PPF at the highest possible level of goods production (furthest from the origin).

The society might then decide that, for any number of reasons, it wishes to introduce environmental regulation. This may be because the society sees that there are alternative uses for the environmental resources, and so the opportunity costs of using them should not be zero. It might also be because the society sees that there is a failure to retain adequate environmental quality to operate the industries themselves efficiently. In any event, the advent of environmental regulation in this scenario creates a constraint on the previously unrestricted use of this factor of production. The impact of environmental regulation in this scenario is straightforward. It shifts "in" the PPF along the axis for Good A (the environmentally-intensive good). Although the economy remains capable of producing the same amount of Good B, it can no longer reach the same levels of production of Good A. In effect, the society has reserved some amounts of environmental resources for other uses, and these restrictions have reduced the level of production in the environmentally-intensive production sector. In this view, environmental regulation is a costly method (to the production sector) for maintaining environmental quality for some sectors of the society.

This is the standard view of the impact of environmental regulation. It includes any attempt to constrain private access to an environmental resource in order to provide it as a public good. For example, the establishment of an ambient air quality standard might be seen as an attempt to constrain private emissions from industry in order to retain the public good of generally available air quality. From this perspective, such a constraint acts to shift "in" the PPF for those goods and services that previously had (and relied substantially upon) unconstrained access to air quality. This is the effect of reducing production, and hence growth, in those industries.

Induced innovation view of environmental regulation – dynamic incentives

The induced innovation perspective on environmental regulation commences from the same starting point as the standard view – the initial impact of regulation is to place a price on the use of environmental resources and to shift in the PPF for goods based upon them. This induced innovation view then deviates from the standard view by emphasizing a second and dynamic effect, whereby the impact of pricing environmental resources is to create incentives for firms and industries to economize in their resource use. In effect, environmental regulation's main impact is to put industry to work on increasing the efficient use of environmental resources in their production systems. Before regulation, firms did not need to think of methods for economizing upon these resources, but afterwards the firms must attempt to solve this problem in the course of their production efforts.

The impact of these dynamic incentives is to cause the PPF to shift twice – once inwards by reason of the pricing of environmental resources, and once outwards by reason of the responsiveness of R&D, and consequently increased efficiency of new methods of production (Figure 4.2). The aggregate impact of environmental regulation may be either negative or positive, depending on which of the two effects outweighs the other. The so-called Porter Hypothesis argues

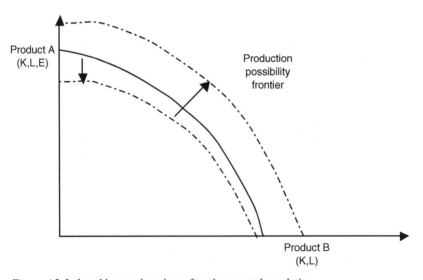

Figure 4.2 Induced innovation view of environmental regulation.

that the impact of environmental regulation is to motivate industries to become more efficient, so that the aggregate impact is positive (Porter and van der Linde 1995). Other economists have argued that, despite the secondary dynamic effects, the overall impact of environmental regulation on industry must be negative (Jaffe *et al*. 1995). The point of environmental regulation, in their view, is to generate the societal benefits from retaining environmental goods and services that outweigh the industrial costs (as discussed above in regard to the static view of regulation). This debate remains unsettled and a significant number of studies have been undertaken. The empirical debate regarding the overall impact of environmental regulation is the subject of the next section.

Market transformation view of environmental regulation – diffusion of standards and technologies

Another view on environmental regulation commences from a very different starting point. In this view, one of the fundamental problems with industry lies in the existence of infra-marginal firms that pursue inefficient methods of production. The inefficiency of these firms may be the result of many factors, such as protective local governments or failures of information flow, but the result is the same. Some firms exist and produce well within the production frontier. This situation is depicted in Figure 4.3, in which firms i, j and k are shown to be engaging in production within the PPF of the economy.

The argument amongst economists on these points concerns "how many dollar bills are left lying around on sidewalks," i.e. why would it be possible for inefficiencies across industries to persist? The diffusion of efficient technologies throughout the industry should be accomplished via adequate competition, given

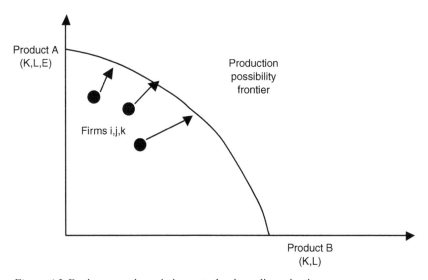

Figure 4.3 Environmental regulation as technology dissemination.

the availability of accurate information. Diffusion may be prevented by either governmental or informational failures. Local governments might act to protect locally inefficient producers, or consumers may be unable to ascertain (from available information) which of the products is most efficient for their own purposes.

Mechanisms may be created that will force these infra-marginal firms toward the frontier. Centralized standards may be adopted to force the firms to employ the best available technologies. Alternatively, market-based measures may force all firms to compete in regard to certain standards, and provide consumers the information on these production qualities in order to aid that competition. Either by resolving the information or regulation problems, the best technologies may be diffused and the firms may be forced towards the frontiers. The discussion of these sorts of (market or governmental) failures and how environmental regulation may cause technologies to diffuse is presented later in the chapter.

It is often debated whether such opportunities for efficiency-enhancement can exist within reasonably competitive economies. The problem is that, in the world of second-best, many economies can have significant local imperfections, due to local governmental protection or local informational imperfections. When this is the case, some sort of centralized efforts at regulation may be able to address these local inefficiencies by means of the diffusion of technologies already available.

Technological or policy leadership view of environmental regulation

One interesting aspect of environmental regulation is its role as an instrument in industrial policy. As mentioned above, the implicit economic function of any environmental regulation is to impose a price on environmental resources within an economy. Many forms of environmental regulation involve the assessment of the *current opportunity costs* of environmental use (in terms of its impacts on health or aesthetics) and then attempt to impose that current cost as a "price" on industries accessing environmental resources. This creates incentives for industries to economize on the use of the environmental resources, to the extent that a price is charged, so technologies are generated that internalize the current price of the environmental resource.

A very different approach to environmental regulation involves an attempt to anticipate future price movements with regard to environmental resources, and then to regulate for the purpose of causing industries to create technologies that internalize *future* prices of environmental resources. The purpose of creating technologies that internalize future prices is to be able to innovate first, patent the technologies, and then to acquire the rents from being an innovator. If the anticipated future prices actually occur, then any firm or industry wishing to possess technology that already incorporates those prices must license it from the leader. In this way, foreseeing future environmental scarcities is a way to assume technological leadership and to earn innovation rents. The manner in which this is done is set forth later in the chapter.

Of course, it is very risky to forecast future price paths, and to invest in technologies based upon these estimates. Guesses about future price trends can be very right or very wrong. If a state leads its industry down the wrong price path, then it leads it toward non-competitiveness.

It can be argued that environmental regulation is an easier approach to technological leadership than some other forms of speculation. This is because there is a reasonably stable relationship between economic growth and the demand for environmental goods and services. As societies' incomes grow, it is reasonably predictable that the prices of environmental goods and services will increase. Anticipating increasing demand for environment-conserving technologies has been a good bet in most of the developed world over the past half-century. Any government that had forecasted that environmental resources would be more highly valued over the last 20 or 30 years would not have been far wrong.

More importantly, even if the demand for the resource does not increase in a given society, it is only necessary that the environmental policy becomes demanded in other countries for the technologies to be sought after. This is the role for "policy leadership" as a means of inducing technology leadership. Policy leadership may also translate into technology leadership, and thus into innovation-based rents. So, technological leadership can be acquired either by foreseeing future resource scarcities or by starting various policy trends.

Technological leadership is an important way in which environmental regulation has actually anticipated and expanded the PPF of various states in particular directions (Figure 4.4). Investment in technologies that deal with forecasted scarcities or enhanced demands creates new means of production, and expands the possibilities of the state concerned. When other states become persuaded to

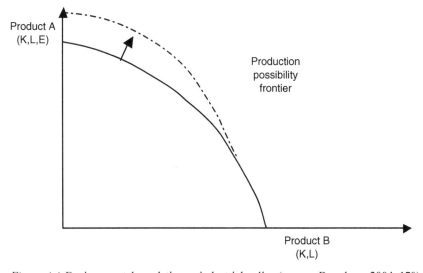

Figure 4.4 Environmental regulation as industrial policy (source: Boardman 2004: 170).

adopt the same technologies, then innovation rents are earned. These are real and important benefits from the strategic adoption of environmental regulation.

Perspectives on the growth impacts of environmental regulation

There are numerous different perspectives on the impact of environmental regulation upon the productive potential of an economy. The most static view sees such regulation as a simple cost upon the productive sectors, in which the government decides to predetermine the amount of environmental goods and services that will be implicitly produced within the economy. Then industry attempts to do the best that it can subject to this constraint. This is the impact set out in Figure 4.1, in which environmental regulation merely constrains the productive part of the economy, by predetermining the amount of environmental goods and services that will be consumed. It is important to recall that this shifting-in of the PPF need not correspond to a loss of societal welfare, only of production possibilities. In fact, it can be assumed that the society's welfare has increased in that it has been willing to trade-off increased environmental goods and services for the foregone production.

The other perspectives on environmental regulation emphasize the secondary, or dynamic, features of state intervention. One aspect of this is that environmental regulation creates incentives to economize on the use of the environmental resources, and so spurs innovation toward more efficient use of the resource. Usually, industries that have not had to consider environmental impacts will be able to economize on resource usage at little cost with initial efforts. In any event, getting industry to work on the problem is almost always an efficient and important means of economizing on the use of real resources. It is argued that the benefits of these dynamic incentives can often outweigh the initial costs of environmental regulation. A large empirical literature has been generated to address the issue, and it is clear that the dynamic benefits exist.

Second, state intervention may be important for growth if the state's industry does not start on the technological frontier. It can sometimes be the case that the country's firms or industries do not all exist upon the PPF, which means that there are local problems that exist which allow the national economy to retain some inefficient firms. When this is the case, environmental regulation can be an important means for diffusing frontier-level technologies throughout the economy, and eliminating local inefficiencies. Centralized intervention can overcome local governmental problems or informational failures to ensure that the best technologies are used in every part of the state.

Third, state intervention may be important for growth if the state wishes to pursue technological leadership. This may be the case if it perceives the movement of important environmental scarcities in a particular direction. It can encourage its industry to develop and adopt new technologies anticipating these scarcities, via environmental policies that encourage this. Then, the industry is put in the position of owning the technologies, should these environmental scarcities occur. All subsequent adopters must then pay the initial innovator a rent for its innovation. In this manner, states may pursue technological leadership via environmental policy leadership.

Finally, environmental regulation is important for growth of global trade in the same way that it is important on the national scale. When environmental regulations are too diverse across countries, this stands as a cost or inhibition to trade. The adoption of a uniform standard, and its diffusion across all countries, is a boon to the trading system so long as the standard is not the most restrictive one. Moving toward uniform standards in environmental regulation on the global level removes inefficiencies of diverse standards, just as it does on the national level.

So, it is only in the most abstract sense that environmental regulation is a pure and simple cost to industry. When a specific context is supplied, it is usually the case that there is some role for the state to be involved in regulation of industry. When other states already have standards, or localities already have problems, or environmental scarcities are changing – in all of these circumstances, it is more important for the state to be involved in environmental regulation for industrial growth than not.

In each of the sections that follow we will consider these contexts in relation to a particular set of case studies. We commence in the next section by looking at the empirical literature on the dynamic effects of environmental regulation. Following this, we look at the impacts of diffusion, examining the case of energy labeling. In the fifth section, we look at the role of technology leadership, examining the anticipatory investments by Denmark in wind turbine technologies. In the sixth section, we examine how the harmonization of standards aids trade and investment, specifically in regard to the regulation of lead and the trade in its products.

Environmental regulation and innovation: contrasting the static view and the dynamic view of regulation

How is environmental regulation related to economic growth? One potential response to this question is that environmental regulation is the primary means of targeting society's desired goods and services, i.e. of making sure that the demanded set of complex goods are produced from the state's combined set of resources. In this view, the role of environmental regulation is to ensure that the economy is producing the precise mix of goods and services that consumers desire (Jaffe *et al.* 1995).

In this static view of regulation, this is the only role that environmental regulation is able to play, and it is an essential role in any economy. A market economy is only able to produce those goods and services that are able to be supplied through private markets and transactions. When this is the case, the market must over-supply any and private-market goods and services relative to public goods such as environmental goods and services. This observation points to the "demand-side" role for cost-benefit analysis and the "supply-side" role for environmental regulation in the mixed economy. Cost–benefit analysis becomes the government's means for assessing the appropriate mix of goods and services actually demanded by consumers. Environmental regulation is the means of supplying that mix of public and private goods that is demanded.

The implied relationship between economic growth and environmental regulation is also apparent from this description. As economic growth advances in an unregulated market, the mix of private and public goods becomes increasingly unbalanced. Since the market will respond to the demand for private goods but not to public, increasing growth must continue to contribute to this unbalance. The unmet demand for public goods then translates into a demand for environmental regulation to supply them (Stokey 1998). Once environmental regulation is in place, it is possible for the economy to produce a more complex mix of goods and services, which it does thereafter.

This shift away from private-only provision and toward mixed goods and services, in combination with increased growth, can then be charted as the Environmental Kuznets Curve (EKC) (Grossman and Krueger 1993). In this respect, the EKC charts nothing other than the simple observation that there are diminishing returns to continuing supplies of unrestricted private goods, and that a more complex mechanism – for registering social demand and generating supplies – is required after private good production has passed some "tipping point."

Environmental regulation in this view is primarily the means for providing the link between societies' demands for mixed goods and the mechanism for the supply of the goods demanded. Economic growth in this view is then the proximate cause through which the demand for environmental regulation is triggered. In an exclusively market-based economy, all production will be private goods production, until environmental regulation is installed to make more complex forms of demand and supply feasible. In this static view of economic growth and environmental regulation, the role of environmental regulation is simply to channel existing demands for complicated goods into their actual supplies.

Environmental regulation and induced innovation – dynamic view

Environmental regulation will register initially as a cost to the economy on account of the reduced production of private goods and services it implies; however, the same shift in emphasis also places a value on public good production. For the first time, the economy is provided with signals and prices that indicate that the public good is valued, and that its production should be targeted. It is the creation of this signal that adds to the efficiency of the overall economy, and provides the potential for dynamic impacts beyond the change in static production priorities.

Of course, the efficiency impact of any signal depends upon the quality of the signal provided, and this, in turn, depends upon the form and substance of the environmental regulation. Nevertheless, movement away from an economy that signals that one set of goods is valued at or near zero (when clearly there exist opportunity costs) must be efficiency-enhancing. It provides the initial signals to the effect that the economy must expend some efforts on conserving these resources, and in investing in their conservation.

The dynamic effect of the introduced signal is to be found in the reports on the initial costs of environmental regulation, in which the various forms of costliness are summarized (Table 4.1).

The important point to take away from this table is that research and development expenditures comprised about 5–6 percent of all expenditures by businesses on abatement costs. This is indicative of the amount of "new thinking" that is being instilled into the US economy, as a result of the introduced regulation. If the shift were solely static, then the expenditure would only be on what was necessary to change the mix of goods today, i.e. static abatement costs. R&D expenditures are evidence of investments into changing the direction of the economy.

An example of such directed innovation might be the use of tradable permit systems to induce innovation in the production of combined energy generation plants in the United States and the European Union (EU). Both jurisdictions imposed aggregate constraints on sulfur oxide (SO_x) production, implying a reduction of about 50 percent in emissions of SO_x over a period of about ten years commencing from the mid-1990s. Such an aggregate constraint on SO_x production places an implicit price on the SO_x generated in energy production, and creates an incentive to invest in techniques capable of reducing SO_x emissions per unit of energy. At the same time a tradable permit system allows many processes and innovations to be considered for these purposes. Innovations may take the forms of new technologies (e.g. high efficiency burners), new inputs (e.g. low-sulfur coal) or new locations (e.g. away from urban areas) as means of meeting the desired production mix. Since SO_x was implicitly priced at zero before the regulatory regime, there was no reason to investigate any of these ideas before. The adoption of environmental regulation has the impact of causing the industry to think, for the first time, about how to be more efficient in the use of these resources. The investments in R&D are indicative of how the adoption of law has shifted the direction of the economy.

Another real indicator of the economic shift resulting from environmental regulation is the decline in abatement costs once investment commences. This is indicative of the way in which innovation becomes a way to substitute away from the impact of the environmental constraint (Table 4.2). In a recent cross-EU study by Oosterhuis *et al.*, the authors charted the decline of abatement costs in several recently regulated industries. They compared the costs of abatement *ex ante* (prior to regulation) to those existing *ex post* (after regulation was imposed). In general, the finding was that the costs of abatement across sectors declined by a factor of two. The introduction of incentives to investigate and to implement resource-conserving technologies was effective in cutting production costs in half, once the regulations were introduced.

In sum, the first and static impact of any new environmental regulation (that creates a non-zero shadow price to resource use) is to increase the production costs to environment-using industries. This must have the static effect of

Table 4.1 Costs of introducing US environmental regulation (1981–90)

Sector	1981	1982	1983	1984	1985	1986	1987	1988	1989	1990
Personal consumption	10,278	10,307	12,119	13,270	14,254	15,349	13,159	14,316	12,278	10,485
Business abatement	48,969	45,726	46,031	49,825	51,314	52,994	53,846	55,615	57,784	60,122
Government abatement	16,446	15,912	15,504	16,760	17,684	18,974	20,727	20,559	21,560	23,122
Regulation and monitoring	2,190	2,068	1,946	1,823	1,647	1,923	1,838	1,988	2,005	1,980
Research and development	2,626	2,484	3,115	2,998	3,017	3,186	3,204	3,216	3,303	3,303
Total	80,509	76,495	78,713	84,677	87,914	92,425	92,773	95,694	96,928	99,024

Source: Jaffe *et al.* (1995).

Table 4.2 Declining abatement costs in regulated sectors

Case study	Directive (sector)	Ex ante/ex post *ratio* Upstream
1	Large Combustion Plant Directive (LCPD) (Power sector)	2 (Germany)
2	Integrated Pollution Prevention and Control (IPPC) (Belgium Ceramics)	>1.2 (operational costs) ~1.1 (capital costs)
3	ODS (Ozone Depleting Substances	2.5 (1.4–125)
4	Transport (Netherlands)	2 (1.4–6)
5	Packaging	–
6	Nitrate's Directive (Agriculture)	~2

Source: Oosterhuis (2006).

reducing the production possibilities in those industries that are resource-intensive; but it is also a way of generating a new mix of goods and services from the affected industry. The second impact of environmental regulation is to enhance the incentives for investments to conserve on the use of these resources. This produces a dynamic impact in which resource-conserving innovations arise over time.

This dynamic impact is important for any economy. It is the signal that the economy must invest in going down a path that recognizes an additional scarcity. Although the introduction of the signal has its costs (as in Table 4.1), the crucial importance of improved allocative efficiency in the economy should not be overlooked.

A major research question over the past 15 years has been how these two impacts aggregate – negative static plus positive dynamic. That is, does the improved efficiency of pricing in the economy compensate for the regulatory costs imposed upon industry? The results of a recent study surveying the empirical work are set out in Figure 4.5.

The one clear conclusion from this mix of evidence is that there is no always-existing positive or negative impact from environmental regulation. Depending upon how it is applied, environmental regulation can lead the economy down both positive and negative growth paths.

Environmental regulation is a means for implementing a particular development path, not just a mix of goods and services. That is, it expressly provides the mechanism for electing the mix of goods and services the society desires to produce (public and private) but it also provides the economic signals for the investments required to shift the economy in the desired direction. It is important that this forward-looking role of environmental regulation is recognized. It is not enough for regulation to be a simple engineering matter of cleaning up already-existing messes from past production. The point of environmental regulation is more directed to selecting the path forward than it is to clearing up the path behind.

In the next few sections we turn to a couple of case studies that illustrate the manner in which environmental regulation may be used to drive technological

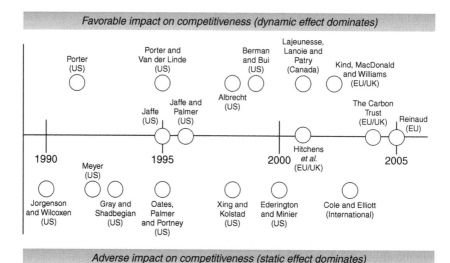

Figure 4.5 Studies on aggregate economic impact of environmental regulation.

change. The simplest approach concerns the encouraged diffusion of some already-existing technologies, when incentives exist to maintain archaic technologies. We turn to this in the next section. The more ambitious approach is to elect policy leadership, and to invest in technologies that are anticipating policy developments generally. In between these examples lies the simple fact of induced innovation as a response to the mixed set of goods and services demanded in the country concerned.

Technology diffusion: environmental regulation as dissemination

The use of environmental regulation to place an economy onto a development path toward increased reliance upon resource-saving technologies may seem a bit abstract, but it is a very concrete affair in many instances. In this section, we will chart the most obvious of instances, where the technology already exists and the goal of regulation is simply to disseminate it. Many times, there are reasons for the slow diffusion of the best available technologies. Sometimes these reasons are regulatory, as in the failure of various agencies to enforce existing standards, and other times they are market-related. In any event, it can often be the case that firms in a given industry are not operating at the technological frontier. When this is the case, the state concerned is able to move the economy toward the preferred technology simply by encouraging its diffusion.

Here we will consider the example of the EU electrical appliance industry as a case study in regulatory diffusion. The EU electrical appliance industry suffers, with other jurisdiction's industries, from the problem of a jointly consumed good. When consumers are purchasing appliances, they are in fact buying two separate things:

1 a particular piece of hardware (the appliance); and
2 a commitment to a particular path of electricity consumption (to support the appliance).

The price perceived by the consumer at point of sale may only refer to the former aspect of the purchase, while the aggregate price of the purchase may be substantially determined by the latter. There are several reasons why it is a relatively complicated matter for the individual consumer to process the information required to make an efficient choice in regard to the joint consumption decision. And, importantly, if the consumer does not make the choice well, then there is little reason for the producer to be concerned with investing in the production of energy-efficient technologies.

The consumer's decision must be able to evaluate the total cost of an appliance which includes its initial purchase price, and also the consideration of:

1 the amount of annual electricity use;
2 for the household concerned;
3 multiplied by the then current price of electricity; and
4 aggregated over the entire life of the appliance.

All of the information above may be unknown to the consumer concerned, and (even if available) the total purchase price requires a significant amount of information processing by the consumer. For this reason, many markets simply leave this information aside, and the consumer is left to focus only on the purchase price of the good concerned.

However, this approach is sub-optimal for the consumer, and for the production of the appliance. Figure 4.6 below shows the total "life-cycle cost" (the sum of initial purchase and aggregate running costs) for a refrigerator-freezer purchased in the European Union (Boardman 2004). The figure shows that initially an energy-efficient product substantially reduces the lifecycle costs of a refrigerator-freezer. That is, the increased purchase price is more than offset by discounted savings in energy bills. However, there does become a point where energy efficiency savings via electricity bills do not offset the additional purchase price involved. Boardman (2004) estimates that the minimum lifecycle cost would be equivalent to an A-rated appliance under the EU labeling scheme with a resultant 46 percent reduction in electricity consumption and over a 10 percent reduction in the lifecycle cost of the appliance. Machines rated above A are not producing cost-savings that compensate for the purchase price change, over a standard life and discount rate.

Such a figure illustrates that improving consumer knowledge on the overall costs of a product can result in a significantly better-functioning market. Once the average consumer is able to see the importance that energy efficiency makes

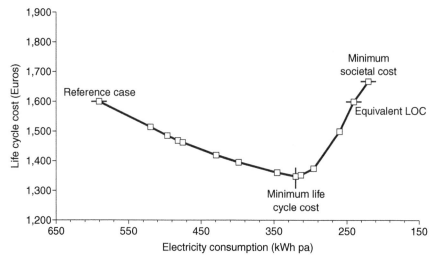

Figure 4.6 Lifecycle costs of a refrigerator-freezer.

to overall costs, the market is able to use this information to drive lesser quality (lower efficiency) products from the market. At current values for the important parameters (energy use, energy price, prevailing interest rates), the minimum aggregate cost is that associated with an A-rated machine.

In order to aid the diffusion of efficient technologies, in 1996 the European Commission announced minimum standards for cold appliances (e.g. refrigerators and freezers) that would come into effect in 1999. The standard prohibited manufacturers and importers from placing D–G rated cold appliances on the EU market. As analyzed by Schiellerup (2002), the minimum standard resulted in reductions in the energy consumption of the average product that were in excess of the aspirations of the regulations. Reductions in energy consumption ranged from 20 percent for upright freezers to 33 percent for chest freezers. Evidence of this can be found in Figure 4.7 that shows the sales weighted average energy consumption for a variety of cold products for the period 1989 to 2000. It can be seen that average energy consumption starts to drop much more rapidly than the historical trend toward the third quarter of 1999.

Is this enhanced efficiency coming at the expense of the industry? On account of information problems or other market failures, there can be many infra-marginal firms operating at a relatively low level of efficiency within the industry. In this case, diffusion of the standard may result in the elimination of the inefficient fringe producers within the industry.

This can be seen in the impact of minimum standards in the EU. If the firms affected were homogenous (and all on the technological frontier), then it would be anticipated that the impact of the standard would be to raise prices as the industry shifted together to higher-cost technologies. Boardman (2004) finds however that despite the shift in production to more energy-efficient products,

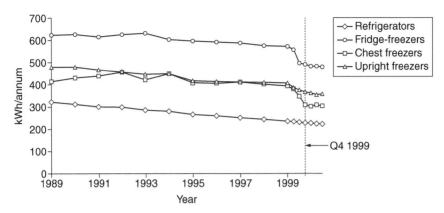

Figure 4.7 Sales weighted average energy consumption of appliances in the United Kingdom (1989–99).

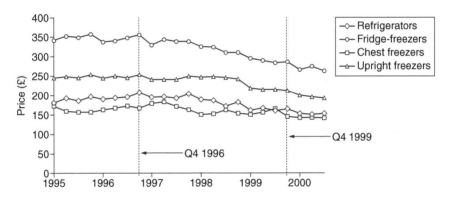

Figure 4.8 Real sales weighted price of cold appliances in the United Kingdom (1995–2000) (source: Schiellerup 2002: 329).

the average purchase price of all cold appliances sold in the United Kingdom dropped by 14 percent over the period of January 1999 to March 2000. As can be seen from Figure 4.8 above, real prices continued their downward trend in the four quarters after the minimum standards came into effect. It can also be seen that the biggest drop in prices has been for refrigerator-freezers, which accounts for the largest share of the market.

This figure conveys the important point that the diffusion of minimum standards can be a means for culling inefficient producers from a diverse industry. There may be many reasons for inefficient producers to exist (and to persist), and so the imposition of a minimum standard on the end-products may be the best means for addressing the problem.

From Table 4.3 overleaf, it can also be seen that the savings to consumers from the 1999 energy-efficiency standards for cold appliances purchased in 2000

Table 4.3 Annual savings from the 1999 minimum energy efficiency standard for the United Kingdom

	Fridge-freezers	All cold appliances
Bought new (kWh per year)		
1998	577	
2000	484	
Reduction	16%	
Lifetime savings of 2000 purchases		
Electricity	1.8 TWh	2.9 TWh
Money	£158 m	£285 m
Carbon	200,000 tC	330,000 tC

Source: Boardman (2004: 172).

in the United Kingdom was £285 million per year. These savings are derived from both reduced up-front purchase costs and reduced energy consumption over the life of the product. (It should also be noted that as the market has been transformed, these annual savings are ongoing.) So, this better-functioning market generated private benefits for consumers of nearly a quarter of a billion pounds per annum.

The combination of labeling and minimum standards has led to a transformation of the cold appliance market in the European Union. Labeling has improved consumer awareness and knowledge of the potential savings from energy efficiency and increased demand for such products. Combined with the labeling, minimum standards have induced research and development that has resulted in cheaper and more efficient cold appliance products being brought to market. The end result of these regulatory measures has been a greater range of consumer products at lower cost and ongoing savings to consumers through reduced energy use. This would also translate into lower resource use and reduced environmental costs due to savings on energy use and its externalities. Finally, it is apparent that the overall industry must be more competitive as a result of these changes rather than less. It is producing a more desirable product at a reduced price and from a set of firms that must have had the least efficient products removed. This is the objective of regulations that are addressed to enhancing technological diffusion.

Technology leadership – regulation as industrial policy

One of the primary reasons that states achieve competitiveness on the world stage is through technological innovation and leadership. There are much-reduced benefits from becoming anything other than first in a new field. Adoption of other countries' technologies may be an avenue to other goals, such as employment or income equality, but it cannot generate the benefits that are derived from actual innovation. Developing countries may have a period of time during which imitation and transfer are the only real options regarding technological change, but (as the technological frontier is approached) there can be no substitute for actual innovation.

Competitiveness in innovation is then determined by the ability of the state to introduce new technologies, rather than simply to adopt pre-existing ones. This can generate competitiveness not only in terms of market leadership in the innovative product but also in terms of the sales of the technology to others who wish to produce it. So, once leadership in a technology is established, competitiveness is measured both in terms of own production, and other countries' production under license.

An obvious example of technology leadership is the case of Denmark and its renewable energy investments. Denmark was the earliest proponent of the wind-turbine technology, and one of the few states to invest in its development from as early as the 1970s (California also offered tax rebates on wind power generation in that decade) (Buen 2006). Figure 4.9 illustrates the range of policies put into place by Denmark across these early decades, and the corresponding level of capacity created in the 1970s and 1980s by reason of these leadership strategies. In this case, Denmark was not leading its industries via policy leadership (as in the case of Japan and energy-saving technologies); it was explicitly investing in particular technologies. This is the distinction between policy leadership and technology leadership. Denmark actually chose the technologies it wished to develop and then invested in those, rather than choosing policies and encouraging investments along those policy pathways.

Denmark's early programs in support of wind power resulted in the development of a new technology a few years before most other countries pursued it. For example, the first installations in neighboring Germany occurred in 1990, and in Spain (a country with vast wind resources) in 1992 (Morthorst 1999). Denmark had a decade-long lead on most other countries by reason of its technological leadership. But timing and technology choice are not sufficient to guarantee the success of leadership. For leadership to take hold, it is also important that the state concerned invests in a certain level of production.

Scale of production is critical in the development of a new technology. The first units of production are always the most expensive in any production process with fixed costs, but especially so when large amounts of R&D are involved in the production process. This is simply by reason of the amount of fixed costs involved in developing ideas for new processes, prototypes for production processes, and trials of the processes and products. All of these costs must be borne as R&D costs before a single unit of real production can occur. For this reason, subsequent units of product (for an accepted technology) will be produced at a much lower cost than the first units. The impact of scale is apparent in Danish wind turbine development after the initial developments in the 1970s. The average real cost of windmill production in Denmark more than halved over the period from 1983 to 1998.

Table 4.4 (from Hansen *et al.* 2003) illustrates the yearly production of windmills in Denmark since 1983, measured by both number of windmills produced and by "total effect" or installation measured in megawatt hours. (It should be

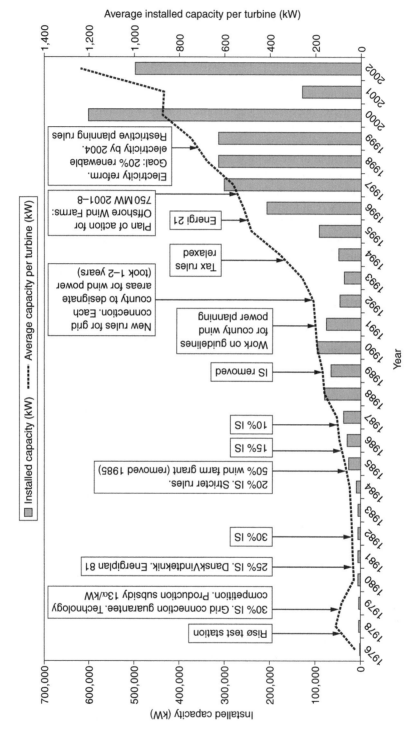

Figure 4.9 Denmark's technology leadership and installed capacity (1976–2002) (source: Buen 2006: 3889).

noted that in the early stages of development, windmills were generally much smaller, albeit larger windmills that required considerably more technological expertise in developing are far more efficient.) Column 5 lists the average real price of a windmill, and column 6 lists the export ratio of windmills produced in Denmark. It can be seen that the price per unit of capacity has fallen by more than half the price of 1983. As noted by Hansen *et al.* (2003), the substantial fall in price points to strong technological progress in the sector, and that the data from statistical regressions they have run are consistent with the hypothesis of productivity growth by learning-by-doing (see below). Table 4.4 also shows that for most of the years, the export share of total production has been above 70 percent – apart from a period in the late 1980s and early 1990s when the industry was in recession, most likely due to a slow response of the industry to demand for larger windmills (Hansen *et al.* 2003).

This is a fairly general phenomenon. Lewis and Wiser (2007), in their survey of wind power policies in 12 different countries, concluded that policies that supported a sizeable and stable market for wind power were the most likely to result in the establishment of an internationally competitive industry. In short, a policy that assures a certain scale of production (after innovation) will both reduce average costs and encourage initial outlays on the R&D required to establish production.

As mentioned at the outset, a state pursuing technological leadership must have a vision of the future and also must have that vision come to pass. In the case of Denmark's investment in wind generation, it has been very lucky in its

Table 4.4 Production, effect and costs of Danish windmills (1983–98)

Year	No. of mills	Effect in MW	Effect per mill in kW	Price per mill in DKK/kW, 1980 prices	Export ratio
1983	1,279	40	31	6,846	0.28
1984	1,694	117	69	6,287	0.93
1985	3,812	243	64	5,598	0.91
1986	2,246	212	94	5,176	0.84
1987	767	88	115	4,845	0.59
1988	597	102	171	3,978	0.23
1989	754	136	180	4,082	0.38
1990	723	162	224	4,323	0.54
1991	778	166	213	4,482	0.54
1992	712	165	232	4,343	0.71
1993	689	210	305	4,142	0.83
1994	1,144	368	322	3,882	0.88
1995	1,530	574	375	3,369	0.87
1996	1,360	726	534	3,433	0.69
1997	1,644	968	585	3,328	0.69
1998	1,742	1,216	698	3,191	0.74

Source: Hansen *et al.* (2003: 327).

leadership. The global investment in wind generation technologies has sky-rocketed in the decades after Denmark's early adoptions.

Figure 4.10 demonstrates how the market for wind-power has grown exponentially since the early 1980s, and of course (given current fossil fuel prices and likely policies) it seems that this growth is likely to continue. Although Denmark probably did not foresee the furor caused by concern over climate change, it did correctly project that excessive worldwide dependence upon fossil fuels would be viewed as increasingly problematic. Betting on this vision a mere ten years before the remainder of the world shared it, has been a boon for its industry.

The vision exhibited by Denmark meant that it had the lead and experience in the technology, when other states turned to it. This could be translated into either straightforward technology licensing or continued leadership in production and export. Denmark has continued to dominate in both. Denmark maintains a position of leadership in the global market for wind turbines, as can be seen from Table 4.5. In 2004, windmills produced in Denmark were estimated to account for 38.7 percent of global market share. This compares to 20.5 percent for Germany and 10.8 percent for the United States. This feat is even more remarkable, given that Denmark is one of the world's smallest states with approximately five million people. In addition, a significant number of the prevailing patents in wind-turbine technology will be held by Danish citizens, so that the use of Danish technology is probably universal. Since 1975, Danish companies have been granted 33 patents relating to wind power (Buen 2006). The importance of

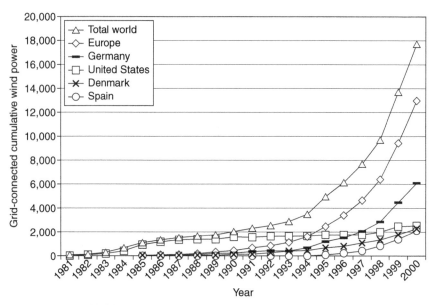

Figure 4.10 Worldwide grid-connected cumulative installed megawatt of wind power (1981–2000) (source: Kobos *et al.* 2006: 1652).

Table 4.5 Top ten wind-turbine manufacturers by country (2004)

	Total sales through 2004 (MW)	Sales in 2004 (MW)	Global market share in 2004 (%)	Global market share through 2004 (%)
Germany				
Enercon (#3)	7,045	1,288	15.1	13.9
Repower (#7)	1,169	276	3.2	2.3
Nordex (#10)	2,406	186	2.2	4.7
Spain				
Gamesa (#2)	6,438	1,474	17.3	12.7
Ecotecnia (#9)	744	214	2.5	1.5
United States				
GE Wind (#4)	5,346	918	10.8	10.5
Denmark				
Vestas (#4)	17,580	2,783	32.7	34.6
	3,874	507	6.0	7.6
India				
Suzlon (#6)	785	322	3.8	1.5
Japan				
Mitsubishi (#8)	1,019	214	2.5	2.0
Others	4,359	334	3.9	8.6
Total	50,765	8,513	100	100

Source: Lewis and Wiser (2007: 1849).

leadership is that it produces value for the state, irrespective of its own production. Other states must purchase the technology, either by license or embedded in the end product.

The example of Denmark, and its development of the wind-turbine industry, demonstrates how a state is able to lead an industry toward innovation. Denmark made specific industrial choices in the 1970s, in which it decided to focus efforts on being the first-developer of a commercially significant wind turbine industry. The competitive success of this industrial policy depends entirely upon the relative price of wind-based energy compared to other sources. As fossil-fuel prices have varied over the past three decades, the industrial decision of Denmark has been a greater or lesser success. The fact that oil prices reached record lows throughout the 1990s demonstrates the weakness of such a strategy. Conversely, the fact that oil prices reached record highs in 2008 indicates that the strategy has also been a success at times. In any event, the extensive range of fossil-fuel prices over this period demonstrates that the approach is a speculative one.

The role of environmental regulation is to lead industries down paths of development. Denmark has speculated on the prospect of rising fossil-fuel prices in the long run, due to increasing scarcities of both fuels and environment. They have invested in technologies that anticipate these scarcities, and generated innovations built around such scarcities. When these scarcities arise, Denmark benefits from these investments and innovations.

Policy leadership – regulation as innovation policy

Regulation is an important means by which a state might drive its industries to develop frontier-level technologies. Placing constraints upon an industry places demands upon it to innovate, i.e. to develop new methods for doing things. These new techniques may then be marketed to other states, if it comes to pass that either:

1   the implied constraint becomes a real one; or
2   other states become convinced to adopt the same constraint.

So, a regulatory policy can be translated into technological leadership if either the regulated resource becomes more scarce or if other countries become persuaded to adopt the regulation. If the state is able to see slightly further than others, or to be persuasive concerning its view, then the technologies it encourages become demanded worldwide.

Policy leadership is then closely related to technology leadership, but involves the widespread recognition of policy-based resource scarcity. For example, one of the ways in which Denmark has translated its success in wind-turbine innovation into industrial success is via the support of EU policies for renewable energy obligations. The EU requires that all member states generate a minimum amount of energy by the use of renewable technologies (such as wind), thereby diffusing the wind-turbine technology throughout the EU irrespective of competing energy prices. This sort of policy diffusion is then as effective a means of generating success as is the anticipation of the actual price path (Brandt and Svendsson 2004).

In this section, we will consider the role of policy leadership in the context of a case study of Japan's use of environmental policy as a means for industrial development. Japan is known for having done this in the case of air pollution technologies as well as energy efficiency technologies. In the 1970s, the country took the decision to pursue policies supporting energy efficiency in its industries, cities and general way of life. At the time, this was a reasonable policy to pursue in the face of high oil prices (on account of the Organization of the Petroleum Exporting Countries crisis) and Japan's famous lack of indigenous oil resources. Japan undertook policy initiatives in industry (development of the hybrid car), in construction (development of solar heating and energy efficient construction) and transportation (development of high-speed rail transit). For many years, these policies seemed poorly designed relative to current prices, as the oil price declined to reach historical lows by the end of the 1990s. Nevertheless, the continued pursuit of the policy gave Japan technology leadership in many of these fields. Its general lead in energy efficiency is indicated by its general level of economy-wide efficiency. As a result of these innovations, Japan now uses one-half the energy per unit of GDP as other developed countries and only one-fifth the energy per unit of GDP as the PRC (International Energy Agency 2007).

More importantly, Japan now possesses the rights over specific technologies that other countries' firms will have to purchase, if they wish to follow in Japan's path. An example of the sheer volume of innovations generated by this campaign is indicated by those cited in regard to automobile energy-efficiency. Note that *hybrid engine technologies* are listed here as only one of 28 different energy-saving technologies developed by the Japanese auto industry (listed second bottom in Figure 4.11).

Finally, these technological leads may then be converted back into policy leadership, when Japan asks other countries to adopt energy-efficiency policies

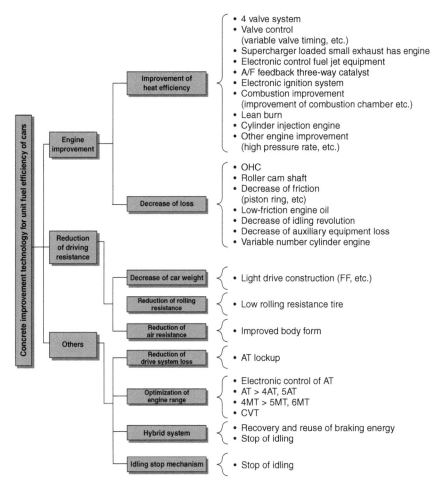

Figure 4.11 Policy-driven innovations in the Japanese auto industry (source: *Japan Energy Conservation Handbook* (2004–5), Energy Conservation Center Japan).

similar to Japan's 20 years later. Persuading other countries to now follow suit in policy means that other governments of other states must require (by parallel policies) their own industries to adopt Japanese technologies (and pay Japanese firms the rents for their innovations). Policy leadership is as important as technology leadership as a means of industrial policy.

There are numerous examples of diffusion of technologies as a result of diffusion of policies. Sticking with the case of Japan, one such example is the policy-related adoption of catalytic converters for the processing of emissions from automobile engines. This technology initially originated from the adoption of clean air emission standards regarding mobile sources (automobiles) in 1970 in Japan and the United States, and then spread later throughout the developed world. Figure 4.12 illustrates the typical diffusion process of innovations, commencing with the states who were policy leaders and then diffusing later to those who were followers. Of course, the diffusion of the policies relating to automobile emissions was reflected in the adoption of the technology as well, and this resulted in the substantial transfer of policy-related rents to the early innovators.

More generally, the role of policy leadership is to anticipate the demands of the citizenry for changes in the sets of goods and services produced by the economy, and to establish the policies that will meet these demands. As societies change, grow and develop, it is predictable that their citizens want and need different things, rather than simply more of the same. For this reason, the income-elasticities of different goods differ substantially over the course of development – some goods are demanded proportionally less as incomes rise (e.g. food), while others are demanded proportionally more as incomes rise (recreation,

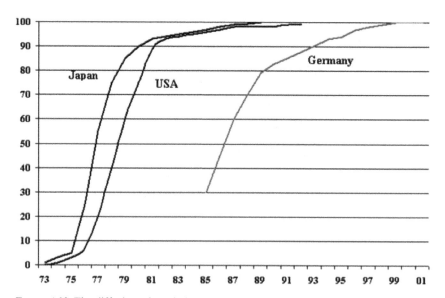

Figure 4.12 The diffusion of catalytic converter technology (1973–2001) (source: Beise *et al.* 2003).

health, environment). One of the basic functions of environmental regulation is to anticipate these changes and to determine the relative proportions of different forms of goods and services produced by an economy (Stokey 1998).

This policy leadership has often been translated into technology leadership, as industries respond to national policies with R&D and resultant patenting. The important consequence of such patenting concerns its adoption by others, and is represented by the proportion of patents won in other countries. In Table 4.6, it can be seen that Japan's miniscule lead in terms of technology resulted in a substantial lead in terms of industrial rents. The proportion of patents for management of "vehicle air pollution" in the United States held by foreign firms jumped from 40 percent to nearly 70 percent at the time of the adoption of catalytic converters, and the proportion of foreign patents held by Japanese firms jumped from 38 percent to 90 percent at the same time (Lanjouw and Mody 1995). Clearly Japan turned this minor technological lead into a major industrial advantage.

And it is important to recognize that the returns from initial policy leadership can be long-lasting, as important patents can have lifetimes of 20 years. It is possible to "innovate around" existing patents, but many times it is necessary to pay the licensing fees to the initial innovator in order to stay in the industry. So, even if a state establishes leadership only briefly, it may be living off the rents of that leadership for decades.

These patterns demonstrate how policy leaders benefit from anticipating emerging trends. The first state to establish an important policy, which then diffuses to others, is presenting its industry with the opportunity to establish technological leadership in an important global industry. A policy-induced patent that is filed first is sufficient not only to grant that industry domestic leadership, but also the opportunity to capture global rents once the policy diffuses internationally.

Both Japan and Denmark have benefited enormously by reason of technology leadership. Japan has done so in the automotive industry. Denmark has made its mark in the wind-turbine industry. In both cases, technology leadership in the domestic industry has resulted in the appropriation of rents from many other countries' industries as the technologies have diffused across the globe. These successes are indicative of the role that states may play in terms of technological leadership, domestically and internationally.

Equally importantly, it is clear to notice the distinction between the approaches taken by the two countries. Japan acted through "policy leadership": adopting environmental regulation before the pack and encouraging its industry to meet the environmental policies through innovation and technology. Denmark acted through pure "technology leadership" initially: adopting the wind-turbine technologies through explicit state-sanctioned investments in a particular technology. Although both have been successful, it is important to see that the main effect of environmental regulation is to operate through policy-induced technological change. That is, the object of environmental regulation is to encourage industries to develop the pathways for future growth and technological change.

Table 4.6 Technology leadership resulting from policy leadership (1972–86/7): sources of foreign patents by nationality of inventor

Source	Industrial air				Water				Vehicle air			
	1972	1977	1982	1986/7	1972	1977	1982	1986/7	1972	1977	1982	1986/7
United States												
Japan	48%	28%	11%	38%	0%	21%	15%	23%	38%	82%	90%	35%
Germany	36	38	64	28	0	21	41	35	45	12	7	51
Other OECD	16	31	25	31	100	49	38	28	18	6	4	11
Other	0	0	0	3	0	9	6	3	0	0	0	2
Foreign/total in field	21%	32%	28%	32%	20%	33%	34%	26%	40%	66%	68%	65%
Japan												
United States	50%	46%	42%	64%	48%	44%	50%	83%	47%	33%	60%	100%
Germany	25	15	42	14	7	22	17	15	47	33	30	0
Other OECD	20	31	16	14	44	44	17	15	7	22	0	0
Other	0	0	0	0	0	0	17	0	0	0	0	0
Foreign/total in field	20%	13	19%	19%	27%	9%	6%	6%	15%	9%	10%	11%
Germany												
United States	37%	34%	45%	15%	40%	20%	22%	19%	35%	34%	70%	19%
Japan	48	34	16	27	10	14	11	3	50	48	11	27
Other OECD	13	32	37	58	50	61	57	71	15	8	20	46
Other	1	0	3	4	0	4	8	6	0	0	0	8
Foreign/total in field	71%	47%	38%	26%	50%	49%	37%	31%	52%	50%	56%	26%

Source: Lanjouw and Mody (1995).

States that select particular technologies for their industries are speculators, and can be wrong as often as they can be correct in their forecasts. States that adopt resource-conserving policies can never be wrong, unless the resources themselves are non-scarce. Then the mandate is for industries themselves to search for the optimal technologies and the correct pathways for future growth and development.

In sum, this section has set out the way in which environmental regulation can induce technological innovation, and hence result in growth, rents and industrial competitiveness. States that adopt environmental policies always encourage their industries to pursue new ways to produce, through innovation or adoption. States that are policy leaders encourage their industries to become leaders in resource conservation by adoption of specific policies for environmental regulation, and then act through the diffusion of those policies.

Conclusion

The PRC has been experiencing growth in a largely unregulated environment for more than two decades. This has generated a vastly more powerful economy at the expense of a much degraded environment. The role of environmental regulation in both regulating the economy and in protecting the environment is the issue at hand.

Clearly, it is important to introduce environmental regulation for the purpose of protecting environmental goods and services. This is the most basic role of environmental regulation – it provides some mechanism for creating the appropriate mix of both private and public goods (such as ambient air and water quality).

Less obvious is the important role that environmental regulation has played in actually managing the overall growth and direction of the economy. Taking Japan as an example, it is clear that growth and development can proceed for some decades by means of simple imitation and general "catching up." For the first two decades of its industrial development, Japan focused primarily on the licensing of overseas technologies and the diffusion of the same throughout its industries. In the 1970s and 1980s, Japan made the transition from imitation to innovation-based growth and development. For this purpose, it commenced investing in various forms of intervention that would drive its industries to innovate.

One of the primary methods that Japan used to encourage innovation then was energy-conservation and environmental policy. It adopted industrial policies to encourage various forms of technological innovation regarding energy policies, and it expended more than any other state in the world on this form of R&D. It also became the first to adopt environmental management policies in important industries, such as automotive exhaust controls. This leadership translated into innovation, growth and global competitiveness in the industries in which it invested.

It is this transition from the backward-looking role of environmental regulation to the forward-looking one that is the core of recognition of regulation's role in growth and development. Once the opportunities for imitation are nearing exhaustion, there are few incentives in competitive economies for growth without governmental intervention. At this juncture, it is important to recognize the role of environmental regulation as one of government's instruments for charting the direction of the future path of the economy.

References

Arrow, K. (1962a) "Economic Welfare and the Allocation of Resources for Invention," in R.R. Nelson (ed.), *American Economic Review* 70, 1089–97.

Arrow, K. (1962b) "The Economic Implications of Learning by Doing," *Review of Economic Studies* 29, 155–73.

Beise, M., Blazejczak, J., Edler, D., Jacob, K., Jänicke, M., Loew, T., Petschow, U. and Rennings, K. (2003) *The Emergence of Lead Markets for Environmental Innovations*, Berlin: Forschungsstelle fur Umweltpolitik.

Blair, R.D. and Cotter, T.F. (2005) *Intellectual Property Economic and Legal Dimensions of Rights and Remedies*, Cambridge: Cambridge University Press.

Boardman, B. (2004) "Achieving Energy Efficiency through Product Policy: the U.K. Experience," *Environmental Science and Policy* 7, 165–76.

Brandt, U.S. and Svendsson, G.T. (2004) "Fighting Windmills: The Coalition of Industrialists and Environmentalists in the Climate Change Issue," *International Environmental Agreements* 327–37.

Buen, J. (2006) "Danish and Norwegian Wind Industry: The Relationship between Policy Instruments, Innovation and Diffusion," *Energy Policy* 34, 3887–97.

Hansen, J.D., Jensen, C. and Madsen, E.S. (2003) "The Establishment of the Danish Windmill Industry – Was It Worthwhile?" *Review of World Economics* 139 (2), 324–47.

International Energy Agency (2007) *World Energy Outlook 2007*, Paris: IEA.

Jaffe, A.B., Peterson, S.R., Portney, P.R. and Stavins, R.N. (1995) "Environmental Regulation and the Competitiveness of US Manufacturing: What Does the Evidence Tell Us?" *Journal of Economic Literature* 33 (1), 132–63.

Kamien, M.I. and Schwartz, N.L. (1982) *Market Structure and Innovation*, Cambridge: Cambridge University Press.

Kobos, P.H., Erickson, J.D. and Drennan, T.E. (2006) "Technological Learning and Renewable Energy Costs: Implications for U.S. Renewable Energy Policy," *Energy Policy* 34, 1645–58.

Lanjouw, J. and Mody, A. (1995) "Innovation and the International Diffusion of Environmentally Responsive Technology," *Research Policy* 25, 549–71.

Lewis, J.I. and Wiser, R.H. (2007) "Fostering a Renewable Energy Technology Industry: An International Comparison of Wind Industry Policy Support Mechanisms," *Energy Policy* 35, 1844–57.

Morthorst, P.E. (1999) "Capacity Development and Profitability of Wind Turbines," *Energy Policy* 27, 779–87.

Mowery, D. (1995) "The Practice of Technology Policy," in P. Stoneman (ed.), *Handbook of the Economics of Innovation and Technological Change*, Oxford: Blackwell.

Oosterhuis, F. (2006) "Ex-post Estimates of Costs to Business of EU Environmental Legislation," Institute for Environmental Studies.

Porter, M.E. and Van der Linde, C. (1995) "Toward a New Conception of the

Environment-Competitiveness Relationship," *The Journal of Economic Perspectives* 9 (4), 97–118.

Porter, M.E. and Van der Linde, C. (2005) "Green and Competitive," *Harvard Business Review* 120–34.

Schiellerup, P. (2002) "An Examination of the Effectiveness of the E.U. Minimum Standard on Cold Appliances: the British Case," *Energy Policy* 30, 327–32.

SQW Ltd (2007) "Phase 2: Exploring the Relationship Between Environmental Regulation and Competitiveness," *Final Report to Defra*, June.

Stokey, N. (1998) "Are there Limits to Growth?" *International Economic Review* 30 (1), 1–31.

Stoneman, P. (ed.) (1995) *Handbook of the Economics of Innovation and Technological Change*, Oxford: Blackwell.

Teece, D.J. (1981) "The Market for Knowhow and the Efficient International Transfer of Technology," *Annals of the American Academy of Political and Social Sciences*.

Part II

Growth and environmental management

The PRC's experiences

5   Air pollution control strategy in the People's Republic of China

Jiming Hao and Shuxiao Wang

Current state and trends of air quality in the People's Republic of China

The urban atmospheric environment of the People's Republic of China (PRC) has been seriously polluted with high concentrations of sulfur dioxide (SO_2) and total suspended particle (TSP) for many years now, due mainly to its coal-dominated energy structure. With rapid urbanization and advancement of transport infrastructure, vehicle exhaust pollution has also aggravated in the PRC. Within the last two decades, all types of environmental problems, which took nearly a century for developed countries to experience, exploded in the developed regions of the PRC. Regional air pollution complex, coal-combustion pollution, vehicle exhaust pollution and pollution caused by multiple other pollutants were experienced in key local and regional clusters of the PRC. It was observed that regional air quality, in particular, has a trend of exacerbating with the frequent occurrence of toxic and hazardous photochemical smog, regional haze and acid deposition which may pose serious health risks to the population.

Urban air pollution

Figure 5.1 shows the movement in air pollutant concentrations in the cities of the PRC from 1990 to 2005. On the national level, urban TSP and SO_2 concentrations began to decrease starting in the year 1990, while nitrogen oxide (NO_x) remained stable, indicating that traditional coal-combustion pollution was abated to some extent. Particulate matter (PM_{10}) is the primary pollutant affecting urban air quality in most cities of the PRC. Figure 5.2 provides the daily average PM_{10} concentrations in the capital cities of the PRC in 2006. Generally speaking, PM_{10} and SO_2 concentrations in the cities of the PRC are between four and six times those of developed countries, and nitrogen dioxide (NO_2) concentration is similar or a little higher than that in the developed countries. Satellite data also present a rapid growth of total NO_2 column concentrations, especially in the eastern PRC and the Pearl River Delta, as shown in Figure 5.3.

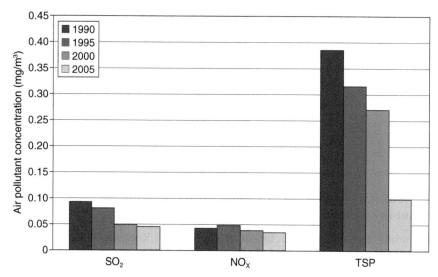

Figure 5.1 Annual average concentrations of air pollutants in the PRC's cities (1990–2005).

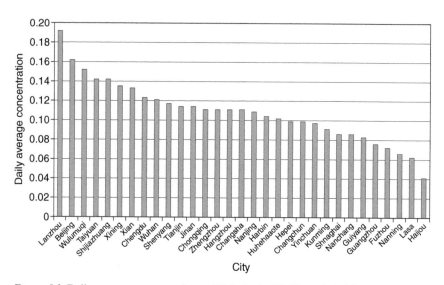

Figure 5.2 Daily average concentrations of PM_{10} in the PRC's capital cities (2006).

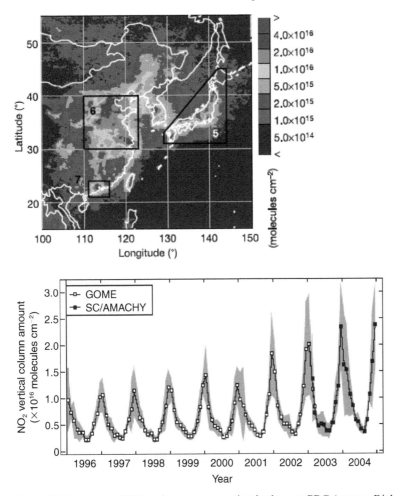

Figure 5.3 Increase of NO$_2$ column concentration in the east PRC (source: Richter *et al.* 2005).

Acid deposition

Figure 5.4 presents the distribution of the pH values of precipitations in the PRC (Meteorological Science Institute of the PRC, 1993–2006). During the period of 1993–2006, the areas with precipitation pH lower than five (also known as acid rain areas) remained stable and made up 30–40 percent of the whole country. However, heavily polluted areas with precipitation pH lower than 4.5 increased. In 2006, the precipitations in some northern cities of the PRC, such as Beijing, Tianjin, Dalian, Dandong, Tumen, Chengde and Shangluo acquired a pH lower than 5.6.

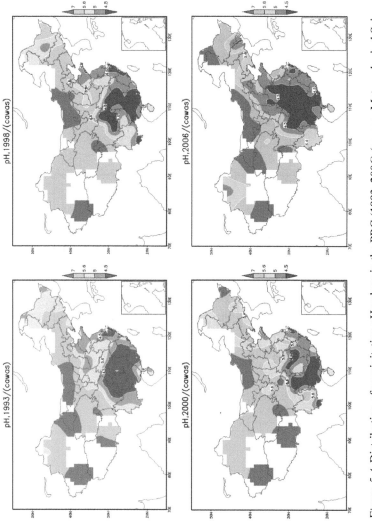

Figure 5.4 Distribution of precipitation pH values in the PRC (1993–2006) (source: Meteorological Science Institute of the PRC (1993–2006)).

Fine particulates, regional haze and visibility decrease

SO_2 and NO_x emitted into the atmosphere can be transformed through chemical reaction into sulphate and nitrate in particles, resulting in regional fine particulate ($PM_{2.5}$) pollution. So far, there are only few data on $PM_{2.5}$ pollution in the PRC. Limited researches show that $PM_{2.5}$ concentrations in some northern cities in the PRC reached as high as 0.08–0.10 milligram per cubic meter (mg/m^3), while those in the south registered 0.04–0.07 mg/m^3, five–six times and two–five times higher, respectively, than the ambient air quality standard in the United States (0.015 mg/m^3, annual average) (see Figure 5.5). The simulation of Congestion Mitigation and Air Quality (CMAQ) model, a regional air quality model developed by the US Environmental Protection Agency (EPA), also indicated that large regions of the PRC were covered with high $PM_{2.5}$ concentrations (see Figure 5.6), signifying that $PM_{2.5}$ pollution is also a severe regional environmental issue in the PRC.

Fine particulates are one of the major factors responsible for regional haze, which is a common turbidity phenomenon characterized by large amounts of imperceptible dry dust particles that float in the air uniformly making the visibility lower than 10 km. Studies indicated that the annual average visibility in the south-east PRC in 2005 decreased about 7–15 km compared with that in the early 1960s.

Ozone and photochemical pollution

Photochemical smog and high ozone concentrations frequently occur in Beijing, Pearl River Delta and Yangtze River Delta. The maximum hourly average value exceeds, in some typical areas, the European alarm level of 240 microgram per

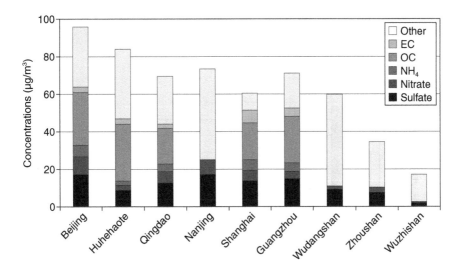

Figure 5.5 $PM_{2.5}$ concentrations in the PRC.

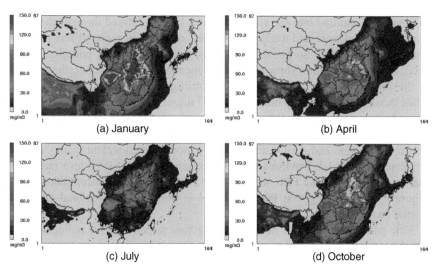

Figure 5.6 Simulated PM$_{2.5}$ concentrations in the PRC by CMAQ model (2005) (source: US EPA 2005).

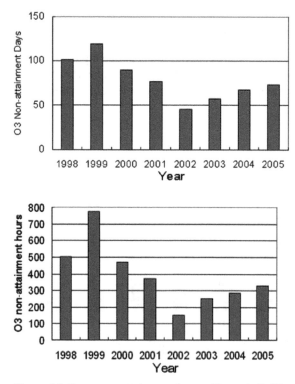

Figure 5.7 Ozone non-attainment days and hours in Beijing (1998–2005).

cubic meter ($\mu g/m^3$). Figure 5.7 shows the ozone non-attainment days and hours in Beijing from 1998 to 2005. In 2005, Beijing experienced more than 50 days or 300 hours of ozone non-attainment.

Future trends

With the continuous increase of the PRC's gross domestic product (GDP) from 1980 to 2006, energy consumption, electricity generation and vehicle population grew dramatically, especially beginning in the year 2000, as shown in Figure 5.8. The government has set as a target by the year 2020 the quadrupling of GDP per capita. If the rapid development of the economy continues, the PRC will face a more severe situation of energy consumption, electricity generation and vehicle population leading to an increase in pollutant emissions.

In the 2007 Edition of the International Energy Agency's (IEA) *World Energy Outlook*, different developing scenarios were set. Under the *baseline scenario*, with the improvement of energy efficiency, the growing rate of energy demand is found to be lower than that of the GDP. Even so, in this scenario, the total energy demand by 2030 was estimated at over 5.1 billion total consumer energy (tce). On the other hand, under the *policy scenario*, with further improvement of energy efficiency and the shift to clean energy, the total energy demand by 2030 will reach 4.3 billion tce only. It is significant to note that under both the baseline and policy scenarios, coal remains the dominant source of energy. Therefore, from now until 2030, the PRC is faced with the task of controlling air pollution from fossil-fuel consumption.

The future energy scenario (see Figure 5.9) estimated the total amounts of

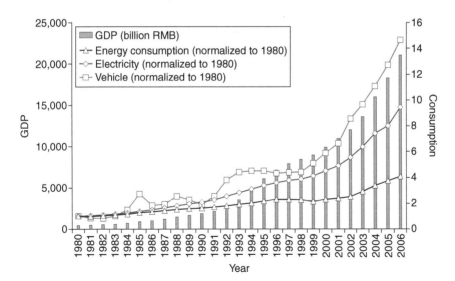

Figure 5.8 Increase of energy consumption, electricity generation and vehicle population in the PRC (1980–2006).

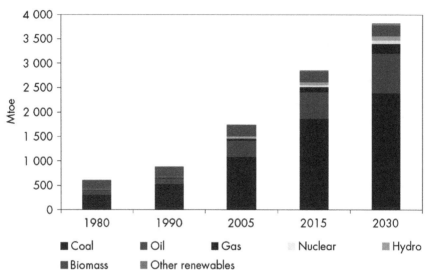

Figure 5.9 Future energy consumption under IEA baseline scenario (1980–2030) (source: IEA 2007, *World Energy Outlook*).

SO_2 and NO_x emissions from 2015 to 2030, with the adoption of different control strategies. According to the current control policy, SO_2 emissions will rapidly increase after 2015 and reach 35 million tons by 2030. This signifies that efforts to strengthen pollution control policies should also consider other sectors beside the coal-fired power plants. Without a national NO_x emission control program and if no measures are taken to stem this kind of pollution, the PRC's total NO_x emissions is estimated to exceed 30 million tons. Air pollution will aggravate due to the pressure and difficulty of emission reduction, so further actions must be taken to improve ambient air quality in the coming three decades.

Goals and strategies

Suggested goals and targets for air pollution control in the PRC

It is suggested that the national strategic target of atmospheric environmental protection be set toward the compliance, by 2050, with the national ambient air quality standard for the entire country, and achievement during the same period of the World Health Organization (WHO) ambient air quality guideline values (see Table 5.1) for most areas of the country. To achieve the targets below, the 2005 levels of SO_2, NO_x, PM_{10} and volatile organic compounds (VOC) should decrease by 60 percent, 40 percent, 50 percent and 40 percent, respectively. The air quality targets for years 2020, 2030 and 2050 are listed in Table 5.2.

Table 5.1 WHO ambient air quality guideline values (in μg/m³)

	$PM_{2.5}$ Annual average	PM_{10} 24-hour average	O_3 Eight-hour average	NO_2 Annual average	NO_2 Hourly average	SO_2 Hourly average	SO_2 Ten-minute average
Phase I	70	150				125	
Phase II	50	100	160			50	
Phase III	30	75		40	200		
Guide value	20	50	100			20	500

Source: WHO (2005).

Table 5.2 Air quality targets (2020, 2030 and 2050)

	2020	2030	2050
Urban air quality	Over 95% of the cities reach the national class II ambient air quality standard; developed areas achieve the phase II target value of WHO guideline.	Over 80% of the cities achieve the phase III target value of WHO guideline.	Most cities in the PRC meet WHO ambient air quality guideline.

Suggested strategies

In order to achieve the strategic target of atmospheric environmental protection, the following four strategies are proposed:

1 whole process control strategy;
2 multi-pollutant co-control strategy;
3 environmental impact based integrated control strategy; and
4 regional air quality management strategy.

The whole process control strategy – by change of economic structure and adoption of clean production technology – aims to establish a whole process emission reduction system which encompasses all the phases from source to emission, and to institute clean energy and new energy utilization, energy-saving technologies, and end-of-pipe control, supervision and management. The end-of-pipe control will translate to pollution prevention and process control, achieving the effective air pollution control in the whole lifecycle.

The multi-pollution co-control strategy – by establishment of a set of scientific air quality and emission standards – aims for a change from single-pollutant control to multi-pollutant co-control, particularly the abatement of ozone and fine particulate pollution. It calls for the development of a comprehensive emission control plan which considers various atmospheric environmental problems, including acid deposition, ozone, fine particles and heavy metals. In the immediate term, this strategy targets to start with the control of NO_x, VOC, ammonia (NH_3) and fine particles, with consideration of their co-benefits on global pollutants such as carbon dioxide (CO_2) and mercury, and establish corresponding multi-pollutant control regulations, policies, technologies and management systems.

The environmental impact based integrated control strategy is to effectively control air pollution by the implementation of total emission control of air pollutants in the important sectors – such as power, metallurgy, petrochemical industry and construction material production – and the concurrent institution of measures to control emissions from other coal-burning sources, area sources and fugitive sources. The strategy also sets out the creation of a total emission control program and work plan for important industrial sectors – such as electric power, steel production and cement production – based on emission and air quality standards. It also aims to improve scientific, feasible and corollary control technologies and emission standards for key industries. It also intends to:

1   speed up the establishment of total amount control regulations and environmental management system;
2   establish an emission inventory;
3   implement a scientific and feasible emission permit system; and
4   develop a source emission monitoring system by training, qualification and sampling inspection.

As to area sources, the strategy proposes to first constitute emission control regulations and standards, increase research and development (R&D) investments, compile emission control plans and develop a simple, economic and practical non-point source emission control technology adapting to local conditions.

The regional air quality management strategy promotes the establishment of regional air quality management coordination systems and institutions in developed city-clusters such as Beijing and its surrounding areas, Yangtze River Delta and Pearl River Delta. It also directs that more attention be paid to secondary pollutants such as $PM_{2.5}$ and ozone, and encourages the design of a dynamic regional air pollution control plan and the setting up of regional total emission cap on PM, NO_x and VOC emissions. To achieve integrated control of regional air pollution complex and improve management capacity, there is a need to establish three-dimensional regional air quality monitoring networks, research and develop regional air quality forecast and alarming systems, and set up regulations, systems and emergency response mechanisms on photochemical smogs and heavy particulate pollutions.

Major policy recommendations

Following our analysis of the air pollution control strategies, three major policies are recommended including:

1   implementing the National Clean Air Action Plan;
2   controlling total coal consumption in heavily polluted areas; and
3   enhancing the vehicle pollution control in megacities.

First, it is imperative that a National Clean Air Action Plan be initiated to improve air quality in the PRC. Air pollution problems are serious in the PRC including urban SO_2, NO_x and PM pollution, sulfate, nitrate, VOCs, acid deposition, regional haze and photochemical pollution. The regional air pollution complex is characterized by multiple pollutants, multiple sources and multiple scales, the scale and complexity of which are highly unusual as compared with the rest of the world. The National Clean Air Action Plan shall:

1   focus on the significant issues which must be resolved within 20–50 years, including urban air quality, regional air pollution complex, acid deposition and climate change;
2   develop a national air pollution control plan;
3   carry out systemic real-time air quality monitoring;
4   identify characteristics and spatial distribution of air pollution;
5   study technologies and methodologies on emission inventory, air quality forecast, and alarming and policy-making;
6   consummate air pollution control regulations and standards;
7   establish regional and urban air quality management systems;
8   enhance technology innovation and application; and
9   establish the R&D bases of air pollution control technologies to promote the air pollution control in key sectors and typical areas.

Second, the total coal consumption in heavily polluted areas should be controlled. The large city-clusters, represented by Beijing and surrounding areas, Yangtze River Delta and Pearl River Delta, are heavily polluted regions. These three regions, accounting for less than 6 percent of national area, consumed 40 percent of coal, produced 50 percent of iron and steel and owned 30 percent of vehicles in 2007. Such intensive coal combustion emits a large amount of air pollutants and results in the regional air pollution complex. Studies indicate that the $PM_{2.5}$ concentrations in these areas are about four times that in the United States, and the days with regional haze are over 100 days each year, posing serious threat to the public health. Therefore, in the institution of an air pollution prevention and control law, it is essential to note the necessity of making a scientific pollution control plan and establishing a regional air quality management mechanism. In the United States where there are no such large-scale regional air pollution issues, Clean Air Intrastate Rule has been issued which plans to invest

US$41 billion to solve the air pollution of 108 "hot spots." In Beijing, over US$30 billion has been spent to control the air pollution and improve the air quality during the 2008 Olympic Games. Researches have unveiled the air pollution issues caused by fossil-fuel burning, especially coal combustion, as fine particles, ozone, acid deposition and regional haze. However, there might be other issues not monitored by current studies, including heavy metals such as mercury and other hazardous air pollutants. It can be said that the control on the total amount of coal consumption is one of the preconditions to solve the air pollution problem in these areas. The actions to be taken shall include three elements:

1   shift from the heavy industrial structure to the service dominated industrial structure;
2   transmission of electricity instead of transmission of coal, coupled with the improvement of energy use structure, control of the development of coal-fired power plants and iron and steel plants, and the promotion of clean energy supply, such as that from renewable energy and nuclear energy; and
3   assurance that during the substitution of the old technology, there shall be no increase of coal consumption by newly-built projects.

Third, the vehicle pollution control in megacities should be enhanced. With the rapid economic development and urbanization, the vehicle population in the PRC has been increasing quickly in recent years. In 2007, the national vehicle population was 160 million, doubling in five years, and the annual average increase rate was as high as 15 percent. In megacities such as Beijing, Shanghai and Guangzhou, vehicle emissions have been one of the major sources of air pollution. Therefore, enhancement of vehicle pollution control in megacities can be an important measure to improve air quality in the PRC. Urban development and economic growth will bring constant growth of urban transport demand over a long period of time. Due to a lag in urban transport planning and public transport facility construction, the private car has played an important role in the urban transportation growth. An urban transportation crisis could not be solved by the mere constant expansion of transport lands and roads. It is necessary to enhance the vehicle pollution control through better traffic plan, strict vehicle emission standards and better fuel quality, which make a long-term sustainable transportation in urban areas possible. Actions to be taken include:

1   improving vehicle emission levels; and
2   improving the fuel quality.

The establishment of the "green transportation" development mode and the implementation of the strategy of public transportation priority are a must to achieve sustainable development of urban transportation. The emission standards for new vehicles in the PRC are still seven years behind those in developed countries. Therefore, strict emission standards for new vehicles should be implemented to attain the same level as that of developed countries by 2020. Meanwhile, the pollution control of in-use vehicles has to be enhanced through the improvement of the vehicle emissions inspection and maintenance (I/M) system. Fuel quality standards intended to reduce the sulfur content in fuel oil and improve fuel quality should also be simultaneously executed with new vehicle emission standards.

Specific measures

Apply clean coal technologies, optimize energy structure and improve energy efficiency

Due to the limited energy resources of the PRC, coal will still dominate energy generation until 2030. Considering that the end use of coal consumption is largely dispersed, it will not only be difficult but will cost highly to control the emissions, thus the effective control measure is to apply clean energy technologies to optimize energy use and generate energy savings. This can be done through the following six measures.

First measure is to control the total energy consumption. The coal-based energy structure is a major cause of air pollution in the PRC. The energy consumption per capita was eight tce in the PRC when the GDP per capita reached US$10,000, as opposed to Japan which only had four tce. The PRC can set as targets three tce for energy consumption per capita and five billion tce for national total energy consumption.

Second, total coal consumption should be limited in regions with severe air pollution. At present, total energy consumption and power generation capacity of the PRC's coastal region is close to or nearing the level of mid-developed countries. Therefore, it is necessary to limit the total coal consumption of those severely air polluted regions.

Third, the PRC should develop and promote clean coal technologies. Coal accounts for 68 percent of the PRC's primary sources of energy, which is not expected to change for a long time. The direct burning of coal has significant impacts on environmental pollution in the PRC. Thus, to improve air quality, one of the most important measures is the promotion of the use of clean coal technologies throughout the country.

Fourth, adjusting energy structure and speeding up the development of solar energy, wind energy, nuclear power, hydropower and other clean energies, will significantly reduce emissions of air pollutants. With governmental support and legal guarantee, renewable energy may account for 15 percent of total energy in the PRC by 2020.

Fifth, adjusting end-use energy structure and increasing the proportion of electricity, natural gas and other clean energies are important measures to reduce various pollutants in the atmosphere. The end-users of coal in the urban centers should be replaced first, followed by those in the marginal areas of the city, and those in the suburban and rural areas.

Lastly, the PRC should improve its energy efficiency. Energy efficiency in the PRC is about 10 percent lower than that of developed countries, a gap that needs to be addressed. High priority should therefore be given to energy conservation. Also, energy savings should be zealously encouraged in all aspects of production, circulation and consumption in various fields of economic and social development, and efforts should be exerted to form an energy-saving consciousness and mechanism, and establish conservation-oriented production and consumption patterns.

Enhance vehicle pollution control

To enhance vehicle pollution control, the first step is to build a green transport system and to prioritize the development of public transport. It is necessary to develop urban public transport through the establishment of a fast and convenient electric railway traffic system in developed areas and the gradual increase of the proportion of railway transportation in the modes of public transportation. Efforts to establish a good public transportation system and to guide the public in choosing more efficient public transportation and in switching from private vehicle to public transport, especially in the urban areas, will help reduce both motor vehicle travel mileage and pollution emissions.

Second, efforts must be directed towards developing and promoting vehicle emission control and testing technologies to speed up the pace of strict emission standards for new vehicles and reach the emission control levels of developed countries by 2020.

Third, there is a necessity to develop fuel quality standards in accordance with the emission standards for new vehicles to gradually decrease the sulfur content and improve fuel quality.

Fourth, priority must be given to the implementation of the I/M system to effectively control in-use vehicle emissions and supplement the positive impacts of the imposition of emission standards.

Fifth, it is also vital to promote compressed natural gas (CNG), liquefied natural gas (LNG), and other clean alternative fuel vehicles in the public transportation system before 2010, as well as to encourage the use of commercialized clean energy vehicles like the hybrid electric vehicles before 2015 through preferential policies such as the grant of tax subsidies and the gradual development of biodiesel and other clean alternative fuels, and to increase the proportion of clean alternative fuels after 2020.

Reinforce SO_2 emission control

Three specific measures can be taken to reinforce SO_2 emission control. First is to implement total emission control on typical regions and important sectors. In order to effectively control acid deposition and other regional environmental problems, national SO_2 emissions and emissions from the power sector have to be reduced and made compliant with the emission caps. For the areas that have implemented the national emission control regulations and standards but still cannot meet the ambient air quality standards, a total emission control target has to be set according to regional air quality and environmental capacity, and stricter control measures have to be adopted to achieve air quality improvements.

The second measure is to strictly control SO_2 emissions from newly-built power plants; phase out small thermal power units with low efficiency, high energy consumption and serious pollution; install continuous environmental monitoring systems (CEMS) at coal-fired power plants with fuel gas desulfurization (FGD); and transmit real-time monitoring data to environmental protection bureaus.

Third, the implementation of SO_2 emission control in non-power industries and the imposition of measures to control SO_2 emissions from ferrous and non-ferrous metal smelting, construction material production, chemical industry, petrochemical industry and other key sectors shall significantly contribute to the reinforcement of SO_2 emission control.

Immediately control NO_x emissions

The first measure to be taken up is to establish NO_x pollution control regulations. The PRC's current NO_x pollution control regulations and policies are inadequate. In the absence of appropriate control policies and regulations, NO_x emissions cannot be fundamentally controlled but will increase yearly. The current "Air Pollution Control and Prevention Law" should be amended to add a clause on NO_x emission control. There is also a need to establish and improve NO_x control regulations and standards to promote NO_x emission reduction.

Second, efforts should be directed towards formulation of NO_x pollution control plan and policies. This calls for researches and the establishment of NO_x emission inventory as soon as possible, as well as the prediction of the future NO_x emissions according to the trend of economic development and energy strategies, and the development of comprehensive NO_x control countermeasures aimed at a long-term NO_x control.

Third, for heavily polluted or high emission sectors, including iron and steel plants, power plants and cement plants, implementation of a total emission control policy to effectively reduce emissions is imperative.

Fourth, NO_x emissions from thermal power plants, which account for 36 percent of the national total emissions and comprise a major source of NO_x emissions in the PRC, should be strictly controlled. Control of NO_x emissions from power plants is essential in easing the growing trend of NO_x emissions in the PRC. NO_x pollution control of thermal power plants should focus on the following endeavors:

1 amendment of NO_x emission standards;
2 retirement of high-emission units; and
3 application of low NO_x combustion technologies.

Strengthen primary particulate emission control

The first measure is to increase use of washed coal, which reduces the ash in coal and will result in the reduction of particulate matter emissions. The second measure is to control particulate emission from the cement and steel industry. Cement plants and iron and steel plants are important sources of particulate pollution in the PRC. The particulate emission control of these sectors shall include: phasing out old production processes with high energy consumption and serious pollution implication; recycling waste heat of dry kilns as low-temperature exhaust heat generation; installing CEMS to monitor the whole process of production; improving the management of current cement and steel plants; installing high efficiency dust removal facilities; and reducing fugitive dust emissions. The third measure is to install high efficiency electrostatic precipitators (ESPs) or fabric filters (FFs) in power plants and industrial boilers, switch the coal use of small boilers to clean fuel, and maintain the installed ESPs or FFs regularly. The fourth measure is to steadily promote the use of clean energy such as biogas and solar energy in rural areas; and forbid the open burning of agriculture residues such as straw, leaves, subtilis and other particulate matter pollution generating material to control primary particulate emission. Fianlly, primary particulate emission control will also be achieved through sustained efforts to emphasize ecological construction and forestation, speed up the virescence in urban areas, gradually eliminate the bare land, and include the dust pollution prevention and control in landscaping technical specifications.

Control VOC emissions

In the control of VOC emissions, it will be necessary to develop VOC emission control laws and regulations; compile and issue a list of VOCs to be controlled; and establish ambient VOC standards, source emission limit standards, and solvent product standards of VOC contents. Moreover, VOC emissions from the use of industrial organic solvents should comply with the national emission standards. Waste gas from industrial processes should be recycled.

Furthermore, to prevent VOC emissions from industrial solvent use, the following steps should be taken:

1   store the organic solvents in sealed containers;
2   minimize the toxic and hazardous gas emissions in the transportation of organic solvents;
3   encourage and promote the use of low-volatile solvent; and
4   prohibit VOC emissions from spraying, sand blasting, glass steel production, and vehicle friction chips in the open air and residential areas.

Oil/gas stations, oil storage tanks and oil tank trucks should use sealing technologies to control VOC emissions and achieve the national emission standards.

Control ozone and fine particulate pollutions

In order to solve the important issues of regional air pollution and provide an important technology base for urbanization in the future, the study of technologies and methodologies on regional air quality monitoring, emission inventory, air quality forecasting and alarming, and regional air pollution control system should be undertaken.

The establishment of systemic, scientific and dynamic air quality standards and objectives shall greatly contribute to the promotion of human health and the protection of the ecological environment. The implementation of the integrated multi-pollutant control strategy instead of the single-pollutant control strategy will significantly help in solving ozone and fine particles pollution.

Moreover, the development of a national pollution control plan of mobile and stationary sources according to environmental impacts and the implementation of an integrated multi-pollutant control program to control pollutants such as PM and its precursors (SO_2, NO_x, organic and elemental carbon), and ozone precursors (NO_x and VOC) shall lead to the achievement of national and regional targets of emission reduction and air quality objectives. A study should be made on integrated regional air pollution control mechanism and management system, starting with typical areas, such as Beijing and surrounding cities, Yangtze River Delta and Pearl River Delta to establish a system for regional coordination and decision making on air pollution control of inter-administrative regions.

Improve air pollution control law and standard system

Many clauses in the "Air Pollution Prevention and Control Law" are principle provisions, which are hardly executory. It is necessary to amend the law to enhance and specify legislative targets, behavior criteria, law enforcement procedures and legal responsibilities. Focus should also be made in the establishment of systematic air quality and emission standards, development of air emission standards targeted at ambient air quality standards, and enhancement of the scientificity, operability and technology support of emission standards. It is also important to strengthen the application, issuance, approval and supervision of pollution discharge permit.

Use the power of environmental economic regulation

The power of economic regulation is that it gives the regulated party the choice in the manner of meeting the regulation. Increase in the industrial air emission charge will result in the internalization of the external costs of air pollution emissions, encouragement for enterprises to improve energy efficiency and reductions in emissions. Other ways to achieve this is to apply fuel taxes on the automotive industry, use differentiated tax rates in accordance with the cylinder capacity based on the principle of "Heavier Emission, More Tax" for cars and motorcycles, and promote production and consumption of high efficiency energy-saving vehicles.

Second, price concession policies will encourage energy end-use sectors to conserve energy and improve the use of clean energy such as electricity and natural gas, as well as solar and wind energy. The same holds true for the promotion of green electricity price policy, increase in parking fees and fuel prices to restrict vehicle use, and implementation of a differentiated price policy for energy-intensive industries (i.e. increase of the price to 1.5 times the average for energy-intensive industries).

The third measure is to establish emission allowance and emission trading programs. In order to push enterprises to control their pollution emission, there is wisdom in implementing an SO_2 and NO_x emission trading program and establishing an emission allowance issuing system in the power sector.

Strengthen international cooperation on global problems

The first step for the effective control of air pollution is to increase knowledge and capacity. Taking mercury as an example, mercury emissions inventory and emission sources should be better understood through international cooperation. It is essential to facilitate mercury monitoring networks to monitor atmospheric mercury pollution and wet deposition. Studies on mercury chemistry, fate and transport shall determine the local, regional and global contribution of emission sources. Moreover, support of R&D programs to improve emission control devices of coal combustion should be encouraged, along with the use of existing control techniques and devices such as gas stream cooling, activated carbon absorbers, scrubbers and mist eliminators to reduce mercury releases to air during manufacturing processes. The use of low-mercury materials and the study of technologies to reduce mercury emissions, use, and contamination shall further this endeavor. Then a mercury pollution management system can be established. This requires putting the mercury pollution control into the current environmental management constitution which includes environmental impact assessment, total amount control and emission allowance, and developing regulations and economic incentives on mercury emission control. International cooperation needs to be strengthened to help increase the understanding of the international community on mercury pollution and control policies in the PRC, and ascertain the international experiences on mercury pollution control technology and policies.

References

Richter, A., Burrows, J.P., Nüß, H., Granier, C. and Niemeier, U. (2005) "Increase in tropospheric nitrogen dioxide over China observed from space," *Nature*, 437, 129–32.
World Health Organization (WHO) (2005) Air quality guidelines – global update 2005. Online, available at: www.euro.who.int/air/activities/20050222_2.

6 Progress and experience

Water pollution control in the People's Republic of China

Beidou Xi and Wei Meng

Current water quality

Despite the government's efforts in strengthening institutions and measures of environmental protection, main river basins in the People's Republic of China (PRC) have increasingly been threatened by complex water pollution problems, which have resulted in quality deterioration of both drinking and underground water, water ecosystem degradation and lake eutrophication. The growth of the economy and urban population has led to the overexploitation of water resources.

Table 6.1 shows water quality observed from 411 monitoring stations in seven main watersheds in 2005. At the national level, 41.8 percent, 30.3 percent and 27.9 percent of the river water is categorized as Class 1–3, Class 4–5 and below Class 5, respectively.[1,2] Across watershed, the water quality in Changjiang and Zhujiang are relatively better – over 70 percent of the river water is categorized as Class 1–3, while less than 10 percent is categorized as below Class 5. Haihe has the worst water quality, with almost 57 percent of its water below Class 5.

Water pollution in the country has changed from simple industrial pollution to integrated complex pollution from industry, agriculture and households. Water pollution in the PRC is increasingly characterized by compound pollution and a high organic basin pollution load which greatly exceeds the ability for

Table 6.1 Water quality in the PRC's seven main watersheds (2005)

Watershed	Class 1–3 (%)	Class 4–5 (%)	Class below 5 (%)
Changjiang	72.1	18.3	9.6
Haihe	25.4	17.9	56.7
Huaihe	19.8	47.6	32.6
Huanghe	36.4	34.1	29.5
Liaohe	32.4	29.7	37.9
Songhuajiang	21.9	53.7	24.4
Zhujiang	78.8	15.1	6.1
National	41.8	30.3	27.9

Source: State Environmental Protection Agency (SEPA), 2004. *State of the Environment Report.*

self-purification. This comes in a situation when infrastructure and capacity in basin pollution prevention and management are weak and lag behind economic development. Serious water pollution has also affected rivers in the country, resulting in water ecological degradation, water quality deterioration and water shortage. Transboundary water environment is also faced with the same huge challenge in pollution control and management.

Various pollutants superposition and new and toxicant presentation have also been observed. Chemical oxygen demand (COD), five-day biological oxygen demand (BOD5), ammonia nitrogen (NH3-N), total nitrogen (TN), total phosphorus (TP) and escherichia coli have alarmingly exceeded the standard and tolerable amounts. Moreover, influence of persistent organic pollutants (POPs) and endocrine disrupters (EDs) is becoming serious. New pollutants, which are harmful to both human health and the safety of drinking water, have also emerged.

At the same time, serious eutrophication problems are observed in lakes. In 1970s, among the 34 lakes surveyed, only 5 percent showed eutrophication problems. The percentage increased to 36 percent during 1986 and 1989, and 75 percent in 2002. In 2005, out of 28 lakes and reservoirs of national importance which are nationally monitored, only two reached water quality of Class 2. Six of the lakes and reservoirs reached water quality standard of Class 3, while three reached Class 4, and another five reached Class 5. The water quality of the remaining 12 lakes and reservoirs, or about 43 percent of the total, was below Class 5. The year 2007 was called the year of Cyanobacteria because of the outbreak of Cyanobacteria in Tai Lake, which seriously threatened the drinking water in Wuxi city.

The frequent occurrence of water pollution disasters has also been noted. From 2001 to 2004, 3,988 disaster events of water pollution have been recorded, which means that nearly 1,000 events occurred each year. While the annual total economic loss in the fields of industry, agriculture and human health caused by water pollution is roughly more than RMB240 billion, or about 3 percent of the country's gross domestic product (GDP), the economic losses due to the water pollution disasters alone was estimated at RMB286 billion in 2004, or 1.7 percent of the national GDP. In 2005, 693 water pollution disasters were recorded, which comprise nearly 50 percent of national pollution disasters during the year.

Causes and challenges

The increasing water pollution in the PRC has been caused by the enormous pressure of economic and population growth, pollution-intensive industrial structure and composition, coupled with outdated technologies, insufficient environmental regulation and management, and inadequate environmental investment. During the past 30 years of economic reform, policy focus has been on economic growth despite the campaign towards environmental protection and pollution treatment. The national GDP has been growing at 7 percent per annum, with many major water-consuming provinces experiencing annual growth rates of 13 percent or above. Both the scale and the composition of the economic growth have brought enormous pressure on water quantity and quality. Water intensity, measured by water consumption per GDP, in the PRC is two to three times that of developed countries, while the corresponding wastewater treatment capacity and technology, especially for the construction of wastewater pipe network, lag behind. Based on the figures in 2005, only about 51.9 percent of wastewater was treated. At the same time, non-point pollution problems have become more serious.

As far as the environmental regulation and management are concerned, the major deficiencies and challenges are discussed from the following six aspects. First, environmental monitoring and enforcement is weak which has lowered the cost of pollution. Second, the integrated approaches using legislative, regulatory, market and technological measures are yet to be developed. Environmental management to date still relies more on command-and-control rather than market mechanism. There is an overall under-pricing of water resources and water environment. There is a lack of understanding of the causes of water pollution such that regional pollution events are either dismissed or regarded through simple methods. Third, institutional and organizational complexities have prevented an integrated water management system which incorporates water supply, water quality, water ecological system and river-basin management. In the current organizational setup the Ministry of Environmental Protection (MEP) oversees water pollution, the Ministry of Water Resources (MWR) is responsible for water supply, the National Development and Reform Committee (NDRC) for project approval and the Ministry of Construction for construction and implementation. Such a fragmented setup impedes the information flow among the agencies, reduces the incentives and accountabilities of the agencies, and discourages public participation in water environment management. Fourth, from the technical perspective, the water environmental standard system is incomplete and lacks operability. The proper link-up is missing between the standard of pollution discharges and of total pollution volume control. The technologies used for pollution control are relatively backward. Fifth, at the provincial and local level, the public investment for environment, despite its growth every year, and the environmental infrastructure are inadequate. The decision-making procedure within the government needs to be improved to reduce incidents of government officials interfering with the enforcement of environmental laws and regulations. The human resource system also has to be improved to align government officials' incentives with environmental protection, rather than mere economic growth.

Water environmental protection strategy

In the face of the current situation of environmental protection, water pollution problems have become more complex and compound, and have transformed into a great obstacle in the economic development process. It has become necessary therefore to establish a macro water environmental protection stratagem, and toward the achievement of which, experts have presented the following seven strategic transformations:

1   transformation of the conflict between environment and economy to amalgamation of these two issues;
2   transformation from pure point source treatment to integrated disposal of watershed pollutants and coordinated management of upstream and downstream water sources;
3   transformation from end treatment to whole process control and water ecology management;
4   transformation from pure water pollution treatment to optimization and coordination of watershed economy distribution and structure;
5   transformation from parallel to integrated management;
6   transformation from goal amount control to capacity amount control; and
7   transformation from the single management to integrated management model with different divisions, classifications and stages.

The ideal water environmental protection strategy for the PRC should address the complex and compound water pollution from the macroscopic standpoint which shall provide sufficient guidance to solve significant water environmental problems on the nationwide, region-wide and basin-wide levels, and to deeply understand the ideological connotation of human eco-civilization. When conceptualizing the nation's water pollution control strategy, it is suggested that the significance of pollution control in the watersheds should be considered. There must be proper implementation of water pollution control measures to safeguard the watershed areas. Efforts must be exerted toward a balance between the benefits of economic development and those of environmental protection in the control and prevention of watershed pollution. In the implementation of watershed pollution control measures, it is also suggested that there be a transformation of the concept of pollution abatement to that of ecological management. Also, transformation of the parallel management of water and land should be undertaken toward a comprehensive management of the two. The implementation of total pollution control is one of the essential measures to protect and restore watershed environment quality in the PRC. In the recent Five-Year Plan, the total amount control theory and the technical methods for pollution control was supplemented and amended further to ensure the scientific implementation of the total amount control system in watershed management. Furthermore, there is also a need to transform pollution point or source treatment to basin integrated measures and upstream–downstream coordination management, and extend mere water pollution control to the optimization of water resources and ecology and adjustment of basin economy, social layout and structure.

Finally, it is suggested that consideration be made on the implementation of water pollution control by establishing ecological zones "by (pollutant) types, (geographic and ecological) regions, (ecological function) grades, and (treatment) stages." Pollutants are classified by types according to the differences in their harmful effects and control requirements. Type classification is essential in drawing up the corresponding control measures and plans. Heavy metal and POPs belong to Class 1 which should be addressed by pollution source and discharge amount controls, while COD and NH3-N are classified as Class 2 pollutants which are controlled through measures that will exact compliance with discharge standards and enhance the construction and operation of the municipal wastewater plants. TN and TP belong to Class 3, the removal of which must be carried out to control the total amount discharged into lakes and reservoirs to maintain the water ecosystem and prevent eutrophication of the bodies of water. Class 4 pollutants are those with hygienic indexes which are best addressed through disinfection that must be carried out before wastewater discharges.

Pertinent regional management of water pollution must be carried out in accordance with the spatial differences of regions and functional areas in the vast territory of the PRC which exhibit different water environmental characteristics. Thus, various total amount control objectives should be identified, and the corresponding control standards should be made according to regional environmental problems and water bodies' functions. And to control pollution by regions, the integrity of the hydrologic process, consistency of ecosystem and water bodies' functions should be taken into consideration. Multiple classifications of water resource regions, water ecological regions and water environment functional regions should be comprehensively adopted to formulate a region classification system for total amount control of water pollution.

Water quality protection targets must also consider the grade classification of different bodies of water according to their functional characteristics. The following are the five grades or functional areas of water bodies:

1   natural conservation area;
2   drinking water resource;
3   fishery;
4   industrial areas; and
5   agricultural areas.

Water quality standards should be set in such a way that the highly functional areas are imposed high and stringent environmental requirements, while the low functional areas are accordingly imposed low and less exacting environmental requirements.

Control measures should also implemented by stages. Differences of water situations in different periods should be taken into consideration in total control, to allow conservation during times of adequate environmental capacity. Near-, medium- and long-term targets for total amount control should be made, and the implementation plan for different stages should be established to facilitate government efforts toward water pollution control.

Case study: Huai River watershed

The Huai River watershed is the first watershed subject of an integrated water pollution control program. This program was launched and headed by the central government in 1994. Around RMB60 billion, or US$8 billion, were invested over a period of ten years, making it the biggest single river watershed pollution control program. Numerous industrial enterprises which contributed to Huai River's pollution were closed down, bringing about far-reaching societal and economic consequences. Both the central and local governments devoted substantial personnel and material resources to this program. Thus, the Huai River watershed pollution control program has become the standard by which the environmental protection measures of the PRC are measured and judged.

The public was made to believe that the program has succeeded, and the water quality of the Huai River highly improved. But in the summer of 2004, the damage brought by flood in the Huai River fueled serious doubts about the effectiveness of the environmental protection measures in the PRC. The highly controversial debate on the success or failure of the Huai River pollution control effort as well as the experiences and lessons from the endeavor provide an opportunity to observe the response of the PRC's government to the challenge of resolving environmental problems during rapid industrialization, urbanization and economic development.

Pollution in the Huai River watershed

The rapid economic development in the surrounding communities of the Huai River watershed made the Huai River the most polluted river in the PRC in the 1990s. Polluted water made up 40 percent of the Huai River in 1980, which increased to 88.1 percent in 1995 and stayed at more than 65 percent in 2004. With the rapid urbanization of the surrounding areas of the Huai River, the load of municipal pollution rose sharply. A study conducted by the PRC's Institute of Water Resources and Hydropower Research shows that the total discharge of sewage increased by 40 percent from 1980 to 1995, more particularly, from 2.55 billion cubic meter per annum (m^3/a) to 3.6 billion m^3/a. At the same time, the discharge of sanitary sewage increased by 132 percent, that is, from 0.434 billion m^3/a to 1.008 billion m^3/a. In some areas of the Huai River, the metallic pollution has also become serious. Until 1997, industrial pollution was the main source of pollution. In response, the PRC government formulated policies to address industrial pollution. But the increasing trend of municipal sewage discharge has been persistent. The COD load from municipal sewage exceeded that from industry sewage. Until 2003, the COD load from municipal sewage was twice as much as that from industry sewage. Beginning in 1996, the pollution load from agriculture and stock farming has also shown an increasing trend.

The highly polluted water of the Huai River watershed brings severe and hazardous effects to public health. Slight water contact brings about immediate health concerns. Children were found to have chafing, turgescent or ulcerated skin after playing in the river. The same symptoms were found among the fisher folks and aquatic-product farmers after harvest. Riverside denizens often complain about the smell which causes headaches, stomach-aches and nausea. Extended exposure to the waters of the Huai River watershed has been observed to bring more severe and dire health effects, especially to those who use the river as their source of drinking water. For instance, the local country-dwellers exhibit higher incidence of diseases such as lung cancer, stomach cancer and intestinal cancer than those living in other areas. CCTV, the biggest television network in the PRC, found that in Huang Meng Ying village, a village beside Ying River which is the largest anabranch of the Huai River watershed, 105 of the 204 villagers died from cancer. For this reason, some surrounding cities had no choice but to cut off their drinking water supply from the Huai River. During the pollution event, some villagers had to run a distance of 15 km to get bottled water for cooking which cost RMB5 per bottle, five times the normal price of RMB1 per bottle.

Huai River watershed pollution control program

At the beginning of 1989, Huai River experienced the most severe pollution in all of the PRC's watersheds. In response, the central government focused on the Huai River watershed pollution problem, and in 1994, the State Council initiated the Huai River Pollution Control Project, which turned out to be the first watershed pollution control program in the PRC. In August 1995, the State Council promulgated the Temporary Act of Huai River Watershed Pollution Control. Thereafter, in June 1996, the Ninth Five-Year Plan was adopted which included water pollution control measures. It acknowledged the severity of water pollution in the Huai River, and indexed the following as causes of the water pollution:

1   the development of the village and town enterprises outpaced the development in technology for the control of the pollution brought about by the enterprises, such that there was an absence of proper sewage treatment;
2   improper industry structure brought low economic benefit and high pollution;
3   rapid urbanization brought about a steep increase in municipal sewage released into the rivers in most cities without proper treatment;
4   lack of environment investment to industries;
5   inordinate implosion of water resources which resulted to seasonal droughts in water supply; and
6   inadequate environmental protection mechanisms and environmental law enforcement.

The pollution control program for the Huai River has three main objectives. The first objective was to close water pollution intensive enterprises such as paper mills and chemical plants. This was attempted in June 1996 when the State

Council carried out a large-scale effort to close such enterprises in the Huai River watershed. The second objective was to improve industrial water treatment processes and ensure that all factories along the Huai River met emission standards at the end of 1997 or face closure or stop production through the campaign code-named "Operation Zero Hour." And the third one was to establish 52 municipal sewage treatment stations to ensure that all municipal sewage were treated before release to the Huai River. Two specific targets were set for the Huai River water pollution control project. First, all industry sewage must comply with emission standards before they are released to the river, and total COD must be decreased from 1.5 million in 1993 to the target level of 0.89 million. Second, total COD must be decreased to 368,000 in the year 2000, and the water quality must ascend to the third level (Huai River was then in the fourth and worst level) of the national environmental standards for surface water.

A unique characteristic of the project is the time constraints. A period of only six years was allotted for the achievement of the objectives. Although the project was given priority by the central government which monitored it closely, the results were not satisfactory, for various reasons.

Outcomes

The primary objective of the Huai River pollution control plan is to restore the water quality to the national standard in both the Huai River and its sub-branches. The PRC government claimed that, after the implementation of the pollution control plan, water quality in the Huai River, as well as 70 percent of water in its sub-branches, had complied with national standards and rated the Huai River watershed pollution control plan successful. However, some governmental documents and media reports revealed differently. According to the Huai River committee, 84.4 percent of the Huai river watershed exhibited more severe pollution before the flood season in 2003, and only 6.2 percent complied with the quality standards.

The pollution control plan heightened the public's awareness of water pollution in the Huai River. By December 31, 1997, 1,562 factories and plants located alongside the river conformed with the national discharge standards. Pollution-intensive enterprises, including about 5,000 paper pulp plants and 4,000 other enterprises, were shut down. The total amount of pollutant discharges in 2003 remained at the same level in 1996, despite the doubling of industrial output during the period. Nevertheless, long-term water quality monitoring indicated that, although there was water quality improvement in the Huai River before 2001, water quality deteriorated thereafter. As soon as public attention on pollution began to wane, pollution problems started to recur.

With the recurrence of the Huai River pollution problems, the PRC's MEP deployed three delegations to inspect factories and water sewerage treatment plants along the stretch of the Huai River. The inspection uncovered that 17 sewerage treatment plants have not been operating, and some closed plants had been undertaking illegitimate production. Furthermore, the investigation disclosed that 52 plants would release into the Huai River polluted water which did not comply with the water quality standards. In contrast to the main anabranch, water quality in small anabranches decreased rapidly.

In actuality, the three main objectives of the Huai River pollution control plan were not successfully achieved. With regard to the first objective of closing down small pollution-intensive enterprises and factories, since the standards varied in the different areas surrounding the river, the enterprises just transferred to areas with lenient standards. One example is the transfer of pollution-intensive small factories from An Hui province which has stringent water quality standards, to He Nan province which has the opposite. It has been reported that 40 percent of industrial factories which were shutdown for being pollution intensive, reopened two years later. Some small factories amalgamated to form a larger enterprise to evade the risk of being closed individually.

Through the "Operation Zero Hour," the PRC government commanded that all factories, by the end of 1997, should comply with wastewater emission standards. In the face of the announcement made by the government that all the factories had achieved the standards, the factories would only stop the emission of wastewater when the monitoring group came, and get back to their pollution-intensive operations once the monitoring group departed after their inspection.

The third objective, which was to establish 52 sewerage treatment plants before 2000, was also not realized. There were only six factories which finished their construction of sewerage treatment plants, while some were still under construction. As mentioned above, according to the results of the investigation conducted by the MEP, only five factories in 2004 operated sewerage treatment plants with reasonable capacity. The failure to achieve this objective was brought about by various reasons. Some factories could not raise the funds for the construction, while some plants lack funding to cover the operation costs. Some plants have all the treatment equipment but no sewerage collection pipe network.

Lessons learned

Despite the strong will and commitment of the government of the PRC, sustainable development was not achieved through the Huai River pollution control project. There are many lessons to be learned from the program. First, objectives were made over-ambitious through the top-down planning process. The central government made the decision to clear the Huai River of pollution before the year 2000, and left it to the scientists to plan out the corresponding pollution control procedure. The major problem encountered was the excessive COD in the river, such that chief scientist Xiaqing made the COD discharge control their final goal. The maximum load limit for COD was set at 368,000 tons, thus scientists were faced with the arduous challenge of having the entire Huai River comply with this limit.

Second, the measures adopted in the Huai River pollution control undertaking superficially addressed the pollution crisis and did not delve into the root causes of the problem. Also, the measures were old-fashioned in that they failed to consider the complexity of the pollution situation and the breadth of the area encompassed by the Huai River watershed. Very little attention was given on the long-term economic development such that support for the development and growth of environment-friendly enterprises was not included in the measures taken. A dynamic problem was thus not addressed by equally dynamic goals and solutions.

Third, the obvious lack of effective coordination between the central government and the local government units was seen as the primary reason for the quite unsuccessful turnout of the project. The local government units failed to carry out the requirements of the central government as embodied in the Temporary Regulations on Huai River Pollution Control issued by the State Cabinet in April of 1995, which clearly outlined the roles of the local government units and the deadline for the accomplishment of each objective. For one, the provincial government units were tasked to disseminate the pollution control objectives to the cities and towns. There was also an absence of continuance mechanisms which made the local governments work half-heartedly.

Fourth, in terms of institutional support, the Huai River pollution control project did not succeed for lack of executive and administrative authority and financial support on the part of the coordinating agency which is the National Environment Protect Bureau (NEPB). The NEPB was not able to effectively coordinate with other departments which argued among themselves and made matters worse. The bureau was also not able to gain the cooperation among the local governments for lack of direct administrative authority over them.

Fifth, local enforcement was weak. Local protection policies obstructed the implementation of the environmental protection laws and regulations and encouraged the illegitimate operation of pollution-intensive enterprises which incidentally are usually run by the large taxpayers in the locality. Local government officials would even be stockholders of these enterprises. In 1997, the criminal laws in the PRC were amended such that enterprises and individuals found guilty of environment pollution may be held criminally liable. However, the close and strong ties between pollution-intensive industries and the local government units rendered the implementation and enforcement of the new law difficult and ineffective.

Sixth, the so called "Operation Zero Hour" of the Huai River plan was scientifically unsound and was only intended to gain media mileage. And indeed, the media became the orchestrator of a grand deception in place of effective supervision.

In the wake of the Huai River project, the PRC government undertook the "Three Rivers and Three Lakes" project which aimed toward the eradication and control of pollution in three major rivers and lakes of the country. The "Three Rivers and Three Lakes" project tried to use the experiences from the Huai River project and promote water environmental protection on a larger scale. This project met the same fate as the Huai River project for failure to implement the following complementary factors:

1   local government cooperation;
2   strategic decision-making which takes into consideration the social and

economic situation and demands to come up with an effective environmental plan;
3 optimization of the industrial structure;
4 due regard to scientific technology; and
5 adequate financial support.

Looking into the future, the government has already realized the necessity for harmonizing both environmental and economic considerations in society building and will build on the lessons learnt. In the new plan for the Huai River pollution control, pollution elimination will be incorporated into the whole integrated river plan which will be headed by the MWR. In this plan, the NDRC will draw up a new industry structure geared toward pollution reduction.

Conclusions and prospects

The current technological level of water pollution control in the PRC is comparatively backward, being short of scientific research at watershed scale. The pollution control countermeasures in use are not able to solve key water environmental problems of watersheds. There is therefore a necessity to carry out research on water environment criteria and standards, and build a suitable system of water environmental quality and water pollutants discharge standards in the PRC. It is also essential to change the traditional concept of pollution control and work toward the harmonious development of pollution control and economy. Pollution control should be implemented by types, regions, grades and stages to respond appropriately to the different classifications and characteristics of water pollution. The formulation of technical norms for total amount reduction of pollutants and the establishment of a technical management system of the PRC's environmental pollution control of watersheds shall contribute greatly to this endeavor. Efforts to further strengthen and promote the supervision, management and implementation of the Environmental Protection Law and the Water Pollution Prevention Law shall be necessary.

The water environmental problems have somehow restricted economic development in the PRC. There must therefore be efforts to adopt a scientific attitude and spirit toward the achievement of a strategic water environmental protection system. Water environmental problems present structural and compound characteristics brought about by various reasons which should be addressed through reformation and innovation of strategic solutions. In order to respond to the social facets of the water environment problems, use of laws, economic techniques and administrative means must be effective and comprehensive. Also, international experiences must be maximized to enable the formulation of a water environment macro-strategy suitable to the PRC with particular focus on science and technology innovation.

The following specific measures should be adopted to attain total water pollution control in the PRC:

1   adoption of financial incentives and contracts;
2   establishment of independent monitoring and enforcement institutions;
3   coordination of independent institutions;
4   enhancement of pollution charges;
5   focus on total emissions; and
6   public disclosure of industries.

The objectives contained in the contracts for local government officials should better reflect the importance of environmental outcomes in their remuneration and reward packages. Specifically, the contracts should ensure environmental outcomes representing "hard" targets to provide a balance in the targets for economic growth, industrialization and infrastructure projects. The threat of budgetary cuts for failure to comply with regulations should be tightened.

International experience shows that effective monitoring and enforcement of environmental policy is usually financially and politically independent of local government, and directly accountable to central government. In this light, the funding and other relationships between the environmental protection bureaus (EPBs) and the local government ought to be reviewed.

A coordinating body is suggested for planning and implementation purposes. This could take the form of the existing River Basin Commission (RBC), only with more power and a greater focus on water quality issues. The coordination of laws is also imperative. Clarification of the jurisdiction roles and responsibilities of the PRC's MWR and the MEP and their implementing agencies is required. The same can be said for the RBCs which are currently weak in the enforcement of border pollution measures.

The enhancement of pollution charges is also suggested. Reflecting the "polluter pays" principle, pollution charges should be applied to all pollutions, not just emissions in excess of standards. The impact of this could be:

1   a larger incentive effect over time, as low performing firms exit the market; and
2   changes in local government revenues.

In particular, the volumetric water prices currently imposed in the PRC should be augmented to reflect the full financial cost of water supply. Overall, full cost pricing strategies have been shown to ensure that limited water supplies are used efficiently, mainly by improving incentives for water saving over time. Furthermore, the strategy can provide adequate financing for reliable service provision.

Focus on total emissions should also be made, such that charges are augmented to reflect total emissions, not solely emissions concentration. This is an important means by which to control total emissions. The establishment and enhancement of water markets and tradable water rights is an important consideration. In recent years, the PRC has undertaken a number of inter-city, inter-sectoral and intra-sectoral water trades. In 2000, the city of Yiwu in Zhejiang province paid RMB200 million to the city of Dongyang to secure 50 million m^3/a of drinking water. The prospect for enabling wider intra-basin, inter- and intra-sectoral water trades should thus be seriously considered. In this connection, tradable permit schemes are more likely to be successful and save costs if:

1 there is an identifiable catchment;
2 the market is not thin;
3 the total pollution/emissions can be easily defined;
4 there is accurate and sufficient data; and
5 there is adequate institutional structure for monitoring and enforcement.

Meanwhile, the total maximum daily loads (TMDLs) have received much interest from the PRC's policy-makers. TMDLs underpinned the design of the Nanpan River permit scheme. It is fair to say that TMDLs provide a clear strategy to convert ambient water standards into emissions targets for point and non-point sources. The strategy also has the potential for application to non-point sources. Nevertheless, the implementation of TMDLs in the United States has been fraught with problems, mainly due to legal uncertainties and their informational intensive nature (see Chapter 7). Given the legislative uncertainties in the PRC, the use of TMDLs should be given extremely careful consideration. If implemented they should apply only to problematic areas of ambient water quality, with the main thrust of pollution control policy aimed at enforcing current emission standards (Houck 2002).

Success of public disclosure schemes will be predicated upon strong monitoring and political will. Information could be shared at the basin level to encourage inter-provincial improvements. These regulations speak of a movement toward a formal role for public participation. Public participation can be used as a means of bridging the implementation gap, which exists for many of the reasons described above. Another means by which accountability can be improved by public participation is through the law courts. Access to legal aid could improve the effectiveness and scope of this measure.

Notes

1 The percentages in 2007 are 49.9 percent, 26.5 percent and 23.6 percent, respectively, for different classes.
2 *Environmental Quality Standards for Surface Water* (GB 3838–2002) defines five water quality classes for different environmental functions: Class I for headwaters and natural reserve; Class II for first class of drinking water sources and habitats of rare aquatic organisms; Class III for second class of drinking water sources, aquaculture and human contact; Class IV for water source of industrial use and recreation area for indirect human contact; Class V for water sources of agriculture use and landscaping requirement.

Reference

Houck, O.A. (2002) *The Clean Water Act TDML Programme: Law Policy and Implementation*, 2nd edn. Washington, DC: Environmental Law Institute.

7 Strategy report for ecosystem management in the People's Republic of China's experience

Jixi Gao and Yongwei Han

Ecological protection problems in the People's Republic of China

In recent years, the People's Republic of China (PRC) has strengthened ecological protection and restoration, launched natural forests protection projects by returning farmlands to forest, grassland and lake projects, and built a number of different types of nature reserves and important ecological function reserves. These efforts have resulted in the significant increase of the national forest coverage and notable achievements in desertification prevention and soil erosion control in major river basins (Chinese State Environmental Protection Agency (SEPA) 2005). Despite these efforts for ecological environmental improvement in the PRC, ecological protection in the country still has a long way to go, with only one-third of the ecological environment of the national territory in good condition and one-third in a severe state (SEPA 2006). The trend of ecological deterioration in some regions has not been effectively curbed, thus the ecological problems therein are still serious. Local ecological problems have eased up, but regional and river-basin ecological damages have worsened. While previous ecological problems have lessened, new ecological problems have emerged. Also, even if there was slight improvement in artificial ecological environment, there was however accelerated degradation in the primary ecological environment. And although individual ecological problems have been controlled to some extent, systematic ecological problems have become more prominent, with dominant ecological problems transforming into hidden ecological problems. Viewed as a whole, the situation of the ecological environment in the PRC is not very optimistic, with the transformation of ecosystem structural damages into functional disorders, intensification of ecological degradation and disasters, and the continuous decline of ecosystem service functions. Ecological problems have become more complex while the ecosystems have continuously become unstable (SEPA 2005).

In the PRC, the regions with fragile ecological environment cover more than 60 percent of the land area. The areas, where soil erosion occurs, account for 37.1 percent of the total land area, with annual soil loss of five billion tons. On the other hand, 90 percent of the natural grasslands have degraded in varying degrees, with annual land desertification rate of 2,460 km². Wetlands have annually shrunk and disappeared, with large areas like the mangrove wetlands in Hainan, Guangdong and Guangxi dropping from 50,000 hectares (ha) to 14,000 ha over the past 20 years. Meanwhile, 90 percent of urban surface waters have been polluted. The per capita arable land area is estimated at merely 1.4 mǔ,[1] which is only 40 percent of the world average level. Furthermore, polluted farmlands make up 10 percent of the arable land area, which is reduced at an annual rate of over ten million *mǔ* due to urbanization and industrialization. Indeed, the rapid economic development has brought great pressure on the ecological environment such that national and regional ecological disasters and environmental pollution events have occurred more frequently since the 1990s (SEPA 2002 and 2006; Du Qinglin 2006; Liu Jiang 2002; The Program Team of Chinese Sustainable Forestry Development 2002).

Continuous vegetation degradation

As a result of climate warming, rapid economic growth, rapid population increase and continuous urbanization, main vegetations such as forests and grasslands have deteriorated seriously. Consequently, forest vegetation functions have also been declining continuously. According to the results of the sixth forestry survey, the forest resources in the PRC are characterized by: insufficient total quantity; uneven distribution; unreasonable forest age group structure composed mostly of young and middle-aged groups; high concentrations of single forest age, species and form in the plantation areas which are mostly simple in stand structure and have low reserves capacity per unit; poor forest quality; low canopy density (the national average level is 0.52 percent); and high timber consumption which outpaces timber growth (The Program Team of Chinese Sustainable Forestry Development 2002).

Among the grassland resources in the PRC, natural grasslands occupy the largest area while artificial grasslands account for only a small portion. It has been observed that the quantity of natural grasslands decreases gradually while the quality declines continuously. Statistics reveal that the degraded grassland area amounted to only 10 percent in the 1970s and increased to 30 percent in the 1980s and 50 percent in the middle of the 1990s. Moderate and severe degradation make up 50 percent of the degraded grassland area, and the present degradation is continuing at a rate of two million square hectometer (hm²)[2] per year (Du Qinglin 2006).

Heightened land degradation

Land degradation in the PRC has become increasingly prominent. There has been continuous increase and aggravation in land salinization and desertification, and soil erosion and pollution. The decrease in arable land area has also been incessant.

By the end of 2005, the area of nationwide land desertification was as high as 1.74 million km², accounting for 18.1 percent of the country's total land area and spanning 30 provinces (autonomous regions and municipalities) and 841 counties (SEPA 2006).

The PRC has joined the ranks of countries suffering from the most serious soil erosion in the world. The nationwide area where soil erosion occurs has reached 3.67 million km², while that where water erosion takes place has amounted to 1.79 million km², accounting for 38 percent of the PRC's land area. Since the 1990s, the annual rate of increase in the area where soil erosion occurs is over 15,000 km², with a volume of more than 300 million tons (SEPA 2006).

Arable land resources in the PRC continue to decrease. Since 1949, 667,000 ha of arable land has become mobile sand. From 1996 to 2006, the average annual net decrease in arable land in the PRC was 820,000 ha. During the same time, the soil pollution has worsened and become increasingly apparent in some areas due to long-term excessive use of chemical fertilizers, pesticides, plastic sheeting and wastewater (Zhao and Zhang 2007).

Declining wetland function

The PRC's wetland area is rapidly and sharply declining. Over the past 40 years, reclamation alone has caused the disappearance of nearly 1,000 natural lake wetlands with total area of more than 1.3 million ha. The area subjected to lake reclamation has exceeded the total area of the five major freshwater lakes, resulting in lost regulation and storage capacity of 32.5 billion cubic meters and the annual loss of freshwater resources of about 35 billion cubic meters. Meanwhile, the area subjected to coastal wetland reclamation has reached nearly half of the total area of the five major fresh water lakes. As a result, the PRC's wetland area has fallen from about 6.9 percent to 3.8 percent of the total land area, much lower than the 6 percent global ratio. With the reduction of wetlands in the PRC, wetland ecological functions have also decreased significantly, resulting in biodiversity reduction and ecological deterioration (Zhao and Zhang 2007; The Program Team of Chinese Sustainable Forestry Development 2002).

Threatened biodiversity

The change of habitat environment has affected biodiversity. Over the years, population growth and rural and urban expansion have destroyed large areas of natural forests, grasslands, wetlands and other natural habitats. Consequently, a large number of wild animals have lost their habitats and are in danger of extinction. There are 4,000 to 5,000 species of endangered or nearly endangered higher plants in the PRC, accounting for 15 percent to 20 percent of the total higher plants. Scientific investigations of the biological and natural resources in the PRC reveal that there are about 398 species of endangered vertebrate animals, accounting for about 7.7 percent of the total number of vertebrate animals in the country, and 258 species of endangered wild animals. It is estimated that only about a dozen are left of the wild South China tiger which is one of the first-class protected animals in the PRC, while only over 100 are left of the white-fin dolphin living in the middle and lower reaches of the Yangtze River from the lower areas of Zhicheng, Hubei. Some species, like the Equus Przeualskii and the high-nosed antelopes, became extinct in the twentieth century. Some common species in the past such as the Mongolian gazelle have become rare species. Out of the 640 species listed in Appendix I of the *Convention on International Trade in Endangered Species of Wild Fauna and Flora*, about one-quarter or 156 species are found in the PRC, and more than 40,000 species of associated biology suffer from survival threat (SEPA 2006 and 2002).

Glacier retreat

The past two to three decades have witnessed significant changes in the glaciers of the western PRC and the extremely severe loss of glacier materials brought about by the climate warming and the environmentally damaging impact of human activities. According to the *Survey on China's Glacier Resources and Changes*, the nearly 20,000 km² of glaciers not covered with moraine are in an overall state of reduction – the reduced area of 1,480 km² translates to an overall reduction ratio of 7.4 percent of the glacier area between the latter part of the 1950s and the 1980s (from the data of the first glacier survey). Apart from area reduction, some glaciers have also thinned. The twelfth glacier, the Tiger Ditch in Qilian Mountain, although not showing any area reduction, exhibited a reduction in ice surface height of 20 to 25 meters (m). As compared with the data in 1984, the Qiyi Glacier has thinned by 19.6 m over the past 23 years, with loss to the end of the glacier exceeding 50 m (SEPA 2005).

The ecological problems discussed above reflect unbalanced ecosystem structure, discordant ecological process and continually declining ecosystem functions in the PRC. For a long time, the PRC's population growth, industrial development, urban expansion and infrastructure construction have brought strong disturbance to the regional ecosystem structures. The landscape and surface structure in the PRC has been significantly and fundamentally changed over the years. Moreover, there is also a perceived incompatibility between the PRC's industrial structure and the carrying capacity of its resources and environment due mainly to the failure to take into consideration the conditions of the resources and environment in industrial structure and layout. Specifically, many high water consumption projects are located in water shortage areas, resulting to aggravation of water resources shortage. Water-intensive metallurgical and petrochemical projects are located in Beijing which is deficient in water resources, while large-scale commodity grain bases are constructed in Xinjiang which is a desert belt province. Rice planting is promoted in the desert areas, and the site of vast rice plantations is in Ningxia which is a province with an arid climate.

In addition to its disturbance on the ecosystem structure, economic growth also impacts on the ecological process in the PRC. Energy- and resource-intensive economies have achieved rapid development over the years as a result of the extensive pattern of economic and social development in the PRC. Excessive and arbitrary exploitation and utilization of water, soil and biological resources brought about uncertain factors which have potential adverse impacts on the material cycle, energy flow and information transmission of regional ecosystems that may lead to an incomplete and uncoordinated ecological process. At present, the most representative situation is the improper development and construction of hydropower and water conservation projects which have made serious disturbances and damages in the river ecosystems. Damming has changed the flow patterns of rivers, shaped and intensified river fragmentation, and changed hydrological characteristics and ecosystem material, energy, chemical and biological fields, which then resulted in changes to species structure, habitat distribution and river ecosystem ecological functions.

As a result of structure damage and process disorder in the regional ecosystems, a continuous recession of ecosystem functions is observed, particularly:

1   the water conservation function of the great rivers source regions;
2   the windbreak, sand fixation, and soil and water conservation functions of the areas rich in important natural vegetation;
3   the flood regulation and storage functions of the wetland areas;
4   the material production function of the grassland, forest and farmland ecosystems; and
5   the biodiversity maintenance and climate regulation functions of the regional ecosystems.

Root causes of ecological problems

Fundamentally unsound ecological conditions

In spite of the vast territory, distinct climatic differences, diverse topography types and complex geological conditions, the PRC's ecological environment on the whole is fragile. The regions with fragile ecological environment such as the arid or semi-arid regions, alpine regions, karst regions and Loess Plateau regions account for 60 percent of the PRC's total land area.

The total area of the north-western regions makes up one-third of the PRC's land area, but water and heat resources are distributed in different regions, thus there is what may be described as an inadequate matching of resources with land area. Also, alpine zones have plentiful precipitation but relatively insufficient heat, while basin areas have rich heat resources but scarce precipitation. Most parts of the north-western regions have a precipitation of 50–400 mm. Under these conditions, vegetation growth and soil development in these regions are subjected to different constraints, such as shortage of water resources, which cause the rather fragile ecosystems. The karst mountainous areas in the south-western PRC have shallow soil and more rainstorms, making them prone to landslides, soil erosion, soil desertification and other consequent ecological problems and natural disasters. Meanwhile, the Qinghai–Tibet Plateau has harsh chilliness, thin air, unpleasant weather, sparse vegetation and low land productivity such that its surface vegetation can hardly recover once damaged. On the other hand, the Loess Plateau has crisscrossed gullies and loose soil making it susceptible to soil erosion, and the regions it cover as among the most seriously eroded regions in the PRC. The eastern PRC is endowed with better natural conditions, but is drought-prone and easily flooded owing to its small area and concentrated rainfall.

Abnormal climate change

During the past 50 years, there have been distinct climate changes in the PRC, corresponding and parallel with the global climate changes (Chinese Weather Bureau 2006; SEPA, 2005). In particular, significant changes have taken place in the average surface temperature, precipitation, severity of weather events and other climatic factors of the PRC. The average surface temperature has increased by 1.1°C with a rate of 0.22°C increase every ten years, significantly higher than the average warming rate of the world or the Northern Hemisphere over the same period. Although the nationwide average annual precipitation has no significant changes, there is an apparent inter-annual fluctuation and regional differences in precipitation. Between 1956 and 2000, there were increases in varying degrees in the annual precipitations in the middle and lower reaches of the Yangtze River, south-eastern PRC regions, most of the western PRC regions, the northern part of north-eastern PRC, and most of Inner Mongolia. The annual precipitations in northern PRC, the eastern part of north-western PRC, and the southern part of north-eastern PRC fell to some extent. The sunshine time, water surface evaporation, average wind speed near the ground and total cloud cover have all been reducing significantly; and the nationwide average frost days have decreased by ten days. With global warming, extreme weather conditions and events such as high temperatures and rainstorms will become more frequent. In particular, there will be severe droughts in the northern and north-eastern parts of the country, and floods in the middle and lower reaches of the Yangtze River and the south-eastern regions.

Resource- and energy-intensive economic growth

The PRC's economic structure has been adjusted to a certain extent, but the industrial structure level is still low and problems like simple quantity expansion are still relatively prominent (Research Center of Environment and Development of Chinese Society Science Research Academy 2004). The average proportion of the PRC's economy to that of the world, and to that of the other developed countries, is diminishing. In 2005, the PRC's gross domestic product (GDP) ranked sixth in the world, but the gap with the GDPs of developed countries or the average GDP level of the world increased. In particular, the PRC's GDP accounted for only 38 percent of Japan's and 14 percent of the United States' while its labor productivity was only 0.03 percent of the developed countries'. The PRC's per capita GDP ranked one-hundred-and-twelfth in the world, accounting for only 3.2 percent of the United States', 3.7 percent of Japan's,

29 percent of Malaysia's and 51 percent of Iran's (Li Wenhua 2007). In contrast, both of the PRC's resource consumption and pollution emission rank high in the world. This is due mainly to the PRC's extensive economic development mode which is characterized by high consumption, high emission and high growth. This development mode has not only brought serious and heavy pressure on the PRC's ecological environment but also made more obvious the contradiction between supply and demand of resources.

Missing market for ecological assets

Although the beginnings of a new socialist market economic system in the PRC were set in motion by the end of 2000, losses in ecological assets have not been covered by the economic costs, and the market mechanism for ecological and resource allocation has not yet been set up resulting in adverse and serious implications on the sustainable development capacity of the country. According to estimates, the losses due to environmental pollution account for about 3–8 percent of the country's GDP while those resulting from soil erosion and ecological destruction of grasslands, wetlands and forests account for about 6–7 percent of the country's GDP (Li Wenhua 2007; SEPA 2002). The monotonic pattern of the environmental economic policies has not been adjusted accordingly and the economic instruments widely adopted in some developed countries have not yet been introduced in the PRC. There is also the difficulty in determining the prices and bases for valuation of natural resources which results in the failure to integrate natural resources into the current economic accounting system. In particular, the pollution charge system has already been in effect for a number of years, but the PRC is still in the "balance compensation" status which is characterized by an imbalance between the charges, the regulatory costs and ecological and environmental losses such that the charges imposed are much lower than the regulatory costs and the losses to ecology and the environment (Ando *et al.* 1998; Baldares *et al.* 1990). This situation has led to a failure to reflect the true value of environmental resources which is the basis for resource economic management (Organisation for Economic Co-operation and Development (OECD) 2003). In the absence of such basis, the effects of economic policies on environment are not significant. The United Nation's *Agenda 21* has proposed the development of national systems of integrated environmental and economic accounting in all countries. In this way, the use of an environmental accounting system and the valuation of natural resources are essential in the realization of environmental resources market allocation (Emerton *et al.* 2006; Wätzold and Schwerdtner 2005; Balmford *et al.* 2002). The PRC however has not yet made any substantial progress toward achieving this goal.

Absence of a strategic and centralized ecological management system

There is an observed lack of integration in the present ecological environment construction management system in the PRC. Several unfavorable factors such as multiple governances, fragmentation, non-cooperation and multiple leaderships have led to scattered investments, ineffective system of accountability and absence of an effective and integrated means of regulation. Construction of the ecological environment requires substantial capital investment and, in recent years, the PRC has increased investments in ecological construction. From 1998 to 2002 alone, the PRC invested more than RMB580 billion in environmental protection and ecological construction, which accounted for more than 1.29 percent of the GDP during the same period and translated to 1.8 times of the total investments in the 47-year period between 1950 and 1997, demonstrating genuine support to the ecological and environmental protection work (Uchida *et al.* 2004). Due, however, to the disjointed use of funds, the investments are dispersed resulting in a failure to come up with an integrated force for effective regulation in a large area. The lack of uniform, systematic and scientific guidelines for decision-making and other practices has resulted in the failure of ecological construction to reference current international advanced concepts on integrated ecosystem management and adopt the multi-element and multi-system integrated management system as opposed to the single-factor management for the protection of the structure and function of regional and river-basin ecosystems. Moreover, sector management has led to overall difficulties in inter-region and inter-project controls of ecological environmental construction, whereby ecological construction projects became overlapping and crosscutting which in turn lead to a lot of wasted time, investments and opportunities. Clearly, merely focusing on construction and ignoring management has adversely affected the effectiveness and sustainability of ecological projects.

The existence of related management organizations for different sectors, including ecological environment in all levels, is another concern. In view of the sector-kind of management which results in several administrative divisions for the different sectors in all levels, the management of different ecological concerns such as water, land, forest and grassland have been separated from each other. In fact, even an individual ecological concern has also been divided into many segments. As a consequence of sector-leaning policy direction and lack of an overall understanding of ecological problems, ecological management in the PRC has not been very effective. Similarly, the regulation system of ecological protection is unsound and regulation capability is weak. In addition, relevant laws, regulations, policies and standards on ecological protection are inadequate. Spot enforcement for ecological protection has not yet been carried out in most regions, and problems such as lack of funds, insufficient vehicles and poor equipment exist throughout the country. Scientific research and technologies for ecological protection are likewise limited. The development of technologies, like ecological monitoring and early warning mechanisms, are still in the initial stages. Also, the ecological information system has not been put in place for being insufficient and having poor channels; therefore, it has been difficult to provide a sound support to ecological management.

Future challenges

Rapid economic growth results to rising ecological impact

Having started later than the already developed world economies, the PRC is just now undergoing the period of accelerated development, industrialization and urbanization which is generally marked by extremely high consumption and demand of resources and energy. In particular, the PRC's economic development is still in the extensive growth mode which is characterized by high input, high consumption and high pollution emission but low cycle and low efficiency. The pressure on the ecological environment of the rapid economic growth is clearly demonstrated in the difficulty in managing high-speed economic growth and intensive resources consumption with ecological destruction and environmental pollution.

As a result of the excessive speed of economic development, domestic mineral resources have fallen far short of the current economic development needs. The total output of mineral mining in the PRC has amounted to five billion tons, with a per capita share of less than 50 percent of the world per capita level, while the unit GDP energy and material consumptions are much higher than the world average levels (Zhang Wenju 2007). In 2006, the PRC's GDP reached US$2.16 trillion which is around 5.5 percent of the world's total GDP, while energy consumption amounted to 24.6 trillion tons of standard coal which is about 15 percent of the world energy consumption. Steel consumption reached 388 million tons which is about 30 percent of the world consumption, and cement consumption totaled 1.24 billion tons which is about 54 percent of the world consumption. With the improvement of the national standard of living and the expansion of the overall size of the economy, the high growth trend of resource consumption will persist for a long time. As a consequence of the limited mineral reserves of the PRC, the degree of dependence of minerals consumption on imports continues to rise. The import ratios of oil, iron ore, copper metal, alumina and potassium salt have reached 45.2 percent, 55 percent, 70 percent, 45 percent and 77 percent, respectively. In recent years, the degree of import dependence of oil, iron ore and copper metal (especially oil and iron ore) in the PRC has been increasing annually. According to forecasts, of the existing reserves, only 24 out of the 45 major minerals in the PRC will be able to sustain the needs until 2010, and only six will have enough reserves to ensure the needs until 2020 (Zhang Wenju 2007).

At the same time, the PRC's energy efficiency is of concern. In comparison with the advanced industrial countries, the per ton steel energy consumption in the PRC's major iron and steel enterprises is 15 percent higher, while thermal power supply energy consumption is 20 percent higher and cement comprehensive energy consumption is 23.6 percent higher (Zhang Wenju 2007). The PRC is still not out of the old path of "pollution first and control last" so there is already a considerable degree of environmental overdraft. Low efficiency will inevitably be accompanied by high consumption, high emission and high pollution. It will take a long time to upgrade and adjust the traditional industrial structure such that the extensive mode of economic development will continue for some time, and there will be no immediate let-up of the pressure of economic growth on the ecological environment which is even foreseen to increase year after year.

Incessant population growth increases consumption capacity

The PRC feeds 22 percent of the world population with its meager share in the world's natural resources – 9 percent arable land, 6 percent water sources, 4 percent forests, 1.8 percent oil, 0.7 percent natural gas, less than 9 percent iron ore, less than 5 percent copper ore and less than 2 percent bauxite (Zhang Wenju 2007). The per capita reserve of most mineral resources is less than half of the world's average level, and the per capita reserve of coal, oil and natural gas is only 55 percent, 11 percent and 4 percent, respectively, of the world's average levels. Continuous growth of population and increase of economic consumption capacity will exacerbate further the pressure on resources and environment.

It is estimated that the total population of the PRC will reach 1.36 billion in 2010 and 1.45 billion in 2020. The national urbanization ratio is expected to rise to 47 by 2010 and to 55–58 by 2020 (Qian Zhengying *et al.* 2001). With the rapid growth of economy, population and urbanization, the PRC's resources consumption demand will intensify further. According to forecasts from relevant departments (Liu Jiang 2000):

1   between 2006 and 2010, the water supply capacity should increase by 30 billion cubic meters (m^3) annually, and water supply capacity for production and living needs should increase by 43 percent;
2   the average annual growth rate of land for urban construction will rise to 5.5 in 2010 and 2.25–2.9 percent in 2020;
3   the energy sources demand will be about 2.61 billion tons of standard coal in 2010 and about four billion tons of standard coal in 2020;
4   the per capita direct and indirect consumption of grain in 2010 and 2020 will be 405 kg and 410 kg, respectively; and
5   the total grain demand will reach 550 million tons of raw grain in 2010 and about 590 million tons of raw grain in 2020.

Growth of demand for land, water and energy resources will increase further the pressure on the regional ecological environment, resulting in an imbalance in the regional ecosystems, and the utilization of lands with high ecological service value such as farmlands, forests and wetlands. Growth in grain demand will cause the farmland reclamation of unsuitable lands and the possible occupation of some important ecological areas such as lakes and beaches. The considerable growth in energy consumption will increase further the emissions of greenhouse gases and aggravate environmental pollution. At present, the emissions of sulfur dioxide and carbon dioxide in the PRC rank first and second, respectively, in the world.

Strict compliance with international agreements

International conventions on the environment have gradually influenced the PRC. With the development of economic globalization, the PRC has further strengthened international collaboration on environmental protection, as proposed in the *Report to the 17th National Congress*. Compliance with international conventions has brought about profound and positive effects on the ecological and environmental protection in the PRC. The PRC is one of the pioneer contracting parties of the Convention on Biological Diversity, the United Nations Framework Convention on Climate Change, the United Nations Convention to Combat Desertification and the Convention on Wetlands. It is observed that influence of international conventions on the ecological and environmental protection in the PRC has become increasingly apparent (SEPA 2006). However, there is a deficiency in the PRC's capability to perform its undertakings under the conventions. The status, system and capacity of ecological environmental protection and management in the PRC are short of the requirements specified in the international conventions. Although efforts toward compliance with the requirements are ongoing, fulfillment of the undertakings shall be very difficult, considering that PRC will be in the primary stage of socialism for a long while, and the country will not only be faced with tremendous development pressure but also be bound by international conventions.

Suggested strategies

It is suggested that the PRC adopt a systematic approach of ecological protection. Through this, the single-factor control is transformed into a comprehensive ecosystem management with integrated structure, process and function; and simple ecological protection is raised to the level which shall optimize economic growth and coordinate effectively the ecosystem structure, process and function to strengthen state ecological safety and provide potent support to sustainable development of the economy and society.

In order to achieve this, we suggest three strategic directions. First direction is to establish a state ecological safety framework system centered on nature reserves and key ecological function zones. Nature reserves currently account for 15 percent of the PRC land area, while key ecological function zones account for 22 percent (SEPA 2006). Nature reserves and key ecological function zones are primary considerations in the ecosystem framework of the PRC, the maintenance of which is crucial to ecological protection efforts such as creature diversity protection, water source conservation, windbreak and sand-fixation, hydrological regulation and ecological safety maintenance. To a certain degree, a good ecological safety framework could be set up by means of establishing nature reserves and key ecological function zones network. It is necessary for the PRC to pursue the strategy of pressure relief and rehabilitation. Efforts to relieve the ecosystems as a whole from extraneous pressure and reformulate the functions of the regional ecosystems after pressure is released from main ecosystem frameworks (such as nature reserves and key ecological function zones) include the following:

1   implementing stricter measures to effectively operate the management system of nature reserves;
2   forbidding development and construction activities in nature reserves;
3   executing effective actions to maintain the ecological service functions of key ecological function zones;
4   guiding industrial development toward a rational direction;
5   restricting economical and social activities in significant function divisions; and
6   releasing artificial pressure over system bearing capacity.

Second direction is to pursue economic growth with due consideration of the ecological bearing capacity of the area. This entails the implementation of the whole process systematical control strategy involving source control, process supervision and terminal regulation. Source control is achieved through the definition of industrial development trend and scale pursuant to regional resource environmental bearing capacity, and the reduction of the impact of industrial development on the ecosystem. Successful process supervision is achieved when:

1   during the natural development process – environmental supervision management is strengthened, resources are utilized properly, and the impact of resource development on the ecosystem is minimized;
2   during the natural resource exploration process – the environmental inspection management is strengthened, resources are used effectively, and the impact of industrial development on the ecosystem is diminished to the utmost extent; and
3   during the resumption and construction process – there are efforts to integrate strengths, optimize configuration and recover ecosystem service function to the utmost extent.

Third direction is to establish a state ecological supervision and management system, and form a structure for the harmonious development of ecology and economy. This will be achieved through the integration and systematization of ecological protection management modes, completion and institution of a mechanism for harmonious development of ecological protection, economy and society. There must also be a social support system for ecological protection and equal attention to the treatment of both symptoms and root causes of ecological problems through a combination of long-term treatment and permanent treatment. Ecological monitoring, evaluation and warning mechanisms must be strengthened, along with resource supervision management; while the ecological compensation mechanism must be completely formulated. The ecological culture and the state ecological protection and construction system must be improved and renovated. On the aspect of social behavior and consciousness, various economic and social actions must be guided toward the maintenance and improvement of ecosystem functions; improvement of ecological culture, consciousness and behavior; formulation of a new and modern ecological culture; and situation characterized by integration among production, human activities and ecology. A complete and effective social support system for state ecological protection will definitely lead to the improvement of the quality of the ecological environment.

Construct a state ecological safety framework centered on nature reserves

Construction of nature reserves allows on-site protection of most ecosystems and rare wild animals and plants as well as important natural relics. At the same time, it plays an important role in maintaining significant ecological functions of the support areas for economic and social development, such as water source conservation, windbreak and sand-fixation, and air purification (Cullen *et al.* 2005; Cavatssi 2004; Brandon *et al.* 1998; McNeely 1994; Dixon and Sherman 1990). However, the existing nature reserves are of low quality and uneven in types, with more forest and morass ecosystem types and less ocean and plain ecosystem types. Thus, the regulation system for nature reserves still needs to be completed while the technological standards still need to be perfected. Meanwhile, the outdated and ineffective management of nature reserves and the weak capability construction with inadequate integrated planning and design at state level should be addressed through reserves development planning for the whole country, with particular focus on state-level nature reserves. There is a need to enhance construction of a nature reserves network and carry out construction engineering of nature reserves which shall optimize space arrangement and improve construction quality and level. There must also be a comprehensive promotion of key breakthroughs and results in reserves construction, as well as emphasis on the importance of reserves construction in the areas with diversified biological structure. A nature reserves system with rational area arrangement, abundant types and strong demonstration function must also be set up, alongside the main framework of state ecological safety.

At present, there are no management organizations for 41.47 percent of the existing nature reserves of the PRC, while there are no professional staff to manage 21.05 percent of the nature reserves (Li Wenhua 2007). Although some nature reserves have management organizations and professional management staff, many of them cannot effectively perform their tasks due to funds shortage and/or failure of management to go beyond the level of mere surveillance work. Therefore, it is necessary to strengthen the construction of management organizations at all levels of nature reserves; optimize and establish state-level nature reserves management organizations; realize the target of all nature reserves of having management organizations with complete functional departments; increase the number of management staff in nature reserves; improve the proportion of professional and skilled staff; discard department benefits; renovate-

management system of nature reserves; attach importance to state-level nature reserves; and explore and establish direct management system of nature reserves.

There is also an urgent necessity for a special law which shall increase technological standards for nature reserve construction and management; revise land management methods of nature reserves; define land ownership; revise nature reserves' assessment standards; establish payment for ecological services system; clarify the management responsibility of nature reserves; establish national standards for general planning, infrastructure construction and function zones of nature reserves; and standardize methods for resource survey, resource quality evaluation and monitoring techniques, as well as sustainable tourism development.

The inadequacy in the management capability and scientific management system for natural reserves has likewise been observed. Uncertain financial support, remote locations, poor working and living conditions, and inadequate and poor infrastructure facilities in most of the natural reserves render the technological personnel incapable of working effectively. It is thus urgent to set up a scientific management system for natural reserves with enhanced scientific research study and adequate basic equipment and internal management and protection facilities, and to intensify fund investments and establish a steady operation guarantee system for natural reserves. The annual investment of RMB250 million by the central finance for the natural reserves construction translates to approximately RMB100,000 of average annual construction fund for every natural reserve under national-level allocation. Meanwhile, the allocation for routine management is less than RMB10,000, while provisions for personnel salary, routine patrolling management and scientific activities implementation are insufficient. In this light, there is a need to include in the national economic and social development plan the construction of the natural reserves, and to increase the central and local financial investments for natural reserves. In the meantime, the social forces at all levels should be mobilized to widen the financing channels and increase the donations and financial aids from national and international environmental protection organizations, financial institutions, volunteer groups, consortiums, major companies and UN organizations (Emerton *et al.* 2006; Emerton 1999; Brandon *et al.* 1998; Hadker *et al.* 1997; Kramer and Mercer 1997).

Strengthen the construction of key ecological function zones

It is also a must that efforts are carried out to strengthen the construction of key ecological function zones and improve the national ecosystem service functions. Ecological function zones or reserves are areas selected and delineated for having important functions in water-resource retention, water and soil conservation, flood regulation, windbreak and sand-fixation, and biodiversity maintenance – which are to be especially protected and subjected to limited development construction. The construction and protection of key ecological function zones is essential to regional ecological safety maintenance and regional economic and social development. Unfortunately, the existing ecological environments of the key ecological function zones are not looking very optimistic due to several factors, which include: absence of a system for comprehensive consideration, coordination and decision-making; weak supervision and management capability; and backward supervision and management means. There is a distinct tendency toward ecological function degradation in the river and lake areas, northern key windbreak and sand-fixation zones, and flood regulating river zones. There must therefore be a reasonable guidance on industrial development through enhanced and comprehensive supervision and management in order to build key ecological function zones. It must be emphasized that the recovery, maintenance and improvement of regional key ecological functions are essential in preventing and reducing natural disasters; coordinating river basin with regional ecological protection and economic development; and ensuring national security.

There is an immediate need to implement national key ecological function zones layout and outline to recover and improve the regional ecological service functions, and identify the areas with significant roles in regional, river basin, local and national ecological safety where key ecological function zones will be built. The immediate implementation of industrial optimization as well as the readjustment and recovery of ecosystem service functions must also be undertaken. At present, the decline of the ecosystem functions in key ecological function zones has mostly resulted from discord between economic activities and ecological protection, inadequate ecological adaptability of the industrial structure and layout, and failure to consider regional ecological bearing capacity in the industrial scope and design. It is suggested that the principles of protection priority, development limitation and spot development be applied to guide industrial development properly. Also, there is wisdom in making full use of the resource advantages of the ecological function reserves, selecting proper development direction and adjusting regional industrial structure and measures in accordance with local conditions and pursuant to the principles of appropriate development. It is also recommended to:

1   develop special industries with resources and environment bearing capability which shall be beneficial to regional primary ecological function realization;
2   launch ecological industries such as ecological tourism, ecological forestry, sand industry, flood prevention, ecological livestock breeding and ecological agriculture;
3   limit the expansion of industries which damage the regional ecological functions;
4   institute legal approval by the relevant state department of regional reserves exploitation activities;
5   eliminate backward industries;
6   close down industries which damage the ecosystem;

7   limit high-consumption industries;
8   spread and promote clean energies such as wind energy, small hydroelectric
    power, solar energy and geothermal energy; and
9   reduce as much as possible the damage to the natural ecosystem (Salafsky *et al.* 2001; Segerson and Miceli 1998; Aylward *et al.* 1996).

There is also a need to immediately formulate a fund investment system and enhance the ecological function supervision and management. The different levels of the government should enhance the fund and policy support to promote the construction of key ecological function reserves. Delineation of the powers and responsibilities between the central and local governments is a must to establish a reasonable fund investment allocation system between these two levels of governments. National investments should be directed toward the institution of supervision and management mechanisms, early warning monitoring, information management, technological support, internal ecological protection and control, and pilot and demonstration engineering of the ecological industrial development. On the other hand, the local governments at different levels should include in the local economic and social development plan the ecological function reserves construction and in the local financial budget the operations costs upon completion of construction, and ensure the installation and construction of internal roads, power, communication and other infrastructures for the successful operation of ecological function reserves. Meanwhile, efforts should also be undertaken to enhance the internal supervision and management capability within the key ecological function zones and establish a comprehensive management and coordination system with the cooperation of several state departments.

Optimize the industrial structure and its geographical distribution according to the ecological function zones

The industrial development should be scientifically planned according to the region's ecological functions. The conduct of overall assessment of ecological sensibility, ecological stress effect and ecological threshold value of the resource exploitation zones should be made upon consideration of the different regional resource endowments, natural environmental characteristics, ecological sensibilities and dominant ecological service functions. The restrictive factors to regional resource exploitation and industrial development must be determined while productivity levels should be conceptualized and set up properly. Resources exploitation space distribution suited to regional ecological function must likewise be confirmed.

There is a necessity to establish an ecological suitability assessment system to provide a scientific guide to the industrial development distribution and provide an ecological suitability division. The assessment factors for various zones must be selected to form an assessment factors database for regional ecological suitability evaluation. Using this system, ecological suitability analysis assessment of the regional and river basin industrial development distribution must be conducted to optimize regional and river basin industrial structure and productivity distribution. In order to reduce regional industrial resemblance and repeated construction and to promote regional economic integration, a multi-level platform for inter-regional industrial development communication and cooperation must be established within areas of same ecological suitability category, and coordinate and integrate among them the regional industrial development distribution.

The formulation of the ecological bearing capability assessment system to define the scope and guide industrial development must also be undertaken through the scientific assessment of the bearing capabilities of the regional resources and environment which should be constantly enhanced and adjusted during actual industrial development and planning to adapt to the resources and environment bearing capabilities of the planned zones.

Regulate industrial development through stringent environmental impact assessment

The current environmental impact assessment in the PRC mainly focuses on the project construction level which falls at the bottom of the decision-making chain, thus the failure of the environmental impact assessment to contribute to the protection of the environment, guide the direction of the development policies or designs, and address the different adverse impacts of the construction activities. It is therefore necessary to enhance the whole environmental impact assessment system, which includes strategic environmental assessment, planning environmental assessment, project environmental assessment and environmental impact evaluation.

The legal status of, and the planning for, the strategic environmental assessment must be strengthened, while the range of strategic environmental assessment must be expanded. Efforts should also be directed toward the development and constant enhancement of a planning technology, implementation mechanism and management system. The integration of the environmental, economic and social subsystems of the areas subject to the environmental impact assessment planning will be achieved through the coordinated development of the regional environment, economy and society. Furthermore, environmental impact assessment planning should take into consideration funds, procedure, content and methods. The environmental impact assessment planning of river basin and regional mineral products development projects should also be enhanced alongside the implementation of the plans for regional resources utilization. There should also be an integration of the environmental impact assessment planning into the management of national mineral resources development, which should proceed in accordance with the environmental bearing capacities of local areas and river basins and the four supervisory grades to be gradually established (country, province, city and county). It is necessary to focus on the reinforcement of the national planning of mining areas for coal, iron and lime, and specific ores development of protective mining such as antimony, tin, gold and ion-type tungsten. There is also a need to strengthen the regional and key sector planning of river basin and key industries such as steel, petrochemical industry, electricity, papermaking and coal industry. A rational arrangement of key industries in the regions and river basins, according to integral bearing capacities of resources such as water and soil, should be made to standardize the development of the key industries and optimize the development and utilization pattern of river-basin resources.

There must be optimization of the project environmental impact assessment and control on the overexploitation of resources on the project level. Newly built, extended and reconstructed projects should strictly observe the relevant regulations on environmental protection. Project environmental impact assessment should precede any construction work. The supervision and process management of project assessment should definitely be strengthened while the results of the project assessment should be strictly implemented. On-site inspection should be done during the course of preliminary acceptance of the project to ensure the implementation of the relevant control measures of project assessment.

In order to complete the environmental impact assessment, a follow-up evaluation system should be established to assess its feasibility and effectiveness. Pursuant to the results of the follow-up inspection and assessment, relevant laws and regulations should be revised accordingly, and the system itself should be adjusted periodically. A management system, along with relevant technical standards, should be put up to fully optimize the follow-up assessment. The gradual standardization of such follow-up assessment should be undertaken to implement and effectively operate environmental protection measures.

Integrate major regional ecological projects

The effective recovery and construction of ecological projects are important measures to improve ecosystem structures and promote ecosystem functions. Under the guidance of the plan for the construction of the national ecological environment and the outline for the protection of the national ecological environment, the PRC has launched the comprehensive soil erosion control pilot project in six key areas and embarked on a series of other key ecological projects. Implementation of these key ecological projects contributes to the protection and recovery of the PRC's ecosystems, and delays the trend of ecological degradation. There is however an absence of a comprehensive planning and design to these ecological projects considering that project proposals originate from different state departments which separately undertake project implementation. This results to repeated construction, dispersed fund allocation and lack of organic combination in the ecological construction areas which lessen the integral benefits of ecological construction projects. There is thus a need to undertake the merger of major ecological projects in the river basins and other regions; establish ecological construction; institute an organization for unified leadership and management; and actively perform ecological recovery and management work in the priority areas and regions. The concrete strategic actions that need to be undertaken mainly include:

1   integration of major ecological projects;
2   resumption and renovation of ecological work in different focus points and areas.

Enhance the ecological monitoring network and establish a national ecological assessment and early warning system

The ideal ecological monitoring network should be comprehensive and systemic, to control and test the types, structures, functions and key elements of the composition of ecosystems, including those which are found in the same regions in order to provide the bases for ecological quality assessment, ecological protection, ecological work resumption, ecological reconstruction and rational utilization of natural resources. Ecological monitoring is one of the important components of, and signifies substantive development of, environmental monitoring. It also serves as the foundation of ecological protection, provides the main basis for the development of an ecological early warning and assessment system, and serves as an important means to strengthen ecological environmental management. At present, although there are many ecological monitoring spots in the PRC, management and authority over such spots are dispersed among the different state departments such as those in charge of forestry, agriculture and the academy of sciences. Ecological monitoring in the PRC has not yet formed a rational network system for lack of unified efforts toward the realization of the ideal ecological monitoring system resulting in low ecological monitoring efficiency, repeated monitoring efforts and lack of the early warning function of real-time assessment. Considering the inadequacy of the present ecological monitoring in the PRC to meet the demand for an effective national ecological protection management, there is a need to refine and enhance the ecological monitoring network to be nationally responsive and to establish an ecological assessment and early warning system to strengthen ecological monitoring efficiency and ecological protection capability. The concrete strategic actions include:

1   integration of the monitoring stations of each state department and establishment of a national ecological monitoring network;
2   compilation of ecological monitoring information and establishment of the ecological monitoring early warning platform to safeguard ecosystem functions and structures; and
3   conduct of comprehensive ecological assessment and establishment of a national ecological security early warning system.

Establish a payment for ecological service system

The basic purpose of an ecological compensation system is to protect the ecological environment and promote harmony between the population and nature. It is an environmental economic policy which is founded on ecosystem service value, ecological protection costs and development opportunity costs. The ecological compensation system comprehensively uses administrative and marketing methods to coordinate the interests of the different parties involved in ecological environmental protection and construction efforts. The Central Committee and the State Council of the PRC lay much emphasis on regional ecological fairness and put forward clear requirements on ecological compensation system. The State Council Working Outline in 2007 (State issue 2007, No. 8) confirms that the endeavor to speed up the establishment of ecological environmental compensation system is a great energy-saving and emission-reduction task. The state's comprehensive work plan for energy-saving and emission-reduction also aspires to improve the ecological compensation system for resource development and to carry out a pilot cross-regional ecological compensation system. President Hu Jintao, in his report for the Communist Party of China (CPC) Seventeenth National Congress, proposes to establish and improve systems for compensable use of resources and for ecological environmental compensation. There is a need to choose a proper ecological compensation mode suitable to local conditions, establish an ecological compensation system to facilitate the promotion of environmental protection, and convert the use of mere administrative means to comprehensive use of legal, economic, technical and administrative means to carry out the ecological compensation system. It is also beneficial to promote sustainable use of resources, speed up the establishment of environment-friendly society, realize the harmonious development in different regions and interest groups, and work toward achieving a balance between regional society and ecology. The diversified ecological environmental problems accordingly require diversified compensation modes and ways (Lee and Mjelde 2007; Goeschl and Igliori 2006; Ninan and Sathyapalan 2005; Flatley and Bennett 1996). The establishment of the following four national compensation systems should be undertaken:

1 financial transfer system based on ecological function protection;
2 policy formulation system based on primary function zones;
3 ecological assets cost internalization system; and
4 river-basin ecological compensation system.

Strengthen national ecological protection laws and policies

The report of the CPC Seventeenth National Congress involves the establishment of an ecological civilization pursuant to the goal of social development. Ecological civilization is so far the highest form of human civilization after primitive civilization, agriculture civilization and industrial civilization. It is a common pursuit of mankind. Overall, the history of human civilization is a history of the co-evolution of human cultures and the environment. Culture is needed to adapt to the ever-changing environment. If cultural development does not come together with environmental development, there will be ecological crisis, resources exhaustion and diseases, as well as all kinds of social ecological crises. It can well be explained by the disappearance of the ancient Babylon civilization, Maya civilization, ancient civilizations described in Greek mythologies, Sahara civilization and many other civilizations. An ecological civilization system should be built on a foundation of laws, regulations, policies and ecological culture construction which addresses serious problems relating to population, resources and environment. This is to promote the harmonious coexistence between society and environment and to gradually influence and guide ecological transformation in the concepts of ecological protection and construction, decision-making process and management, people's value orientation, production modes and consumption behavior (Toman and Ashton 1994; Caldecott and Program 1988; Alcorn 1989). The main detailed strategic actions include:

1   enhancement of ecological protection laws and regulations;
2   establishment of an economic policy system along the concept of ecological civilization; and
3   establishment of an ecological protection persuasion mechanism.

The above eight strategic actions for preserving the PRC's ecosystem clearly suggest four common crosscutting themes for policy improvement. The first theme is that the government needs to intensify its efforts in ecological construction and preservation. Ecological construction and preservation should be strengthened through the continued implementation of major ecological projects, such as the protection of natural forests and return of farmlands to forests and grasslands. The industrial structure and layout should be adjusted with due consideration of the ecological carrying capacity. A national ecological safety framework should be put up, centered on nature reserves, ecological function zones, scenic spots and forest parks. Full restoration of degraded natural ecosystems should be done through proper focus on fragile and critical ecological areas. All these call for government investments and coordination of different regions and line ministries.

The second theme is that ecological construction and preservation should aim at recovery of the ecosystem functions. Ecological construction direction must be transformed toward the recovery of ecosystem functions such as the natural, economical and social service functions. The resources for ecological protection, construction and management – which are dispersed among different state departments such as those for environmental protection, agriculture, forest industry and water conservation – should be pooled together to be used for national implementation of ecological construction, recovery and protection. An integrated decision-making mechanism for ecological protection and development should be constituted, while the relationship between ecological protection and economic development should be harmonized. Local governments need to establish the corresponding integrated administrative setup to coordinate the relevant state departments to increase the efficiency of ecosystem function maintenance.

The third theme is that a stocktaking and accounting system of ecological assets is the basis for all future strategic actions. An accounting system for ecological assets at the central and local government level should be launched along with a GDP accounting system. The consumption of ecological assets during economic development should be accounted for as costs in the scheme of economic development. The repair and loss of natural resources and ecological assets should be taken into consideration in the formulation of the price mechanism and structure of ecological assets. A compensation system for the use of ecological assets must be established and ecosystem services used as agents of production should be regarded as production costs. Business enterprises should be encouraged to develop eco-friendly operating procedures through staged price and market trade system.

The fourth theme is to establish a centrally managed ecological safety framework. A national ecological safety network system should be established in nature reserves, areas with important ecological functions, forest parks, ecological tourism zones and geological parks. The construction of an ecological safety system should be integrated into the general construction category of national safety under national management. A special fund for the construction and maintenance of a national ecological safety system should be set up. Financial expenditure should be integrated toward the stabilization of the ecosystem structure in nature reserves, areas with important ecological functions, and other similar areas which are important to national ecological safety. This would ensure the regularity of the ecosystem service functions such as biodiversity protection, water resource conservation, windbreak and sand fixation, and climate regulation, and also lay the foundation for economic and social sustainable development.

Notes

1 *mǔ* is a widely used (modern Chinese) unit for measuring land area, 1 *mǔ* = 1/15 ha.
2 It is a unit for measuring land area under the metric system, 1 hm^2 = 1 ha.

References

Alcorn, J. (1989). "An Economic Analysis of Huastec Mayan Forest Management." In *Fragile land of Latin America: Strategies for Sustainable Development*, ed. J. Brouwer. Boulder: Westview Press, 182–206.

Ando, A., J. Camm, S. Polasky and A. Solow (1998). "Species Distributions, Land Values, and Efficient Conservation." *Science* 279(5359): 2126.

Aylward, B., K. Allen, J. Echeverria and J. Tosi (1996). "Sustainable Ecotourism in Costa Rica: the Monteverde Cloud Forest Preserve." *Biodiversity and Conservation* 5(3): 315–43.

Baldares C., M.J. Laarman and J.G. Laarman (1990). "User Fees at Protected Areas in Costa Rica." FPEI Working Paper No. 48. The Forestry Private Enterprise Initiative. Southeastern Center for Forest Economic Research, North Carolina.

Balmford, A., A. Bruner, P. Cooper, R. Costanza, S. Farber, R.E. Green, M. Jenkins, P. Jefferiss, V. Jessamy, J. Madden, K. Munro, N. Myers, S. Naeem, J. Paavola, M. Rayment, S. Rosendo, J. Roughgardenn, K. Trumper and R.K. Turner (2002). "Economic Reasons for Conserving Wild Nature." *Science* 297(5583): 950–3.

Brandon, K., K.H. Redford and S. Sanderson (1998). *Parks in Peril: People, Politics, and Protected Areas*, Washington, DC: Island Press.

Caldecott, J.O. and I.T.F. Program (1988). *Hunting and Wildlife Management in Sarawak*, imprint unknown.

Cavatassi, R. (2004). *Valuation Methods for Environmental Benefits in Forestry and Watershed Investment Projects*, FAO Agricultural and Development Economics Division. ESA Working Papers.

Chinese Weather Bureau (2006). Chinese climate communique. Beijing: Weather Press.

Cullen, R., E. Moran and K.F.D. Hughey (2005). "Measuring the Success and Cost Effectiveness of New Zealand Multiple-species Projects to the Conservation of Threatened Species." *Ecological Economics* 53(3): 311–23.

Du Qinglin (2006). *Chinese Strategy for Grass Sustainable Development*, Beijing: Chinese Agriculture Press.

Dixon, J.A. and P.B. Sherman (1990). "Economics of Protected Areas: Approaches and Applications." East–West Center, Washington, DC, 243.

Emerton, L. (1999). "Mount Kenya: The Economics of Community Conservation." Evaluating Eden Series Discussion Paper No. 4. Evaluating Eden Project and Community Conservation Research Project (Universities of Manchester, Zimbabwe and Cambridge and the African Wildlife Foundation). Online, available at: www.iied.org/pubs/pdfs/7797II.pdf.

Emerton, L., J. Bishop and L. Thomas (2006). *Sustainable Financing of Protected Areas: A Global Review of Challenges and Options*, The World Conservation Union (IUCN).

Flatley, G.W. and J.W. Bennett (1996). "Using Contingent Valuation to determine Australian Tourists' Values for Forest Conservation in Vanuatu." *Economic Analysis and Policy* 26(2): 111–27.

Goeschl, T. and D.C. Igliori (2006). "Property Rights for Biodiversity Conservation and Development: Extractive Reserves in the Brazilian Amazon." *Development and Change* 37(2): 427–51.

Hadker, N., S. Sharma, A. David and T. Muraleedharan (1997). "Willingness-to-pay for Borivli National Park: Evidence from a Contingent Valuation." *Ecological Economics* 21(2): 105–22.

Kramer, R.A. and D.E. Mercer (1997). "Valuing a Global Environmental Good: US Residents' Willingness to Pay to Protect Tropical Rain Forests." *Land Economics* 73(2): 196–210.

Lee, C.K. and J.W. Mjelde (2007). "Valuation of Ecotourism Resources Using a Contingent Valuation Method: The Case of the Korean DMZ." *Ecological Economics* 63 (2–3): 511–20.

Li Wenhua (2007). *The Research of Chinese Ecological Compensation Mechanism and Policy*, Beijing: Science Press.

Liu Jiang (2000). *21st Century Strategy for Chinese Agriculture*, Beijing: Chinese Agriculture Press.

McNeely, J.A. (1994). "Protected Areas for the 21st Century: Working to Provide Benefits to Society." *Biodiversity and Conservation* 3(5): 390–405.

Ninan, K.N. and J. Sathyapalan (2005). "The Economics of Biodiversity Conservation: a

Study of a Coffee Growing Region in the Western Ghats of India." *Ecological Economics* 55(1): 61–72.

OECD (2003). *Harnessing Markets for Biodiversity Towards Conservation and Sustainable Use*, Paris: OECD Publications.

Qian Zhengying and Zhang Guangdou (2001). *The Strategy Research of Chinese Water Resource and Sustainable Development*, Beijing: Chinese Water Conservancy Press.

Research Center of Environment and Development of Chinese Society Science Research Academy (2004). *Comment on Chinese Environment and Development*, Beijing: Society Science Press.

Salafsky, N., H. Cauley, G. Balachander, B. Cordes, J. Parks, C. Margoluis, S. Bhatt, C. Encarnacion, D. Russell and R. Margoluis (2001). "A Systematic Test of an Enterprise Strategy for Community-Based Biodiversity Conservation." *Conservation Biology* 15(6): 1585–95.

Segerson, K. and T. Miceli (1998). "Voluntary Environmental Agreements: Good or Bad News for Environmental Protection?" *Journal of Environmental Economics and Management* 36: 109–30.

State Environmental Protection Agency (2002). *State Report of Chinese Sustainable Development*, Beijing: Chinese Environment Press.

State Environmental Protection Agency (2005). *Evaluation and Investigation of the Ecosystem in China*, Beijing: Chinese Environment Press.

State Environmental Protection Agency (2006). *Chinese Report of Environment Status*, Beijing: Chinese Environment Press.

The Program Team of Chinese Sustainable Forestry Development (2002). *The Sustainable Strategy Research of Chinese Forestry Development*, Beijing: Chinese Forestry Press.

Toman, M.A. and P.M.S. Ashton (1994). *Sustainable Forest Ecosystems and Management: A Review Article*, Resources for the Future.

Uchida, E., J. Xu and S. Rozelle (2004). 'Grain for Green: Cost-effectiveness and Sustainability of China's Conservation Set-aside Program.' *Land Economics*, 81(2): 247–64.

Wätzold, F. and K. Schwerdtner (2005). "Why be Wasteful when Preserving a Valuable Resource? A Review Article on the Cost-effectiveness of European Biodiversity Conservation Policy." *Biological Conservation* 123(3): 327–38.

Zhang Wenju (2007). *Chinese Mine Resource Sustainable Development*, Beijing: Science Press.

Zhao, Shidong and Yongming Zhang (2007). *Millenary Ecosystem Evaluation Report*, Beijing: Chinese Environment Press.

Part III

Pathways to a brighter future?

International experiences in environmental regulation

8 International experiences in air pollution management

Haakon Vennemo and Shaun Larcom

Introduction: the experience with air management

Even in late 1970s, emissions of pollutants into the atmosphere in Europe and the United States remained very high. For instance, in 1978 sulfur dioxide (SO_2) emissions in Europe stood at 70 million tons (Figure 8.1), almost three times higher than current emissions in the PRC. Not only were emissions very high, but any impartial observer, basing his views on trends in European SO_2 emissions from 1945–78, would have forecasted that emissions would continue to grow. Only the bravest would have suggested that, come 25 years later, emissions of SO_2 in Europe would stand at 15 million tons, similar to the level of 1930.

Yet this is what happened. In Europe, a mountain of SO_2 has disappeared since 1978. The story is the same although less dramatic in the United States – emissions of SO_2 in the United States have fallen by about 50 percent since

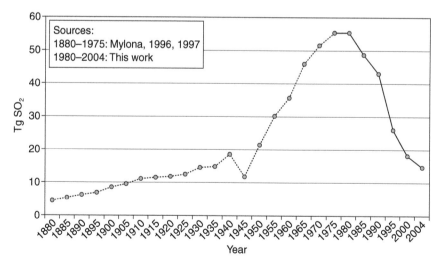

Figure 8.1 SO_2 emissions in Europe (1880–2004) (source: Vestreng *et al.* 2007).

Note
* 1 Tg = one million tons.

1990. In fact, the dramatic fall in emissions of SO_2 in Europe and the United States is a main inspiration of the now famous Environmental Kuznets Curve (EKC), depicting that emissions first rise and then fall as gross domestic product (GDP) per capita grows (Grossman and Krueger 1995).

Emissions of most other polluting compounds to air, with the notable exception of carbon dioxide (CO_2), have also fallen in Europe and the United States. Meanwhile, emissions of SO_2 and many other compounds to air are increasing fast in the People's Republic of China (PRC). Thanks to the double impact of lower emissions in Europe and the United States and higher emissions in the PRC, SO_2 emissions in the PRC are now higher than in Europe and the United States combined, see Figure 8.2.

Trend extrapolation suggests further growth in the PRC's emissions, similar to what an impartial European observer would have said in 1978. But the Western experience shows that trends may be broken. This chapter asks what were the reasons for the trend disruption in Europe and the United States? Why did things change so dramatically, and what transpired to make this happen?

In order to answer these questions, we examine the experiences of the developed countries in controlling air pollutants over the past 20 years, including:

1   SO_2 management in both the United States and the European Union (EU);
2   urban air pollution (particulates and ozone) in the EU; and
3   mercury emissions to air in the United States.

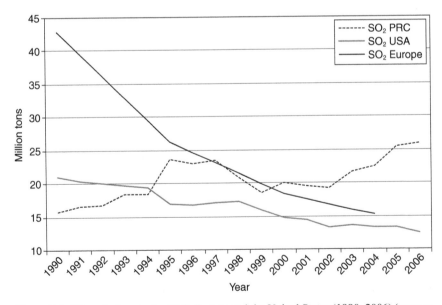

Figure 8.2 SO_2 emissions in the PRC, Europe and the United States (1990–2006) (source: Vestreng *et al.* 2007; US EPA 2007; Vennemo *et al.* 2009).

The lessons we find in this survey are two. First, it is important to manage the pollutant at the scale that it requires. If the problem is local, then local management will suffice. If it is regional or national, then a higher level of regulation is required. We see the importance of this fact in both the study on SO_2 and in the study on mercury. Sometimes air management needs regional or international coordination in order to be effective. Second, we find that the best approach to pollution management is not a given. Both command and control (standards, monitoring and enforcement) and cap-and-trade have been tried and used successfully. What will work in a particular jurisdiction and for a particular pollutant depends upon the context. It is clear that there are substantial cost-savings from cap-and-trade based approaches, but there are also significant costs (if there are varying deposition costs, as is usually the case). It is important to select the system that works in the jurisdiction where it will be applied.

In the following sections we now examine three specific case studies in air management: SO_2 management; urban air management (particulates and ozone); and mercury management. These case studies provide the basis for illustrating the lessons we have learned over the past 20 years in the developed world.

Regulation of SO_2 in Europe and the United States

Immediate reasons why SO_2 emissions are falling

To understand the regulatory success behind falling emissions in Europe and the United States, it is useful first to review the immediate and concrete reasons. We use SO_2 emissions in Europe as our example since, as noted, the break in the trend has perhaps been the most dramatic there. However, what we have to say in this section applies quite generally to emissions in Europe and the United States. The next chapters will make that clear.

There are many sources of SO_2 emissions including industrial sources, household consumption, possibly gasoline and diesel. But Figure 8.3 shows that emissions in Europe primarily are falling because emissions from power plants are falling.

Emissions from power plants have in fact fallen from a little over 25 million tons in 1990 to around ten million tons in 2004. That is an elimination of 15 million tons of SO_2. Lower emissions from non-industrial combustion plants, in particular, also matter percentage wise, but less so in an absolute sense since initial emissions were much lower.

Why have emissions from power plants gone down? There are several possible reasons – e.g. fuel switch from coal to natural gas, or from high- to low-sulfur coal; introduction of renewables. But the records show that in Europe, end-of-pipe *abatement* of SO_2 emissions is the overwhelming reason why emissions have gone down (see Figure 8.4). In the United States, the introduction of low-sulfur coal at the expense of high-sulfur coal is an additional reason. We will see later that this particular difference between Europe and the United States is related to the different regulatory environments of Europe and the United States.

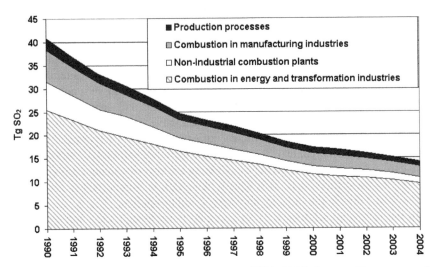

Figure 8.3 Industrial SO$_2$ emissions in Europe (1990–2004) (source: Vestreng *et al.* 2007).

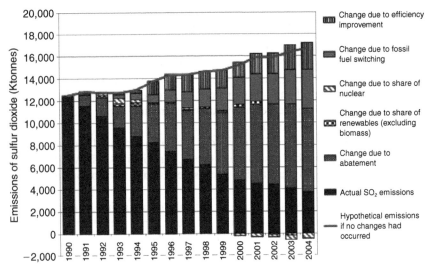

Figure 8.4 SO$_2$ emissions from power plants in Europe (1990–2004) (source: European Economic Agency).

The heavy impact of end-of-pipe abatement is due to the fact that a convenient technique was found to reduce SO$_2$ emissions from power plants and large industrial sources. Called flue gas desulfurization (FGD), this technique is capable of reducing SO$_2$ emissions from a power plant by 95 percent. The capital cost of FGD is approximately US$100–US$150 per kilowatt (kw) (World Bank

1997; Vennemo and Yan 2008), meaning it adds about 10 percent to the capital cost of a power plant.

The line in Figure 8.4 indicates the underlying demand for electricity in Europe. We see that demand has grown since 1990, but "only" by around 2 percent per year.[1] Demand growth would have been higher but for the economic downturn in (Eastern) Europe and the impacts of general energy efficiency.

In summary then, we have the following reasons for the dramatic reduction in SO_2 emissions in Europe and the United States:

1   end-of-pipe abatement technology;
2   fuel switching;
3   power sector efficiency improvements;
4   economic cycles and especially restructuring in Eastern Europe; and
5   energy efficiency improvements.

This list of mitigating factors applies to many air pollutants, and so the example of SO_2 is instructive on many accounts. The immediate reasons for reduction in SO_2 and other pollutants did not emerge spontaneously. Rather, they have been pushed through by various policies. Based on the SO_2 example, the next section describes which general policies have been pursued to control priority substances in Europe and the United States, and this is followed by a closer examination of the role of a cap-and-trade system in the cost-effective management of SO_2 in the latter jurisdiction.

Policy reasons why emissions of priority substances have been falling in Europe

Emission reduction protocols coordinated action

When emissions stood at their peak in 1978, damages from acid rain, in particular, were generating considerable concern all over Europe. In continental Europe, the so-called black triangle of dead forest emerged in Germany, Austria and the Czech Republic. This was a large region in which forests were damaged in leaves, in growth, etc. and in the worst cases, only dead trunks remained. Acid rain was suspected as the primary culprit. In Scandinavia, acidification of lakes emerged as a huge concern. The problem here was that the water in freshwater lakes became too acid for fish to live, and the thousands of small lakes that are spread in Norwegian mountains and Swedish forests were declared "dead." The loss of trout, in particular, was considered significant since recreational trout fishing is a popular pastime that is engraved in national identity.

The main driver of acid rain was clearly SO_2. SO_2 also led to local air pollution in urban areas, and reports at the time from cities such as Athens in Greece and Krakow in Poland emphasized that SO_2 was eating up millennia-old statues and cultural relicts. Something had to be done. But action was not easy, both because Europe seemed dependent on large amounts of SO_2 emissions for its standard of living and because acid rain, in particular, was a transboundary problem. For example, the emissions causing damage to Scandinavian lakes were mostly coming from Great Britain, Poland and other European countries. With hindsight, maybe the main achievement of the concerted European action to reduce SO_2 emissions was that it overcame the twin obstacles of the seemingly high cost to the standard of living and the transboundary character of the problem.

The SO_2 protocols

What happened? In the words of Menz and Seip (2004),

> the necessity of international cooperation in dealing with acidification problems in Europe led to a ministerial meeting in Geneva in November 1979 within the Framework of the United Nations Economic Commission on Europe (ECE) on the Protection of the Environment.

"The necessity of international cooperation" simply is to say that the situation was considered so grave that something had to be done. An economist would interpret this sentence in cost–benefit terms: the benefits of emission reduction had become sufficiently obvious that action was taken. Maybe it also mattered that coal-mining in Europe, in particular, was not as profitable as it once had been, bringing down the cost of emission reduction in important emission source countries. Finally it is interesting that in the ECE the countries had available an institutional framework for organizing cooperation on SO_2 control.

The meeting in Geneva led to the ECE Convention on Long-range Transboundary Air Pollution, more commonly known by its acroynym LRTAP. LRTAP, which entered into force in 1983, established general principles for international cooperation on air pollution issues. This was necessary since LRTAP was the first legally binding convention to deal with air pollution on a broad international basis (Menz and Seip 2004). Second, LRTAP established an institutional framework bringing together science and policy. The framework was centered at the International Institute for Applied Systems Analysis (IIASA) in Austria and in particular the part of IIASA operating the air pollution model known as the Regional Air Pollution Information and Simulation model (RAINS).[2] IIASA with RAINS has later been important as a generally accepted impartial referee on what is the science of acid rain, its causes and effects.

Since 1978, LRTAP has been followed by a number of conventions and agreements on emission reduction in Europe. The Helsinki Protocol of 1985 committed participants to reducing their SO_2 emissions by 30 percent within 1993. The Oslo Protocol of 1994 committed participants to further reductions in SO_2 emissions. In the Oslo Protocol, emission reduction targets were differentiated and based on the notion that some emissions are more harmful than others due to prevailing winds, accumulation of emissions in hotspots, etc. The concept of critical loads, that is, how high pollution loads can a region tolerate, developed at IIASA was the basis of the so-called effect-based approach of the Oslo Protocol.

Protocols on other substances

The most recent agreement is the Gothenburg Protocol of 1999, which seeks to reduce Europe's SO_2 emissions by a further 63 percent by 2010. The Gothenburg Protocol has similar, if less ambitious, reduction targets for nitrogen oxide (NO_x) of −41 percent, non-methane volatile organic compounds (NMVOC) of −40 percent, and ammonia (NH_3) of −17 percent. The Gothenburg Protocol continued the effects-based approach of the Oslo Protocol and extended it to a cost–benefit-based approach. Menz and Seip (2004) posit that, in setting differentiated emission ceilings, both effects and abatement costs were taken into account.

As the Gothenburg Protocol indicates it is not only SO_2 that has been subject to regional agreements on emission reductions in Europe. An important landmark in NO_x reduction was the Sofia Protocol of 1988, which required signatories not to increase their NO_x emissions between 1987 and 1994. Signatories also committed to introducing emission standards and control measures, including catalytic converters for vehicles, which were uncommon in Europe at the time. The Geneva Protocol of 1991 is the similar landmark for reductions in volatile organic compound (VOC) emissions. The Geneva Protocol required signatories to reduce VOC emissions by 30 percent between 1988 and 1999. The 1998 Protocol on Heavy Metals targets cadmium, lead and mercury. Signatories promise to reduce their emissions of cadmium, lead and mercury compared to 1990 levels, and agree on a number of interventions for doing so. Finally, the 1998 Protocol on Persistent Organic Pollutants (POPs) specify 16 substances that signatories should ban, and a number of other substances that they should restrict.

One noteworthy aspect of the protocols is that as a rule they do not detail policy instruments and there are no penalties. Rather, they are coordinating devices that in the end rely on the trust and goodwill of signatories to follow up on their promises. Fortunately, countries have indeed been following up on their promises, perhaps because it has been easier (cheaper) than feared, or perhaps because of the peer pressure that is characteristic of such agreements. So what were the policy instruments countries chose?

The EU approach: command-and-control at the emission level

While they do not detail policy instruments, the protocols do include some statements about policy. We have already noted the call of the Sofia Protocol to introduce emission standards and facilitate catalytic converters. Similarly, the Oslo Protocol "requires Parties to take the most effective measures to reduce (SO_2) emissions. It cites controlling the sulfur content of fuel, energy efficiency measures, the promotion of renewable energy, and the application of best available technology (BAT)" (ECE 2006). However, the main policies for emission reductions in Europe have been laid down in a number of directives of the EU.

Directives are turned into national law and as such are binding for all member states. They can be supplemented by national policies, but remain the drivers of European policy in the area.

Important directives for air pollution control in Europe are set out in Table 8.1. As can be seen, the EU directives prescribe typical command-and-control policies such as BAT in the case of the Integrated Pollution Prevention and Control (IPPC) directive, and emission limit values and standards in the case of the Large Combustion Plant (LCP) directive and the successive generations of EURO standards. The exception is the National Emission Ceiling (NEC) directive, which gives member states a freedom of choice in how to meet the national emission ceilings.

With the prominent role of command-and-control policies, one may ask what is the role of economic incentives and regulations in European policies for air pollution control. The answer is that some environmental levies exist in some countries. For instance, Norway has long had a levy on the sulfur content of oil products, and recently introduced a NO_x-levy, which Sweden has had for several years. Denmark and some other European countries also have levies on air pollutants including sulfur. The Organisation for Economic Co-operation and Development (OECD) has a useful database that provides an overview of environmental economic instruments in member countries and tracks recent developments (www2.oecd.org/ecoinst/queries/index.htm).

Incentive-based regulation at the energy level

The main area of economic regulation in Europe, however, is at the energy level. European countries have levies on gasoline and diesel that currently bring

Table 8.1 Important EU directives for air pollution control

EU directives, instruments	Type of measure	Pollutants covered
National Emission Ceiling (NEC) Directive (2001)	Binding emission ceilings, which EU member states will have to meet by 2010	SO_2, NO_x, NMVOC, NH_3
Large Combustion Plant (LCP) Directive (1988, 2001)	Emission limit values	SO_2, NO_x, dust
Integrated Pollution Prevention and Control (IPPC) Directive (1996)	Integrated permit based on Best Available Technology (BAT)	Not specified: "overall environmental performance"
EURO standards (1992 and onwards) for passenger cars and other light duty vehicles, heavy duty vehicles (e.g. lorries, buses) and motorcycles	Emission standards and testing Fuel regulations	NO_x, CO, HC, HC + NO_x and PM

Source: European Economic Area (EEA) (2007).

consumer prices up to about two dollars per liter.[3] The high prices on gasoline and diesel are quite remarkable given that Europe has a large and vibrant car industry. Second, the EU has set up the European Trading System (ETS) for CO_2 trade, clearly the most ambitious economic regulation of a pollutant that the world has ever seen. Since there is currently no economical way of reducing CO_2 per unit of fossil energy, the ETS is, in practice, an economic regulation at the energy level. European customers also pay high levies on stationary electricity consumption, and important EU countries such as Germany have generous feed-in tariffs of up to 0.49 euros per kilowatt hour (kWh) for renewable energy (*The Economist* 2008). Other EU countries such as Sweden have started up a market for green certificates, whereby qualified green electricity supply technologies sell not just a kWh of power, but in addition sell a green certificate that obtains a price in the market since purchasers of electricity are required to buy a certain quantity of them. Finally, in new member states of the EU, schemes such as Joint Implementation for CO_2 and green investment schemes are taking hold.

These are just a few examples to demonstrate that economic regulation is pervasive at the energy level in Europe. Economic regulation has helped to reduce demand for fossil energy. In other words, it has stimulated energy efficiency. By stimulating energy efficiency, economic regulation lays the foundation for successful reductions in emissions. But in Europe, it is command-and-control policies that have realized the potential offered by end-of-pipe technologies like FGD (SO_2) and catalytic converters (NO_x), and turned limited energy demand growth, which we recall has been 2 percent per year in terms of electricity, into radical emission reductions.

Policy reasons why priority emissions have been falling in the United States

Public concern and the Clean Air Act shaped regulatory response

The chain of events for emission control in the United States was in many ways similar to Europe. Similar to Europe, public opinion in the United States was alerted by visible signs of environmental damage attributable to acid rain and SO_2 emissions. In the mid-1970s, it became clear that lakes were acidic in the Adirondack Mountain Region in New York State (Menz and Seip 2004). Several north-eastern states and the province of Ontario, Canada, sued the US Environmental Protection Agency (EPA) in 1980 to take action to control emissions against states in the Midwest.

However, prior to these developments the Clean Air Act was approved by the US Senate in 1970. The Clean Air Act set a timetable for compliance with the nationwide ambient air quality standard (NAAQS) and required states to work out implementation plans for stationary emission sources. The Clean Air Act was amended in 1977, primarily to give states more time to comply with the nationwide air quality standard, but the amendment also went some way toward requiring end-of-pipe abatement technology. This was done through the New

Source Review, which requires coal-fired power plants and industrial facilities to install end-of-pipe technology whenever they make a "significant modification" that would result in a net increase in emissions.

These initial efforts at legislation were followed by a big scientific program enacted in 1980. Called National Acid Precipitation Assessment Program (NAPAP), the scientific program was designed to inform about the effects of acid rain, whether these effects really were due to acid rain, whether they were serious enough to warrant interventions, and what emission control technologies were available to reduce emissions. The NAPAP assessments ten years later included a cost–benefit analysis with the conclusion that a 40 percent cut in sulfur emissions would give benefits of US$0.6–US$2.5 billion annually (Menz and Seip 2004).

To this point, the developments in the United States resemble those in Europe with the Clean Air Act playing the agenda setting role of the Helsinki Protocol and subsequent protocols; and NAPAP providing the science similar to IIASA, RAINS and the scientific community in Europe. In 1990, however, events in the United States took a different turn from Europe. That year, the US Congress approved new amendments to the Clean Air Act that introduced an emission trading system for SO_2. This means that in terms of SO_2 control, the United States opted for an incentive-based regulatory approach as opposed to the command-and-control strategy of Europe. In the next section, we turn to how this approach differed from that employed in Europe, and why this mattered.

Moving toward cost-effective regulation: SO_2 cap-and-trade system in the United States

Introduction

The Clean Air Act Amendments of 1990 in the United States represent perhaps the best example of how a well-designed pollution abatement policy can deliver large net benefits to society. Further, Title IV of the Amendments, which allowed for sulfur trading, is potentially the best large-scale example of how economic instruments can deliver a certain level of pollution abatement at a lower cost to society than more traditional (command-and-control) regulatory measures. In this section, we describe the way in which these Amendments provided economic incentives, and how this was accomplished.

The SO_2 trading regime emanating from Clean Air Act Amendments of 1990 was the world's first large-scale cap and trade program for air pollution. As noted by Carlson *et al.* (2000: 1293), for years economists had urged policymakers to use market-based approaches to control pollution (taxes or tradable permits) rather than relying on uniform emissions standards or uniform technology mandates (command-and-control). However, this advice was largely ignored until the 1990 Clean Air Act Amendments that established a market for SO_2 emission permits in the United States. Along with capping overall emissions, the 1990 amendments allowed emitters (power plants) to trade emission permits rather than forcing them to install uniform emissions reduction or emissions reductions technologies. This case study summarizes the key features of the Article IV amendments, analyzes the net benefits achieved and the cost savings generated by SO_2 trading, discusses the regional effects of the program, and discusses recent regulatory changes such as the Clean Air Interstate Rules (CAIR).

Background to the regulations

Acid deposition (acid rain) occurs when SO_2 and NO_x emissions react with water, oxygen and oxidants in the atmosphere to form various acidic compounds. These compounds are transported by winds (often hundreds of kilometers) and fall to earth in either wet form (rain, snow and fog) or dry form (gases and particles). The compounds have many detrimental effects on human health and the environment. These include increases in mortality and morbidity, the impairment of air quality, acidification of lakes and streams, forest and coastal ecosystem harm, the reduction of visibility, and the acceleration and decay of buildings and cultural artifacts. Electric power generation accounts for approximately 70 percent of US SO_2 emissions (EPA 2007: 7–8).

As mentioned earlier, until 1990, the regulatory developments in the United States were similar to those in Europe, with the Clean Air Act playing the agenda-setting role similar to that of the Helsinki Protocol and subsequent protocols; and NAPAP providing the science similar to IIASA, RAINS and the scientific community in Europe and with a focus on command-and-control regulatory instruments to reduce SO_2 emissions. However, in 1990 the United States took a different course from Europe.

In 1990, the United States Congress approved the Article IV Amendments to the Clean Air Act which saw the introduction of an emission trading system for SO_2 emissions from electric power generation in 1995. Given that electric power generation accounts for approximately 70 percent of US SO_2 emissions (EPA 2007), it can be said that in terms of SO_2 control the United States opted for an economic instrument approach as opposed to the command-and-control strategy of Europe. The focus of this case study is on the SO_2 emissions trading regime.

Key features of the regulations

Under Title IV of the 1990 Clean Air Act Amendments, a cap was set on the total amount of SO_2 that could be emitted by electric-generating units in the United States. Emission reductions have been phased in, with the 2010 cap set at 8.95 million tons, approximately a 50 percent reduction in emissions from power generation in 1980 levels (EPA 2007: 7). An emitter subject to the scheme is required to hold one permit for each ton of SO_2 it emits. The bulk of emission permits have been and are allocated free of charge (grandfathered) to electricity generators based on their share of heat input during the baseline period (1985–7) each year. In addition, a small portion of permits (around 3 percent) are auctioned each year. Electricity generators and members of the public are free to bid for the permits, in addition to purchasing them from the generators themselves via a clearing house (Napolitano *et al.* 2007: 49).

Regulated sources must monitor, quality assure and report emissions to the EPA. If a liable generator's emissions exceed the number of SO_2 permits it holds, it has to pay a shortfall penalty. Title IV of the Amendments set the shortfall penalty at US$2,000 per ton, which is indexed to inflation. In 2006, the shortfall penalty was US$3,152 per ton. Given that permits were trading at under US$500 per ton in December 2006, it is not surprising that compliance rates with the allowance holding requirements for 2006 were 100 percent (EPA 2007: 11).

The trading scheme has consisted of two phases to date. In Phase I, the 263 largest and most SO_2 emissions intensive generating units (operated by 63 different electricity companies) located largely in the east of the United States were included in the scheme. After January 1, 1995, these electricity companies could only emit SO_2 if they had a sufficient quantity of permits to cover their emissions. Phase II began in 2000 with 9.97 million permits being allocated. This will decline to 8.95 million in 2010. The number of generators affected by Phase II is considerably more than those in Phase I, with 3,520 generating units affected (Napolitano *et al.* 2007: 49; EPA 2007: 8).

As shown in Figure 8.5 below, Phase I and Phase II sources have reduced their SO_2 emissions by 40 percent compared to 1990 levels. Phase I sources reduced their emissions considerably with the advent of emissions trading; while Phase II sources increased their emissions slightly from the period of 1990 to 1999, indicating the powerful effect of the regulations, and some regulatory "leakage" from regulated to unregulated sources. Another large reduction in emissions occurred in 2000 when Phase II sources were brought into the emissions trading scheme.

Figure 8.5 also shows that during Phase I, emissions were consistently less than the annual allowances allocated; whereas in Phase II, emissions were, up

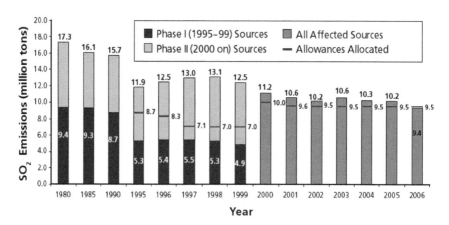

Figure 8.5 SO_2 emissions reductions from Phase I and II sources (1980–2006) (source: EPA 2007: 8).

until very recently, more than the annual allowances allocated. Such events are possible as the SO₂ trading regime also provides emitters with temporal flexibility through the allowance of "banking," where permits can be saved and used in future years.

Because market participants knew that the SO_2 cap was to shrink considerably between Phase I and Phase II, some banking of allowances was in general optimal as the expected benefit of banking a credit is greater than acquitting or selling it (Carlson *et al.* 2000: 1298). Figure 8.6 shows that the bank of unused permits did indeed peak during 1999 and 2000. Allowing the banking of credits also allows generators to directly insure against unforeseen events and potential future permit price volatility.

One risk of banking is that allowances could be considerably higher than the yearly issue of permits in any one year. As can be seen from Figures 8.5 and 8.6, this has not been the case and banking has mainly been used to smooth emissions reductions and costs. Another reason why banking is unlikely to generate a spike in emissions in any one year is that emission reduction efforts are likely to be "lumpy" in nature and often have a long timeframe (e.g. installation of large and expensive desulfurization equipment or the commissioning of a new generator). Also, as electricity cannot be stored for any meaningful period of time, the risk of large increases in any one year is not significant.

As shown in Figure 8.7 overleaf, a mature and liquid SO_2 market has developed. Trading volumes between distinct (arm's length) entities have increased considerably since the beginning of the scheme. In 2006, there were 6,400 transactions exchanging 22.4 million allowances. About 9.5 million (or 43 percent) were transferred between distinct entities, indicating an active, functioning and liquid market. The depth of the market is considerable, given that total permits issued in 2006 was 9.5 million units. The decline in permits transferred since 2001 is attributed to the collapse of Enron (EPA 2007: 12).

Parties to a trade can enter the transactions electronically, allowing trades to be processed in less than one day. The cost of transactions is estimated to be less

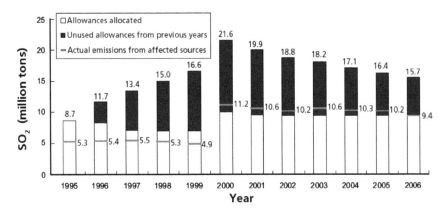

Figure 8.6 SO₂ emissions and the allowance bank (1995–2006) (source: EPA 2007: 9).

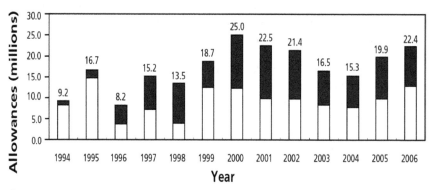

Figure 8.7 Trading volume in SO_2 allowances (1994–2006) (source: EPA 2007: 13).

than 0.1 percent of the cost of a permit, and administering the millions of transactions in permits requires less than one full-time employee at the EPA (Napolitano *et al.* 2007: 49).

Emissions reductions achieved at least cost

By the end of 2006, regulated power plants had decreased their annual SO_2 emissions by more than 40 percent from 1990 levels. Figure 8.8 also shows that these emissions reductions occurred while electricity generated from fossil fuel combustion increased by almost 40 percent, demonstrating the effective decoupling of electricity generation from SO_2 emissions. While there are a number of factors that affect electricity prices, it can also be seen from Figure 8.8, that these marked reductions in SO_2 and NO_x emissions were achieved during a period when the real price of electricity fell.

One reason that emissions reductions did not result in large price increases was that the emissions trading enabled the regulatory goals to be met at least cost to the economy. Since the late 1960s, economists have been advocating the use of cap-and-trade instruments to reduce pollution levels. This is so as they have the theoretical advantage (along with emissions charges) of achieving a given level of pollution abatement at least cost to the economy. For those whose cost of abatement is less than the market price, they will opt to pursue abatement and then sell their permits to those whose cost of abatement is higher than the market price. The free trade of permits should see the marginal cost of abatement equal across all polluters.

If marginal abatement costs were not equalized, then the overall level of pollution could be achieved at a lower cost by having low-cost abaters reduce their emissions more and high-cost abaters reduce their emissions less. Such a concept can be demonstrated in Figure 8.9 where there are two power plants and where $MD(x)$ represents the marginal aggregate damage of SO_2 emissions and we wish

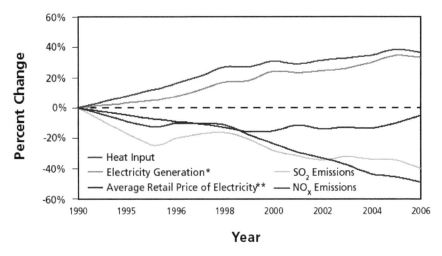

Figure 8.8 Trends in electricity generation and emissions (1990–2006) (source: EPA 2007: 7).

Note
* Generation from fossil fuel plants.
** Real year 2000 dollars (adjusted for inflation).

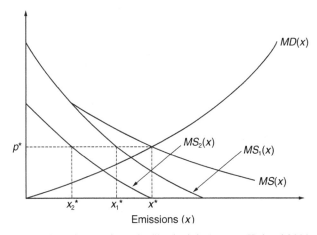

Figure 8.9 The "equimarginal" principle (source: Kolstad 2000: 122).

to cap emissions at X*. Also shown are the benefit curves (MS₁ and MS₂) to each of the two plants in generating the pollution. An aggregate marginal benefit curve is also drawn (MS), which depicts the aggregate benefit of the two power plants if they increase emissions by one extra unit. Under a command-and-control approach, one option would be to divide the pollution reduction among the emitters equally so that power plant 1 has a higher marginal cost of pollution control than power plant 2. However, we can reduce the overall costs without changing the overall amount of pollution by increasing emissions from the low-cost abater (plant 2) by one unit and decreasing emissions from the high-cost abater (plant 1) by one unit. Pollution costs will fall while the total amount of pollution stays the same. This can be continued until the marginal costs for the two power plants are equalized at p* through the free trade of emissions permits.

SO_2 trading in the United States provides a vivid demonstration that the theoretical benefits of economic instruments, as demonstrated above, can be realized. The gains from emissions trading over traditional command-and-control measures (such as the mandatory installation of desulfurization units or the uniform emissions reductions) arise from the fact that emissions control costs vary considerably across generation units and firms.

The flexibility of the trading scheme has driven down the cost of abatement by offering a wide range of control options and has encouraged innovation. Importantly, the trading regime allowed *both* the use of desulfurization units (scrubbers) and fuel switching as viable options in reducing emissions. Stavins (2005) considers that one of the most significant benefits of the trading regime was that technology standards requiring scrubbers for SO_2 for all plants was avoided.

The continuing price incentive to find cheaper emission reduction options also led to the improved understanding and wider use of fuel blending that reduced the cost of emissions abatement. Innovations in the fuels market also led to lower compliance costs as producers in the west of the United States who produced low-sulfur coal make large productivity gains to make their coal competitive in the midwestern and eastern US markets. Also, some suppliers of high-sulfur coal started to bundle permits with their coal, which reduced transaction costs and enabled arbitrage between fuels and the permit market (Napolitano *et al.* 2007: 52). Competition among the railroads freighting low-sulfur coal led to significant reductions in transport costs. This solution would not have been possible if a command-and-control approach was chosen. Furthermore, the flexibility in the regime also enabled the use of boiler adaptations and flexibility in the operation of gas desulfurization equipment (i.e. scrubbers) coupled with design advances, all of which further decreased costs. It is estimated that the capital costs of pollution control equipment responded by falling to around 50 percent of their pre-regime level (Napolitano *et al.* 2007: 51–2). It is this incentive to technological choice and change that generates much of the cost-savings from this approach.

Accurately measuring the cost savings from SO_2 trading is difficult as it requires a number of assumptions, particularly concerning the marginal abatement cost curves of various power plants. As a result, the estimated savings vary a lot, ranging from US$0.9 billion per year to US$5.9 billion per year. The most accurate cost-saving estimate is generally accepted to be that of Carlson *et al.* (2000). Their estimation is considered to be the most accurate as it uses a simulation model based on marginal abatement cost functions derived econometrically from a sample of more than 800 power-generating units. Importantly, this allows them to account for input substitution due to changes in relative prices.

Most of the other estimates are based on engineering models that allow little or no substitution due to price changes (Burtraw and Palmer 2005: 49).

In estimating marginal abatement cost curves for all generation units in the permit market, Carlson *et al.* (2000) separated plants into those that reduce SO_2 emissions via fuel switching (substituting low-sulfur coal for high-sulfur coal) and those who install scrubbers. Fuel switching is the main method of reducing SO_2 emissions in power plants. Carlson *et al.* (2000: 1299) find that in 1995 only 17 percent of all generating units in the United States used scrubbers and 86 percent of these were required to do so by law, with only 15 percent of units installed scrubbers to specifically comply with Title IV.

In order to estimate the cost savings, an estimate of the cost of achieving the emissions reduction using command-and-control policies is also needed to compare with the costs of complying with the cap-and-trade scheme. Therefore, as noted by Carlson *et al.* (2000), the command-and-control policy which the SO_2 trading regime costs are measured against is key to their analysis. Carlson *et al.* (2000) use two benchmarks in comparing the gains from emissions trading forced scrubbing and a uniform emissions rate standard. However, their main results estimate how much cheaper the chosen level of emissions could be achieved through trading rather than through a uniform emissions standard (which they refer to as an "enlightened" form of command-and-control).

Table 8.2 lists the long-run costs estimated by Carlson *et al.* (2000) and compares them with two previous EPA estimates. Column 1 lists the costs under a uniform emissions rate standard (command-and-control), and Column 2 lists the estimated costs under an efficient trading regime. Columns 3 and 4 list the estimated marginal and average cost of SO_2 abatement, respectively. Column 5 lists the potential gains from the emissions trading regime (Column 1 minus Column 2) in 1995 dollars. The estimated savings are considerable, and are almost half the total "enlightened" command-and-control costs and are well over US\$1 billion per year in current prices.

Also it is important to note that the compliance cost estimates of Carlson *et al.* (2000) are considerably less than the earlier *ex ante* EPA estimates. One reason for the divergence in cost estimates arises from the technologies assumed to exist under both scenarios. Before emissions trading occurred, the prevalence of fuel switching was not envisaged, nor were the large reductions in the capital costs of scrubbing. This highlights a considerable advantage of economic instruments in that the flexibility allows for creative abatement solutions, while the constant incentive to reduce emissions induces technological advances. Inducing industry-based investments and efforts into the regulator's objective (here, reduced cost abatement) is the main objective of the economic approach to regulation.

Benefits of SO_2 emissions reductions

Substantially reducing SO_2 emissions is one thing, but delivering environmental and health benefits is another. Data collected from EPA monitoring networks

Table 8.2 Long-run annual cost estimates (1995 dollars)

	Total cost under "enlightened" command and control (billions)	Total cost under efficient trading (billions)	Marginal cost per ton SO_2 ($/ton)	Average cost per ton SO_2 ($/ton)	Potential gains from trade (billions)
	(1)	(2)	(3)	(4)	(5)
Preferred estimate	1.82	1.04	291	174	0.78
1995 technology	2.23	1.51	436	198	0.72
1989 prices and 1989 technology	2.67	1.90	560	236	0.77
EPA (1990)	–	2.3–5.9	579–760	299–457	–
EPA (1989)	–	2.7–6.2		377–311	–

Source: Carlson et al. (2000: 1313).

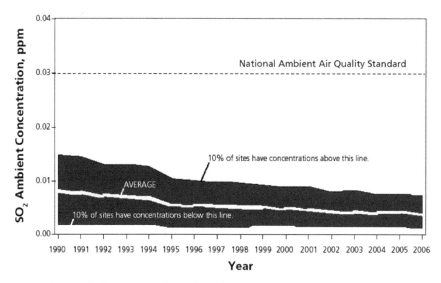

Figure 8.10 United States SO_2 air quality (1990–2006) (source: EPA 2007: 25).

show that the decline in SO_2 emissions from power plant emissions has improved air quality. This can be readily seen from Figure 8.10 which demonstrates that the US national composite average of SO_2 decreased by 53 percent between 1990 and 2006.

Figure 8.11 shows that there has been a visible reduction in wet-sulfur deposition of between 25–40 percent from the early 1990s to 2005 (Napolitano *et al.* 2007). Chestnut and Mills (2005) also report that the reduction in sulfur deposition is up to 50 percent lower from what it would have been in 2010 without the Title IV Amendments over most Midwest and Mid-Atlantic states.

The most comprehensive estimate of the benefits of the Article IV Amendments of the Clean Air Act has been undertaken by Chestnut and Mills (2005). Unfortunately, their estimates do not separate the benefits of SO_2 and NO_x reductions. Table 8.3 provides a summary of annual benefits and costs of Title IV emission reductions. While the estimates are subject to considerable uncertainty, the aggregated benefits of US$122 billion far outweigh the aggregated costs of US$3 billion. The vast bulk of the benefits are derived from health benefits from reduced formation of fine particulate matter ($PM_{2.5}$) due to lower SO_2 and NO_x emissions, which are discussed in more detail below.

Of the non-health benefits, the quantified benefits from improved visibility are significant. Sulphate aerosols are particularly effective at scattering light, which creates a hazy look to the sky, reduces the clarity of sight and reduces visual range. Visibility conditions directly affect people's enjoyment of a variety of activities. The estimated annual value held by all households in the United States for the Title IV improvements in visibility at national parks and wilderness areas is estimated at US$2 billion (Chestnut and Mills 2005).

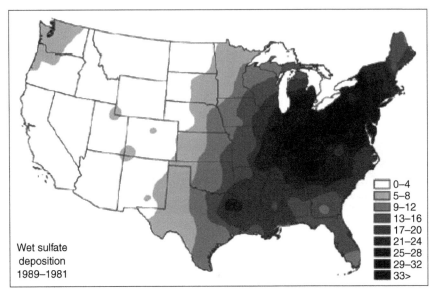

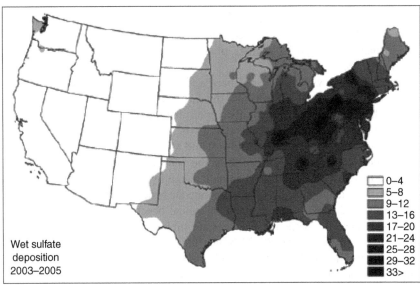

Figure 8.11 Annual mean wet sulphate deposits (1989–91 and 2003–5) (source: Napolitano *et al.* 2007: 48).

Table 8.3 Summary of annual benefits and costs of Title IV in 2010 (in millions US 2000 dollars)

Quantified benefits[a]		
PM$_{2.5}$ mortality (United States and southern Canada)	$107,000	
PM$_{2.5}$ morbidity (United States and southern Canada)	$8,000	
Ozone mortality (eastern United States)	$4,000	
Ozone morbidity (eastern United States)	$300	
Visibility at parks (three US regions)	$2,000	
Recreational fishing in New York	$65	
Ecosystem improvements in Adirondacks (New York residents)	$500	
Total annual quantified benefits	$122,000	
Quantified costs		
SO$_2$ controls	$2,000	
NO$_x$ controls	$1,000	
Total annual quantified costs		$3,000

Source: Chestnut and Mills (2005: 265).

Note

a These are central estimates but are subject to uncertainty and should not be interpreted as exact point values; we have therefore rounded for summary purposes. Many categories of expected benefits are not quantified due to insufficient data. Some, such as urban visibility, are quantified only as sensitivity tests due to uncertainty; these sum to about $4 billion. Other unquantified benefits include improved health and environment due to mercury reductions; improved health of natural forests and improved water quality in lakes, streams and coastal estuaries from reductions in acid and nitrogen deposition; and increased longevity and reduced soiling of painted surfaces and stone materials.

The value of ecosystem services, including wildlife habitat, biodiversity, water cycling and purification, along with recreation and aesthetic appreciation, are considerable. However, quantification remains problematic due to a lack of measurement units to gauge changes in the quality and quantity of ecosystem services and a lack of "dose-response" in how the services may change as a result of pollution exposure. However, willingness-to-pay surveys have found for example that New York residents may be willing to pay US$300 to US$700 million for the reduced acidification of lakes and improvements in forest health in the Adirondacks similar to that achieved through the Article IV reductions. Other benefits include US$65 million dollars from recreational fishing in New York State (Chestnut and Mills 2005: 263).

While the estimated environmental benefits are substantial, the great bulk of the estimated benefits come from the prevented health effects of the Clean Air Act. Chestnut and Mills (2005) estimate this to be US$108 billion for the United States, with an additional US$6 billion for the Canadian population. From Table 8.4, it can be seen that the estimated health benefits include 18,000 deaths prevented, 11,000 new cases of chronic bronchitis avoided, and 24,000 non-fatal heart attacks prevented. The mortality estimates play a particularly important role in the benefits analysis, making up about 90 percent of the total value of the health benefits.

Chestnut and Mills (2005) conclude that the available literature suggests mortality risk reduction has a high monetary value. A central estimate used in recent

Table 8.4 Estimates of annual benefits as a result of Article IV related fine particulate reductions

Avoided health effects	Number of cases of avoided health effects[a]		Monetary value (millions US 2000 dollars)	
	US	Canada	US	Canada
Mortality (adults)	17,000	1,000	100,169	6,002
Infant mortality (children less than one)	100	5	751	28
Chronic bronchitis (adults)	10,400	600	4,056	218
Nonfatal heart attacks (adults)	22,800	1,200	1,917	101
Respiratory hospital admissions (all ages)	8,300	400	123	7
Cardiovascular hospital admissions (adults)	10,800	600	233	13
Emergency room visits for asthma (children)	14,100	600	4	0.2
Acute bronchitis (children)	26,600	1,100	10	0.4
Asthma exacerbations (children with asthma)	28,200	1,200	1	0.1
Upper respiratory symptoms (children with asthma)	338,200	15,200	9	0.4
Lower respiratory symptoms (children)	287,300	12,200	5	0.2
Minor restricted activity days (adults)	12,130,300	636,100	643	34
Work loss days (adults)	2,090,400	109,600	228	12
Total monetary value			108,148	6,416

Source: Chestnut and Mills (2005: 258).

Note
a Rounded to nearest 100. Source: calculated by the authors using REMSAD results provided by US EPA, Clean Air Markets Division.

US EPA analysis suggests that the value of reducing the risk of mortality of one in 100,000 is equal to US$60. The average per capita risk reduction calculated for Title IV in 2010 is about six per 100,000; therefore, the average per capita value is about US$300. While there is considerable controversy over monetary valuations in the reduction of risk, even if one of the lowest monetary values reported is used, the health benefits would still be in the order of US$50 billion in 2010 and many times greater than the costs.

It should be noted that a key uncertainty in estimating the benefits of the Clean Air Act Article IV Amendments is determining what emissions would have been in the absence of the intervention as benefits are derived not just from reductions but also foregone increases.

Regional effects

Flexibility under emissions trading, where any emitter in the country can sell a permit to anywhere else in the country, has the potential to lead to increases in localized pollution, or "hotspots." However, the SO_2 trading experience seems to indicate this has not been the case. Rather, as can be seen from looking at Figure 8.12 overleaf, the largest SO_2 emissions reductions have been achieved in the regions that prior to the scheme being in place had the highest SO_2 emissions. It can also be seen from looking at Figure 8.12 that acid deposition decreased and environmental benefits were delivered where most needed. Research about trading under SO_2 program has found no hotspot problem caused by emissions trading (Banzhaf *et al.* 2004). Along with emissions and wet sulphate deposition, wet sulphate concentrations have also decreased significantly in all the main monitoring regions. Since 1989–91 to 2004–6, average levels have decreased 40 percent in the Northeast, 31 percent in the Mid-Atlantic and 33 percent in the Midwest (EPA 2007: 30).

While there is no evidence of emission "hotspots" resulting from the SO_2 market, the benefits of reductions in SO_2 vary between regions and states. Banzhaf *et al.* (2004) estimate the benefits of a one-ton reduction of SO_2 emissions allowing for weather patterns and population levels. As can be seen from Figure 8.13, reductions in emissions in California, the Carolinas, Tennessee and Kentucky derive the largest benefit because they lead to reductions in exposure to a large population. Emissions reductions in the western states (excluding California) have the lowest gains. As noted by Banzhaf *et al.* (2004: 330), the large variation in benefits across regions illustrates the potential usefulness of segregating the permit market into regions.

Originally, the SO_2 trading program was designed with two regions (east and west) to ensure that emissions were adequately reduced in the east, where damages from acidification were the most severe. However, a single national market was introduced to generate greater cost savings from allowance trading (Burtraw *et al.* 2005: 259).

SO₂ Emissions in 1990
SO₂ Emissions in 1995
SO₂ Emissions in 2000
SO₂ Emissions in 2006

Scale: Largest bar equals
2.2 million tons of SO₂
emissions in Ohio, 1990

Figure 8.12 SO₂ emissions from electric power (1990–2006) (source: EPA 2007: 9).

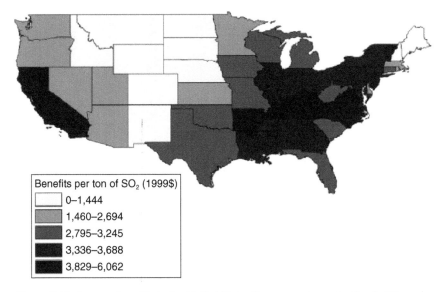

Benefits per ton of SO_2 (1999$)
- 0–1,444
- 1,460–2,694
- 2,795–3,245
- 3,336–3,688
- 3,829–6,062

Figure 8.13 Average benefits to the United States from a one-ton reduction in SO_2 emissions (source: Banzhaf *et al.* 2004: 329).

Future developments and the Clean Air Interstate Rule (CAIR)

While the Article IV amendments have seen dramatic reductions in SO_2 and NO_x emissions and hotspots have not been generated, there are still quite large areas that do not meet air quality standards. As shown in Figure 8.14 there are still large areas mostly in "downwind states" that still exceed national air quality standards for ozone and particulate matter (i.e. non-attainment areas).

In response to this, the EPA plans to implement the CAIR that is expected to see further SO_2 and NO_x emission reductions of approximately 70 percent and 60 percent, respectively, based on 2003 levels. In its current form, the CAIR will require 25 eastern states and the District of Columbia to reduce and cap annual SO_2 and NO_x emissions and to reduce ozone levels. The CAIR states, with the exception of California, are broadly those states that receive the highest benefit from reductions in SO_2 as calculated by Banzhaf *et al.* (2004), demonstrating the potential welfare gains of the program. The CAIR program will also increase the scope of generating units captured by the regulations, with approximately 320 sources added (EPA 2007: 39).

SO_2 emissions trading in the CAIR region will face a tighter regional cap in 2010 and then a further reduced cap in 2015. Title IV emissions trading will continue after CAIR SO_2 trading begins in 2010. It is planned that generators will use Title IV SO_2 allowances to demonstrate compliance with both programs. As a result, banked Title IV allowances can be used for CAIR compliance, and generators in CAIR states will be subject to two SO_2 trading programs that "share

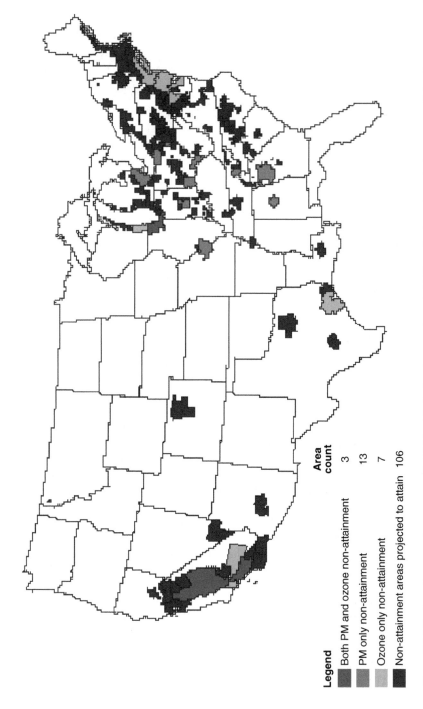

Legend	Area count
Both PM and ozone non-attainment	3
PM only non-attainment	13
Ozone only non-attainment	7
Non-attainment areas projected to attain	106

Figure 8.14 Projected non-attainment areas in 2020 with the implementation of CAIR and other planned abatement policies (source: EPA 2007: 39).

the same currency." However, under CAIR, it is planned that one permit will no longer always equal one ton of emissions. Rather, SO_2 allowances of 2009 vintage and before will cover one ton of emissions, 2010–14 vintage permits will cover 0.50 tons of emissions, and 2015 vintage and later will cover 0.35 tons of emissions. (It is worth noting that the CAIR program remains under consideration, and continues to be altered through regulatory and judicial consideration).

Conclusion

The Title IV amendments to the Clean Air Act in the United States are given as an example of how well-designed environmental policies based on science and pragmatism can lead to large welfare gains to society. Furthermore, the reductions were achieved during a period where real energy prices actually fell. Interestingly, most of the gains to society from the emissions reductions have been driven through public health improvements, which at the time was not the key catalyst for taking action. Rather, as Menz and Seip (2004) note, the momentum for the regulations came from the environmental movement and public opinion concerned about the acidification of freshwater and forests.

SO_2 emissions trading provides an ongoing case study on how economic instruments can indeed move from the textbook into real life and achieve large reductions in compliance costs compared to traditional command-and-control regulations. In particular, SO_2 trading achieved large cost savings largely due to differing abatement costs among polluters. If abatement costs were uniform across polluters, there would be no point in adopting a market-based approach. Also, SO_2 trading also demonstrated how economic instruments, through their non-prescriptive nature, encourage innovation such as the transportation of low-sulfur coal from the west to the east of the United States. Such an outcome considerably lowered the costs of compliance, however unforeseen at the time.

The SO_2 trading experience also highlights a potential tension associated with emissions trading. Allowing a nationwide emissions trading scheme significantly lowered the costs of the scheme, as it allowed more low-cost emitters to meet the standard. However, as the gains from emissions reductions vary considerably, with the highest gains coming from "up wind" emitters in the east of the United States, it also reduced the potential benefits of the scheme. Resolving this tension between simplicity with lower costs versus more sophistication in design (including trading regions) and higher costs is an ongoing task.

Regulation of urban air pollution – fine particles and ozone – in Europe

The size of the problem

Urban air pollution involves a cluster of compounds including SO_2, NO_x, particulate matter (PM), and ground-level ozone (O_3). Current attention in Europe is on PM and O_3 since pollution levels of SO_2, in particular, have gone down and because PM and O_3 increasingly are associated with health damage. This section addresses these problems of urban air pollution, especially PM and O_3. In both cases, we confine the discussion to European policies.

It might be useful to start off with a brief discussion of the extent of the current urban air pollution problem in Europe. As noted, the urban air pollution problem involves a lot more than SO_2. Figure 8.15 gives one indicator in the form of the percentage of urban Europeans exposed to air quality levels above the EU limit values. We see that the percentage is around 30 percent on average, which we think is fairly high. Moreover, the long-term trend in population exposure seems to be increasing for PM (measured as particle matter less than 10 microns in diameter, PM_{10}) and for O_3. Exceedance levels of SO_2 are very low, and for NO_x the trend is down.

In this context, it matters what the limit values are (see Table 8.5). The limit values obviously are somewhat lower than the corresponding levels in the PRC. For instance, to reach Class II air quality a city in the PRC limited by PM would have to reach below 150 micrograms per cubic meter ($\mu g/m^3$) in PM_{10} concentration, which is obviously a bit more lax than the European 24-hour limit of $50 \mu g/m^3$. The World Health Organization (WHO) recommends an even lower limit value of $20 \mu g/m^3$.

It is also interesting to view the trend in European PM emissions (see Figure 8.16). Emissions of PM have fallen by 50 percent in the period 1990–2005. It is

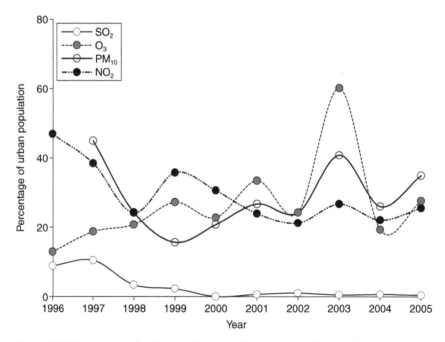

Figure 8.15 Percentage of urban population resident in areas where pollutant concentrations are higher than selected limit/target values, EEA member countries (1996–2005) (source: EEA).

Table 8.5 Limit values for pollutants in Figure 8.15

Pollutant	Concentration	Averaging period	Legal nature
Sulfur dioxide (SO_2)	$125\,\mu g/m^3$	24 hours	Limit value enters into force 1.1.2005
Nitrogen dioxide (NO_2)	$40\,\mu g/m^3$	One year	Limit value enters into force 1.1.2010
PM_{10}	$50\,\mu g/m^3$	24 hours	Limit value enters into force 1.1.2005
Ozone	$120\,\mu g/m^3$	Maximum daily eight-hour mean	Target value enters into force 1.1.2010

Source: EEA.

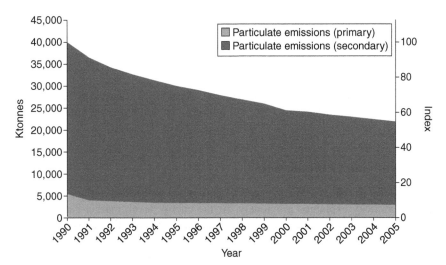

Figure 8.16 Emissions of primary and secondary fine particles, EEA member countries (1990–2005) (source: EEA).

mainly the so-called secondary particle emissions that have gone down. Secondary particles are typically formed from SO_2 and NO_x in the atmosphere. In other words, the reduction in PM emissions reflects lower emissions of SO_2 and NO_x.

This point is reinforced if one looks at the contribution to PM reductions by source (see Figure 8.17). The figure shows that road transport is by far the largest source of reductions. Road transport is important not because it has contributed to reductions in primary PM, but because it has contributed to reductions in secondary PM through NO_x. Road transport used to be a big source of NO_x emissions, and although it is still a considerable source, the introduction of catalytic converters, in particular, in the 1990s have greatly reduced the problem. Note also that the energy industries contributed to higher PM_{10} concentrations.

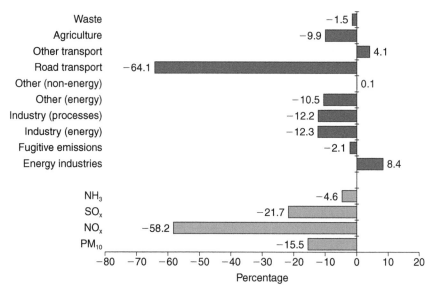

Figure 8.17 Contribution to change in emissions of primary and secondary fine particulates (PM$_{10}$) for each sector and pollutant, EEA member countries (1990–2005)
(source: EEA).

Policies to reduce PM emissions

The policies to reduce PM emissions in Europe are embedded in the general air-
quality strategy explained previously. At the energy level, market-based incentives are used to control fossil-fuel consumption. At the emission level,
command-and-control is used to further reduce emissions per unit of fossil fuel.
Key EU level policy interventions were summarized in Table 8.1. The large
combustion plant directive (CPL) and the Euro standards for cars affect primary
PM directly and secondary PM indirectly. The NEC directive and the IPPC
directive affect PM indirectly, the latter by requiring best available technology.
These directives, which member states adopt in their national legislation, are
complemented by EU-level legally binding air-quality standards.

The EU has for some years had the limit value we mentioned above for PM$_{10}$ of
50 µg/m^3 24-hour average. For each year, 35 exceedances are allowed. The annual
mean limit value is 40 µg/m^3. Recently, in April 2008, the EU Commission
approved a directive for PM$_{2.5}$ emissions.[4] Recent research suggests that PM$_{2.5}$
should take over from PM$_{10}$ as the main health concern with respect to particles.
PM$_{2.5}$ is a measure of smaller particles than PM$_{10}$. The new directive says that levels
of PM$_{2.5}$ should not exceed 25 µg/m^3 by 2015 – a limit value for that year. Since
meteorological conditions tend to influence PM levels in any given year, the "2015-
level" is actually the average of 2012, 2013 and 2014.[5] If possible, the 25 µg/m^3
level for PM$_{2.5}$ should be achieved as early as 2010 – a target value for that year.

The problem of ozone pollution

Recall from Figure 8.15 that more than 30 percent of the population of Europe experiences O_3 levels above limit values, and the number is increasing. Figure 8.18 presents this information from another angle, by focusing on the number of days Europeans experienced health-threatening ground-level O_3 levels in 2007. We see that in most of Southern and Continental Europe inhabitants experience health-threatening levels 25 days per year or more. This is worrying, but actually, in terms of ozone levels, 2007 was a good year for Europe. In 2006 and earlier years, levels were higher.

The European Economic Area (EEA) says that the long-term objective for protection of human health is exceeded when the daily, maximum eight-hour average concentration of ozone is higher than $120 \, \mu g/m^3$ (see Table 8.5).

As is well known, ground-level O_3 is created when pollutants mix with sunlight. The O_3 precursors are VOC and NO_x, followed by carbon monoxide (CO) and methane (CH_4). Figure 8.19 shows that emissions of the O_3 precursors have been falling in Europe over the last 15 years. The fall in VOC and NO_x has been about 25 percent, and hence lower than the fall in other substances.

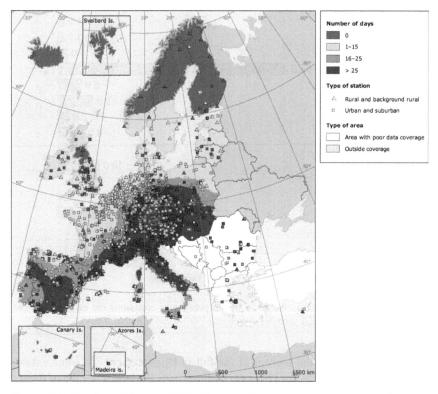

Figure 8.18 Number of days in 2007 with ground-level ozone concentrations above the long-term objective for the protection of human health (source: EEA 2008).

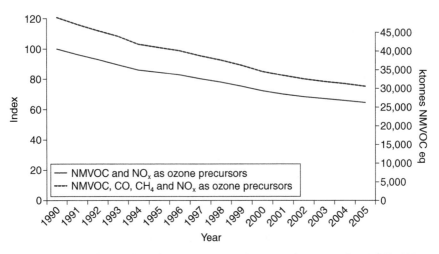

Figure 8.19 Emissions of ozone precursors, EEA member countries (1990–2005) (source: EEA).

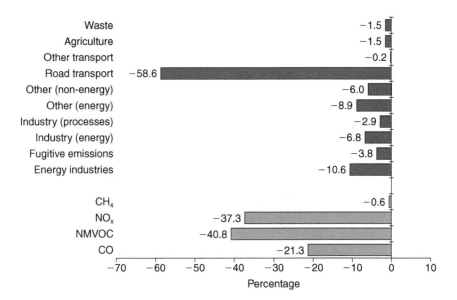

Figure 8.20 Contribution to change in ozone precursors emissions for each sector and pollutant, EEA member countries (1990–2005) (source: EEA).

Figure 8.20 shows the sources of the fall in O_3 precursors. To some extent, the picture is the same as for PM – i.e. road traffic is the largest source of reduction. The overall reduction is evenly split between NO_x and VOC.

Policies to reduce VOC emissions in Europe

We focus the discussions of O_3 precursors on VOC emissions. Like the PM regulation, VOC regulation is embedded in the general framework of Europe – Fossil-fuel consumption is regulated via economic incentives and pollutants are regulated via command-and-control.

Recall that in the case of VOC, international emission reduction efforts are coordinated by the Geneva Protocol of 1991 and the Gothenburg Protocol of 1999. The Geneva Protocol promises 30 percent reduction by 1999, and the Gothenburg Protocol promises a further 40 percent reduction by 2010. ECE (2006) contains an interesting discussion of how countries have approached the targets of the two protocols. The 30 percent reduction goal of the Geneva Protocol was met by 19 of 21 countries. Sources of VOC are to some extent different between countries. For instance, in Norway, loading and storage of crude oil is by far the largest source of VOC. In neighboring Finland, solvents, the transport sector and residential consumption are the largest sources.

Since emission sources differ and because of national differences in policy practice, countries developed different strategies to meet the Geneva target. For instance, Austria has a special ozone law of 1992 to tackle ozone reductions. In 2000, Switzerland introduced a VOC incentive tax on solvents. In Finland, the Environmental Permit Act requires installations using more than ten tons of organic solvents per year to apply for a special permit. In Canada, solvent emissions have been tackled by a "Federal Agenda for the Reduction of VOC Emissions from Consumer and Commercial Products." The ECE (2006) gives the following summary of EU regulations:

> EU Directive 99/13/EC on the limitation of emissions of VOCs due to the use of organic solvents in certain activities and installations was applied at the national level in Cyprus, Denmark, Estonia, Germany, Hungary, Norway, Slovakia, Spain, and the United Kingdom. A complementary EU directive (2004/42/EC) on the limitation of emissions of VOCs due to the use of organic solvents in certain paints and varnishes and vehicle refinishing products and amending directive 1999/13/EC, required additional labelling on products to show the sub-categories and the relevant limit values. It also required labelling of the maximum VOC content in products. Depending on the type of coating material, EU directive 2004/42/EC set different limit values for the content of VOCs, taking effect in two steps in 2007 and 2010.

The Geneva Protocol asked countries to apply best available technologies for reduction of VOCs. The ECE (2006) reports that the following technologies were among the ones chosen: "leak repairs, operating and performance standards, biofiltration, vapor processing at tank loading, end-of-pipe technology, low-solvent alternatives, new drying technology, less volatile cleaning agents, incineration and closed moulding in polyester processing and recycling."

Several measures were taken to reduce VOC emissions associated with gasoline and diesel. According to the ECE (2006),

> Canada reported that federal regulations from 1997 ensured that new light-duty vehicles and light-duty trucks were designed to limit hydrocarbon emissions during refuelling. A national regulation was adopted in 2000 to limit the dispensing flow rate of petrol and petrol blends to a maximum of 38 litres per minute. Regulations also effectively limited benzene in gasoline to 1 percent volume since 1999.

Vapor recovery systems were mandated in several countries.

The Gothenburg Protocol of 1999 not only stipulates that VOC emissions should be cut 40 percent by 2010, it also goes some way in indicating how emissions should be cut. According to the ECE (2006),

> for VOC emissions, the Gothenburg Protocol sets emission limit values for several sources, such as solvents used in the car, the printing and the dry cleaning industries. In the United States, top coat operations in the automobile and light duty truck sector set the VOC discharge limit at 1.47 kg/litre of applied coating solids for those vehicles which construction, reconstruction, or modification commenced after 5 October 1979. In the Netherlands and Slovakia, this value was $45\,g\,NMVOC/m^2$ or $1.3\,kg/item$.

As these examples show, the command-and-control approach to VOC reduction entails very detailed regulations at the source and product level, and this is the route followed by authorities in Europe, as well as in the United States and Canada. In other words, the incentive-based regulation popular in the United States for SO_2 does not extend to VOC. The command-and-control approach presumes monitoring and enforcement, but if those are in place the European experience shows that the approach works in reducing VOC.

Conclusion – regulating urban air pollution in Europe

The experience of managing the various urban air pollution problems in Europe is indicative of how many of these pollution problems are "tied together." The typical pollutants contributors to urban air pollution – particulates and ozone – are closely related to the problems of SO_2 and NO_x discussed earlier. Many of these problems can and do move together, as the solutions applied to one work toward solving the others. In addition, this section also indicates that it is important to undertake coordinated monitoring, standard formulation and control strategies in regard to these associated pollutants. This enables the overall air management strategy to be undertaken in an efficient and coordinated manner. In these cases, where monitoring and enforcement are critical, the standard command-and-control approach is adequate for most purposes.

The approach taken by Europe has been a general emphasis on market intervention to encourage energy efficiency, through energy pricing policies, combined with command-and-control policies at the level of the primary industries concerned. The command-and-control policies have usually required some specific abatement technologies to be adopted across industries in Europe. This combination of resource pricing and standard technology adoption is more palatable to a community of competing states, and it tends to work well in terms of producing environmental improvements. The conclusion is that these sorts of policy combinations might work well in jurisdictions, such as the PRC, where there is a tendency for regions to compete.

Regulation of mercury emissions to air – examining command-and-control in the EU and cap-and-trade in the United States

The size of the problem

Hg (mercury) is a heavy metal that is known to damage the central nervous system. Symptoms include impairment of vision, hearing and speech; disturbed sensation; and a lack of coordination. A child exposed to mercury as a fetus may later experience loss of intelligence quotient (IQ) points, attention deficits and decreased performance in tests of language skills and memory function (Axelrad *et al.* 2007).

Hg is both a local and global pollutant. Elemental Hg (Hg^0) emitted to air may have a residence time in the atmosphere between one half and two years and is transported over vast areas. Significant concentrations of Hg from all over the globe are found at remote locations including the Arctic and Antarctic.

Globally, Asia is by far the largest emission source of Hg, with the PRC important among Asian sources (Pacyna *et al.* 2007). European emissions have gone down by 45 percent since 1990 (see Figure 8.21).

The EEA does not publish data on mercury emissions by source, but the US EPA publishes such data for the United States. Table 8.6 shows that in 1999 the category utility coal boilers, that is, coal-fired power plants, was the main source of US mercury emissions followed by industrial boilers, some of which may also be fired by coal. Medical waste incineration has seen a major reduction in Hg emissions, and contributes significantly to the overall reduction of almost 50 percent. Percentage wise, the reduction in total US Hg emissions is similar to Europe. Europe also has its share of coal-burning power plants that are a source of Hg.

Atmospheric mercury from coal-fired power generation falls to the ground through rain, snow and dry deposition, and enters lakes, rivers and estuaries. Figure 8.22 shows mercury deposits in the United States from US power plants.

Once deposited, the mercury can transform into methylmercury, and can build up in fish tissue. People are exposed to methylmercury primarily by eating contaminated fish. Developing fetuses are the most sensitive to the toxic effects of methylmercury. Children who are exposed to methylmercury before birth are at

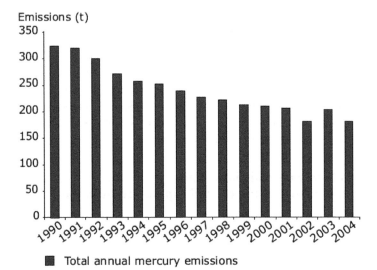

Figure 8.21 Emissions of mercury (Hg) in Europe (source: EEA 2007).

Table 8.6 Sources of mercury emissions in the United States

Source category	1990[a] (tons)	1999 (tons)[f]	% reduction
Utility coal boilers[b]	51.1	47.9[a]	6
Industrial boilers[b]	12.0	12.0	0
Medical waste incinerators	49.7	1.6	97
Municipal waste combustion	56.7	4.9	91
Hazardous waste incinerators[b]	6.6	6.6	0
Chlorine production	10.0	6.5	30
Electric arc furnaces[c]	6.9	n/a	n/a
Gold mining	3.4[d]	11.5	n/a
Other[e]	23.5	21.6	6
Total	219.9	112.6	45

Source: US EPA (2006).

Notes
a 1990 estimate derived using a different methodology.
b Regulations for these categories finalized after 1999.
c Electric arc furnaces data not available for 1999. The 2002 estimate is ten tons per year.
d The 1990 emissions estimate is a preliminary estimate and is based on back calculations and assumptions using data from 1999 along with information about types of processes, production rates and ores used in 1990 compared to 1999.
e Other includes, but is not limited to such items as, Portland cement production – 2.36 tons per year (tpy), pulp and paper production – 1.69 tpy, and over 219 miscellaneous industrial processes.
f One ton equals 0.9070 metric ton.

increased risk of poor performance on neurobehavioral tasks, such as those measuring attention, fine motor function, language skills, visual-spatial abilities and verbal memory, and will have lower IQs. The pathway from reduced mercury emissions to health outcomes is depicted in Figure 8.22 below.

Although mercury emissions have been sourced in many different processes, the continued emission of mercury from coal-fired power generating plants continues to be a problem. The need to address the problem of mercury emissions to air has generated environmental policy in both the EU and the United States, although the approaches once again are very different.

Policies to reduce emissions of Hg in Europe

Hg to the atmosphere is released during several stages of the lifecycle – during production as a point-source; during consumption as a non-point source; and during destruction (waste) as a point or non-point source depending on circumstance. Authorities in Europe and the United States have policies and regulations directed at each stage as well as the different sector sources of Hg emissions.

The international response to Hg emissions is set out in the 1998 Protocol on Heavy Metals. Besides requiring signatories to emit less than in 1990, the protocol provides detailed guidance based on BAT including dust-cleaning devices, "bio-treatment," fabric filters and scrubbers to reduce emissions, particularly focusing on the iron and steel industry, the non-ferrous metal industry, power generation, road transport and waste incineration. The Protocol also introduces measures to lower the mercury content in batteries, thermostats, switches, thermometers, fluorescent lamps, dental amalgam, pesticides and paint.

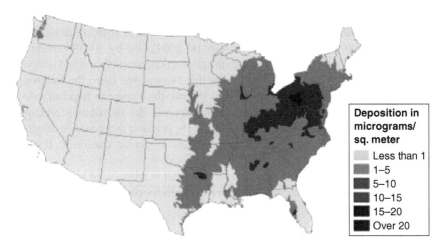

Figure 8.22 Mercury deposits from US power plants (2001) (source: EPA 2005; www. epa.gov/camr/pdfs/NationalDepositionMaps3.pdf).

The ECE (2006) makes reference to reports sent in by a sample of countries to show how they have responded to the protocol:

> Austria reported that mercury content was limited to 0.0005 percent in batteries and to 2 percent in button cells. Furthermore, capture of waste-water from dental surgeries was compulsory. In the Netherlands, the production and import of goods containing mercury has been banned since 2000. The use of products containing mercury was banned three years later (2003), except for fluorescent lamps, films and some specific professional products for which specific limits applied. In the Czech Republic, the Ministry of the Environment and Czech Dental Chamber signed a voluntary agreement in 2001 (the Czech association of drinking water and wastewater companies joined in 2004) to facilitate the removal of mercury from their clinics. By the end of 2004, more than half of the 6,500 dental clinics had installed mercury separators with above 95 percent efficiency rates for mercury removal. In 2002, 1.1 tonnes of dental amalgam waste containing mercury was collected and by 2003 this figure had risen to more than 34 tonnes. In the United Kingdom (UK), a burden-sharing scheme has been implemented by the crematoria industry to achieve a 50 percent reduction in mercury from gas emissions by 2012 as per the UK Pollution Prevention and Control Act of 1999. This scheme will allow greater choice to the industry in deciding how to meet the national 50 percent mercury emission reduction target. Operators will be able to meet the industry's target by either fitting abatement mechanisms, sharing the cost of abatement fitted by other crematoria (whether or not owned by the same operator) or a combination of both.

The OECD (2007) discusses the instrument mix addressing Hg to air in Norway, Sweden and the United States. Norway and Sweden are, in this context, fairly representative countries of Europe. Hg emissions in both countries have fallen since 1990, by 50 percent in Norway (to 2004), and by 50–55 percent or more in Sweden. Distinguishing between the production, consumption and destruction stages of the lifecycle, the report notes that Norway has taken the following actions toward Hg releases. First, Norway follows the European trend of using command-and-control in emission regulation. Second, the substitution principle offers a way of thinking consistently about the Hg problem that could be adopted elsewhere. Third, the take-back principle offers a similar consistent line of thought.

For Sweden, the OECD (2007) gives a table that is reproduced here as Table 8.7. Several intervention measures are the same in Sweden as in Norway, and indeed the whole of Europe.

Proposed cap-and-trade system for mercury in the United States

The OECD (2007) also reviews policies in the United States to limit emissions of Hg. Many policies are similar to those found in Europe and target dental amalgam waste, batteries, pesticides, paint, waste incineration and other source categories. However, as was pointed out above, it is coal-fired power plants that form the largest source of Hg emissions in the United States. In 2005, the US EPA announced a cap-and-trade system for Hg emissions from power plants. The system is closely modeled on the system for SO_2 emission trading. The announcement confirms the willingness in the United States to make use of market-based instruments and incentive regulation at the emission stage (as opposed to the energy stage). In this section, we examine the way in which the US EPA has proposed to use cap-and-trade in the management of Hg and what, if any, benefits there may be from this approach.

During the 1990s, the United States significantly reduced mercury emissions through the near elimination of medical waste incineration containing mercury and drastically reducing municipal waste combustion. As shown in Figure 8.23, emissions fell by 45 percent in 1990 and left mercury emitted from coal-fired power plants as the main source.

Despite the increased management of mercury within the United States, depositions of mercury remain a problem within the jurisdiction and one that is largely outside of its unilateral control. While the largest single source of mercury emissions in the United States is the US-based coal-fired electricity generation sector, the sector contributes only a small portion of total mercury deposits. This is so as mercury deposits come from a number of natural and human sources, from both inside and outside the United States. One of the problems with managing mercury depositions is the extent of this "background" pollution.

Mercury deposition is a management problem that is more like the "global pollutants" (such as CO_2) or the "regional pollutants" (such as SO_2). Most of the US emissions are not deposited in the country and, conversely, a significant portion of deposits in the United States are sourced from other countries. Over 60 percent of mercury deposits comes from other countries. Also, it is estimated that only 34 percent of US emissions are deposited locally. The other 66 percent contributes to the global pool of elemental mercury (Gayer and Hahn 2006).

The US anthropogenic emissions account for only 3–5 percent of total global emissions, with about one-third of these arising within the energy sector. Asia accounted for about 54 percent of global anthropogenic mercury emissions, followed by Africa who account for around 18 percent, and Europe who account for around 11 percent. The PRC is the largest anthropogenic emitter, producing more than 600 tons of mercury per year and contributing around 28 percent to the global emissions. Fossil-fuel electricity production is the largest source of mercury emissions in all continents. However, in the PRC, emissions from combustion of poor quality coal mixed with various

Table 8.7 Policies to address mercury emissions in Sweden

Year	Source	Major initiatives on mercury use in Sweden
1979	Dental releases	A voluntary agreement was made with dentists associations, requiring all dental clinics to be equipped with amalgam separators.
1979	Seed dressings	The use of mercury-containing seed dressings was banned (SFS 1979: 349).
1985	Biocides	Import, sale, transfer and use of mercury and mercury compounds as biocides were not approved (SFS 1985: 836).
1990	Goal setting – phase-out	Government Bill 1990: 91/90 proposed a numerous set of legislative and voluntary actions, with the ultimate aim of a total phase-out of mercury use.
1991	Dental amalgam	The overall goal of a phase-out of mercury also included dental amalgam, as a precautionary measure to minimize the exposure of these groups to metal mercury vapour. This led to a voluntary reduction of new amalgam fillings in children's teeth from 30 to 1.5 percent between 1991 and 1995. The use in adult's teeth decreased from 32 to 15 percent.
1992	Clinical thermometers	The import, professional manufacture and sale of clinical mercury thermometers were prohibited.
1993	Thermometers, measuring instruments and electrical equipment	Professional manufacture, import and sale of thermometers, level switches, pressure switches, thermostats, relays, electrical contacts and other measuring instruments were banned (Ordinance 1991: 1290). Some exemptions, mainly for spare parts, still exist. (Ordinance 1998: 944). Time-schedule for phase-out is stipulated for each exemption (Regulation 1998: 8).
1993	Goal setting – timing of phase-out	Government Bill 1993/94: 163 set a goal of phase-out of mercury and mercury-containing products by the year 2000. After that date, mercury should be offered for sale only in vital products and for uses to which no alternative techniques were known or fully developed.
1995	Dental amalgam	An agreement was reached between the state and the county councils that amalgam should be phased out of children's and young people's dentistry as a precautionary measure to minimise the exposure of these groups to metal mercury vapour.
1998	Batteries	The EU Battery Directive that also applies in Sweden was amended in 1998. Batteries with mercury content in excess of 0.0005 percent by weight are defined as dangerous for the environment and may not be marketed as such or incorporated into appliances. Button cells with a mercury content of no more than 2 percent by weight are exempted. The rules meant that mercury oxide batteries may no longer be sold – such batteries accounted for 700 of the 800 kg of mercury in batteries in 1997. The new rules led to a sharp reduction in sold quantities of mercury in batteries in 1999, the amount of mercury in batteries sold is estimated to approximately 100 kg.

Table 8.7 continued

Year	Source	Major initiatives on mercury use in Sweden
1998	Sewage sludge	In Ordinance 1998: 944 the contents of heavy metals in sewage was regulated in cases where sewage sludge was sold or conveyed for agricultural purposes. Regulations for when, where and how much sludge may be used in agriculture are found in SNFS 1994: 2 (changed SNFS 1998: 4). At present the maximum content of mercury allowed in sludge is 2.5 mg per kg dry matter and the maximum application is 1.5 g per hectare and year.
1997	Export of mercury	As of July 1, 1997 mercury and chemical compounds and preparations containing mercury may not be commercially exported from Sweden. Also, mercury-containing measuring instruments and electrical components may not be exported (Ordinance 1998: 944).
1999	Dental amalgam	Dental care compensation ceased to be paid for amalgam fillings, which made the cost for a composite filling and amalgam about the same for the patient. In 2003, amalgam was used for 0.05 percent of the fillings in children and young people and 1.8 percent of the fillings in adults in Sweden [see Keml (2004)].
2000	New products containing mercury	Bill 2000/01:65, Chemical Strategy for a Non-Toxic Environment requires that new goods put on the market should be, as far as possible, free from mercury by 2003, at the latest.
	Production processes	Also, mercury should not be used in production processes, unless the producer can prove that neither human health nor the environment would be harmed.
2006	All product uses and production processes	Proposal of a national general ban on the marketing and use of mercury and mercury-containing products, export and import. The proposal has been notified to the European Commission and to the WTO.

Sources: various, as stated in the table.

kinds of wastes in small residential units to produce heat and for cooking in rural areas produce an equivalent amount of mercury emissions as power generation.

As can be seen from Figure 8.25 below, Asian emissions increased by more than 50 percent in the five years between 1990 and 1995, then started to stabilize. Half of this increase was due to increases in the PRC's emissions. The primary reason for the large increase was due to the increased demand for electricity and heat, mostly based on coal combustion. The stabilization is in part due to anti-pollution technology used in new power plants in the PRC. However, emissions are still growing from small residential furnaces used to burn coal for heat and cooking. During 1990 to 2000, emissions also increased in Africa, South America and Australia mainly due to increased populations, increases in

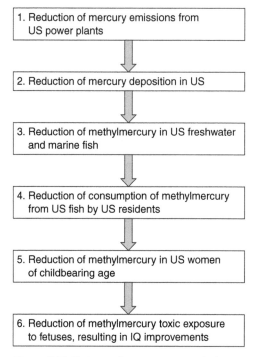

Figure 8.23 Pathway from mercury emissions to health outcomes (source: Geyer and Hahn 2006: 303).

demand for electricity fired by coal, and the increased use of mercury in gold mining. A continuous decrease of Hg emissions in Europe since the 1980s is due mainly to the installation of emission control equipment in Western Europe and a change from coal to oil/gas for energy production in several countries. Similar trends are observed for North America.

For these reasons, some sort of coordinated action on mercury will be necessary for its efficient management. As in the case of SO_2 management, the management regime must span the entire set of jurisdictions that share the problem. In European SO_2 management, this required the establishment of several international protocols that coordinated management efforts and systems. The problem of mercury appears to require a similar sort of approach on account of the shared nature of the problem. At some point in the future, it will be necessary to join all of the above regions in addressing this common problem. Any individual state acting unilaterally must necessarily be addressing its own problems with mercury in a very partial manner.

Irrespective of the need for coordinated action, the United States has proceeded to regulate mercury emissions on a national basis. It is notable that it has proposed a very different approach to the one that has been adopted in the EU,

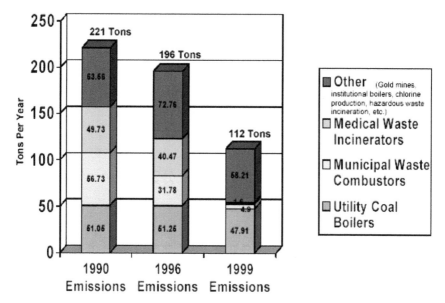

Figure 8.24 Drop in mercury emissions from human sources (1990–9) (source: EPA 2008; www.epa.gov/camr/pdfs/slide1.pdf).

once again advocating the importance of cost-effectiveness in the control methodology. On December 15, 2003, the EPA proposed two mutually exclusive options for regulating mercury emissions from electric utilities. The first option proposed establishing uniform limitations on mercury emission rates across utilities, based on the type of coal the utilities use. This standard is known as the "maximum achievable control technology" (MACT). It is a standard sort of command-and-control approach to controlling the level of mercury emissions from US power plants.

The EPA also proposed a possible cap-and-trade system that would apply initially to new plants and then be expanded to others. This system would place a "cap" on national mercury emissions from power generation, and then issue permits corresponding to that cap. It would be required of emitters that they either be issued a permit, or acquire one from another power generator that will not be used (or has gone unused, and been "banked"). The proposed cap-and-trade system would occur in two phases. In the first phase scheduled to commence in 2010, utility mercury emissions are capped at approximately 34 tons per year. The second phase of the mercury cap-and-trade program, scheduled for 2018, caps utility mercury emissions at 15 tons per year.

As in the discussion of the cap-and-trade scheme applied to SO_2 above, the role of a trading system is to enable the firms in the industry to cooperate in attaining the national standard. Under such a system, they may allocate the burden across the industry in any way that they see as most cost-effective, so long as the aggregate standard is met. The costs of standard attainment falls by a

Table 8.8 Global anthropogenic mercury emissions (2000) (in tons)

Continent	Stationary combustion	Cement production	Non-ferrous metal production	Pig-iron and steel production	Caustic soda production	Mercury production	Gold production	Waste disposal	Other	Total
Africa	205.2	5.3	7.9	0.4	0.3	0.1	177.8		1.4	398.4
Asia (excl. Russia)	878.7	89.9	87.6	11.6	30.7	0.1	47.2	32.6	0.9	1,179.3
Australasia	112.6	0.8	4.4	0.3	0.7		7.7	0.1		126.6
Europe (excl. Russia)	88.8	26.5	10.0	10.6	12.4			11.5	15.3	175.1
Russia	26.5	3.7	6.9	2.7	8.0		3.1	3.5	18.2	72.6
South America	31.0	6.5	25.4	1.4	5.0	22.8				92.1
North America	79.6	7.7	6.4	4.3	8.0	0.1	12.2	18.7	8.8	145.8
Total	1,422.4	140.4	148.6	31.3	65.1	23.1	248.0	66.4	44.6	2,189.9

Source: Pacyna et al. (2006: 4052).

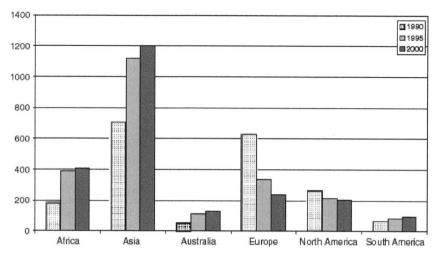

Figure 8.25 Changes in anthropogenic mercury emissions (1990–2000) (source: Pacyna *et al.* 2006: 4057).

factor of 4–8, depending upon the assumptions used in evaluating the system. This is illustrative of the cost-effectiveness attained by allowing industry to cooperate in meeting imposed standards.

Conclusion – international experiences in air management

It is remarkable that although both Europe and the United States have managed to reduce emissions of SO_2 and other local air pollutants as well as mercury, they have approached the problem in opposite ways: Europe relies on incentive-based regulation of energy and command-and-control of the pollutants. The United States relies on command-and-control of energy and (mainly) incentive-based regulation of the pollutants. Equally remarkable, each is proud of its economic regulation, the ETS system in Europe and the SO_2-emission trading in the United States.

The main conclusion for us to draw is that command-and-control and economic incentives both work. They are both able to obtain the desired emission reductions if appropriately strict. The exception to this conclusion could be energy consumption in the United States, but there the problem is that emission limits and fuel economy standards, which are the typical command-and-control measures, are not sufficiently strict.

It is sometimes claimed that a precondition for economic regulation, such as emission trading, to work is that emissions must be thoroughly monitored. That is true. The idea that one must pay for emissions will encourage cheating in the form of unreported emissions. For this reason, the SO_2-trading scheme of the

Table 8.9 Present value costs of MACT and cap-and-trade (2005–20) (in billions of 2004 dollars)

Discount rate (%)	Using Model 1 estimates		Using Model 2 estimates	
	MACT costs	Cap-and-trade costs	MACT costs	Cap-and-trade costs
3	$23.2	$3.3	$20.7	$5.5
5	$19.5	$2.7	$17.8	$4.3
7	$16.5	$2.3	$15.4	$3.4

Source: Gayer and Hahn (2006: 300).

Notes
These costs are computed by using the cost estimates from Charles River Associates, EPA, and the Clean Air Task Force listed in Tables 8.1 and 8.2. Cost figures represent incremental costs compared to a baseline scenario that assumes the Clean Air Interstate Rule is in effect. We computed the present value of the sum of these annual costs, summing from 2005 to 2020, and we converted to 2004 dollars.

United States requires units to install continuous monitoring of emissions. Fines and penalties for units that are caught cheating are also necessary in an emission trading scheme.

However, monitoring for violations and penalties are equally necessary in a command-and-control scheme. Command-and-control in the form of an emission standard or a best-available technology requires companies to take on some costs of end-of-pipe abatement and appropriate technology that they would rather not take on. This gives a company under command-and-control exactly the same marginal incentives to cheat as a company under incentive-based regulation. If anything, the marginal incentives to cheat are higher under command-and-control since compliance costs are higher in this case. Not only in the United States but also in Europe, continuous monitoring is an integral part of the system both on the energy side and on the emission side. On the energy side, every gasoline station is for instance required to have a meter surveying how much gasoline is sold and, by implication, how much tax should be paid. The meter is sealed with state-of-the-art technology and the penalty for breaking the seal is high. Similarly, on the side of emissions, a large apparatus of monitoring and surveillance makes sure that emissions are reported correctly. Sometimes, when continuous monitoring is considered too expensive, firms are given the choice between evaluation based on monitoring and evaluation based on default emission factors. Firms are then able to choose the monitoring scheme that is to their favor. This seems an advantage for the firm, but it is also an advantage for the regulator since the choice reveals characteristics of the firm. The regulator may then use the information about characteristics when regulation is designed.

Perhaps it is the deficiencies in monitoring and enforcement that traditionally have been the biggest problems in the PRC system. It has been described how local Environmental Protection Bureaus (EPBs) are sometimes caught between vertical pressure from the Ministry of Environmental Protection (MEP) to enforce pollution regulation rigorously and horizontal pressure from provincial and local governments to enforce environmental regulations flexibly (World Bank 2001). It is also known that emission levies are not always collected as intended if the perceived costs are high on companies. Without appropriate monitoring and enforcement, neither command-and-control nor incentive-based systems will work.

It is also noteworthy that, while both Europe and the United States combine command-and-control and incentive-based regulation, the PRC almost entirely relies on command-and-control. Sometimes economic incentives actually encourage higher emissions. In the energy field, important command-and-control measures in the PRC include the Action Plan for energy conservation in 1,000 large industrial enterprises, and the policy to close small, inefficient power plants. (See State Council (2008: Section IV) for current policies.) Reductions in transport emissions are attempted via strict emission standards in Beijing and elsewhere. Meanwhile, electricity prices are subject to negotiations between the provincial power bureaus and the electricity generation companies. Lately, the generation companies have not been allowed to increase their prices on par with increased prices of coal. This amounts to a subsidy of electricity consumption. Not only that, it also encourages generation companies to cut costs and cut corners by looking for cheap coal supplies (Steinfeld *et al.* 2008). Cheap coal means low quality coal that is high in sulfur and impurities. These incentives are counterproductive to emission control and make the task of emission reduction harder. Gasoline offers a similar story: for fear of protest from, e.g. taxi drivers, gasoline prices have not been allowed to increase on par with oil prices. Inflationary pressure has been cited as another reason. This amounts to a subsidy to private transportation. In fact, the government of the PRC has recently reimbursed oil refineries' value-added tax (VAT) in order to cover some of their losses. The taxi drivers, in turn, are regulated with respect to the fare they are allowed to charge. Even taxi fares are in effect subsidized.

The PRC's SO_2-control policy also relies on command-and-control. To cope with cost and effect differences, the command-and-control policy is very detailed. Emission standards are differentiated according to size, age, region, etc. There is a requirement that all power plants should install FGDs, but again there are exceptions. If you are a mine-mouth plant in a western region burning coal of less than 0.3 percent sulfur, you do not after all need to install an FGD. These are burdensome ways of handling the inherent inflexibility of the command-and-control system. There are some economic incentives as well, including a RMB0.6 per kilogram (kg) SO_2 emission levy and a feed-in tariff of RMB0.15 per kWh to power plants with FGD installed. However, the feed-in tariff does not specify that the FGD should be operated, and a recent survey found that only half of FGD units were in fact operated (National Development and Reform Committee (NDRC) 2006). The failure to operate FGDs points back to the monitoring and enforcement aspect. The command-and-control fashion of regulation is not by itself an impediment to meeting environmental goals. It just makes it more expensive, especially when economic incentives run in the opposite direction.

The lessons from the developed world on air management are three. First, air pollution management is possible. Most regions of the developed world have vastly improved air quality over what was deemed possible 20 or 30 years ago. Second, both command-and-control and economic incentives are feasible approaches to effective regulation. The EU has relied primarily on the former, and the United States primarily on the latter, but both have been equally effective. The benefits of the economic approach lie not in effectiveness but in cost-effectiveness, especially the reduction of the costs of abatement and the creation of new abatement approaches and technologies. The costs of the economic approach lie in the differences across communities that they must gloss over, and this may result in significant increases in deposition costs or "hotspots." To date, this has not been seen to be a large problem in the United States, although there is nothing within the regulatory regimes that would prevent it from occurring. Finally, the case studies demonstrate the importance of regulation occurring at the appropriate scale: local, regional, national, international. Problems in the atmosphere do not stop at boundaries, and cooperation and coordination are often necessary to get the best outcomes.

Notes

1 Thirty-five percent compounded over 14 years.
2 RAINS is a tool for analyzing alternative strategies to reduce acidification, eutrophication and ground-level ozone. The RAINS model is the outcome of a multi-year scientific effort of an interdisciplinary and international team of researchers at IIASA.
3 In the course of a few months in 2008 the dollar equivalent of European gasoline prices has fluctuated between 1.5 and 3. The reason is of course the sharp volatilities in both the price of oil and in the euro/USD exchange rate.
4 http://ec.europa.eu/environment/air/quality/legislation/directive.htm.
5 http://ec.europa.eu/environment/air/quality/standards.htm.

References

(All Internet links accessed July 2008)

Axelrad, D.A., D.C. Bellinger, L.C. Ryan and T.J. Woodruff (2007) "Dose–Response Relationship of Prenatal Mercury Exposure and IQ: An Integrative Analysis of Epidemiologic Data," *Environmental Health Perspectives*, 115, 4, 609–15.

Banzhaf, H.S., D. Burtraw and K. Palmer (2004) "Efficient Emission Fees in the US Electricity Sector," *Resource and Energy Economics*, 26, 317–41.

Burtraw, D. and K. Palmer (2004) "SO$_2$ Cap-and-Trade Program in the United States: A Living Legend of Market Effectiveness," in *Choosing Environmental Policy: Comparing Instruments and Outcomes in the United States and Europe*, Winston Harrington, Richard D. Morgenstern and Thomas Sterner (eds.). RFF Press.

Burtraw, D. and K. Palmer (2005) "Cost-effectiveness of Renewable Electricity Policies," *Energy Economics*, 27, 6, 873–94.

Burtraw, D., D.A. Evans, A. Krupnick, K. Palmer and R. Toth (2005) "Economics of Pollution Trading for SO_2 and NO_x," *Annual Review of Environment and Resources*, 30, 253–89.

Chestnut, L.G. and D.M. Mills (2005) "A Fresh Look at the Benefits and Costs of the US Acid Rain Program," *Journal of Environmental Management*, 77, 252–66.

ECE (2006) *Strategies and Policies for Air Pollution Abatement. Review 2006*. Economic Commission for Europe.

Economist, The (2008) "German Lessons," *The Economist*, April 3. Online, available at: www.economist.com/business/displaystory.cfm?story_id=10961890.

EEA (2007) *Air Pollution in Europe 1990–2004*, EEA Report 2007/2, European Environmental Agency, Copenhagen.

Environmental Protection Agency (EPA) (2007) *2007, Acid Rain and Related Programs: 2006 Progress Report*, Washington, DC.

Grossman, G.M. and A.B. Krueger (1995) "Economic Growth and the Environment," *Quarterly Journal of Economics*, 110, 353–77.

Kolstad, C.D. (2000) *Environmental Economics*, Oxford: Oxford University Press.

Menz, F.C. and H.M. Seip (2004) "Acid Rain in the United States and Europe: An Update," *Environmental Science and Policy*, 7, 253–65.

Napolitano, S., J. Schreifels, G. Stevens, M. Witt, M. La Count, R. Forte and K. Smith (2007) "The U.S. Acid Rain Program: Key Insights from the Design, Operation and Assessment of a Cap-and-trade Program," *The Electricity Journal*, 7, 47–58.

NDRC (2006) *The Current Situation of FGD at Coal-fired Power Plant in China and Suggestions* (in Chinese), September 4. Online, available at: www.ndrc.gov.cn/hjbh/huanjing/t20060904_82826.htm.

OECD (2007) *Instrument Mixes Addressing Mercury Emissions to Air*, ENV/EPOC/WPNEP(2006)8/FINAL, OECD, Paris.

Pacyna, E.G., J.M. Pacyna, J. Fudala, E. Strzelecka-Jastrzab, S. Hlawiczka and D. Panasiuk (2006) "Mercury Emissions to the Atmosphere from Anthropogenic Sources in Europe in 2000 and their Scenarios until 2020," *STOTEN 370*, 147–56.

Pacyna, J.M., E.G. Pacyna, F. Steenhuisen and S. Wilson (2007) "Global Anthropogenic Emissions of Mercury to the Atmosphere," in *Encyclopedia of Earth*, C.J. Cleveland (ed.). Washington, DC: Environmental Coalition, National Council for Science and the Environment.

State Council (2008) *White Paper: China's Policies and Actions on Climate Change*. Online, available at: www.chinadaily.com.cn/china/2008-10/29/content_7153800.htm.

Steinfeld, E.S., R.K. Lester and E.A. Cunningham (2008) "Greener Plants, Greyer Skies? A Report from the Frontlines of China's Energy Sector," Working Paper 08–003, China Energy Group, MIT Industrial Performance Center. Online, available at: http://web.mit.edu/ipc/publications/pdf/08-003.pdf.

US EPA (2006) *EPA's Roadmap for Mercury*, July, US EPA, USA. Online, available at: www.epa.gov/mercury/roadmap.htm.

US EPA (2007) *National Emission Inventory Air Pollutant Emission Trend Data*. Online, available at: www.epa.gov/ttn/chief/trends/index.html.

Vennemo, H. and Q. Yan (2008) "Co-benefits of Mercury Control in Guizhou Province," *mimeo*, Econ Pöyry, Oslo.

Vennemo, H., K. Aunan, H. Lindhjem and H.M. Seip (2009) "Walking the Line – Environmental Pollution Trends in China," *mimeo*, Econ Pöyry, Oslo.

Vestreng, V., G. Myhre, H. Fagerli, S. Reis and L. Tarrasón (2007) "Twenty-five Years of Continuous Sulfur Dioxide Emission Reduction in Europe," *Atmospheric Chemistry and Physics*, 7, 3663–81.

World Bank (1997) *A Planner's Guide for Selecting Clean-Coal Technologies for Power Plants*, Washington, DC: World Bank.

World Bank (2001) *China – Air, Land, Water*, Washington, DC: World Bank.

9 International experience to inform the People's Republic of China's water pollution and water resource management policy

Ben Groom

Introduction

Although the People's Republic of China (PRC) has sustained an average of 10 percent annual economic growth between 1978 and 2006, it had been clear for some time that this has come at the expense of environmental integrity. Water pollution and water scarcity are perhaps the most pervasive problems that have emerged, ranging from point-source municipal and industrial pollution to non-point agricultural pollution. Pollution accidents and environmental disasters, such as the benzene spill which contaminated the Songhua River in 2005 leading to the temporary loss of drinking water in downstream Harbin, and the toxic algal blooms which affected Lake Tai in 2007, are high profile, albeit extreme, examples of a general trend in the state of the aquatic environment in the PRC. These trends in water quality and environmental accidents, of which there are over 500 every year, are the consequences not only of the underlying technologies employed in the PRC, but also the inadequacies of the current institutional structure and policy environment and associated weaknesses in the regulation of industrial and agricultural water pollution (Palmer 2007; Woo 2007).

Water shortages are also extremely common in parts of the PRC and are widely regarded to represent an important constraint to economic development. At present, the PRC uses around 70 percent of its available water resources and around 400 of the PRC's 660 cities face water shortages (Woo 2007; Economy 2007). In the north of the PRC, in particular, this has led to the unsustainable mining of groundwater with all the attendant problems of land subsidence. Similarly, water resource management in the PRC is undertaken within an institutional framework which evolved during a time when the development of water resources, rather than their efficient allocation or conservation, was the primary objective (Maria Saleth and Dinar 2006; Woo 2007). The tendency remains to approach water resource scarcity from the perspective of supply augmentation rather than demand management, as evidenced by the advance of the recent south–north conveyor project in parallel with continued subsidies for water consumption to industry, agriculture and households, and major losses from reticulation systems (Tsur and Dinar 1995; Cook 2007).

The importance of the environment and environmental damage was recognized in the aftermath of the Environmental Protection Law of 1979, during which time economic reforms followed a policy of "coordinated development" (*xietiao fazhan*). This policy emphasized the need for a balance between economic growth and the environment. Nevertheless, the policy did not stress the needs of future generations nor their rights to environmental quality, and focused more on economic growth and the reduction of poverty (Palmer 2007). It was in the early 1990s that the notion of "sustainable development" (*chixu fazhan*) entered into the parlance of economic development policy reforms. More recently, and in light of emerging environmental constraints, at the 2006 Plenum of the Chinese Communist Party, the Hu-Wen leadership announced that the chief task of development policy was the establishment of a "harmonious society" (*héxié shèhuì*) whose objectives include the establishment of a society in which humans live in harmony with nature (Woo 2007). Despite previous references to environment and sustainable development, this announcement was widely seen as a turning point in the PRC's development policy.

Nevertheless, the institutions, policies and legislation underpinning the regulation of water pollution and water resource management, while ostensibly strong and coherent, appear to have been extremely slow to reverse the worsening trends in water quality and water scarcity of recent decades. In short, the PRC has found it difficult to decouple economic growth from environmental degradation in the manner that appears to have happened in many developed countries. While the reasons for this are numerous, perhaps the chief problem is a regulatory institutional structure that is unable to enforce central policies for water pollution control at the local level (Woo 2007; Wu 2008). For instance, the dependence of the Ministry of Environmental Protection's (MEP) implementing agencies, the Environmental Protection Bureaus (EPBs) and Environmental Protection Offices (EPOs), on funding from local government and pollution taxes and fines places these bodies at the mercy of local governments whose objectives are almost always to enhance growth, while making them dependent upon, and partially therefore legitimizing, polluters (Palmer 2007; Wu 2008). This is compounded by lack of coordination between different governmental institutions responsible for different aspects (e.g. spatial, sectoral) of water pollution and water resource management. The continued lack of coordination between the MEP and the Ministry of Water Resources (MWR) and their implementing agencies is one example, as is the ill-defined jurisdiction of the River Basin Commissions (RBCs), and hence their inability to deal successfully with cross-boundary pollution and water allocation issues (MacMahon 2005).

The PRC's macro-environmental policy is the most recent movement to address the important and often puzzling link between economic growth and the environment. *Inter alia*, the development of this policy has sparked a renewed interest in the broader questions surrounding water resource management, water pollution and economic development, such as: what do we know about the relationship between economic development, water resources and water pollution? Does environmental policy in the water sector necessarily inhibit economic growth? What can be learned from international experience, both successes and failures, in the water sector? This chapter draws from international experience to provide some answers to these questions in the context of the issues currently facing the PRC.

Macro-perspectives on water resource management

Income–environmental relationships

The relationship between environmental resource use and economic development is often captured in an empirical Income Emission Relationship (IER). The most frequently cited IER is the Environmental Kuznets Curve (EKC): an inverted U-shaped relationship between income level and measures of environmental damage. In the past, economists and policy-makers have been tempted to interpret empirical evidence of an EKC as a sign that economic growth alone will remedy environmental degradation over time. There are at least two problems with this. First, the empirical evidence varies across pollutants and countries and has been fraught with technical difficulties (Stern 2004). Second, close inspection of the relationship between economic development and environment makes clear that IERs are determined via *inter alia* changes in the **composition, technique and scale** of the economy by complicated interactions between the underlying institutions, policies, political economy and individual preferences. In short, IERs are not necessarily good predictors of the future. There is no guarantee that growth will improve environmental quality, and governments have an important role to play in determining the IER. IERs do not have the status of a physical law but are rather dependent on economic and environmental policy responses superimposed on the economic environment (Stern 2004; Copeland and Taylor 2004).

Water quantity, water quality, growth and income

The availability of **water quantity** is widely seen as an emerging constraint to growth and development. Cross-country analysis of this constraint suggests that low-growth countries either have failed to develop their water resources, or are approaching domestic water constraints. High-income countries have moderate water use intensity. These findings suggest that water scarcity has an important influence on growth (Barbier 2006: 242). At the country level, the extent of the constraint will depend on transboundary resources, the spatial distribution of water resources, ecological services and specific sectoral constraints (e.g. in agriculture). Recent research has shown that there are no hard and fast rules for IERs for water withdrawals. Much depends on the scale and composition of the economy and, in particular, the composition of trade relative to endowments of water resources (Gleick *et al.* 2006).

In the PRC, water scarcity is widely understood to be one of the most important constraints to economic growth. As described above, two-thirds of the more than 600 cities in the PRC are described as water scarce, 100 of these acutely so.

Up to 70 percent of the total renewable water resources are currently being exploited, and groundwater is being unsustainably exploited in many areas (Economy 2004). By these measures, if we take Barbier's (2006) analysis literally and assume that all countries have the same relationship between growth and water scarcity, long-run economic growth in the PRC may well be inhibited by scarcity of water resources as the country approaches the resource constraint.

The relationship between economic growth and **water quality** is another important IER and a great deal of research has been undertaken to understand its determinants. Estimates of the IER for water quality also vary across pollutants, sectors and countries. A regional analysis of the PRC shows a strong negative IER between income and industrial wastewater due to a composition effect: the richer regions have specialized in light, export-oriented industries. Also, foreign direct investment has introduced newer technologies, and public preferences shaped policy (De Groot *et al.* 2004). However, it is doubtful that rich and poor regions are on the same development path due to different economic compositions and unequally enforced environmental standards. Poor regions need not exhibit the same IER.

EKCs have been found for chemical oxygen demand (COD), arsenic (AS) and cadmium (Shen 2006). One channel for this was the policy response to municipal pollution in the 1990s by the PRC government which induced a *technique effect*: a 40 percentage point increase in wastewater treatment (Vennemo *et al.* 2008). Another is the changing proportion of secondary industry: the *composition effect*. However, the turning points are at relatively high income levels and often at high levels of pollution (see Figure 9.1). A deeper analysis shows that most regions are currently on the upward portion and, putting empirical issues aside and assuming that each region follows the same path over time, the results suggest that pollution levels in most regions will get worse before they get better.

While more recent analyses have looked at a wider range of pollutants and found similar patterns, many important pollutants have been ignored to date (Song *et al.* 2008). The so-called "new toxics," such as carcinogenic chlorine compounds (e.g. polychlorinated biphenyls (PCBs)) and carbon dioxide (CO_2) have been widely shown to have a positive IER, that is they increase with income (Stern 2004; Dasgupta *et al.* 2002). The new toxics are often associated with some of the more advanced industries that tend to occupy developed countries, and for this reason it might be expected that these toxins become more prevalent with economic growth over time. However, the main point is that these toxins are frequently monitored and regulated in developed countries, but frequently overlooked in developing countries and not regulated (Dasgupta *et al.* 2002). The fear is that economic development will always generate new pollutants and risks. Such pollutants are only reduced by the counteracting forces of sustained technological change and more rigorous standards. The prospect of "new toxics" sounds a cautionary note for the PRC (Dasgupta *et al.* 2002).

Last, just as for water quantity, there are good reasons to suspect that the patterns observed in developed countries will not be exhibited in developing countries in the future. One of the main channels through which developing countries were able to decouple water pollution and scarcity (indeed, environmental deg-

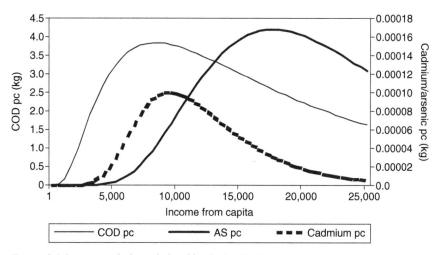

Figure 9.1 Income emission relationships in the PRC (source: author's calculations, from Shen 2006).

radation in general) from economic growth was via trade and the movement of "dirty" industries overseas. This option is no longer available for many developing countries, and the PRC is no exception. This only goes to emphasize the importance of environmental policy in achieving sustainable development and a harmonious society.

In summary, the reasons for the observed declining IERs are numerous, interlinked and complicated. Growth alone will not induce water quality improvements and ameliorate water scarcity. Water institutions and water policy will be important determinants. The lesson of the IER and EKC literature is that we cannot have our cake and eat it too (Stern 2004).

International experience in water management

The aim of water policy is to ensure efficient allocation of limited water resources between competing economic sectors and the environment, while ensuring water quality is maintained at low cost. Water policy is increasingly concerned with the distributional effects of water constraints. The overall aim is to limit the impact of water resource constraints and pollution control policy on economic growth and well-being. International experience provides numerous lessons in this regard. We first summarize general experience in water policy and then turn to three specific case studies.

Water quantity

Water pricing should, in principle, reflect the full economic cost. By providing information to consumers on the cost and scarcity of water, water pricing allocates scarce water between competing uses more efficiently. This can limit the impact of environmental constraints on economic activity. Water pricing influences water consumption decisions, such as investment in water-saving technologies in industry, more efficient irrigation technology as well as crop choice (Briscoe 1996; Moore *et al.* 1994). Water pricing provides finance for maintaining reliable supply. Indeed, water pricing policy should reflect the desired policy goals – e.g. allocation, revenue sufficiency, prevention of shortages and conservation (Horbulyk 2005).

In practice, full cost pricing of water is far from universal. That is, water is subsidized leading to excessive consumption, particularly in agriculture (Dinar and Subramanian 1998). Volumetric pricing is also infrequent. Water in irrigated agriculture is frequently priced on the basis of area cultivated. While residential and industrial water is sometimes charged volumetrically, fixed charges are more common. This reflects, *inter alia*, the political economy of water reforms: governments are reluctant to embark on water pricing reforms because of their large welfare effects. Historically, low prices as well as rising incomes have increased demand and caused scarcity and drought in the PRC. Volumetric water pricing has been successful throughout the world in managing demand for water, improving efficiency and financing supply. Although water is in general effectively subsidized in the PRC, there is some evidence that farmers who irrigate actually bear a substantial proportion of the supply cost already, and hence efficiency gains can only really be made through improved applications (Webber *et al.* forthcoming).

Objections to water pricing arise on distributional grounds since poor households/farmers are affected disproportionately by price increases. To combat this, subsidies are often used. Recent analysis shows that quantity-based subsidies such as IBTs are in fact *regressive* in many cases, and often exclude the poor completely (Groom *et al.* 2008). Consideration should be given to alternative pricing strategies such as payment rebates, "end user" schemes, or connection subsidies which help extend service provision to poor households (Fankhauser and Tepic 2005).

Water markets can also allocate scarce water supplies between competing users, leading to efficient water use and limiting the impact of environmental constraints on economic activity. Formal water markets require well-defined water rights, ideally separated from land rights. Water markets decentralize water allocation and are informationally less unwieldy than centralized allocations or pricing. Also, water markets can strengthen and formalize rights and are responsive to changing economic circumstances – e.g. crop prices and seasonal water scarcity – yet require institutions to monitor trades and limit third-party effects (Hearne and Easter 1995).

Successful water markets can be found in many arid countries. In the United States, formal and informal trading of water rights along the Colorado River has occurred for years. Trade has occurred between users within and between sectors with large gains from trade – in 2002, water supplied to urban areas sold for US$0.35 per cubic meter (m^3) compared to US$0.011 per m^3 for irrigation (Mohanty and Gupta 2002). Trades are monitored and agreed by the state.

Water markets have a long history in Chile where water rights changed from being centrally allocated, state-owned and non-transferable, to being fully privatized, separate from land and tradable. As well as individual trades between irrigators and sectors, auctions for water rights are overseen by the government. Water trades have lead to a more efficient allocation of water, especially in water scarce areas (e.g. Hearne and Easter 1997). Demand for water has expanded with economic growth, and now 20 percent of water needs are met by water trading (Hearne and Donoso 2005). The success of the Chilean Water Code stems from the security of rights that it has provided water users.

Water markets have limitations however. In both the United States and Chile there is evidence of adverse distributional and environmental consequences arising from the unfettered trade in water rights (Hearne and Easter 1995). Trading has been limited by speculative behavior (Bauer 1997 and 2004), while ill-defined user rights (e.g. absence of requirements to approve changes in water uses) have led to adverse third-party consequences. The overall message is clear: successful water markets need to be mindful of the institutional and practical requirements as well as the distributional effects of this allocation mechanism.

In recent years, the PRC has undertaken a number of inter-city, inter-sectoral and intra-sectoral water trades. In 2000, the city of Yiwu, in Zhejiang province, paid RMB200 million to the city of Dongyang to secure 50 million m^3 of drinking water per annum. In 2006, the Beijing water authority paid RMB20 million to the neighboring province of Hebei and purchased water from both Hebei and Shanxi province. More recently, Tongliang county water authority in Chongqing, south-west PRC, sold water rights to industry. In February of 2008, a new interim measure for water quantity allocation was promulgated by the MWR for the purpose of facilitating water markets and further trades.[1] The PRC seems to have recognized the gains from trade that such markets can enable in times of scarcity.

Water quality

International experience with the regulation of water quality is also extremely varied. Market-based instruments (MBIs) include pollution taxes and tradable pollution permits. User fees also play an important role in financing water and sewerage treatment. MBIs can check the social costs of pollution efficiently compared to command-and-control regulation. Nevertheless, mixtures of instruments have proven successful, especially in trying to combat non-point source pollution.

Pollution taxes should reflect the full economic cost of the marginal unit of pollution. Similarly, **wastewater treatment user fees** should reflect the economic cost of treatment. International experience shows that pollution taxes have been levied in order to generate revenue rather than induce a behavioral response from polluters. In Europe and the PRC, taxes and charges are set at low levels. In France, Germany and the United Kingdom, taxes are approximately one half the level of measurable social damages (Boyd 2003). For many years in the

PRC, pollution taxes only applied to emissions in excess of the standard, thereby providing no incentives for reductions below the standard. They are also not well-enforced and often were negotiated between the firm and the local government to a level acceptable to the former (see, for example, Wu 2008). For these reasons, they have historically provided little incentive for abatement, and this is unlikely to change even though pollution charges are now applied to total emissions (Pei Xiaofeng 2008, personal comment).

For similar reasons pollution taxes were unsuccessful in reducing emissions in Europe for many years. The Netherlands provides a good example of the successful implementation of pollution taxes where pollution fees levied on biochemical oxygen demand (BOD) and heavy metals are higher, have increased over time in real terms, and have reduced effluent flows and industrial pollution by 70 percent between 1976 and 1996 (Organization for Economic Co-operation and Development (OECD) 2007; Boyd 2003). Pollution taxes are appealing since they are administered by existing taxation frameworks and regulatory bodies. However, they have also been employed successfully in countries with weak regulatory bureaucracies. For instance, via a system of pollution charges for BOD and toxic shock syndrome (TSS), Colombia managed to reduce pollution loads by 28 percent, despite weak regulatory agencies and strong economic growth. Pollution charges were periodically increased until pollution reduction targets were met (Sterner 2003).

Alongside pollution charges, the Netherlands employed the principle of full cost recovery for users of wastewater treatment. This was far more effective and required less investment than the "end-of-pipe" technology standards employed in nearby Denmark. Canada provides an example of bad practice where subsidized water treatment led to a drastic deterioration of drinking water quality due to lack of funding. Increased scope and level of pollution taxes is required to make the existing pollution pricing strategy successful. Recent improvements in wastewater treatment in the PRC can be financially sustainable if user fees are increased from currently low levels.

International experience shows that industry tends to lobby against pollution taxes and other environmental charges. Resistance can be diffused by adapting economic instruments. **Refunded Emissions Payments (REP)**, which refund taxes to firms in a manner which does not affect the incentive to reduce pollution levels, are a good example. They have been employed successfully in Sweden and have reduced the need for industry to lobby for weak targets (Sterner 2003). The PRC employs a similar system, and yet the patchy enforcement and low taxes translated to lesser success.

Non-point source pollution is pervasive in the PRC, and has proven difficult to regulate the world over. The US Environmental Protection Agency (EPA) claims that non-point source (NPS) is the last remaining pollution problem in the United States. International experience suggests that NPS can be addressed by a mixture of instruments. Denmark, the Netherlands and the UK have all employed mixed strategies to comply with the various pollution directives of the European Union (EU). The Netherlands employed command-and-control standards, such as a quota on animals per hectare, employed alongside large fees for excess emissions. Furthermore, emissions and applications standards were gradually increased in stringency over time. Using mixtures of instruments to address complicated issues such as NPS has been successful in reducing NPS in many countries in Europe.

In selecting the appropriate instrument, or mixture thereof, a trade-off exists between determining the extent and certainty of the environmental outcome and the costs of implementation in terms of monitoring, enforcement and political economy. International experience shows that this trade-off is resolved in many different ways.

Tradable pollution permits represent an alternative market-based instrument for regulating water pollution. First, a property right must be defined – the pollution permits, which give the holder the right to pollute the environment in a predefined manner. These rights are limited in number to some aggregate target or "Cap," e.g. for emissions. By setting up a market for these rights, firms, factories and municipalities, for whom reducing emissions is costly, will purchase permits from those who can abate pollution at low cost. This process decentralizes the allocation of emissions between firms, and leaves the role of monitoring and enforcement to the government authority.

The success of such schemes depends upon how well the market functions and the institutional capacity to monitor and enforce property rights. Well-functioning schemes benefit from being cost effective and inducing efficiency gains over time. Permits can be auctioned to raise revenue, or distributed on the basis of historical use to reduce resistance from industry. In the United States, pollution trading schemes exist for BOD, COD and nutrients (N and P), and, in recent years, non-point sources have started to participate. In Australia, several schemes exist, including one for salt. In each case, success has varied inversely with the rigidities in the market. For example, thin markets prevented the US Fox River scheme from operating efficiently, while the Hawkesbury–Nepean River (HNR) scheme in Australia is expected to afford costs savings in the order of US$50 million (37 percent) in the long run among three participating treatment works (Kraemer *et al.* 2003).

In the PRC, pollution trading schemes have been proposed for the Upper Nanpan River (Tao *et al.* 2000) and, more recently, for polluters around Lake Taihu, both for COD. Trading schemes offer a means by which total emissions can be regulated efficiently. This is a departure from the historical focus on concentrations in the PRC.

International experience suggests that successful pollution trading schemes have had the following features:

1   clearly defined property rights;
2   clear protocol for trading;
3   a competitive market with many participants;
4   information provision;
5   strong institutions for monitoring, enforcement and conflict resolution.

For this mechanism to be implemented in the PRC, a system of pollution permits would have to be defined for potential polluters.

Alternative regulatory instruments

Liability rules present firms with the prospect of footing a bill for environmental damage and compensation of third parties. Such rules are usually applied in the case of hazardous waste. The Comprehensive Environmental Response, Compensation and Liability Act of the US EPA (or CERCLA 1990) lists chemicals and makes companies that have contributed to environmental pollution liable for the costs of clean up. Whilst sensible in principle, the impact of CERCLA has been mixed. One study suggests that hazardous waste spills have increased for small firms since 1990 as large firms place hazardous activities in small subsidiaries. In short, care should be taken in designing any similar scheme in the PRC.

Public Disclosure (PD) and **Pollution Ranking (PR)**. The attraction of these instruments is that they are administratively straightforward, require only limited expertise, and are low cost. This makes them attractive to developing countries where expertise is often limited. The objective is to place information on performance in the public domain so that polluters can be subjected to public scrutiny and encouraged, via moral suasion and share prices for example, to clean up their act. Successes include the US EPA Toxic Release Inventory (TRI), the Program for Pollution Control Evaluation and Rating (PROPER) in Indonesia and, in the PRC, the "GreenWatch" program. Preliminary empirical evidence shows that when firms were listed on the TRI, stock prices fell, followed by a proportional fall in emissions. But this is only one mechanism through which this instrument might work.

Public Participation. In all of the following case studies, the success of environmental policy and water resource management is built on public participation. Many economists agree that an important influence on the Income Environment Relationship (IER) comes from changing preferences for the environment as incomes grow. For these preferences to be felt at the policy level, and hence influence environmental outcomes, these preferences need to register with policy-makers. In the Murray–Darling River Basin (see case study below, pp. 237–40), the Community Advisory Committee registered public preferences. In the Rhine case study, the International Commission for the Protection of the Rhine (ICPR) had forums for public participation, while the Arles declaration made public participation more important and explicit still. In the United States, as discussed above, the courts provide one such route for public perceptions.

In the PRC, moves have already been made in some circles to enlist public participation in environmental decision-making. Most recently, in 2006, the State Environmental Protection Administration (SEPA) announced Provisional Measures for Public Participation in Environmental Impact Assessment. In May 2008, the Regulations of the PRC on Open Government Information also encouraged greater public participation as well as the spread of information. The non-governmental organization (NGO) sector is also growing, e.g. the Institute of Public and Environmental Affairs which has a web-based pollution map derived from public data. Another example is the "Green Choice Initiative" which informs consumers about these issues. At the local level, public participation could be enhanced.

International experience: case studies

Case study 1: the Murray–Darling River Basin

The Murray–Darling Basin (MDB) in Australia is an example of the successful introduction of cutting-edge MBI for the management of water quantity and quality. The scale of the MDB made this unlikely. It covers an area of one million square kilometers (km^2) and contains 45 percent of all irrigated land in Australia. The combined value of agriculture is said to be US$7.5 billion. In recent years, water demands and threats to general water quality have increased. This has led to the application of a number of innovative water management instruments, the most important of which is a market for water extraction permits. The innovations were part of broader economic and environmental reforms taking place at the time. On the one hand, the National Competition Policy (NCP) aimed to increase the competitiveness of all sectors including irrigation over time. On the other, the 2004 National Water Initiative (NWI) emphasized full cost recovery for water supply and market-based instruments for water allocation.

The case study shows how tradable permits can be successfully employed to allocate water. It also illustrates that this success depends on well-defined policies, laws and institutions, including the river basin commission.

Institutions: Australia is a Commonwealth of States. The MDB covers several states and territories each of which have separate water laws and regulations. For this reason, coordination is required between basin states. This is facilitated by three well-defined institutions: the Council of Australian Governments (COAG); the Murray–Darling River Basin Commission (MDBC); and the Murray–Darling Basin Ministerial Council (MDBMC) which acts as a conduit between them. The latter contains members from a number of relevant ministries (land, environment and water) in order to limit duplication and conflict. Decisions made at the basin level by the MDBMC require unanimity among basin states. Community interests are represented within the Basin Commission by the Community Advisory Committee (CAC).

In short, all stakeholders are represented at the basin level upwards and can participate in decision-making concerning water policy. The roles of the institutions are clearly defined allowing coordination among basin states without contravening other national state interests or policies.

Water laws and policy: since 1994, Australia and its States and Territories embarked on a process of reform in the water sector. In recent years, the NWI of 2004 has guided reform. One of the main goals of the NWI is to improve

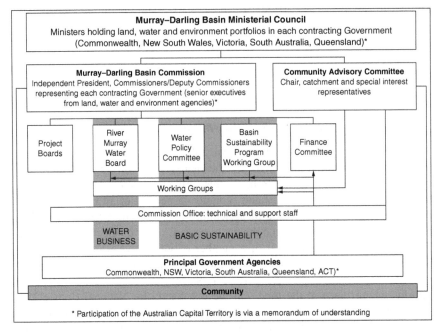

Figure 9.2 Institutional arrangements for the Murray–Darling River Basin Commission (source: Macdonald and Young 2001).

efficiency of water use by facilitating trade in water between sectors to achieve an efficient allocation of water. In order to facilitate this, *property rights* reform will take place, starting with separation of rights from land and culminating with harmonization of rights across basin states to facilitate water trade.

Water policy has changed radically in Australia and in the MDB since the 1994 COAG agreement, and this process of reform remains a feature of the NWI, particularly in relation to water quantity and allocation. The overall ethos of water law and policy has shifted away from the need to develop water resources at government expense, toward an ethos of conservation of water resources, control of pollution and full-cost recovery of water supply. It has also emphasized efficient allocation of water.

Tradable water rights: in 1994, the MDBC agreed that extraction within the MDB should be capped at 1993 levels. The impact of the cap has been manifold; however, the main impact has been the increase in the trade of water rights facilitated recently by the NWI. Water rights are now traded between basin states and both within and between sectors according to general strict rules, including absence of environmental impacts, and state water laws.

Intra-state trading, within Victoria and New South Wales (NSW) is well developed, with trades easily facilitated on the Internet.[2] In NSW between 1997–8, total sales of water rights amounted to 11 percent of the total entitle-

Table 9.1 Intra-state water trades (2003–4)

State	Permanent		Temporary		Total (Ml)
	Million litres	Percent of trades	Million litres	Percent of trades	
New South Wales	20,077	15.9	604,059	84.1	624,136
Victoria	52,212	3.2	275,446	96.8	327,658
South Australia	23,818	21.4	87,522	78.6	111,340
Queensland	–	–	15,585	100	15,858
Total basin	96,107		982,612		1,078,719

Source: PWC (2005).

Table 9.2 Inter-state water trading (2003)

Origin	Destination (million litres)			
	NSW	SA	Victoria	Total
New South Wales	–	7,310	345	7,655
Southern Australia	100	–	2,074	2,174
Victoria	3,040	9,936	–	12,976
Total	3,140	17,246	2,419	22,805

Source: PWC (2005).

ments to consumptive users. Most trades at that time were temporary "leases" of water, rather than permanent trades, and involved low security rights. Since that time, the volume of temporarily traded water has increased by 8.8 percent, while permanent trades increased by 7.9 percent (PWC 2005). **Inter-state water trading**, on the other hand, has only recently started as part of a pilot project between South Australia (River Murray) and Victoria and New South Wales (Mallee Regions).

The economic value of water trades is revealed by the gravitation of water rights toward Southern Australia from New South Wales and Victoria. The economic benefits of inter-state trade are estimated to be in the order of US$50 million per annum in agriculture alone (Beare and Heaney 2002). It has also been estimated that the cost of the cap has been reduced by 40 percent as a result of water trading. This represents a cost saving of around US$350 million. On the ground, irrigation technology has improved, and higher value crops are more prevalent.

The major shortcoming of water trading in the MDB has been the emergence of several related environmental problems, particularly salination of surface water. Ironically, increased efficiency in irrigation has reduced the return flows which formerly diluted the salt levels in the main rivers (Beare and Heaney

2002). The tradable water entitlements do not explicitly consider these third-party effects, and this leads to problems in trading off consumptive uses with the environmental flows which were formerly partly return flows from irrigation.

Lessons for the PRC: despite the potential problems of federalism in Australia, water reforms have proceeded apace with what some authors have called a spirit of "cooperative federalism" (Macdonald and Young 2001). The main factors facilitating this:

1   Clear institutional structure at the river basin level:

    a   The Commonwealth Government acts via the COAG to create river basin institutions.

    b   The MDBMC and MDBC are well defined legal entities with representation from community to government level. This facilitates coordination.

    c   The Community Advisory Committee facilitates public participation.

2   National policies reflected in well-defined state water laws:

    a   The impetus for water reform was driven by the NCP.

    b   Water and land rights are separated in all basin states. This enables trade.

    c   The NWI has removed further hindrances to water trade.

3   Strong enforcement of NWI:

    a   The Commonwealth Government can withhold funding (via the COAG) if states are slow to reform.

    b   Under the NWI, policy reforms are now consolidating the river basin approach and sub-basin catchment organizations have emerged.

The Australian case study provides a good example of how to deal with issues of federalism and inter-state water resource management. Not only is the institutional arrangement conducive to clear vertical lines of responsibility from the federal government to the state and district level implementing agencies, it also allows both bottom-up interactions through community interaction and horizontal coordination of national policies between relevant ministries and between basin states. The PRC could learn as much from this robust coordinating institutional structure as it could from the instruments that are employed under its watch. One outcome of this institutional arrangement is the successful deployment of tradable permits for water quantity and quality, with considerable benefits for agriculture, despite increased openness to international trade.

Case study 2: the Rhine River Basin

The Rhine River Basin contains nine separate countries, up to 60 million people, supports industry in the Ruhr valley as well as being an important trade link. (Möllenkamp *et al.* 2007). It is a classic transboundary water resource with all the attendant problems associated with international cooperation. The main players on the Rhine in terms of area are Germany, Switzerland, France and the

Netherlands. Despite the upstream–downstream issues associated with water pollution, the Rhine River has changed from being the "sewer of Europe" to being one of the cleanest rivers in the world. While much of this change has happened as a matter of course, much has arisen as a consequence of international cooperation between the main basin states. Today, some see the Rhine Basin as a prototype of international cooperation.

The earliest treaty among the basin states was in 1816 and established the Rhine as a freely navigable waterway (Huisman *et al.* 2000). This established a culture of cooperation and a succession of further international treaties followed in the twentieth century (Barrett 2003). Cooperation on the Rhine started with the establishment of the ICPR in 1950 in response to rising pollution levels. At this point, basin states agreed to monitor water quality and report to the ICPR.

In the 1970s and 1980s, several events marked a distinct change in the approach taken to river basin management in the Rhine and the fortunes of the ICPR. First, in 1976, the EU joined the ICPR. The presence of this broader international body lent more authority to the ICPR, and in, 1976, two important initiatives commenced. First, the ICPR basin states agreed to put in place actions to limit chloride emissions, formalized in the Convention on the Protection of the Rhine Against Pollution from Chlorides and Thermal Pollution. Second, basin states signed the Convention on the Protection of the Rhine from Chemical Pollution.[3] Therein, chemicals were ranked in terms of their toxicity, while standards were set for cadmium, mercury and other harmful substances. In fact, these Conventions marked the beginning of a lengthy process of negotiation. Final agreement on chlorides was only met in 1998, for instance.

The impact of these international agreements was mixed. Between 1970 and 1990, the countries along the river spent US$38.5 billion on building a string of purification plants to reduce chemical and biological oxygen demand. As a consequence, oxygen concentrations rose, and some life returned to the Rhine. However, the impact on heavy metals was minimal, and levels of mercury, cadmium and zinc, and harmful substances, including PCBs, benzene and atrazine (from pesticides) remained high.

The Sandoz chemical spill in 1986 marked the turning point of international cooperation in the Rhine River Basin. The pollution traveled the length of the Rhine in around ten days, and such was the toxicity of the spillage that an estimated half million fish were killed. This disaster sparked a change in the way in which the ICPR operated and was the starting point for an Integrated River Basin Management approach for the Rhine. The Rhine Action Plan (RAP) for Ecological Rehabilitation was agreed by the ICPR secretariat in response and signed by the European Union in 1987. The objective of the RAP was summarized by the phrase "salmon 2000," that is, the river should be habitable by salmon by the year 2000 (Sadoff and Grey 2002). Technical standards and increasingly stringent pollution standards were agreed by the ICPR leading to almost 70 percent reductions in the listed pollutants (see Table 9.3).

A second series of disasters prompted a review of water *quantity* management in the Rhine basin. In 1994 and 1995, the Rhine was beset by severe flooding.

Table 9.3 Changes in major pollutants on the Rhine between 1972 and 1995

Pollutant	Percent change between 1972–95	Percent change between 1985–95
Mercury	−97	−50
Cadmium	−98	−69
Chromium	−93	−34
Lead	−83	−22
Copper	−84	−34
Nickel	n/a	−38
Zinc	−88	−42
Total Organic Carbon	−72	−38
Oxygen	+127	+25
Phosphate	−62	−50
Nitrogen	−50	−64

Source: Huisman *et al.* (2000).

The 1995 floods exposed the weaknesses of the existing flood management system. The costs to the Netherlands were 250,000 people evacuated, while the rehabilitation of dykes, floodplains and other areas cost over US$100 million. As with the Sandoz disaster, these events lead to national and basin wide responses. At the basin level, the 1995 declaration of Arles agreed basin wide changes to spatial planning and other technical solutions to flood management within the framework of the existing ICPR. This accompanied individual national responses, such as compulsory insurance.

In 2000, the EU adopted the **Water Framework Directive (WFD)**.[4] The purpose of the Directive is to establish a framework for the protection of inland surface waters (rivers and lakes), transitional waters (estuaries), coastal waters, and groundwater. The WFD emphasizes river basin management and states that the release of untreated water is prohibited throughout the EU to ensure "good status" for water ecosystems. The most recent plan for sustainable development of the Rhine was agreed in light of the ecological and sustainability focus of the WFD and is embodied in the ICPR "Rhine 2020" agreement.

The evolution of the Rhine River Basin and its institutions is a very particular one. It speaks to the difficulties surrounding international cooperation as well as how successful cooperation can be arrived at and sustained. Pollution has declined since the ICPR was established and the rigorous monitoring began. The standards applied under the RAP appear to have had an important impact on pollution levels. The responses to accidents and disasters, alongside the gradual evolution of thinking toward maintenance of environmental quality has shaped water quality in the Rhine. Progress has been facilitated through institutions such as the ICPR, through which standards were agreed and monitoring verified among basin states, and through supra-national legislation such as the WFD, which has provided a uniform water quality objective for EU members on the Rhine, and facilitated cooperation as a result.

Lessons for the PRC: the lessons from the Rhine case study concern the attainment of cooperation between provinces on water resource management and pollution control. Cooperation in the Rhine case study followed from several crucial factors:

1   Clear agreement on the **science** of pollution through:

   a   A credible basin level monitoring institution: the ICPR;
   b   Monitoring practices accepted by all parties via the ICPR;
   c   Agreement on the level of standards.

2   Cost-sharing agreements and interlinked policies:

   a   The costs of environmental clean-up were shared between upstream polluters and downstream pollutees.
   b   Polluters contributed to the clean-up despite not being beneficiaries of the program, while the "victim pays" principle was accepted when downstream parties contributed to the costs.
   c   The rationale for such action included reasons such as "solidarity," but in general side payments and interlinked policies/agreements are important components of many solutions to transboundary problems.

3   Adversity can be used to encourage policy changes and cooperation:

   a   The Sandoz incident in 1987 and the floods of 1995 spurred the Rhine River Basin into action on environmental policy.

4   Overarching institutions (the EU) can consolidate cooperative agreements:

   a   Many agree that the EU WFD provided additional impetus for cooperation on the Rhine by providing a common set of objectives for all members.
   b   Since joining in 1976, the EU has always added credibility to the ICPR which itself has no power to enforce its recommendations.

The Rhine River Basin provides a useful historical perspective on the evolution of water pollution policy as well as providing insights into the process of generating consensus among competing and sovereign users of transboundary water resources. The Sandoz disaster caused countries to cooperate and resulted in agreed standards. The lessons on cooperation can be applied to issues of inter-province cooperation in the PRC, involving river basins such as the Pearl River, in which cooperation so far has failed to achieve agreement on pollution limitations despite the creation of a River Basin Commission.

Case study 3: Total Maximum Daily Loads (TMDLs)

Total Maximum Daily Loads (TMDLs) represent the maximum pollution loads that water bodies can receive and yet maintain ambient standards. TMDLs need to be calculated in full, and a pollution reduction plan presented to the EPA for any water bodies not meeting ambient standards. TMDLs were a long-neglected aspect of the

US Clean Water Act of 1972 (CWA) (Boyd 2000). The CWA emphasized techno-logical standards. As a consequence of technological improvements between 1972 and 1981, municipal and industrial biological oxygen demand loads decreased by 71 percent and 46 percent, respectively, while the US economy grew by 25 percent (Boyd 2000). Nevertheless, Section 303(d) of the CWA made reference to a back-up program in the event that the technological solutions aimed at point sources should fail – the TMDL program. It was the intention of several states that this scheme provide them with greater autonomy in addressing pollution problems.

While providing a useful means of converting ambient standards into emis-sions standards, the implementation of TMDLs has been fraught with problems. The problems have stemmed largely from legal uncertainties and consequent tensions between the three layers of governance shaping US environmental policy – federal, state and local government.

Implementation of TMDLs: the Long Island Sound case study provides a good example of how TMDLs can be implemented. Long Island Sound is an estuary of national significance. The main pollution issue concerns nitrogen pollution from point and non-point sources. The point sources are mainly public treatment plants for effluent. The Long Island TMDL scheme was implemented in three phases:

1   pollution loadings were frozen at 1990 levels;
2   in 1994, nitrogen removal investments were made, mainly involving retro-fitting of the public treatment plants, and generally at low cost; and
3   in 1998, a TMDL was calculated for nitrogen and reductions were agreed in 2001 – 58.5 percent reduction overall, 10 percent from non-point source, 65 percent from point sources (see map in Figure 9.3).

Even these reductions did not guarantee that the ambient water standards were achieved, and so in Phase (4), reductions from point and non-point sources outside of the state were introduced, and in Phase (5), alternative technologies were planned. Curiously, there is no provision in the CWA for a phased approach to TMDLs. However, on this occasion, the EPA acted flexibly and allowed the approach to continue. Indeed, there appears to be a preference for a phased approach when a mixture of point and non-point sources is involved.

In 2001, the Nitrogen Credit Exchange Program, a tradable permit scheme, was initiated in order to help achieve the nitrogen standards. Such were the dif-ferences in abatement costs, the Department of Environmental Protection (DEP) estimated that savings of around US$200 million in avoided capital costs would be possible over 15 years. Tradable permits were issued in accordance with the TMDL. Permits were then traded in the usual way, except that an exchange rate is used for trades to and from particular geographical zones.

The scheme has been somewhat successful. Of the 79 plants involved, sellers and buyers were more or less in equal number, although the initial allocation of permits was excessive because firms made their own capital investments in nitrogen reduction. In sum, the scheme has reduced nitrogen below the levels specified by the TMDLs.

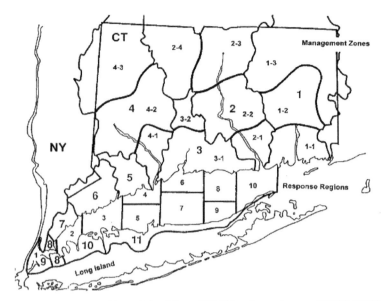

Figure 9.3 Zones of Long Island Sound TMDL scheme (source: NYSD 2000).

Lessons for the PRC: TMDLs have had limited success in the United States, despite the positive example described above. The main problems are:

- **Legal uncertainty**: the history of TMDLs has been fraught with inertia on the part of the states and the EPA, and litigation by agricultural lobbyists to inhibit the program and citizens to encourage it. Much of this stems from problems in the drafting and interpretation of the CWA, particularly in relation to the introduction of non-point sources to the TMDL program.
- **Informational intensity**: many believe that TMDLs are too complicated and onerous a means by which to regulate water quality. The scientific uncertainty surrounding ambient standards and the difficulties encountered when monitoring and enforcing such standards make implementation extremely difficult practically, as well as politically (Boyd 2000; Houck 2002).
- **Monitoring and enforcement**: the costs of enforcement can be high in large watersheds because the measurement of ambient standards can be extremely time-consuming for a central agency.

In sum, the case study shows clearly how TMDLs have been utilized in water management, and how trading programs have been incorporated into these sorts of standards. The lessons from the Long Island case study show that TMDLs:

1 provide a means by which ambient standards can be converted into emissions equivalents;

Table 9.4 Nutrient loads for Long Island Sound zones (in tons/year)

Zone	Non-point sources				Point sources			Total load
	Pre-colonial	Terrestrial	Atmospheric	Total	WWTP	CSO	Total	
1	991.3	251.6	604.7	1,852.1	1,242.6	0.0	1,242.6	3,094.7
2	1,158.6	479.5	835.1	2,473.2	2,805.0	0.0	2,805.0	5,278.2
3	408.0	235.5	355.7	999.2	2,103.3	0.0	2,103.3	3,102.5
4	808.2	305.7	538.0	1,651.9	1,668.6	0.0	1,668.6	3,320.5
5	179.1	121.2	174.3	474.6	947.9	0.0	947.9	1,422.5
6	195.9	146.8	202.2	544.9	1,108.0	0.0	1,108.0	1,652.9
7	43.5	68.7	77.3	189.5	837.0	0.0	837.0	1,026.5
8	n/a	n/a	n/a	n/a	17,502.2	578.5	17,502.2	18,080.5
9	n/a	n/a	n/a	n/a	9,103.0	314.1	9,103.0	9,417.1
10	81.9	84.2	108.6	274.7	484.0	0.0	484.0	758.7
11 – west	104.0	133.5	155.2	392.7	191.0	0.0	191.0	583.7
11 – east	9.1	11.6	13.5	34.2	13.9	0.0	13.9	48.1
12	1,785.8	0.0	3,699.2	5,485.0	0.0	0.0	0.0	5,485.0
Total	5,765.4	1,842.8	6,763.8	14,372.0	38,006.3	892.6	38,006.3	53,270.9

Source: NYSD (2000).

2   can form the basis for the pollution cap and the distribution of permits in any given scheme;
3   can deal well with non-point source pollution;
4   should be reserved for extreme cases of severely low water quality;
5   can only be implemented if the legislation associated with implementation specify clear roles and responsibilities for all regulatory institutions backed up by enforcement.

In short, the Long Island case study demonstrates the usefulness of the approach, but the history of the TMDL program shows that the approach is complex and (often) costly (Malone 2002; Houck 2002). Indeed, on account of administrative difficulties and onerous informational requirements, pollution policy in the United States and the EU has tended to emphasize pollution standards to achieve ambient water standards (Houck 2002).

Conclusion

This chapter represents an attempt to contribute to the PRC's macro-environmental policy by reviewing international experiences in water resource management and water pollution control. As the review of IER explains, growth will not necessarily lead to the improvement of environmental outcomes. A concerted and coordinated effort will be required to monitor and enforce pollution control and facilitate efficient water allocations. The international experiences described here provide some important pointers for the PRC in this regard and lessons can be learned from them to ensure sustainable development and a harmonious society.

Notes

1   Order No. 32 of the Ministry of Water Resources: www.lawinfochina.com/law/display.asp?id=6623andkeyword=.
2   See, for example, www.watertrading.com.au and www.waterexchange.com.au.
3   Convention on the Protection of the Rhine from Chemical Pollution, December 3, 1976 (Bonn).
4   Directive 2000/60/EC of the European Parliament and of the Council establishing a framework for the Community action in the field of water policy.

References

Barbier, E. (2006). *Natural Resources and Economic Development*. Cambridge: Cambridge University Press.
Barrett, S. (2003). *Environment and Statecraft*. Cambridge: Cambridge University Press.
Bauer, C. (1997). "Bringing Water Markets Down to Earth: the Political Economy of Water Rights in Chile, 1976–95." *World Development*, 25(5), pp. 639–56.
Bauer, C. (2004). *Siren Song: Chilean Water Law as a Model for International Reform*. Washington, DC: Resources for the Future Press.
Beare, S. and Heaney, A. (2002). "Water Trade and the Externalities of Water Use in

Australia – Interim Report." ABARE paper for Natural Resource Management Business Unit, AFFA, Canberra, July.

Boyd, J. (2000). "The New Face of the Clean Water Act: A Critical Review of the EPA's Proposed TMDL Rules." RFF discussion paper 00–12. Resources for the Future, Washington, DC.

Boyd, J. (2003). "Water Pollution Taxes: A Good Idea Doomed to Failure?" Discussion Papers dp-03–20, Resources For the Future, Washington, DC.

Briscoe, J. (1996). *Water Resources Management in Chile: Lessons from a World Bank Study Tour*. Washington, DC: World Bank.

Cook, I.G. (2007). "Environment, Health and Sustainability." In *China's Post Reform Economy: Achieving Harmony, Sustaining Growth*, Richard Sanders and Yang Chen (eds.). New York: Routledge.

Copeland, B.R. and Taylor, M.S. (2004). "Trade, Tragedy and the Commons." NBER Working Papers 10836, National Bureau of Economic Research.

Dasgupta, S., Laplante, B., Wang, H. and Wheeler, D. (2002). "Confronting the Environmental Kuznets Curve." *Journal of Economic Perspectives*, 16(1), pp. 147–68.

De Groot, H.L.F., Minliang, Z. and Withagen, C.A. (2004). "The Dynamics of China's Regional Development and Pollution: An Empirical Investigation into the Existence of an Environmental Kuznets Curve for China." *Environment and Development Economics*, 9, pp. 507–37.

Dinar, A. and Subramanian, A. (1998). "Water Pricing Experiences." World Bank Technical Paper.

Economy, E. (2007). *The River Runs Black: The Environmental Challenge to China's Future*. Ithaca: Cornell University Press.

Fankhauser, S. and Tepic, S. (2005). "Can Poor Consumers Pay for Energy and Water? An Affordability Analysis for Transition Countries." EBRD Working Paper No. 92.

Gleick, P. H., Cooley, H. and Katz, D. (2006). *The World's Water, 2006–2007: The Biennial Report on Freshwater Resources*. Washington, DC: Island Press.

Groom, B., Liu, X., Swanson, T. and Zhang, S. (2008). "Equity versus Efficiency? The Impact of Increasing Block Tariffs for Residential Water in Beijing." In *Facing Water Scarcity*, P. Koundouri (ed.). Dordrecht: Kluwer.

Hearne, R. and Donoso, G. (2005). "Water Institutional Reforms in Chile." *Water Policy*, 7, pp. 53–69.

Hearne, R. and Easter, K. (1995). "Water Allocation and Water Markets: An Analysis of the Gains from Trade in Chile." World Bank Technical Paper No. 315.

Hearne, R. and Easter, K. (1997). "The Economic and Financial Gains from Water Markets in Chile." *Agricultural Economics*, 15(3), pp. 187–99.

Horbulyk, T. (2005). "Markets, Policy and the Allocation of Water Resources Among Sectors: Constraints and Opportunities." *Canadian Water Resources Journal*, 30(1), pp. 55–64.

Houck, O. (2002). "The Clean Water Act TMDL Program: Law, Policy, and Implementation." Environmental Law Institute.

Huisman, P., Jong, J. and Wieriks, K. (2000). "Transboundary Cooperation in Shared River Basins: Experiences from the Rhine, Meuse and North Sea." *Water Policy*, 2(1–2), pp. 83–97.

Kraemer, R.A., Pielen, B. and Leipprand, A. (2003). "Global Review of Economic Instruments for Water Management in Latin America." Working Paper for the Inter-American Development Bank Regional Policy Dialogue, Environment Network

Meeting II: Application of Economic Instruments in Water and Solid Waste Management, February 25–6, 2003, Washington, DC.

Macdonald, D.H. and Young, M. (2001). "A Case Study of the Murray–Darling River Basin." Report for the International Water Management Institute by CSIRO.

MacMahon, G.F. (2005). The Yellow River Law: A Framework for Integrated River Basin Management. Proceedings of the 2005 Georgia Water Resources Conference, University of Georgia.

Malone, L. (2002). "The Myths and Truths that Threaten the TMDL Program." *Envt'l L. Rep*, (Envtl L. Inst.) 11133.

Maria Saleth, R. and Dinar, A. (2006). "Water Institutional Reforms in Developing Countries. Insights, Evidences and Case Studies." In *Economic Development and Environmental Sustainability: New Policy Options*, Ramon Lopez and Michael Toman (eds.). Oxford: Oxford University Press.

Mohanty, N. and Gupta, S. (2002). "Breaking the Gridlock in Water Reforms through Water Markets: International Experience and Implementation Issues for India." Working Paper, Julian Simon Centre for Policy Research. Dehli. Online, available at: www.libertyindia.org/policy_reports/water_markets_2002.pdf.

Möllenkamp, S., Lamers, M. and Ebenhöh, E. (2007). "Institutional Elements for Adaptive Water Management Regimes. Comparing Two Water Management Regimes in the Rhine Basin." In *Adaptive and Integrated Water Management: Coping with Complexity and Uncertainty*, C. Pahl-Wostl, P. Kabat and J. Möltgen (eds.). Springer Verlag, pp. 147–66.

Moore, M.R., Gollehon, N.R. and Carey, M.B. (1994). "Multicrop Production Decisions in Western Irrigated Agriculture; the Role of Water Price." *American Journal of Agricultural Economics*, 76, pp. 859–74.

NYSD (2000). "A Total Maximum Daily Load Analysis to Achieve Water Quality Standards for Dissolved Oxygen in Long Island Sound Prepared in Conformance with Section 303(d) of the Clean Water Act and the Long Island Sound Study." Report prepared by the New York State Department. Online, available at: www.longislandsoundstudy.net/pubs/reports/tmdl.pdf.

OECD (2007). "Instrument Mixes Addressing Non-Point Sources of Water Pollution." *OECD Papers*, 7(8).

Palmer, M. (2007). "Towards a Greener China? Accessing Environmental Justice in the Peoples Republic of China." In *Access to Environmental Justice: A Comparative Study*, A. Harding (ed.). The Netherlands: Koninklijke Brill.

PWC (2005). "Water Trading." In *National Water Initiative Water Trading Study Final Report*. Water for the Future Publications Commissioned by the Australian Government. Online, available at: www.environment.gov.au/water/publications/action/nwi-wts-report.html.

Sadoff, C. and Grey, D. (2002). "Beyond the River: the Benefits of Cooperation on International Rivers." *Water Policy*, 5, pp. 389–403.

Shen, J. (2006). "A Simultaneous Estimation of Environmental Kuznets Curves: Evidence from China." *China Economic Review*, 17(4), p. 383.

Song, T., Zheng, T. and Tong, L. (2008). "An Empirical Test of the Environmental Kuznets Curve in China: A Panel Cointegration Approach." *China Economic Review*, 19(3), pp. 381–92.

Stern, D.I. (2004). "The Rise and Fall of the Environmental Kuznets Curve." *World Development*, 32(8), pp. 1419–39.

Sterner, T. (2003). *Policy Instruments for Environmental and Natural Resource Management*. Washington, DC: Resources for the Future.

Tao, W., Zhou, B., Barron, W.F. and Yang, W. (2000). "Tradable Discharge Permit System for Water Pollution: The Case of the Upper Nanpan River." *Environmental and Resource Economics*, 15, pp. 27–38.

Tsur, Y. and Dinar, A. (1995). "Equity and Efficiency Considerations in Pricing and Allocating Irrigation Water." *World Bank Policy Research Working Paper* 1460.

Vennemo, H., Aunan, K., Lindhjem, H. and Seip, H.M. (2008). "Environmental Pollution in China: Status and Trends." *Economics and Policy*, 3(1), pp. 1–22.

Webber, M., Barnett, J., Finlayson, B. and Wang, M. (forthcoming). *Pricing China's Irrigation Water. Global Environmental Change* (in press).

Woo Thye Wing (2007). "The Origins of China's Quest for a Harmonious Society: Failures on the Governance and Environmental Fronts." In *China's Post Reform Economy: Achieving Harmony, Sustaining Growth*, Richard Sanders and Yang Chen (eds.). New York: Routledge.

Wu, J. (2008). "Public Participation in the Enforcement of China's Anti-Pollution Laws." *Law, Environment and Development Journal*, 4(1), p. 411.

10 International experiences in ecosystem management

Andreas Kontoleon

Introduction

This chapter reviews international experiences for ecosystem management as well as their finance mechanisms. We discuss how policy options can be classified and then proceed with more detailed sections on international experiences with specific policy and financing options. We then provide some insights from two specific case studies that were chosen as being particularly pertinent for the case of the People's Republic of China (PRC). Lastly, we provide policy recommendation for the ecosystem management in the PRC. This review focuses on evaluating international experiences for terrestrial (mainly forest-related) ecosystems and provides a summary of work undertaken for the Asian Development Bank (ADB)-funded project on evaluating the PRC's macro-environment strategy.

An instructive way to classify environmental policy options is to do so in accordance with the *nature* and *degree* of regulatory intervention which would classify environmental policy options into three broad categories – namely:

1   command-and-control (CAC) regulation;
2   regulatory incentive-based policies; and
3   market-enabling policies – as shown in Figure 10.1 (Kolstad 2000).

This chapter reviews international experiences on how these alternative policy and finance mechanisms for conserving ecosystems are likely to fare in terms of their effectiveness in meeting environmental objectives; the cost effectiveness of doing so; distributional impacts; long-term sustainability; and the sufficiency of funds mobilized.

Protected areas and land use restrictions

Under CAC, the regulator determines the target (or quantity) of ecosystem protection, then specifies the relevant actions that need to be taken to meet this target, and, lastly, "commands" land users to take these actions. Experience suggests that the main problems with CAC approach are:

1   they can imply substantial informational requirements; and
2   they can be highly inflexible.

International experience points to two commonly-used forms of CAC responses – protected areas and land use restrictions (Kontoleon *et al.* 2008). The former have been prone to high transactions, monitoring and enforcement costs (leading to so-called "paper parks") which affect both their cost and environmental effectiveness. Further international experience shows that the introduction of protected areas can impose substantial costs on people living in (and nearby) ecosystems, who often have very low levels of income, particularly in the tropical regions. The distributional impacts of this can be highly negative because the benefits of protected areas often accrue to wealthier groups, nationally or internationally. In terms of the sources of finance for protected areas, international experience suggests that funding from traditional government and intergovernmental sources is not growing in line with expansion, or possibly even ongoing maintenance requirements, of protected areas. This suggests that either alternative policy mechanisms that directly capture demand for ecosystem protection must be used, or that funding for protected areas needs to come from new (marked-based and private) sources. Lastly, the long-term sustainability of protected areas depends on the extent to which ongoing sources of funding can be accessed. This may further necessitate the use of markets to capture demand for ecosystem conservation.

The second form of CAC response, i.e. the land use restrictions, includes those that state that certain proportions of land must be kept under forest cover. This is a typical condition of logging concessions on public forest land in many countries, together with riparian buffers. Other regulations that can contribute to the protection of ecosystems are regulations about how private forests are managed. These are generally focused on sustainable forest management and

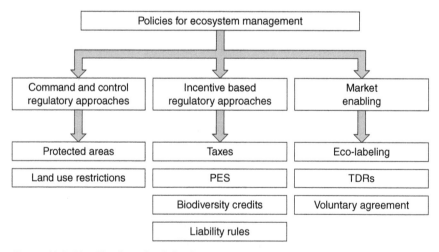

Figure 10.1 Classification of policies for ecosystem management (source: Kolstad 2000).

pollution control. Such regulations may relate to the holders of logging concessions, and determine the extent of logging that is allowed or the methods that
should be used. These include, among others, minimum size class restrictions,
prohibition of harvesting certain species, and restrictions on logging equipment.
Another notable international experience of land use regulation for protecting
forest ecosystems is the Endangered Species Act in the United States.

The costs of forest regulations may be difficult to quantify because they often
include the opportunity costs of land for individual landowners as well as direct
spending on compliance. However, international experience suggests that cost
effectiveness is low in many cases because the regulations are imposed across all
locations, regardless of the magnitude of the costs (Ferraro and Kramer 1997).
Where costs are relatively homogeneous, forestland regulations may be efficient;
but if costs vary widely, then it would be more cost effective to account for those
costs in determining which land should be regulated for biodiversity protection
purposes. One advantage of such regulations is that they may be less costly than
other policy mechanisms to implement, although if landowners believe they are
unfair, they may be costly to enforce. An additional disadvantage of forestland
regulations is that they do not provide incentives for dynamic cost reduction
because once they are met, landowners do not benefit from further improvements
to diversify their forestland, or other environmental benefits arising from it. A
further disadvantage of regulation as a means of protecting ecosystems is that, if
it is not compensated, it may create perverse incentives for habitat destruction.

In terms of the implementation of ecosystem regulation, its funding generally
comes from domestic government budgets. However, funding may also come
from private land users, especially where compliance incurs direct costs.
Funding may be required only for implementation and monitoring, or possibly
for compensation as well. Where compensation is not paid, there may be limits
to the extent of the regulatory requirements that can be placed on forest landowners without being perceived as unfair. This in turn limits the extent to which
regulation can be used as a biodiversity conservation mechanism. Lastly, in
terms of their viability, provided ecosystem regulations are accepted by private
landowners, they can, in principle, operate indefinitely. However, if they are perceived to be excessively restrictive, there may be political pressure for them to
be removed. In addition, the existence of particular standards for land management in one time period may create a perception of entitlement, making it difficult to implement more stringent standards in future (Aylward *et al.* 1996;
Emerton *et al.* 2006; Lapham and Livermore 2003)

Regulatory incentive-based instruments

International experience suggests that, although CAC approaches still dominate
environmental policy, incentive-based approaches have been widely embraced
by most governments and environmental non-governmental organizations
(NGOs) (such as the Consumers International (CI), World Wildlife Fund (WWF)
and Greenpeace, who up until recently were highly opposed to the use of such

instruments). The realization of the potential benefit of such instruments is attributable partly to enhanced awareness (proliferation of relevant graduate courses and government training schemes) and partly to the negative experiences with CAC measures (most notably the failure of many protected areas or "paper parks"). Use of incentive-based measures may include taxes and tax breaks, payments for ecosystem services (PES) and systems of biodiversity credits. Such interventions can be seen as entailing some form of "price" and "quantity" rationing. The regulator is required to define the amount and nature of the subsidies to be deployed or, in the case of biodiversity credits, the regulator needs to define what is to be traded (quantity and quality of credits or permits) and how trade is to be undertaken (e.g. how the permits are allocated, how compliance is monitored).

The provision of tax breaks to those who undertake various forms of biodiversity conservation is an established method for encouraging voluntary action. For example, in the United States, landowners receive reductions in income tax, and, in some cases, property tax and inheritance tax, if they donate a conservation easement. This involves a permanent transfer to an approved conservation organization of part of the rights to their land. The effect is that, while the land may continue to be used for some purposes (such as residential uses), other activities (such as commercial development or industrial uses) are prohibited. As these rights have been permanently relinquished, the restrictions apply to all future owners of the property and become part of the land title. Conservation easements that benefit from tax breaks in this way are similar to other charitable donations of land or money, which may also contribute to biodiversity conservation. However, conservation organizations may also purchase conservation easements directly. In this case, they would fall into the category of payments for ecosystem services (Wunder 2007). Biodiversity conservation may also be aided by reforming taxes or subsidies that have perverse environmental impacts. One commonly cited example is production-based agricultural subsidies that can encourage the destruction of woodlands as well as intensive farming methods that reduce biodiversity. Another less obvious example is if concessions for logging on state lands are offered at prices that are lower than the rents that can be obtained, or that do not account for the social costs of the activities (Kontoleon *et al.* 2008; May *et al.* 2002).

Payments for ecosystem services (PES) is the most widely used fiscal instrument for ecosystem conservation (Wunder 2007). PES schemes do not have a single, universal definition, and, as such, the term may be used to describe a wide range of programs, including the "Pagos por Servicios Ambientales" (PSA) program in Costa Rica, agri-environment schemes in the European Union, and the Conservation Reserve Program in the United States.

PES mechanisms can be used as a policy tool for state intervention, or as a way for the private sector to provide incentives for biodiversity conservation. In the former case, the government is the buyer of the services on behalf of the national population, while in the latter case, the buyer of the services may be one or more private sector firms, individuals or donor institutions. It is also possible to combine funds from different sources to create a single payment for landowners. For example, the Costa Rican National Forestry Financing Fund (FONAFIFO) is a government agency that makes payments to landowners for forest protection and reforestation. The majority of its funding comes from a national tax on fuel, but it also receives income from donors such as the Global Environment Facility (GEF), and from public and private companies with specific interests such as watershed protection for hydropower operation, or conservation of areas of scenic beauty that are used for ecotourism purposes (Rojas and Aylward 2003). The private donors can choose to target particular forest locations through FONAFIFO in order to obtain specific environmental services.

Due to the local nature of many ecosystem services, PES schemes are frequently implemented at the local level, although they may be funded at the local, national or international level. For example, in the case of the Pimampiro watershed in Ecuador, the Pimampiro municipality has established a fund, into which domestic water users in the town pay a fee for water provision. This fund is used to make monthly payments of US$0.5–US$1 per hectare (ha) to upstream landowners for managing forestland (Echevarria *et al.* 2004). Similar schemes, involving payments from urban residents to upstream farmers, have been developed in many other locations including Nicaragua, India and Brazil (Perez 2005; Kerr 2002; Landell-Mills 1999).

PES agreements can also be made between individual companies and upstream landowners. For example, in Mount Kanlaon National Park in the Philippines, conservation of forestland within the park is financed by charges that are levied by the park board for use of the park's natural resources, including watershed protection benefits. These are then used to compensate residents in the park for conservation activities. It was estimated that the benefits of forest protection for SMC-Viva, a mineral water company, were approximately US$4,000–US$18,000 per year (Rosales 2003).

The main strength of PES-type schemes is argued to be their cost effectiveness (as compared to more indirect ways of conserving ecosystems) (see Ferraro and Simpson 2002). Cost effectiveness depends on whether the land that is targeted has the lowest opportunity costs. The nature of PES programs is such that if a flat-rate payment is used, information does not need to be collected on the opportunity costs of land. This is an advantage relative to protected areas, where the value of alternative land uses is generally unknown, making it difficult to minimize opportunity costs. A PES scheme involves offering a payment at a particular level so that only those with opportunity costs below that level will choose to participate, and high-value land is automatically excluded. Costs of financing the program can potentially be lowered further with differentiated payments based on the opportunity costs of conservation on individual plots of land, or for individual households. However, this will also affect transactions costs (Wätzold and Schwerdtner 2005).

Theoretically, we would expect the environmental effectiveness of PES schemes to be high relative to other mechanisms as they directly pay for the environmental service required, and they are conditional on the delivery of that service. However, international experience suggests that effectiveness is determined in practice by the way the scheme is designed. Where links between changes in land management and environmental outcomes are uncertain or variable, paying landowners for outcomes rather than actions means that they bear the risk of not receiving payment if those outcomes are not achieved, even if they did everything possible to achieve them. In this case, they would require a premium to account for the risk of not receiving payment, which raises overall program costs. The second consideration in relation to environmental effectiveness is that the voluntary nature of PES schemes means that it is more difficult to target the land of greatest biodiversity value than in the case of protected areas (Wu and Boggess 1999).

PES schemes operate on the basis of "beneficiary pays." In the case of ecosystems, it is commonly the case that the beneficiaries of conservation are wealthier than those who bear the costs. To this extent, we would expect PES schemes to have positive distributional impacts, particularly relative to protected areas, in which those who incur the costs may or may not be compensated. Even where compensation does occur, we can argue that PES schemes will tend to be more beneficial because of their voluntary nature: if a landowner chooses to participate, it suggests that they expect to be better off as a result. As compensation for the introduction of protected areas is not voluntary, landowners will have to participate even if they are worse off as a result (Wunder 2006).

Market-enabling instruments

The third category of policy instruments involves providing incentives for ecosystem conservation *via* enabling private market forces. These instruments require only indirect or supplementary forms of government regulation (e.g. defining property rights, providing information such as certification labels) and limited (and in principle only temporary) government financial support (e.g. access to micro-credit, training, and other such forms of business start-up support). As in the case of incentive-based regulation, the acceptance of such market instruments has arrived with a considerable time lag stemming partly from ideological and political reason. Yet, as the need for using a mixture of both public *and* private funds to provide all forms of public goods (from health to military services) has become widely the norm, the acceptance of using these instruments for ecosystem conservation came naturally. Beyond this, the rise in the interest of market-based instruments also reflects the evolution of public preferences and the increase in demand for environment-friendly goods (in accordance with the logic of the Kuznets Curve paradigm). Moreover, market-enabling schemes have been argued to entail less lobbying costs (both from the regulated and regulators' perspective) as well as being perceived as aligned with the current mode for less *direct* government intervention and an enhanced role for NGO and stakeholder group involvement. In this chapter, we focus on reviewing two forms of market-enabling instruments – certification schemes and tradable development rights – as being more relevant for ecosystem management.

Eco-labels are mechanisms that allow consumers to express their values for environmental protection by discriminating among products and services, while producers may be able to capture part of those values. They operate on the basis of a price premium paid and improved market access for products that are certified as having been produced in an environmentally (and/or socially) benign way. This has the effect of creating a separate market for goods that are produced in combination with environmental protection in order to meet consumer demand for conservation. The increased consumer demand for such certified goods could be motivated by different forms of values, including use and non-use values.

The main costs involved in a certification scheme are the initial set-up costs and the ongoing monitoring and inspection process. If the scheme is successful, the cost-effectiveness should be relatively high because market demand directly provides the financial incentives for biodiversity conservation. However, the credibility of the certification process is extremely important in determining success, so it is crucial that sufficient investment is made in the monitoring process. In addition, expenditure on raising awareness of the availability of the certified products and the differences in the production systems will also be necessary.

Some certification schemes include social, as well as environmental, requirements for the producers. For example, the Forest Stewardship Council (FSC) certification includes commitment to recognizing local and indigenous rights to forestland, as well as protection of worker rights. In the case of shade-grown coffee, many of those using the technique are small farmers without the capital to convert to a higher-yielding production technology. If these farmers can earn a premium price, the distributional impacts are likely to be positive although, as mentioned above, so far consumers have not proven willing to pay premiums. More generally, where environmental certification can be gained for low-intensity production processes, it has the potential to benefit small-scale producers who use those processes out of necessity (Moguel and Toledo 1999; Pagiola and Ruthenberg 2002).

A disadvantage for small-scale farmers or producers will be that there are likely to be fixed costs associated with undergoing the certification process, making it more difficult to access the market than for larger producers. The FSC has a special set of policies and standards for small and low-intensity producers, and encourages them to form groups for the purposes of certification, but they are likely to still face relatively high costs of participation. Obtaining certification may also require initial investment in changes to production processes, in the anticipation of higher future returns. This also has the potential to burden poorer producers if they have limited access to credit or relatively high aversion to risk (Kontoleon *et al.* 2008).

In principle, the market for eco-labeled products should be relatively large as it is capturing the non-use values of conservation. In practice, this will depend on how well those values can be captured, which in turn relies on the size and nature of consumer segments for these products. One related issue of particular concern is on consumer awareness and understanding of the environmental impacts of alternative production methods. Experience with schemes so far suggests that the greater complexity of issues surrounding biodiversity means that eco-labels relating to biodiversity are likely to be more difficult to develop than those relating to other social or environmental issues such as organic production or sustainable fishing. However, the high non-use values relating to ecosystems suggest that the potential exists to develop a substantial market, if the information difficulties can be overcome. Yet, this discussion is still somewhat speculative since, as discussed above, there is a further need for gaining better understanding on how consumer markets with respect to such certified goods are segmented as well as the dynamics of these segments. Such information from detailed segmentation analyses is particularly absent from the current literature.

Tradable development rights (TDRs) for management of ecosystems have been established in many developed countries, such as schemes for wetland mitigation and endangered species conservation in the United States and biodiversity credits in some Australian states. These operate by placing limits on the amount of land that can be developed, or habitat that can be destroyed, and allowing trading within that limit. The intended effect is that those who invest in biodiversity protection can sell credits to those who wish to develop land, which creates a financial value for ecosystem conservation. The other objective is to minimize the cost of regulations that limit the extent to which natural habitat can be converted by allowing conservation to take place in the locations where opportunity costs are low (Organisation for Economic Co-operation and Development (OECD) 2003; Chomitz *et al.* 2004).

So-called "biodiversity offset" schemes involve developers (broadly defined to include miners, energy companies, commercial foresters, real estate firms, large public works companies) incurring the costs of conservation or restoration of forestland of equivalent quantity/quality to the one converted. Where such offsets are required by law, they can be viewed as a form of trading scheme and would be classified as a quantity rationing incentive-based regulation. In cases where the offset scheme is not legally binding (which is normally the case) but is designed and enforced by the industry itself or some other non-governmental authority (such as the Business and Biodiversity Offset Program (BBOP)), then it can be viewed as a voluntary environmental agreement and would be classified under market-enabling schemes (Pagiola *et al.* 2002).

TDRs are theoretically more cost effective than non-tradable development restrictions, as they allow the mitigation of environmental damage to be achieved at lowest cost. This is because those who own land with high opportunity costs of conservation will purchase development rights, while those with low opportunity costs will sell them, minimizing the total opportunity cost of conserving a given amount of land. For TDRs to work effectively, they require clear property rights. This means that transactions costs may be high if the appropriate institutions do not exist. They also require sufficient buyers and sellers to avoid monopoly outcomes.

Further international experience suggests that the environmental effectiveness of TDRs will depend on the spatial distribution of ecological benefits and opportunity costs, with the greatest scope for trading without compromising conservation either where costs and benefits are inversely related, or where costs are heterogeneous and benefits are relatively homogeneous.

Unlike PES schemes and other market creation options, the costs of conservation with TDRs are borne by land developers rather than by the beneficiaries of forest protection (in essence we have a form of "polluter pays" market). The restriction on development that results in habitat loss has led to significant debate in US courts about whether the Endangered Species Act constitutes a "taking" or a diminution of private property rights (Innes *et al.* 1998). This may be the reason why they are more widely used in developed countries, where there may be less of an income disparity between those using land of ecological value in rural areas and the wider population, than in developing countries.

In terms of the distributional impacts between landowners, TDRs are often seen as benefiting those who wish to develop land because if the benefits of development exceed the costs of purchasing the rights, then land development is permitted, unlike with non-tradable restrictions or protected areas. These are likely to be wealthier landowners because land clearing and other related activities rely on initial investments of capital or labor. However, some argue that poorer landowners also benefit because they receive compensation for not converting their land.

As with protected areas and PES schemes, if TDRs are environmentally effective, this may reduce incomes for households in rural areas who do not own land if economic activity relating to timber harvesting or agriculture is reduced.

TDRs can be expected to have positive long-term effects because once the regulation is in place and the rights have been allocated, then the sale and purchase of rights should occur without intervention beyond monitoring and enforcement. In addition, they provide ongoing incentives for habitat protection. In the United States, long-term sustainability is achieved by requiring an easement and a trust fund for management of land used as compensation.

Financing options for ecosystem management policies

The policy options discussed above all require the relevant financial means for them to be designed, implemented and enforced. Ultimately, financing is about some form of compensation. For example, in the case of protected areas, compensation (say in the form of royalties) is required to be offered to those who have incurred a loss in user rights. In the case of PES schemes, compensation (most notably in the form of direct subsidies) is required to induce participation and compliance; while in the case of certified products, compensation (in the form of a price premium) is required to induce adherence to specific production practices. The sources of such financing schemes can vary, including charities, sale of non-timber forest products, tourism revenues and carbon markets. Different ecosystem management policies may be financed via the *same* type of financial instrument. For example, environmental funds and charities can be a source for subsidizing protected areas, PES schemes and/or certification schemes

(Kontoleon *et al.* 2008; Pearce 2007). International experiences suggest that, most commonly, financing mechanisms for ecosystem policies are as follows.

Non-use benefits

Mechanisms that aim to capture non-use benefits represent the purest form of public good values associated with ecosystems. Some of these non-use values (NUVs) can be captured *indirectly* through market instruments as they are often coupled with private goods (such as ecotourism). Yet, as is the case with most pure public goods, they mainly must be *directly* provided. There are two financing instruments for the direct provision of pure public goods: public taxation, and private (national and international) donations. International experience suggests that all of these mechanisms are failing to appropriate substantial amount of non-use benefits, and that so-called Environmental Funds could provide a promising avenue for addressing this shortfall (Pearce 2007).

Non-timber forest products

Non-timber forest products (NTFPs) have the potential to be harvested without compromising ecosystem integrity. Furthermore, the overall diversity of the ecosystem may contribute to its value in relation to the provision of NTFPs. As such, income from NTFPs may provide incentives to maintain large and diverse areas of ecosystems, rather than clearing for timber or agriculture. This may provide justification for encouraging the development of markets for NTFPs or assisting forest-based communities with participation in NTFP markets. The private good characteristics of NTFPs means that markets can and do exist without any outside intervention. However, these markets commonly occur only at the local level, indicating that support for harvesters in the form of improved availability of information or product marketing skills, or provision of infrastructure, could potentially increase the size of the market across which NTFP values could be captured, and therefore the prices received (Angelsen and Wunder 2002).

The extent to which the harvest and sale of NTFPs can deliver funding for ecosystem conservation depends on the potential value of the flow of products. A review of case studies on values of forest ecosystem benefits suggested that the gross value of NTFPs in tropical forest areas averaged around US$40 per ha per year. In some areas, this exceeded US$100 per ha per year, while in others the values of harvests were only a few dollars per hectare. In many areas, the value of forest land for NTFP harvests does not match the value of the land if converted to agricultural production. Certain products do have high levels of demand, but frequently supply cannot be met by sustainable use of natural forests, in which case rising prices will lead to pressures for cultivation of products rather than wild harvest (OECD 2003).

Support for the creation of a market for NTFPs will only be effective if there is genuine potential for a profitable activity that can continue after the initial assistance has ceased. However, if the harvest and sale of NTFPs is not profitable in the absence of subsidies, then supporting the development of NTFP markets will be less cost effective than a PES scheme aimed at biodiversity protection.

Historical patterns of the harvest and sale of NTFPs such as rubber, cocoa and cashews have shown that growth of demand is often followed by overexploitation of the natural resource base, and then the development of domesticated varieties (Goeschl and Igliori 2006). This suggests that high-value NTFPs are unlikely to be a long-term mechanism for forest ecosystem conservation. As discussed above, low-value NTFPs will not provide sufficient incentive for forest conservation unless the opportunity costs of not converting to agriculture are also low.

Ecotourism

A long-established method of encouraging the conservation of ecosystems has been to use mechanisms that create a connection between conservation and income from tourism. Capturing the benefits of nature-based tourism can occur in various ways. One option is to charge entrance fees for national parks and other protected areas. It is not necessary to charge entrance fees to protected areas to benefit from the tourist enjoyment of diverse forest areas. This is because the protection of natural resources that attract tourists to an area can also create economic opportunities in that area. There has been fairly extensive experience with community wildlife conservation projects, where communities protect wildlife in return for income and employment as safari or hunting guides, and earnings from tourist lodges, often in cooperation with the private sector. A third financing alternative is that private companies that earn income from tourist activities may compensate landowners for forest conservation. This method of conservation is not widespread, in part because of difficulties in overcoming free-riding.

In order for ecotourism to act as an effective method of protecting ecosystems, there needs to be a clear link between tourist demand and ecosystem conservation. However, it is not clear that tourists value the diversity of the forest as opposed to the presence of the forest resource, in many cases. More significantly, it may be difficult to separate the value of forests from other characteristics of a particular site. To illustrate, we consider the case of nature-based tourist activities in Costa Rica, a key destination within the global ecotourism market. According to Aylward *et al.* (1996), two-thirds of visits to Costa Rica's National Park System were to Manuel Antonio, Volcan Poas and Volcan Irazu. While these three parks all contain important forest habitats, the primary purpose of visiting Manuel Antonio National Park is to access its beaches, while the other two parks are marketed specifically on the grounds that they are volcanoes. Tourist visits to parks such as these, where forest attributes are less important than other physical characteristics, are likely to provide incentives for basic levels of forest conservation, as conversion to alternative land uses could diminish their attractiveness; but they are unlikely to encourage conservation of, or improvements to, the levels of diversity within the forested areas.

In contrast to sites where diverse forest areas are simply one of many attributes that are attractive to tourists, there would be a more direct link with protection of biodiversity in forests where wildlife viewing is an important tourist activity. This would particularly apply to cases where bird-watching is an attraction, as it relies on the presence of a wide variety of species. However, where tourists visit in order to view particular species, such as lemurs in Madagascar or gorillas in Uganda, the protection of the species also provides incentives for maintaining the quality of the forest ecosystem (Wunder 2000).

In addition to the issue of whether the demand for ecotourism relies on maintaining forest quality and diversity, there is also a risk that tourist activities may lead directly to degradation of the forest ecosystems the activities are based on. Ultimately, optimal pricing of the reserve that would aim to extract the highest possible consumer surplus would need to take into account the carrying capacity levels of a particular site.

Carbon markets

Deforestation is the largest source of carbon dioxide (CO_2) emissions from developing countries, contributing an amount greater than the total US fossil-fuel emissions. For example, deforestation rates found in Indonesia make it the world's third largest emitter after the United States and the PRC. Not surprisingly, in academic circles (most notably the recent Stern review), the idea of using carbon markets as a vehicle for investing in new or in preserving existing forests to be used as carbon sinks is gaining prominence, while the issue is also increasingly being elevated on the climate change policy agenda.

Whether such carbon markets that invest in maintaining or increasing forest land could benefit conserving ecosystem integrity is not straightforward. At the same time, there is strong evidence to support that tropical forests have a higher carbon absorption potential and, hence, there is scope for coupling of objectives and policies so that carbon markets that are designed for climate change mitigation could have a beneficial impact on ecosystem biodiversity (Matthews *et al.* 2002; Caparros and Jacquemont 2003).

The cost-effectiveness of such schemes would depend on the opportunity costs of land as well as on monitoring and enforcement costs. Both of these are context specific so carbon markets would not be equally cost effective across regions. A related issue to cost effectiveness has to do with that of "additionality." In theory, carbon credits should be awarded to a country for creating or maintaining forest sinks that would not have been created or maintained in the absence of carbon-uptake incentives. Yet, determining such additionality is far from easy as, in many cases, reforestation or forest-preservation activities are motivated by other reasons and would have taken place even in the absence of a carbon market. The issue of additionality perplexes even further when we consider so-called "co-benefits" of reforestation such as wildlife habitat or water quality improvements. International experience suggests that many programs or activities that promote ecosystem services would, on their own, not pass a benefit–cost test without consideration of their carbon benefits. For example, payments for private habitat restoration undertaken by non-governmental agencies would in many cases be neither efficient nor cost-effective without considering carbon benefits. In such cases, carbon is a valuable co-benefit and carbon financing may in fact provide a valuable vehicle for accomplishing a dual objective (Van Kooten and Shogren 2007).

Case study: evidence from payments for ecosystem services schemes in the United States

International experience suggests that PES schemes have become the most discussed areas of ecosystem management, reflecting the wider appeal within policy circles of the "beneficiary-pays principle," an enhanced interest in finding alternative sources of conservation financing, greater private sector engagement and changing governance structures which are more compatible with the development of PES schemes (Wunder 2005). Here, we summarize some key lessons from looking at PES schemes in the United States. There are various reasons why this case study is of particular interest for the PRC. First, it is perhaps the most insightful example of the "beneficiary-pays principle". Second, it is highly applicable to ecosystems (e.g. grasslands) that are of interest for the PRC. Third, the issue of "compensation" is increasingly becoming pressing in the PRC (e.g. social unrest in rural areas). Fourth, as the PRC becomes wealthier, citizens would be increasingly willing to pay more for environmental services to those who bear the cost of their provision. Last, PES scheme allows for the possibility for balancing economic development, poverty alleviation and environmental protection.

Though PES schemes have been developed in the United States since the 1930s, we focus in this chapter on the so-called Conservation Reserve Program (CRP), a land set-aside program which started in 1985. The broad underlying characteristics of this agro-environmental program is that it is voluntary in nature; it is financed via general taxation; it uses various environmental indices to rank contracts that are offered to farmers in terms of environmental gain and cost; and that it also has other social (equity) objectives built into it.

In the US program, cost-effectiveness implies:

1 targeting payments to those lands that yield the largest environmental benefit per dollar spent; and
2 offering payments that just equal the minimum amount necessary to encourage farmers to adopt the desired practices on the targeted plots.

This entails a huge informational cost as it is necessary to identity those combinations of lands and practices that would yield the greatest environmental benefit relative to cost (Claassen *et al.* 2008). This, in turn, requires understanding the relationship between environmental benefits and costs (Wu *et al.* 2001). As these programs are limited in scale, enrollment into the scheme is done on a competitive basis. Through various bidding mechanisms, the regulator can ascertain the services that land producers are willing to offer for program enrollment, the practices they are willing to adopt and the minimum level of payment they are willing to accept (WTA).

The process of establishing these programs involves considerable amounts of information gathering but also a considerable degree of stakeholder involvement and participation. Figure 10.2 shows the steps this process involves. It starts with all farmers and ranchers as potential entrants and concludes with selecting a group of program participants based on the highest benefit–cost ratio as revealed through the consultation and bidding process. Bids are then ranked according to their ability to deliver environmental gain per dollar spent, and contracts are issued until the budget is exhausted or the acreage cap is reached.

As stated, the CRP was initiated in 1985 mainly to combat soil conservation (though in its present form, it also aims at promoting water quality improvement and wildlife habitat). It provides 10–15 year contracts to farmers for retirement of agricultural land. Farmers receive financial assistance to plant and maintain grass or forest in previously cultivated land, as well as an annual cash subsidy determined through competitive bids. Land that is eligible for enrollment into the CRP is that which has a history of crop production and is deemed to be environmentally important (either by being highly erodible, located in a Conservation Priority Area, or being intended for use as wetland restoration area or

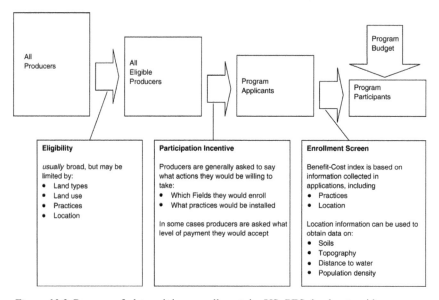

Figure 10.2 Process of determining enrollment in US PES land set aside programs (source: Claassen *et al.* 2008).

streamside or conservation buffers). Land can be re-enrolled after another round of bidding.

In practice, enrollment is determined on an assessment of offers from farmers using the Environmental Benefits Index (EBI), a benefit–cost index that accounts for a broad range of environmental concerns and the cost of the contract to the government (US Department of Agriculture-Farm Service Agency (USDA-FSA) 2003).[1] In 2005, 14.5 million hectares (ha) were enrolled. The bid that each farmer submits specifies the amount of land being offered, the type of land cover that would be established (grass or trees), and their WTA. The regulator then ranks offers using the EBI, with bids gaining EBI scores above a predetermined cut-off level (selected for each sign-up period after bids are received) being accepted (Claassen *et al.* 2008). A farmer could improve his/her bid (and their overall EBI score) by accepting lower annual payments, foregoing cost-sharing on establishment of grass or tree coverage, or by establishing cover that is more suitable for wildlife habitat.

The PES schemes serve as useful examples of the efficiency and effectiveness of PES schemes for ecosystem management in the PRC. Following Claassen *et al.* (2008), we can consider the following questions for determining the efficiency of various market-based systems:

- Has benefit–cost targeting enhanced the environmental gains per dollar spent? In what ways could targeting be improved?
- What are the cost-savings that have resulted from bidding? Has bidding managed to reveal true WTA?
- Is monitoring adequate to ensure contracted actions are being implemented?
- Have programs resulted in environmental gains that would not have otherwise been obtained (i.e. additionality)?

Assessing benefit–cost targeting under CRP

Undertaking benefit–cost targeting using EBI has brought about a shift in emphasis from enrollment of low-cost land (that in many cases was also low quality and highly erodible land) to enrolling land that yields broader environmental benefits. EBI points are assigned to a series of environmental and cost considerations. These are highlighted in Table 10.1. As can be seen there, the most heavily weighted are the environmental factors (receiving 100 maximum points) of wildlife habitat, water quality and soil erodibility. Various farm features (such as plot location, slope) determine the size of the points attributed to each factor. The number of points offered to the cost factor (i.e. the WTA bid made) can vary, but a general trend is for this to be assigned around 150 points.

There is considerable research to show that the EBI system has led to an increase in the environmental benefits provided by the CRP (as compared to a pre-1986 benchmark). For example, initial research estimating improvements in recreational benefits found that (Feather *et al.* 1999; Claassen *et al.* 2008):

Table 10.1 Main factors and points determining EBI

EBI factors	Definition	Features that increase points	Maximum points
Wildlife	Evaluates the expected wildlife benefits of the offer.	• Diversity of grass/legumes • Use of native grasses • Tree planting • Wetlands restoration • Beneficial to threatened/endangered species • Complements wetland habitat	100
Water quality	Evaluates the potential surface and ground water impacts	• Located in ground- or surface-water protection area • Potential for percolation of chemicals and the local population using groundwater • Potential for runoff to reach surface water and the county population	100
Erosion	Evaluates soil erodibility	• Larger field-average erodibility index	100
Enduring benefits	Evaluates the likelihood for practice to remain	• Tree cover • Wetland restoration	50
Air quality	Evaluates gains from reduced dust	• Potential for dust to affect people • Soil vulnerability to wind erosion • Carbon sequestration	45
Cost	Evaluates cost of parcel	• Lower CRP rent • No government cost share • Payment is below program's maximum acceptable for area and soil type	Varies but normally set to 150

Source: Claassen et al. (2008); US Department of Agriculture-Farm Service Agency (USDA-FSA) (2003).

- total freshwater-based recreation benefits attributable to the CRP increased by US$92 million (a 255 percent gain);
- benefits due to increased opportunities for wildlife viewing increased by US$287 million (83 percent); and
- pheasant-hunting benefits declined by US$10 million (13 percent).

In aggregate, the Feather *et al.* (1999) study estimates recreational benefits to be in the order of around US$400 million in 1999 alone, a figure, however, that may be less than the CRP costs. Hence, focusing just on recreational benefits (though admittedly more easy to measure) does not provide an adequate picture of the entire potential environmental benefits. In more recent studies, researchers have estimated wider environmental benefits. For example, Sullivan *et al.* (2004) estimate CRP environmental benefits to be around US$1.2 billion, but even this estimate masks the true benefits of the CRP as it does not include possible benefits such as groundwater quality and carbon sequestration. Nonetheless, Claassen *et al.* (2008) suggest that additional improvements in the environmental cost-effectiveness of the CRP could be attained by further shifting emphasis from maintenance of soil productivity to improving water quality and wildlife habitat. Overall, the message from the use of a benefit–cost targeting strategy is that, for the case of the CRP, it definitely has led to significant environmental benefits.

Efficiency of the bidding process

Opting for some form of competitive auctioning of PES contracts is a recurring theme in the literature, as it is considered the most cost-effective way of utilizing a (normally fixed) program budget (see Ferraro 2008 for a review of bidding alternatives). The aim of the auction would be to induce farmers to reveal their latent true WTA. Though such bidding presupposes a specific institutional and legal framework that is often not present in developing economies, it is something that should nevertheless be considered and planned for when undertaking a long-term environmental strategy exercise.

In the case of the CRP, the final bid submitted by the farmer could be determined in several ways. CRP applicants can offer to receive a discount, that is, a WTA that is below the maximum payment that has been established by the regulator for the specific type and location of plot that is offered for inclusion in the CRP. These so-called "bid caps" reflect county average cropland rental rates at average productivity. When a farmer increases the discount they would be willing to accept, they increase the EBI score (keeping everything else fixed). Alternatively, a farmer may cover all (or a large share) of the cost of land cover (growing grass and planting trees). Also, the farmer can increase the EBI score by offering to enhance wildlife habitat or to improve water quality. The bidding process reveals to farmers their *environmental scores* on their EBI before they finalize and submit their bids. Hence, farmers must submit their best bid given their environmental scores. The speculative element of the CRP auctions has been shown to be reduced through the learning achieved through repeated sign-ups.

Bidding is only as effective as the auction structure and the competitive nature of the process. Strategic bidding by insufficiently motivated participants may explain findings by Kirwin *et al.* (2005) that sequential sign-ups may lead to significant premiums being awarded. Further, Claassen *et al.* (2008) find that:

* Despite the auction program, competition has not been particularly intense with nearly 75 percent of applicants accepted in 1997 and almost 50 percent in 2003.
* The proportion of acres offered with discounts has declined over the years.
* Farmers accepted in the CRP did not offer discounts more frequently or discounts that were larger than farmers who were not enrolled.
* EBI scores were significantly higher for farmers who were enrolled in the program.

The experience from the CRP shows that (despite theoretical predictions) the auctioning of contracts has been largely unsuccessful at reducing program costs. There is too much room for learning and strategic behavior in these simple auction procedures. Conversely, competitive bidding might also lead to situations where farmers end up bidding so close to their true WTA that small changes in economic conditions may significantly alter their willingness to carry out the contracted practices. (Claassen *et al.* 2008). The overall message that can be deduced is that bidding is a complex process with many pitfalls, even in economies with a long tradition in competitive tenders.

Monitoring and enforcement costs

PES schemes are essentially contracts, and hence monitoring and enforcement are essential for the contract to be effective. The main issues involving monitoring and enforcement include the cost of monitoring, the frequency of monitoring, the form and amount of penalty, and the risk aversion of the farmers. These are crucial issues as the monitoring of imperfections can lead to perverse outcomes including adverse selection problems (Ferraro 2008).

In the case of the CRP, monitoring is undertaken via random inspections. Claassen *et al.* (2008) report on the findings from a recent assessment that identified serious deficiencies in the monitoring and enforcement of US cross-compliance requirements – and the main finding of which is that the amount of payment deducted was a more important determinant of compliance compared to the expected likelihood of inspection. Various measures to reduce the cost of monitoring and boost compliance have been investigated including the use of low-cost proxy variables. The message here is that even in cases such as the CRP and Environmental Quality Incentives Program (EQIP), which have been implemented with advanced monitoring and enforcement mechanisms and technologies, monitoring and enforcement remain cumbersome and costly matters.

Transactions costs

Transactions costs include the cost of designing the program (e.g. setting up the EBI system), the farmer's cost of submitting an application, and the cost of processing applications, selecting participants, entering into contracts, making payments, monitoring compliance and taking enforcement actions when necessary (Claassen *et al.* 2008). Though the actual total size of transactions costs is hard to assess, some indication is available on the magnitude of certain components. For example, conservation-related salaries and expenses are estimated to be around 1 percent of the CRP expenditure. These expenditures are in fact modest and can be explained on the basis of the availability of existing large databases on soil and land quality which can be combined with geographic information system (GIS) technology to estimate EBI scores. Still, the research and data collection efforts that are required to assess EBIs remain significant (reaching US$530 million in 2004 alone). Yet, these research efforts have wider applications beyond the CRP, and the exact share attributed to the CRP is unknown. The message that can be derived is that transactions costs have an inverse relationship with investment in research and development. Hence, the implementation of such PES schemes, even in the developed world context, depends on the availability of extensive databases on the quality of soils, topography, the location of land, local land rental conditions, etc. that can be readily accessed using GIS to quickly and inexpensively estimate benefit–costs indices and (when necessary) costs (Claassen *et al.* 2008).

Additionality, post-program retention and slippage

As discussed above the requirement of "additionality" refers to assigning contracts to those farmers who would not adopt the environmentally-friendly production practices without the extra incentive provided by the program (Wunder 2005). To adhere to this principle, the EQIP offers payments only for practices that were not previously applied by the farmer. This is easier to determine in regard to structural practices (e.g. riparian buffers) and less so for management practices (e.g. nutrient management). In the CRP case, farmers applying for enrollment into the program must show that the land offered has been under cultivation before 2002.

Yet, as Claassen *et al.* (2008) note, whether gains are truly additional can only be measured by comparing land use changes undertaken under an agro-environmental program with regard to a baseline of land use changes that would have occurred in the absence of the program. Establishing such a baseline is not trivial. For example, in a study conducted by Lubowski *et al.* (2003), they found that approximately 15 percent of the land enrolled in the CRP would have been retired even if it were not included in the CRP.

The issue of post-program retention concerns what farmers will do in cases where their application for re-enrollment of land is rejected. There is ample evidence to suggest that more than 50 percent of CRP land would be returned to crop production in the absence of CRP payments (Sullivan *et al.* 2004). Other effects related to possible perverse incentives for increasing crop land for future enroll-ment into the CRP also had to be addressed. This was done via a series of meas-ures which discourage expansion of crop production on highly erodible lands and wetland so that they can gain CRP eligibility status.

Lastly, "slippage" is another adverse effect that has been studied in the context of such ecosystem management related PES schemes. Slippage refers to the practice of some farmers increasing the area used for cultivation as they intend to benefit from possible crop price increases due to the supply reduction that was induced by the PES scheme. Yet, estimates of the magnitude of this problem for the case of PES schemes vary. For example, Wu (2000) estimates that for every 100 acres retired in CRP there are another 21 which are brought into cultivation; however, others such as Roberts and Bucholtz (2005) (using the same data as Wu) dispute these estimates.

In sum, the CRP case study demonstrates the costs and complexity involved in providing an incentives-based conservation scheme. It clearly has significant benefits compared to CAC approaches to conservation, but also with significant costs and complexity as well.

Case study: biodiversity offsets in the United States

The second case study examined here concerns biodiversity offsets in the United States (also referred to as land development rights). This focus on biodiversity offsets was chosen for several reasons. First, offsets are "polluter-pays" type of instruments, and so offer a natural counterpart to the PES schemes discussed above which are underpinned by a "beneficiary pays" rationale. Second, offsets and banking are policies that, perhaps more explicitly than others, try to address the challenge of reconciling the need for economic development and use of ecosys-tems, on one hand, and the aim for conservation, on the other. In terms of the sus-tainability literature, offsets fully embody the notion of "weak sustainability," a notion that in the face of current economic realities and social norms appears to be adopted by most policy-making centers in both the developed and developing world. Third, offsets and tradable land use rights are increasingly being discussed in the context of optimal selection of protected areas (PAs) and networks of nature reserves. As in many other countries (including the EU, United States and Canada), PAs and nature reserve networks constitute one of the cornerstones of long-term ecosystem management policies. Last, offsets are an instrument that is much more related to the issue of *regional ecosystem planning* which is of considerable focus in the PRC's long-term environmental strategy for ecosystem management.

The International Union for Conservation of Nature (IUCN) defines biodiver-sity offsets as "conservation actions intended to compensate for the residual, unavoidable harm to biodiversity caused by development projects, so as to ensure no net loss of biodiversity."[2] To set these ideas, we focus on one particu-lar type of offset banking in the United States, namely wetland banking. Devel-opers whose plans may cause damage to wetlands must obtain permits from the

US Army Corps of Engineers under the US Clean Water Act 1972 and the US Army Corps of Engineers regulations. The Corps follows a sequential approach in granting these "wetland permits" (ten Kate *et al*. 2004; Salzman and Ruhl 2000 and 2005). First, developers must prove that the damage to the wetlands is "unavoidable." They must then try to minimize any negative impacts on those wetlands that cannot be reasonably avoided. Finally, they must offer "compensatory mitigation" for the damages that they cannot avoid after all minimization measures have been pursued. In principle, for every unit of wetland destroyed (say one hectare), an equivalent unit (but usually more) of a comparable wetland must be restored or regenerated within the defined "service area" (ten Kate *et al*. 2004).

Initial experience with in-kind and on-site offsets highlighted various problems. For example, there was a lack of know-how amongst developers, and the monitoring and enforcement efforts were stretched across too many relatively small mitigation projects. This resulted in a low quality of restoration from initial wetland offset schemes which resulted in a new generation of policies, including Wetland Mitigation Banking (WMB).

In practice, developers may meet their "compensatory mitigation" obligations themselves (usually at or near the development site), or they can pay third parties to do this instead. In the latter case, they can either:

1 purchase "wetland credits" from a mitigation bank;
2 pay fees (determined by the Corps) to public entities or private not-for-profit organizations that use the fees (known as "in-lieu-fees") to "protect, enhance, or restore" wetlands; or
3 pay a third party that is neither a mitigation bank nor an in-lieu fee provider to undertake the mitigation (these are referred to as "ad-hoc" arrangements) (ten Kate *et al*. 2004).

The United States has witnessed the development of a whole new industry of wetland banking (see Table 10.2).

There are two main benefits to wetland banking:

1 they allow for maintaining the integrity of the aquatic ecosystem by consolidating compensatory mitigation into a single (or a few) large parcel(s); and

Table 10.2 Growth of wetland banking in the United States (1992/3, 2001/2)

	1992/3	*2001/2*
Approved banks	46	219
Wetlands restored	17,664 acres	139,896 acres
Participating states	18	40
Size of banks (% > 100 acres)	35%	57%
Private commercial banks	1	135

Source: Wilkinson *et al.* (2002).

2   they lead to consolidation of financial resources, planning and scientific expertise.

Both of these features lead to more effective management. Also, banking increases the efficiency of limited agency resources for monitoring and enforcement. Last, banking schemes contribute towards attainment of "no-net-loss" of the nation's wetlands (Salzman and Ruhl 2005).

Experience with commercial mitigation banking suggests that costs linked to risk from future demand uncertainty can lead to increased permit prices which in turn may act as a barrier to entry (market thinness). Further, we could be faced with significant credit demand uncertainty, mostly due to regulatory issues (e.g. the sequencing process continues to prefer on-site credits). As a result of these shortcomings, the share of Commercial Wetland Banking (out of total credits) remains relatively small (10–20 percent). In response to these problems, alternative banking schemes are being developed. One such development is Credit Resale Mitigation Banking.

Under this scheme, the central government must allocate some initial funding for setting up the scheme. This start up fund is allocated between assessing the likely demand for credits and setting up an implementing agency. The implementing agency sells credits sold to agency via auction. The agency receives bids from potential credit suppliers who bid for credits in auction. The agency purchases the best "value for money" credits. The agency then resells credits (so as to recover full costs) to future developers or permit-holders. An important feature of the program is that it allows for up front payment from the credit supplier (in total or in predefined installments). It also entails limited credit demand uncertainty as well as full cost recovery on behalf of the government. As the credit inventory is depleted, new auctioning of credits is offered. The scheme offers a promising avenue for securing the supply, quality and price advantages of a competitive market for wetlands credits. An example of this scheme is the North Carolina Ecosystem Enhancement Program (NCEEP).[3] Shabman and Scodari (2005) observe that, under the NCEEP, the auctioning process can be costly (though this could be reduced as prospective bidders increase and more experience with auctioning attained). Also, this may bring about the exhaustion of permitted wetland restoration sites in one area. They argue that extending the program to providing other forms of mitigation credits (e.g. stream restoration, nutrient reduction) required by different pollution control programs could add to the number of auctions issued in any year. Also, expanding the wetlands credit resale program concept regionally or nationally should be considered (see Shabman and Scodari 2005).

Further, the auctioning process has focused on a very limited geographic area. This means that the availability of suitable lands for credit production decreases and undermines the market for credits. This could be mitigated by developing credits for "wetlands functions and services" rather than wetland assets (e.g. land area) – for example, Shabman and Scodari (2005) suggest water quality and hydrologic services (these are site dependent) as well as habitat services (less site dependent). Also issuing credit auctions for wetlands habitat services at larger eco-region scales could lead to an increase in the pool of land parcels that would be suitable sites for credit production, and this would enhance competition for credit supply contracts. Last, there is need for auxiliary regulation for securing the provision of local site dependent watershed services (e.g. for non-wetland alternatives such as riparian buffers).

Conclusions on international experiences on ecosystem management

Overall, international experience suggests that we cannot argue in favor of a single policy mechanism, because the features of each mean that they are likely to be appropriate in different situations. For example, market creation will be more effective where property rights are well defined and enforced; regulatory mechanisms may be the best option if benefits are very heterogeneous; and PES schemes will have favorable distributional impacts if those who are providing the biodiversity benefits are poor relative to the beneficiaries. In addition, multiple instruments can frequently complement each other. For example, PES-type transfers may be used at the international or regional level to purchase environmental services from national or local governments. These governments may then either set up further PES contracts with individual landowners, or they may implement regulations, or use the ecosystem payments to fund one or more protected areas.

The type of benefit will also determine the appropriate policy instrument. Market creation options are desirable because they ensure that conservation only occurs when net benefits are positive, and because they do not require (as much) public finance as other mechanisms. However, some benefits can be captured more easily than others through the use of markets. This suggests that encouraging markets for private goods and services, such as tourism benefits, and for goods and services where the necessary institutions already exist, such as carbon benefits, would give the highest returns. Public goods such as watershed services or non-use values may need greater levels of local or national government intervention. For watershed services, experiences with local PES schemes appear promising, although there is often a need for clearer understanding of the ecological processes. For non-use benefits, eco-labeling schemes can capture part of the values of ecosystems, but international financial flows from developed country governments (through institutions such as the GEF), on behalf of their residents, will also be necessary.

Notes

1 Other forms of auctions for assigning PES contract are reviewed in Ferraro (2008).
2 This section is based on ten Kate *et al.* (2004) and Salzman and Ruhl (2000 and 2005).
3 See www.nceep.net.

References

Angelsen, A. and S. Wunder (2002). "Exploring the Forest – Poverty Link," *CIFOR Occasional Paper.*

Aylward, B., K. Allen, J. Echeverría and J. Tosi (1996). "Sustainable Ecotourism in Costa Rica: the Monteverde Cloud Forest Preserve," *Biodiversity and Conservation* 5: 315–43.

Caparros, A. and F. Jacquemont (2003). "Conflicts between Biodiversity and Carbon Sequestration Programs: Economic and Legal Implications," *Ecological Economics* 46(1): 143–57.

Chomitz, K.M., T.S. Thomas and A. Salazar (2004). *Creating Markets for Habitat Conservation when Habitats are Heterogeneous,* World Bank, Development Research Group, Infrastructure and Environment Team.

Claassen, R., A. Cattaneo and R. Johansson (2008). "Cost-effective Design of Agri-environmental Payment Programs: U.S. Experience in Theory and Practice," *Ecological Economics* 65: 737–52.

Echevarría, M., J. Vogel, M. Albán and F. Meneses (2004). *The Impacts of Payments for Watershed Services in Ecuador: Emerging Lessons from Pimampiro and Cuenca,* London: International Institute for Environment and Development (IIED).

Emerton, L., J. Bishop and L. Thomas (2006). *Sustainable Financing of Protected Areas: A Global Review of Challenges and Options,* The World Conservation Union (IUCN).

Feather, P., D. Hellerstein and L. Hansen (1999). "Economic Valuation of Environmental Benefits and the Targeting of Conservation Programs: The Case of the CRP," Agricultural Economics Report No. 778, April 1999.

Ferraro P.J. (2008). "Asymmetric Information and Contract Design for Payments for Environmental Services," *Ecological Economics* 65: 810–21.

Ferraro, P.J. and R.A. Kramer (1997). "Compensation and Economic Incentives: Reducing Pressures on Protected Areas," in *Last Stand: Protected Areas and the Defense of Tropical Biodiversity.* R. Kramer, C. van Schaik and J. Johnson (eds.), New York: Oxford University Press, pp. 187–211.

Goeschl, T. and D.C. Igliori (2006). "Property Rights for Biodiversity Conservation and Development: Extractive Reserves in the Brazilian Amazon," *Development and Change* 37(2): 427–51.

Innes, R., S. Polasky and J. Tschirhart (1998). "Takings, Compensation and Endangered Species Protection on Private Lands," *Journal of Economic Perspectives* 12: 35–52.

Kerr, J. (2002). "Sharing the Benefits of Watershed Management in Sukhomajri, India," in *Selling Forest Environmental Services: Market-based Mechanisms for Conservation and Development.* S. Pagiola, J. Bishop and N. Landell-Mills (eds.), London: Earthscan.

Kirwan, B., R.N. Lubowski and M.J. Roberts (2005). "How Cost-Effective are Land Retirement Auctions? Estimating the Difference between Payments and Willingness to Accept in the Conservation Reserve Program," *American Journal of Agricultural Economics* 87(5): 1239–47.

Kolstad, C.D. (2000). *Environmental Economics,* Oxford: Oxford University Press.

Kontoleon, A., K. Mullan and J. Bishop (2008). "Economics of Forest Biodiversity Conservation," Report for the IUCN and the EU EA.

Landell-Mills, N. (1999). "Country Profile for Brazil," Report prepared within the project "Instruments for Sustainable Private Sector Forestry" (unpublished). London: IIED.

Lapham, N.P. and R.J. Livermore (2003). "Striking a Balance: Ensuring Conservation's

Place on the International Biodiversity Assistance Agenda," Center for Applied Biodiversity Science, Center for Conservation and Government. Conservation International. Washington, DC.

Lubowski, Ruben, Andrew Plantinga and Roberts Stavins (2003). "Determinants of Land-Use Change in the United States, 1982–1997," Discussion Paper 03–47, Resources for the Future, Washington, DC.

Matthews, S., R. O'Connor and A. Plantinga (2002). "Quantifying the Impacts on Biodiversity of Policies for Carbon Sequestration in Forests," *Ecological Economics* 40(1): 71–87.

May, P.H., F.V. Neto, V. Denardin and W. Loureiro (2002). "Using Fiscal Instruments to Encourage Conservation: Municipal Responses to the Ecological Value-added Tax in Paraná and Minas Gerais, Brazil," in *Selling Forest Environmental Services. Market-based Mechanisms for Conservation and Development*. S. Pagiola, J. Bishop and N. Landell-Mills (eds.), London: Earthscan.

Moguel, P. and V.M. Toledo (1999). "Biodiversity Conservation in Traditional Coffee Systems of Mexico," *Conservation Biology* 13(1): 11–21.

OECD (2003). "Harnessing Markets for Biodiversity Towards Conservation and Sustainable Use," Paris: OECD.

Pagiola, S. and I.M. Ruthenberg (2002). "Selling Biodiversity in a Coffee Cup: Shade-Grown Coffee and Conservation in Mesoamerica," in *Selling Forest Environmental Services: Market-based Mechanisms for Conservation and Development*. S. Pagiola, J. Bishop and N. Landell-Mills (eds.), London: Earthscan.

Pagiola, S., J. Bishop and N. Landell-Mills (2002). *Selling Forest Environmental Services: Market-based Mechanisms for Conservation and Development*, London: Earthscan.

Pearce, D. (2007) "Do We Really Care About Biodiversity?" in *Biodiversity Economics: Principles, Methods and Applications*. A. Kontoleon, U. Pascual and T. Swanson *et al.* (eds.), Cambridge: Cambridge University Press.

Perez, C. (2005). "Recovering Positive Mountain Externalities: Reversing Land Degradation through Payments for Environmental Services at Local Level," Report for the Program for Sustainable Agriculture in the Hillsides of Central America.

Roberts, M.J. and S. Bucholtz (2005). "Slippage in the Conservation Reserve Program or Spurious Correlation and Quest; A Comment," *American Journal of Agricultural Economics* 87(1): 244–50.

Rojas, M. and B. Aylward (2003). *What are We Learning from Experiences with Markets for Environmental Services in Costa Rica? A Review and Critique of the Literature*, IIED.

Rosales, R. (2003). "Mt Kanla-On: Bearing the Costs," *World Conservation* 1: 21.

Salzman, James E. and J.B. Ruhl (2000) "Currencies and the Commodification of Environmental Law," *Stanford Law Review* 53(3): 607–94.

Salzman, James E. and J.B. Ruhl (2005). " 'No Net Loss' – Instrument Choice in Wetlands Protection," in *Moving to Markets in Environmental Regulation: Twenty Years of Experience*. Jody Freeman and Charles Kolstad (eds.), Oxford: Oxford University Press.

Shabman, L. and P. Scodari (2005). "The Future of Wetlands Mitigation Banking," *Choices* 20(1): 65–70.

Sullivan, P., D. Hellerstein, L. Hansen, R. Johansson, S. Koenig, R. Lubowski, W. McBride, D. McGranahan, M. Roberts, S. Vogel and S. Bucholtz (2004). "The Conservation Reserve Program Economic Implications for Rural America," US

Department of Agriculture, Economic Research Service, Agricultural Economic Report Number 834. Online, available at: www.ers.usda.gov/publications/aer834.

ten Kate, K., J. Bishop and R. Bayon (2004). "Biodiversity Offsets: Views, Experience, and the Business Case," IUCN, Gland, Switzerland and Cambridge, UK and Insight Investment, London.

USDA-FSA (2003). United States Department of Agriculture. Fact Sheet. Conservation Reserve Program, April 2003. Online, available at: http://farm.ewg.org/CRP.pdf.

van Kooten, G.C. and B. Shogren (2007). "Economics of Forest Ecosystem Carbon Sinks: A Review," *International Review of Environmental and Resource Economics* 1(3): 237–69.

Wätzold, F. and K. Schwerdtner (2005). "Why be Wasteful when Preserving a Valuable Resource? A Review Article on the Cost-effectiveness of European Biodiversity Conservation Policy," *Biological Conservation* 123(3): 327–38.

Wilkinson, J., C. Kennedy, K. Mott, M. Filbey, S. King and J. McElfish (2002). *Banks and Fees: The Status of Off-site Wetland Mitigation in the U.S.*, Washington, DC: ELI.

Wu, J.J. and W.G. Boggess (1999). "The Optimal Allocation of Conservation Funds," *Journal of Environmental Economics and Management* 38(3): 302–21.

Wu, J.J., Richard M. Adams and William G. Boggess (2000). "Cumulative Effects and Optimal Targeting of Conservation Efforts: Steelhead Trout Habitat Enhancement in Oregon," *American Journal of Agricultural Economics* 82(May 2000): 400–13.

Wu, J., D. Zilberman and B. Babcock (2001). "Environmental and Distributional Impacts of Conservation Targeting Strategies," *Journal of Environmental Economics and Management* 41: 333–50.

Wunder, S. (2000). "Ecotourism and Economic Incentives – an Empirical Approach," *Ecological Economics* 32(3): 465–79.

Wunder, S. (2005). "Payments for Environmental Services: some Nuts and Bolts," CIFOR Occasional Paper No. 42, Center for International Forestry Research, Jakarta, Indonesia.

Wunder, S. (2006). "Are Direct Payments for Environmental Services Spelling Doom for Sustainable Forest Management in the Tropics?" *Ecology and Society* 11(2): 23.

Wunder, S. (2007). "The Efficiency of Payments for Environmental Services in Tropical Conservation," *Conservation Biology* 21(1): 48–58.

Part IV

Institutional development for a regulated environment

11 Institutional development of environmental management in the People's Republic of China

Keyong Dong, Wenzhao Li, Zhong Ma and Shuming An

Institutional development overview

The system of environmental protection generally consists of legislation, administration and judicial interventions. This chapter focuses on the institutional development of environmental protection and management at the central government level of the People's Republic of China (PRC).

History

The environmental protection system in the PRC traces its roots to the 1971 stewardship of Premier Zhou Enlai, when the Environmental Protection Leading Group Office (EPLGO) was established under the State Planning Commission (SPC). This was the first time that environmental protection was made an endeavor by the PRC government. Thereafter, in 1972, a government delegation was sent as observer to the Stockholm Conference on Human Environment in Sweden. In August 1972, the State Council held a national environmental protection conference, wherein the regulation for environmental protection and improvement was approved. In 1974, the EPLGO was transferred to the State Construction Commission (SCC).

On September 13, 1979, the standing committee of the National People's Congress (NPC) promulgated the Environment Protection Law of the PRC, the first ever comprehensive environmental protection law in the country. This marked a milestone in the PRC's environmental protection efforts which paved the way for environmental protection management to be brought into the legal system.

Within the 20-year period that followed, seven specific laws on environmental protection, such as the Air Pollution Prevention and Control Law, were enacted, while more than 20 other laws were amended to accommodate stipulations and items in relation to environmental protection. The State Council also issued more than 20 rules and regulations to enforce the national environmental protection law. Likewise, the ministries and departments under the State Council, which are responsible for environmental protection, also issued a series of administrative regulations in relation to environmental protection. The passage of these laws, rules and regulations has brought about the establishment of a basic environmental protection legal system in the PRC, providing adequate legal and policy support for the implementation, enforcement and development of the national environmental protection agenda.

During the national institutional reform in 1982, the EPLGO under the State Council was replaced by the State Environmental Protection Bureau (SEPB), and this was placed under the Ministry of Urban and Rural Construction (MURC). The Bureau was accorded independence in planning, finance and personnel selection. In May 1984, the State Council created the State Environmental Protection Commission, which was attached to the MURC and placed under the supervision and authority of the SEPB. In December 1984, the SEPB was renamed National Environmental Protection Agency (NEPA), but remained under the MURC.

During the institutional reforms in 1988, the NEPA was detached from the MURC, and was elevated to the status of an independent agency under the State Council. This significantly contributed to the improvement of the PRC's environmental protection administration. The main function of the NEPA was the conduct of unified supervision and management over environmental protection work, particularly in the formulation of laws for the purpose of institutional reform. The NEPA had other 12 basic functions and more than 400 detailed tasks, for which internal departments and more than 260 positions were created and set up. Ten years later, in 1998, the NEPA was elevated to the ministerial level as the State Environmental Protection Administration (SEPA), ushering in a new developing stage in the PRC's environmental protection administration. Finally, in 2007, SEPA was recognized as a full-fledged ministry, and re-titled the Ministry of Environmental Protection (MEP).

Rules configuration

The state laws, State Council-issued ordinances, administrative regulations, state planning and state standards are the five legal components to the institutional establishment of the PRC's environmental protection administration. There are four legal governance levels of the PRC's environmental protection system – namely, the Constitution; the basic laws of environmental protection; specific environmental protection laws; and provisions and stipulations in relation to environmental protection in other laws.

The administrative ordinances issued by the State Council and the regulations released by the component and relevant departments under the State Council provide great legal support to the operation and the enforcement of environmental protection administration. Meanwhile, a series of important plans and programs have been formulated pursuant to the objectives of the environmental protection administration, such as the National Program on Environmental Protection, the National Program on Ecological Environmental Protection, the National Tenth Five-Year Plan (FYP) for Environmental Protection, the Cross-Century Plan of Green Engineering and the National Program for Total Amount

Control of Pollutant Discharge. A total of 395 environmental standards, including 361 *national* environmental standards and 24 *industry* environmental standards, have been promulgated as of 1998. In 2001, the number of environmental standards had reached 459.

Organizational structure

The national environmental protection system consists of several key governmental organizations.[1] Pursuant to Article 7 of the Environmental Protection Law of the PRC, the MEP (SEPA) and other local-level departments of the environmental protection administration are the principal bodies tasked with environmental protection administration. Also involved are the comprehensive economic management organizations – such as, the State Development and Planning Commission, the State Economic and Trade Commission, and the Ministry of Finance. Sectoral departments – such as the Ministry of Agriculture and the Ministry of Construction – also make up the national environmental protection system. Finally, resource exploitation administrative departments – such as the Ministry of Water Resources, the State Forestry Administration and the Ministry of Land and Resources – complete the system.

In 2001, the State Council instituted a mechanism for cross-ministry-level meeting which eventually evolved into a coordination mechanism among the ministries composing the environmental protection system.

Capacity building

There has been gradual improvement in recent years of the PRC government's capacity for, enforcement of and information release on, environmental protection. In 2006, member organizations at various levels have reached 11,321, with a total of around 1,702,906 personnel.[2] Environmental monitor stations total 2,322 nationwide, with 44,689 personnel. Monitor centers have also been established, the composition of which are as follows: a national-level monitor center with 108 personnel; 39 provincial-level monitor centers with 2,825 personnel; 39 municipal monitor centers with 16,143 staff; and 1,886 local-level monitor centers with 28,613 staff. All the monitor centers formed a relatively perfect monitoring team at the preliminary stage.[3]

For better monitoring capacity, the MEP (SEPA) began to periodically (weekly and daily) issue reports, forecasts and prevention measures on the PRC's environmental status, such as urban air quality, through the National Report on Environmental Status. It also formulated and implemented the Plan of Capacity Building for National Environmental Monitor Network.

In 2006, environmental supervision stations at various levels totaled 2,803 with 52,845 personnel all over the country – and these stations are broken down as follows: 32 provincial-level supervision stations with 772 personnel; 404 municipal/local-level supervision stations with 9,169 personnel; and 2,366 county-level supervision stations with 42,859 personnel.[4]

On July 17, 1998, the first environmental pollution criminal case was heard in a court in Shanxi with the support and participation of MEP (SEPA) until judgment was promulgated.[5] On January 1, 2001, the original NEPA imposed for the first time an administrative punishment for an environmental offense after the conduct of a hearing attended by witnesses in consideration of the rights of the person charged.

According to statistical data, between 1999 and 2001, 179,399 environmental administrative punishments were enforced; 799 environmental administration reviews were accepted; 1,897 environmental administration lawsuits were completed; 175 environmental administration compensations were given out; and five environmental criminal cases were concluded.[6]

Roles and responsibilities

In the current environmental protection system for pollution prevention and control, the responsibilities and authority for supervision and administration have been concentrated in the MEP (SEPA) and the environmental protection departments of various levels in the local governments. Meanwhile, the responsibilities for nature and resource conservation are spread out among the departments of environmental protection, resource, agriculture, forest, water resource and land. Table 11.1 shows the detailed tasks of MEP (SEPA) in the 1998 State Council's "Three Determination Program" (*Determination of Functions, Staff and Personnel*) for institutional innovation.

Lessons and challenges of institutional development

Important contributions

The unrelenting efforts of the PRC government to strengthen environmental protection administration and institutions contributed to the significant progress and achievements of the country's environmental protection efforts during the past 30 years. The Communist Party's Central Committee and the State Council attached great importance to environmental protection when they included it in the national policies. The third generation of party leaders gave environmental protection more prominence when the National Symposium on Population, Resources and Environment was incorporated during the annual conference of the NPC and the Chinese People's Political Consultative Conference. This raised the responsibility mechanism of environmental protection to the level of the party leaders, and clearly defined the responsibilities on environmental quality of the different local levels of governments. The State Council emphasized the importance of environmental protection when it promulgated the Determinations for Strengthening Environmental Protection to improve guidance on environmental protection efforts.

The environmental protection legislative system was established, and powerful legislative supports were provided for the implementation of environmental protection administration. Based on the PRC's Environmental Protection Law, a series of related laws were also promulgated – e.g. the Prevention and Control of Air Pollution Law; Prevention and Control of Water Pollution Law; Marine Environment Protection Law; Prevention and Control of Noise Pollution Law; and Prevention and Control of Solid Waste Pollution Law.[7] Legislative organizations also supervised and urged the enforcement of environmental protection laws by local governments.

Judicial agencies dealt with civil, administrative and criminal lawsuits to ensure adherence to national laws, and guarantee fairness in the implementation of the policies on environmental protection.

Administrative and environmental management regulations were gradually formulated. A series of policies and actions were also promulgated to implement environmental management, such as the environmental impact assessment, design, construction and operation standards for construction projects; pollutant emissions charging; pollutant discharge permit, license and reporting; pollutant total amount control; deadlines for standards compliance; responsibility attribution to meet the objectives of environmental protection; and quantitative examination of comprehensive control on urban environment.

The management functions of the departments in charge of environmental protection administration were improved constantly, and the levels of the departments went up gradually. In particular, the MEP (SEPA), which was upgraded to ministerial level in 1998, had fundamental functions on policies formulation, planning, supervision and coordination, although it was still not a member of the State Council. At present, there is a team in charge of environmental protection administration with more than 70,000 personnel all over the country.

The State Council distributed among the different departments the functions of environmental protection. There were some overlapping of functions among the departments, but the administrative supervision on pollution prevention and control was concentrated on the MEP (SEPA) and the environmental protection agencies in different levels of governments. The functions of preservation of nature and resources were given to the departments of environmental protection, agriculture, forest, water resources and land.

Environmental protection strategies were constantly adjusted to keep up with the times. Based on the development of the environmental situation, the key efforts of environmental protection were transformed from the original point pollution source control to a combination of point pollution source control and comprehensive prevention and control, alongside macro-environmental management and control of key regions and river basins. During the Ninth FYP period, an environmental protection guideline was issued to ensure that equal attention is given to pollution prevention and control, on one hand, and ecological protection, on the other hand. In order to promote economic and social development, the following measures were undertaken:

1   industrial pollution prevention and control;
2   total pollutant discharge control, through air and water pollutant emission standards and ambient air and water surface quality standards for key cities;

Table 11.1 Detailed tasks of the MEP (SEPA) in the "three determination program"

Main responsibility	Detailed task
Unified supervision and management of the environmental protection work throughout the country	1. Drafting guidelines, policies, laws and regulations on national environmental protection, formulating administrative regulations, carrying out environmental impact assessment for important economic and technological policies, development planning, and key economic development planning with the endorsement of the State Council, drafting National Planning for environmental protection, organizing to draft and supervising the implementation of the plan of pollution prevention and control and the plan of ecological protection for key regions and basins identified by the state, and organizing to formulate the program for environmental functional area.
	2. Formulating and organizing the enforcement of the pollution prevention and control laws and regulations on air, water, soil, noise, solid waste, hazard waste and vehicle, and guiding, coordinating and supervising the efforts on marine environmental protection.
	3. Supervising the exploitation of natural resources with ecological environment impact, important ecological environment construction and recovery of ecological damage, overseeing various types of natural reservation zones, scenic and historic sights and forestry park pursuant to environmental protection efforts, supervising biodiversity protection, wild plant and animal preservation, wetland environmental protection, desertification prevention and control, recommending approval of the establishment of various kinds of new national natural reservation areas, and supervising national natural reservation areas.
	4. Guiding and coordinating efforts to deal with major environmental problems involving different departments, localities, river basins and regions, investigating and dealing with major environmental pollution and ecological damage accidents, resolving interprovincial environmental disputes, organizing and coordinating efforts to prevent and control water pollution in national key basins, taking charge of environmental supervision and environmental administrative examination, and organizing to carry out the examination on the enforcement of environmental protection laws.
	5. Formulating and promulgating national environmental quality and pollutant emission standards pursuant to the national objectives, taking charge of documenting local environmental protection standards and examining the content in relation to environmental protection within the urban comprehensive plan, organizing to formulate national environmental protection report, promulgating national environmental status report, publishing periodically environmental quality conditions of major cities and basins, and participating in the compilation of a national sustainable development profile.
	6. Formulating and organizing to implement the regulation on environmental protection management, examining and approving the environmental impact assessment reports of new construction events according to the national requirements, guiding urban and rural environmental protection comprehensive control, spearheading the efforts of rural environmental protection, guiding the construction of national ecological pilot areas and promoting eco-agriculture.

7. Organizing the efforts to develop environmental science and technology, important research projects and technological pilot engineering, guiding the development of the environmental industry, managing the national certification on environmental management system and environmental signs, building up and organizing the qualification approval system on environmental protection and guiding and promoting the development of environmental protection industry.

8. Overseeing environmental monitoring, statistics and information, formulating the regulations and norms on environmental monitoring, organizing the set-up and management of the national environmental monitoring and information networks, organizing and supervising the national environmental quality monitoring of pollutant sources, organizing, guiding and coordinating the efforts of environmental education and publicity and promoting public and non-governmental organization participation in environmental protection.

9. Formulating national principles for addressing global environmental issues, managing international cooperation on environmental protection efforts, taking part in the coordination of major events on environmental protection, participating in the negotiation for international environmental protection agreements, managing and coordinating the implementation of international environmental agreements, coordinating and implementing foreign-funded environmental projects, dealing with foreign affairs in relation to environmental protection upon the endorsement of the State Council, and corresponding with international environmental organizations.

10. Managing and formulating relevant guidelines, policies, laws and standards on nuclear safety, radioactive wastes and nuclear materials, participating in the emergency measures in case of nuclear and radioactive accidents, undertaking unified supervision and management of nuclear facilities safety, utilization of electromagnetism radioactive effects and development of mineral resource with radioactive contents, and supervising the safety assurance of unclear pipes and pressure-bearing facilities.

Source: State Council (1998), *Determination of Functions, Staff and Personnel.*

3   comprehensive control on urban environment;
4   establishment of national model cities on environmental protection;
5   construction of economic pilot areas;
6   cleaner production;
7   certification under the environmental management system; and
8   implementation of international agreements on economic and social development.

With limited management capacity and financial resources, the PRC focused on addressing its most prominent environmental problem – i.e. the serious industrial pollution brought about by the early stages of industrialization. This was done by mobilizing the state, localities and enterprises; centralizing limited funds; and balancing environmental protection inputs with national economic development. Between 1981 and 1995, environmental protection funds reached 0.5 percent of the gross domestic product (GDP). During the Ninth FYP period, which was characterized by the rapid development of the national economy, investments for environmental protection increased rapidly. In 2000, investments for nationwide environmental protection reached RMB106.07 billion, accounting for 1.1 percent of the GDP.[8]

Key problems

Although the environmental administration and institutions are capable of meeting the basic requirements of environmental protection, having been improved and strengthened constantly, the lack of management instruments and the conflicts among departments prevent the relevant authorities from properly addressing new environmental problems and meeting the actual needs of environmental protection.

There is observed lack of a clear and focal legislation which would serve as a basis for the institution for environmental protection administration. Among the national administrative legislations, there is no specific law or regulation on environmental protection administration at both the national and local levels. Provisions on the institution for environmental protection administration and its divisions are referenced in various relevant laws, legislations, regulations and official party committee or government documents. But these provisions are dispersed and have not been systematically compiled, thereby making integration of these different, and sometimes divergent, legislations difficult.

The laws on environmental protection administration are either too simple or abstract to provide clear and competent definition of the functions and responsibilities of relevant departments on environmental protection. Considering that each of these relevant departments have their own management capabilities, the institution for environmental protection administration will have unified supervision and responsibility over these departments, as provided for in various environmental protection legislations. However, with the PRC's current transition from a planning system to a market-oriented system, the legislative foundation of the environmental protection administration has been rendered unstable.

There is also an observed lack of necessary instruments to facilitate the integration of environmental protection work with social and economic development decision-making. As opposed to economic development, environmental protection has not been properly integrated with the comprehensive decision-making. Thus, in 1998, in order to improve the capacity of integrating environmental protection into comprehensive decision-making, the institution reform of the State Council prescribed that MEP (SEPA) should carry out environmental impact evaluation (EIA) for all significant economic and technology policy-making and development planning, in behalf of the State Council. At present, environmental protection has been integrated into social and economic development decision-making to foster balance among environmental protection, social development and economic progress.

Another observation is the decline of the environmental protection coordination ability. The previous Environmental Protection Committee was repealed after the institutional reform of the State Council in 1998 and its basic competency was handed over to MEP (SEPA). As a non-member of the State Council, the MEP (SEPA) does not have the necessary implementation authority or instruments to carry on the coordination function previously held by the Environmental Protection Committee. Before the economic institution reform, each trade department managed an environmental protection unit, which has the authority to organize and provide guidance on environmental protection work in its jurisdiction. After the institution reform, some of the trade departments were merged or repealed, resulting in a decrease in their influence and authority. The environmental protection units within the trade departments were merged or repealed as well, thereby slowing down the implementation of environmental protection regulations and laws in the departments, particularly in the department in charge of industrial management. In 2001, the State Council approved an affiliation scheme among ministries on the issues of national environmental protection, but it will take some time before the success of the scheme can be established. The task of environmental protection cannot be handled solely by an organization with environmental management capacity but requires cooperation among different departments. It would not matter what kind of institution for environmental protection administration is laid out, as long as an effective cooperation scheme is established.

The absence of a competent definition of the functions and jurisdiction of the environmental protection department and the natural resources management department makes it impossible to have unified supervision on ecological conservation. Of the many issues which caused ecological degradation in the PRC, such as the lack of funds and environmental awareness, the most problematic is the unsound administration institution of ecological conservation. The institution for ecological conservation lags behind that of pollution control. Government functions for ecological conservation are scattered among different departments, thus there is no strong or unified supervision mechanism for ecological conservation. The lack of a unified decision-making and supervision mechanism in environmental management at the national level brings about overlapping of functions, if not malfunction, among different governmental departments, lack of specific authority for management work, and conflict between public and departmental benefits. All these make it difficult to implement the ideas of "unified law making, unified planning, unified supervision and management" and "enhanced standard making, enhanced information releasing, enhanced monitoring instrument, enhanced scientific research ability, and enhanced propaganda and education" (Three Unifications and Five Enhancement Principle), which were initiated by the State Council. Also, the departments made their own resource management regulations to strengthen their respective power and authority, causing conflict among departmental laws and regulations and rendering enforcement at the local level next to impossible. Moreover, the departments, without consultation and linkage among each other, formulate their own plans and policies resulting in incompatible handling of issues, like ecological exploitation and conservation planning. This became an extreme disadvantage to the national macro-control of ecological conservation. There are also problems of overlapping management and project construction – such as in the water resources management and pollution control, species protection, and natural conservation area management – which, to some extent, aggravate the degradation of the ecosystem. The lack of a clear and competent definition of natural resources management and exploitation, which results in the conflicting functions of the natural resources department in natural resources management and natural resources exploitation, also blocks ecological conservation. Proceeding from the experiences of pollution control, the enhancement of the administration institution is essential to fundamentally change the situation of ecological degradation.

There is also a perceived necessity for reforms in the regional and watershed management institution. A comprehensive environmental protection administration institution for regional and river basin management has not been set up in the PRC. There is also an absence of comprehensive planning for watershed management. The difficulties of coordinating environmental protection efforts between regions and watershed areas, as well as the absence of an ecological compensation mechanism, aggravate the problem of ecosystem degradation. Plans for land use, forest, agriculture, irrigation and ecological functioning are normally implemented in the same area at the same time without an integrated environmental plan.

The PRC's environmental protection administration is seriously fraught with lack of both personnel and fund resources, thus the urgent need to augment financial and human resources support to realize the goals of environmental protection. The budget allocated for environmental protection administration in the national financial plan is insufficient. For a country with a population of 1.3 billion, it is unbelievable that only about 200 formal staff are employed in the environmental protection administration at the national level. The percentage of professional staff to the total population is only one-tenth, or less, of that of the developed countries. Because of this apparent lack of human resources, only urgent issues and concerns are attended to, and the more vital task of formulating long-term development plans and strategies are left by the wayside.

Proposals on institutional development reform

The PRC needs to identify and establish the country's principal administrative authority for environmental protection to facilitate the effective management and implementation of the various functions and programs of the nation's environmental protection system.

Rapid development in the PRC's political, economic, social and environmental situations have brought about several unprecedented new challenges in the nation's environmental protection administration. In dealing with these challenges, the MEP (SEPA) has improved and matured in its working capacity, but it has also encountered some institutional obstacles which necessitate timely reforms to reinforce the country's environmental protection administration institution.

Positioning of the nation's principal administrative authority for environmental protection

In reforming the nation's environmental protection administration, the key problem is the positioning of the nation's principal administrative authority for environmental protection. There are several important factors to consider.

International environmental diplomacy and cooperation

The increasingly active international environmental diplomacy and cooperation are prompting the PRC's environmental protection agency to improve its international status in the field of environmental protection. The PRC's political, economic, legal and institutional conditions are exerting pressure on the country's environmental rights and interests, and introducing new challenges on the country's environmental protection management system. Provisions on developmental rights and benefits of countries contained in international environmental and resource protection conventions (e.g. Convention on Climate Change and its Protocol; Convention on Biological Diversity; Montreal Protocol on Ozone Depletion Substances; Stockholm Convention on Implementing International Action on Certain Persistent Organic Pollutants; and Convention to Combat Desertification) wield certain legal influences and effects on signing countries to strengthen their relative position in the international environmental diplomatic negotiations. As implementation of agreements set forth in the conventions is primarily carried out by the environmental protection departments, the signing countries should set a high level of standards and professionalism on their respective environmental protection departments.

Since 1980, the PRC has signed and approved 29 international environmental and resource protection conventions and treaties, the implementation of which is being carried out by the country's national environmental protection agency. With the accelerated institutionalization of environmental management in the world, the establishment of the world environmental organization and the international environment court has been repeatedly proposed to strengthen the mechanism for environmental protection execution in the international arena. Such a trend has exerted pressure on developing countries, especially those who, like the PRC, are opposed to having environmental execution mechanism used as a pretext to intervene in their internal affairs. To keep its sovereign right of national environmental management, the PRC should reinforce the capability of its national environmental protection agency, enhance its unified position in the field of domestic environmental protection, and strengthen its voice in international dialogues.

After joining the World Trade Organization (WTO), the PRC has gradually become the "world factory." One of the effects of economic globalization is the remarkable increase in the influence of external industries and the entry of new species and foreign wastes into the country's environment. This situation calls for the PRC to establish an evaluation system for environmental safety in the field of international trade. The PRC government also needs to strengthen its environmental supervision and control in order to:

1   prevent the transfer of severely polluted enterprises and products into the country;
2   thwart the introduction of invasive species into the country's environment;
3   strengthen the examination and approval of imported wastes and prevent foreign wastes pollution; and
4   protect the genetic resources of the country.

The functions of existing environmental agencies, unfortunately, do not fully reflect these necessary measures. Thus, the institutional reform should accordingly include them.

In the course of development of environmental protection agencies in several countries, the management of global environmental problems has become a focus and the jurisdictional authority of said agencies has broadened continuously. In the Republic of Korea, for example, the reform of governmental organizations in 1994 witnessed the enhancement of the functions and rights of the Environment Ministry. In Japan, the Environment Agency was upgraded into the Environment Ministry in 2001, while the original Terrestrial Environment Department under the Environment Agency was upgraded into the Terrestrial Environment Bureau under which the Countermeasure Department for Preventing the Earth Warming Up was established. A new position was even created under the Japan Environment Ministry with the rank of vice minister to actively participate in the international negotiations for the prevention of global warming.

During the central government reforms of various countries, the upgrading in the ranks of their respective environmental protection agencies has become a common phenomenon. Statistical data from 17 countries[9] reveal that most of the environmental protection agencies are of ministry level and officials in charge of these agencies are mostly governmental cabinet members. Because the PRC's environmental protection administrative agency holds a relatively lower rank than the environmental protection agencies of major countries such as Japan and the Republic of Korea, it has already been relegated to a disadvantageous position in international environmental exchanges. In this way, there is a need to accordingly and appropriately upgrade the rank and position of the national environmental protection agency of the PRC, thereby reflecting the importance given to environmental protection and improving its state image.

As the new century ushered in international environmental diplomacy, conventions and cooperation, the PRC needs to face the vital task of enhancing its environmental protection authority to bring it up to par with international standards. More importantly, the establishment of its environmental protection agency should take into account political, economic, population and environmental considerations, so as to protect both the country's national interest and international image.

Environmental and developmental comprehensive decision-making

One of the causes of environmental problems stems from the failure to fully consider, during the decision-making process, the environmental consequences of economic and social development, thereby resulting in an imbalance between economic development and environmental protection. In order to guarantee national environmental security, environmental and developmental concerns should both be considered in a comprehensive decision-making mechanism. Such a mechanism should be established through a set of procedures and institutions wherein environmental protection agencies can participate, to a certain extent, in discussions on economic and social development – especially those which have a major influence or impact on the environment – and accordingly render recommendations, suggestions and advice on environmental protection and affairs.

The central government has always paid great attention to environmental protection, and has also repeatedly advocated the perfection and implementation of the mechanism for comprehensive environmental and developmental decision-making. The "Agenda of China 21st Century" points out that the existing development strategies, policies, plans and management systems cannot satisfy the demand for sustainable development. To achieve the coordinated development of population, economy, society, ecology and environment, the concept of sustainable development should be fully embodied in the PRC's general development strategy, goal and action plan. In this respect, the direction of environmental actions should be to:

1   carry out institutional reforms and establish a comprehensive decision-making mechanism favorable to sustainable development;
2   adjust functions of existing departments;
3   reinforce extensive negotiation and cooperation among departments; and
4   establish coordination between management and operation mechanism, on one hand, and feedback mechanism, on the other, to harmonize the operations of various departments.

If necessary, new organizing and coordinating institutions should be established to guarantee the successful realization of the strategic objective of sustainable development. In fact, the Fourth National Environmental Protection Conference made the same call for the establishment of the mechanism for comprehensive environmental and developmental decision-making.

The main approach of the comprehensive environmental and developmental decision-making is to implement the system of environmental impact assessment of important policy decisions – such as, the plans and programs for the national economic and social development; comprehensive economic policies; industry development policies; plans for natural resources exploitation; and plans for regional development. There must also be improvement on the role of science in the evaluation process. Considering the requirements of a scientific and comprehensive decision-making, the positions, authorities and capabilities of relevant environmental protection administration departments should be strengthened further.

At present, however, the MEP (SEPA) is not armed with sufficient and suitable mechanisms and methods to properly carry out environmental impact assessment of relevant national policies and plans. Its capability to participate effectively in the integrated decision-making for socio-economic development is at a low level, while the strength of its policy research, organization and staff is comparatively weak. Moreover, the guarantee function of the MEP (SEPA)'s technical support units has not been fully maximized, and the related departments have prioritized policy formulation and study. All these factors have adversely affected the MEP (SEPA)'s implementation of its functions of macro-policy management and its performance and effectiveness in instructing and guiding local environmental protection works.[10]

Clearly, during the institutional reform, there is a need to enhance the authority and capacity of the MEP (SEPA) to enable it to successfully participate in and implement integrated decision-making.

Management of environmental social affairs

Environmental social affairs management refers to the function of the state environmental protection administrative departments to manage certain social affairs to further environmental protection objectives. This includes important undertakings such as promoting education and public awareness programs on environmental protection; settling environmental disputes; upholding the environmental rights and interests of the public; steering environmental protection efforts of non-governmental organizations (NGOs); and developing the environmental culture.

The Party's Central Committee attaches great importance to "improving the Party's capability of administration and level of leadership," and emphasizes that the Party should run the state in the interests of the public and "listen to the voice of the public, respect their will and cherish their resources."[11] From the perspective of the development trend of the socialist market economy, the government needs to gradually veer away from its practice of closed management in its social administration and take greater efforts to encourage public participation. If necessary, the government should set up certain establishments to function as "windows" between the government and the society so as to better serve the people. Environmental protection translates to the protection of the vulnerable, which in a sense refers to the public.[12] The assumption by environmental protection organizations of the new function of managing environmental social affairs is in line with the objectives of institutional reform. By the end of June 2001, over 2,000 environmental protection bodies had been set up in the PRC, which are all required to conform with the new situation in a timely manner and attach greater importance to the enhancement of the administration of environmental social affairs.

After an analysis of the foregoing three considerations to improve the positioning of the state administrative departments in charge of environmental protection, coupled with the need to strengthen unified supervision of environmental protection efforts, the following general propositions are made:

1   there should be immediate reform of the state environmental protection departments to strengthen the government's macro regulation and public management capability, build an efficient and honest government operating at low expense, and intensify the uniformity, authority and international capacity of the state environmental protection; and
2   there must be prioritization of the resolution of key problems such as difficulties in making, coordinating and implementing decisions due to the lack or overlap of responsibilities, inefficiency in environmental protection management, and lack of a solid organizational guarantee to maintain state interests and environmental safety and realize the goals and tasks of environmental protection.

These suggestions can be summarized as "uniformity and high efficiency" goals. During the new institutional reform of governmental institutions, the establishment of a more comprehensive state environmental protection administrative department with higher position and greater authority, and the transformation of the department into a constituent of the State Council, will hasten the proper execution of the basic functions of a state environmental protection agency.

Major suggestions for further reform of the environmental protection agency

There must be reform of the environmental management system to make it more effective and responsive to the realization of the objectives of environmental protection and governance.

Reconstructing the strategic objectives and goals of environmental management system

Environmental and human health protection should be made the primary objectives of the environmental management system. Economic development should be achieved without sacrificing environmental protection. To realize environmental protection and improvement, specific targets should clearly be set with respect to clean water, clean air, clean and safe food, and robust ecology. Prevention, rather than governance, of environmental problems should also be made a goal. The importance of public participation in the achievement of environmental protection objective, as well as its corresponding goals and targets, should not be overlooked.

Reforming the legislative and judicial systems

The legislative and judicial systems should also be allowed to participate in environmental protection work. The legislative bodies should create more laws for environmental protection to provide a robust legislative foundation for the environmental protection system. Congress should also coordinate the different laws and statutes in order to promote cooperation among administrative bodies of environmental protection. The role of judicial bodies in the enforcement of environmental protection rules, laws and standards should be strengthened. Enterprises and firms violating environmental standards should be brought to court and duly sanctioned.

Adopting reform strategies for the National Environmental Protection Agency

In the Seventeenth National Conference of the Communist Party, administrative reforms for the National Environmental Protection Agency were proposed. The most prominent of which is the "Big Ministry" strategy. This strategy entailed the establishment of the NEPA as the "Big Ministry" of environmental protection undertaking administrative reforms, and the transfer of administrative agencies relating to environmental protection to the NEPA.

Cultivating environmental protection in civil society

The effective dissemination of information on environmental issues and concerns will help raise public awareness on these issues, which in turn will encourage citizen participation in the environmental protection efforts. This being the case, the government should provide the citizens with more access to environmental information. Public participation is essential to the realization of environmental protection objectives. Citizens should also be afforded the rights to self-organization and association to allow them to participate in relevant environmental protection initiatives.

Notes

1 See Xia Guoguang, *Research on the Relationship between National Environmental Protection Policies and Environmental Protection Administration*, 2002.
2 *National Environmental Statistic Communiqué for 2006*, China State Environmental Protection Administration, Beijing, 2007.
3 *National Environmental Statistic Communiqué for 2006*, China State Environmental Protection Administration, Beijing, 2007.
4 *National Environmental Statistic Communiqué for 2006*, China State Environmental Protection Administration, Beijing, 2007.
5 *Environmental Status Report for 1999*, China State Environmental Protection Administration, Beijing, 2007.
6 *National Environmental Statistic Communiqué for 2000, 2001, 2002*, China State Environmental Protection Administration, Beijing, 2003.
7 Environmental Protection Law of the People's Republic of China.
8 *National Environmental Statistic Communiqué for 2002*, China State Environmental Protection Administration, Beijing, 2003.
9 *The State Environmental Protection Administration Report on the Functional Operation Status of the State Environmental Protection Administration*, 2002, p. 10.
10 Jiang Zhemin, *The Speech on Conference Celebrating the 80th Anniversary of the Foundation of CPC*, July 1, 2001, Renmin Publication House, separate edition.
11 The Politics Study Center of the State Bureau of Environmental Protection, *To Go with the Time and to Counter Power by the Aid of Power – the Study on Environmental Management Strategy in the New Century*, Research Report, April 2002, p. 51.
12 The Research Team on the "Well-to-do" topic of the State Bureau of Statistics, *China's "Well-to-do" Process Has Entered the Last Sprint*, China Information Newspaper, November 28, 2000.

12 International experiences to inform the People's Republic of China's institutional choices for environmental policy

Timo Goeschl

Introduction

It is a widely acknowledged fact that the People's Republic of China's (PRC) macro-environmental policy faces a number of institutional challenges in developing its "capacity for environmental protection." This capacity, defined as "a society's ability to identify and solve environmental problems" (Organization for Economic Co-operation and Devlopment (OECD) 1994), is a key determinant of the PRC's conditions for environmental action in the long term. Meeting the present institutional challenges is likely to help improve both the environmental quality in the PRC and the efficiency of its environmental policy.

For a country's capacity for environmental protection to perform satisfactorily, institutions have to be in place that would enable all of the necessary stages of the environmental policy cycle to function. The PRC's capacity for environmental protection is to a significant extent a question of:

1 what is the **internal** organization of institutions of environmental policy vis-à-vis each other; and
2 what is the **external** relationship of these governmental institutions vis-à-vis other stakeholders such as businesses, non-governmental organizations (NGOs) and private citizens.

The internal organization of the PRC's environmental policy raises three key issues, among others. The first issue is whether the governmental institutions that the PRC has developed to carry out its environmental policy are of the appropriate number, size and scope. The second issue concerns the question of whether the governmental institutions that the PRC has developed to carry out its environmental policy do interact in a way that promotes the country's macro-environmental objectives. The third issue is whether macro-environmental objectives are addressed by governmental institutions at an adequate spatial level and, if so, how governmental institutions at different spatial levels interact.

The external relations of the PRC's institutions of environmental policy concern the relationship between governmental and non-governmental players. In the external context, several distinct issues likewise arise. One is what governmental institutional solutions are in place in order to ensure adequate monitoring and enforcement of environmental policies. Another important issue is what role non-governmental players such as private citizens, corporations and NGOs are expected to play in supporting the PRC's capacity for environmental protection.

This chapter will set out a range of international experiences to inform how these key questions can be answered in a way that allows building on the PRC's existing institutional capacity for environmental protection in a continuous and meaningful way. These experiences are not in short supply. The key questions being asked in the PRC context have been asked in many other countries before, and several successful solutions have been developed as a result. At the same time, in areas where other countries have failed to tackle environmental challenges fully, international experiences also help anticipate problems at an early stage and build realistic expectations on the timescales involved in building a functioning environmental policy system.

Institutions for environmental policy

Capacity for environmental policy and its importance

Successful environmental policy requires a national institutional capacity that allows a country to respond to the need for environmental management by designing and implementing suitable policies. Accordingly, the OECD defines a country's *capacity for environmental protection* as "a society's ability to identify and solve environmental problems" (OECD 1994).

Increasing a country's capacity for environmental protection has two key benefits. The first is that a greater capacity for environmental protection will lead to higher environmental quality for the same level of output. The second benefit derives from the fact that a greater capacity for environmental quality will allow a society to achieve a desirable level of environmental quality at a lower overall cost to both consumers and producers.

A growing capacity for environmental protection has enabled OECD countries to decrease concentrations of many pollutants and reduce pressure on pristine habitats and ecosystems during a process of macroeconomic expansion. For example, emissions of so-called "criteria" pollutants in OECD countries has been falling, with the relevant improvements in environmental quality accruing to these countries. Figure 12.1 shows, as an example, current trends regarding sulfur oxide (SO_x) and nitrogen oxide (NO_x) intensities in OECD countries for 2002 as well as the change in these two emissions since 1990. Improvements in environmental quality within countries and differences in the environmental performance across countries of the type shown in Figure 12.1 reflect, to a significant extent, the quality of institutions set up domestically for the purpose of environmental protection.

Countries also differ in the amount of resources they devote to environmental protection. Here again, institutional quality matters. More stringent environmental

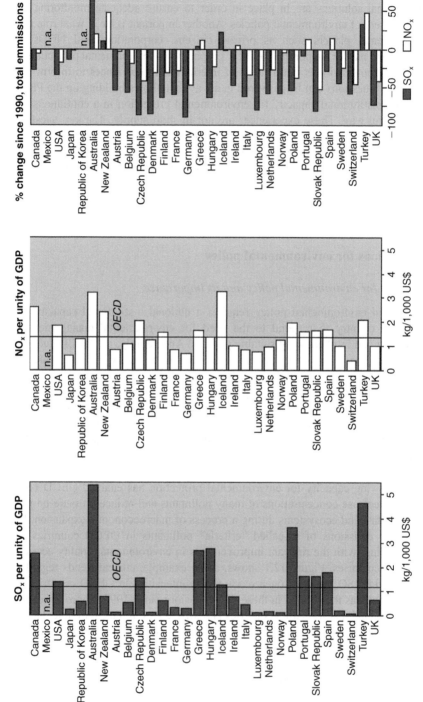

Figure 12.1 Emission intensities in 2002 and percent change since 1990 (source: OECD 2007).

regulation will be more expensive. Therefore, higher expenditures on environmental protection reflect the ability of institutions to channel national resources both at the public and the private level toward environmental improvement. On the other hand, countries may achieve comparable levels of environmental quality at very different cost. Lower environmental expenditures at similar levels of environmental quality are therefore also indicative of high institutional quality. These cost reductions generated by high environmental capacity originate from two sources. One source is *direct savings*, which results from reductions in the cost of those that have to comply with the regulation. An example is the cost of installing filters under a policy that sets a technical standard. The second source is *indirect savings*, which come from reductions in the cost to the taxpayer of administering the policy. A suitable example of indirect savings are reductions in the cost of auditing firms regarding their installation and maintenance of the required filter.

International organizations such as the OECD collect data on environmental expenditures for member countries. A cross-section of data on pollution abatement and control expenditure of industrialized and industrializing countries, such as that shown in Table 12.1, leads to three key observations:

1   expenditures for environmental protection are often significant, reaching up to 2 percent and more in highly developed countries;
2   higher levels of environmental expenditures go broadly together with higher environmental quality; and
3   at similar levels of environmental quality, countries sacrifice significantly different levels of resources for environmental protection.

Improving on a country's capacity for environmental protection entails not only devoting more resources toward this objective, but also doing so in an efficient manner. The key question for policy-makers is then: what is the institutional framework that effectively delivers environmental improvements at the lowest cost possible? Addressing this question has implications both for the level of environmental quality that a country can implement and for the sacrifices it has to make in order to achieve this level.

The key features

The institutional framework that delivers capacity for environmental protection has to fulfill a number of requirements. One concerns the question of the optimal set of institutions. This set has to form a framework that is open enough to make use of as much relevant information as practicable, but sufficiently structured to deliver actionable decisions. At the same time, it has to be large enough to realize economies of scale and scope in carrying out environmental policy, but differentiated enough in terms of spatial and sectoral coverage to reflect heterogeneities of costs, preferences, income and wealth, and environmental conditions.

Table 12.1 Data on pollution abatement and control expenditure (2002)

| | PAC expenditure, early 2000s or latest available year | | | | | | | |
| | as % of GDP | | | | in US$ per capita | | | |
	Public	Business	Private specialized producers	Total*	Public	Business	Private specialized producers	Total*
Canada*	0.6	0.5	–	1.1	173	144	–	316
Mexico*	0.2	–	–	–	19	–	–	–
Japan*	0.6	0.8	–	1.4	144	202	–	346
Republic of Korea*	0.8	0.7	–	1.5	133	111	–	244
Australia*	0.5	0.3	–	0.8	118	63	–	181
Austria*	1.3	0.5	0.6	2.4	358	131	157	646
Belgium*	0.7	0.3	0.4	1.5	192	89	109	390
Czech Republic*	0.3	0.3	0.6	1.2	50	50	91	192
Denmark*	1.4	–	0.9	–	386	–	264	–
Finland*	0.5	0.3	–	0.8	122	68	–	183
France*	1.0	0.3	0.4	1.7	282	94	109	484
Germany*	1.3	0.3	–	1.6	321	70	–	393
Greece*	0.5	–	–	–	76	–	–	–
Hungary*	0.5	0.3	0.6	1.4	55	32	63	150
Iceland*	0.3	–	–	–	93	–	–	–
Ireland*	0.4	0.2	–	0.6	102	52	–	153
Italy*	0.7	0.1	–	0.8	182	24	–	175
Luxembourg*	0.6	–	–	–	219	–	–	–
Netherlands*	1.1	0.5	0.4	2.0	268	127	89	484
Norway*	0.3	–	–	–	101	–	–	–
Poland*	0.8	1.2	–	2.0	78	120	1	199
Portugal*	0.5	0.3	–	0.8	90	48	–	138

Slovak Republic*	0.1	0.7	–	0.8	15	70	5	89
Spain*	0.6	0.2	–	0.8	118	37	–	155
Sweden	0.7	0.4	–	1.1	192	107	–	300
Switzerland*	0.8	–	–	–	234	–	–	–
Turkey*	0.9	0.2	–	1,1	55	13	–	68
United Kingdom*	0.4	0.3	–	0.7	110	65	–	175

Source: OECD (2007).

Note
* excluding households.

These countervailing requirements mean that the institutional framework has to strike important trade-offs that will typically result not in a monolithic organization, but in a variety of institutions with overlapping, competing and complementary functions along sectoral and spatial lines, and relying on both governmental and non-governmental stakeholders to contribute to the policy.

Given the conclusion that a framework of several institutions is needed, the second concern is then what the coordination of institutional activity within this framework should look like. This means:

- ensuring that the environmental policy cycle is followed through;
- ensuring that environmental issues do not fail through gaps in mandates and responsibilities that may exist between institutions; and
- ensuring that overlapping mandates and competition are conducive to environmental protection and to reduction in costs.

The objective of ensuring coordination is known as the problem of *environmental policy integration* (EPI) (Müller 2002). Integration of policies across sectors is commonly referred to as *horizontal* EPI. This cross-sectoral coordination requires specific institutional provisions for linking institutional processes together that cross traditional institutional boundaries at the same level of hierarchy. The integration of policies occurring at multiple layers of government, such as national and regional governments, is commonly referred to as *vertical EPI*. This objective requires aligning processes at different levels of government in the face of structural constraints. The question of how best to combine governmental institutions and non-governmental stakeholders is a question about the external integration of environmental policy (interface). There, issues of instrument choice and about the role of legal instruments are at the fore of the debate.

Areas of institutional choice

Institutional frameworks for environmental protection are complex and multifaceted. In light of the specific challenges facing the PRC, this chapter concentrates on five sub-areas where experiences of foreign governments that have developed institutions of environmental policy are likely to be of greatest assistance to the PRC government as it develops its own framework.

The first area concerns the institutionalization of environmental policy. The overriding question in this area is which branches of government should be involved in environmental policy (EP) and what their specific roles are. Particular attention is paid to the role of the administrative and judicial wings of government. Reasons for the different choices adopted in different countries are hereby made explicit.

The second area focuses on the challenge implicit in horizontal policy integration. Environmental policy frequently interacts with other important policy sectors such as energy, agriculture and infrastructure planning. How do countries design cross-sectoral governance across different sectors and different ministerial domains? What instruments do governments use to coordinate and integrate the environmental policy internally? The chapter studies the institutional, strategic and procedural measures in place in different countries in order to effect the integration of environmental policy objectives into the total of governmental policies.

Related to, but distinct from the challenges of, horizontal policy integration is the issue of vertical policy integration. Environmental policy is carried out at very different levels of spatial aggregation, ranging from the purely local to a provincial or frequently to a national level. What choices do countries arrive at in terms of assigning responsibilities to governmental institutions at the various spatial levels? What instruments are used to coordinate decisions at these different levels such that both spatial heterogeneity and national consistency are adequately reflected? Here, we consider the different designs pioneered in other countries for ensuring consistent and effective environmental governance at multiple spatial levels in terms of the choice of institutions and mechanisms for their coordination. This comprises both the spatially-devolved enactment of national environmental policy along vertical lines and the horizontal coordination of environmental policies carried out at lower levels of spatial aggregation.

The fourth area of particular importance to building capacity for environmental protection in the PRC is openness. Governments rely on non-governmental players such as firms, NGOs and private citizens for information and cooperation in effecting environmental policy. Many countries have developed mechanisms for harnessing the potential contributions these players can make, and have demonstrated their potential for policy improvement. Here, we discuss various international experiences in integrating non-governmental players into environmental policy-making in order to establish public acceptance and legitimacy for policy action as well as to utilize to its best potential information relevant for policy solutions that exists in society, but is not immediately available to policy-makers.

The final key area of concern is the role of legal instruments in environmental policy. Countries understand that compliance with environmental laws and regulations requires mechanisms for monitoring and enforcement. Here, we discuss various approaches employed by different countries for building monitoring systems and for sanctioning non-compliance.

Institutionalizing environmental policy

Successful environmental policy is the product of a multi-staged process, the typical stages of which are captured in the "environmental policy cycle" (Howlett and Ramesh 1995; Jänicke *et al.* 1999: 52), and are as follows:

1   problem perception;
2   agenda-setting;
3   policy formulation;

4   decision-making;
5   implementation;
6   evaluation;
7   modification or termination.

It is evident that institutions that perform the various steps need to be in place to complete the policy cycle. However, there is a considerable heterogeneity in how countries respond to this requirement. While most industrialized countries share the common feature of having three branches of government (legislative, executive, judicial), countries differ in terms of the roles these different branches play in the environmental policy cycle, and under what constitutional constraints these branches operate.

In some countries, notably Germany, the constitution predetermines the relative involvement of the legislative and executive branches in various stages of the cycle. In others, such as the United States, the set of possible configurations of involvement is considerably larger. Countries also differ in the way the judiciary branch interacts with the policy cycle. In some countries, courts are simply an additional enforcement device in the implementation stage of environmental policy, or are there to protect individual citizens from unconstitutional policies. In others, courts provide additional checks and balances to the executive branch prior to policy implementation.

Rose-Ackerman (1995), in an influential comparative study of environmental policy-making in Germany and the United States, pointed out the central tension in environmental policy between legitimacy and competence of the process, on the one hand, and the need for environmental institutions to provide meaningful trade-offs between these objectives, on the other. Table 12.2 reproduces the central matrix by Rose-Ackerman (1995), with issues on substance in the rows and issues on process in the columns. The function of the matrix is to highlight the findings that depending on the substance expected from the policy-making process, whether it is the establishment of scientific validity ("technical"), the protection of individual rights, or the decision on the identity of policy winners and/or losers ("political"), some processes are better suited than others to deliver that substance. Marked cells indicate those cases of "best fit."

Different countries choose different environmental policy-making processes to generate what they regard as the most suitable in meeting their idiosyncratic substantive objectives. This reflects the inherent heterogeneity of objectives across different countries. However, it is not always the case that countries choose the processes that are best suited to meet their objectives, as Rose-Ackerman shows. Decisions about how to involve experts, parliaments, courts and the executive branch of government are decisions about the nature of policy processes. In other words, these choices determine the ability of the institutions of environmental policy to perform as desired, thereby underscoring the critical importance of well-designed institutions.

Table 12.2 Matching substance and process

Substance	Process				
			Bureaucrat-led		
	A		*B*		*C*
	Peer review	*1 Court-like*	*2 Quasi-legislative*	*3 Administrative balancing*	*Consensual*
A. Technical	X				
B. Individual Rights		X			
C. Political					
1 Distributive			X		
2 Net benefits possible					
a All interests not well-represented				X	
b All interests well-represented					X

Source: Rose-Ackerman (1995).

Types of institutions

As a rule of thumb, there is broad consensus that a minimum set of institutions needs to be created nationally in order to carry out environmental policy successfully. These institutions are the following:

1   a ministry of the environment;
2   a national environmental agency;
3   a national environmental report;
4   a national environmental framework law;
5   a national sustainability strategy; and
6   a council of environmental experts to advise the government.

Additional institutions that have proved to be highly conducive to environmental policy-making are the integration of the environmental dimension into constitutional law and the drawing up of a national environmental plan. Finally, at least one of these institutions has to be charged with the overriding task of monitoring and measuring the state of the environment, both as a quantitative input into the status quo of environmental quality and in order to track progress against policy targets. The presence of this set of institutions can be regarded as a prerequisite for effective environmental policy implementation. However, to add subtlety, some of the international leaders in environmental policy have succeeded without some of these institutions in place. The United States is a case in point. The formal act of institutionalization is a necessary, but not a sufficient, condition for better environmental policy. Likewise, as long as the institutionalization of environmental policy is substantive (rather than purely formal), other institutions can perform functions within the policy cycle that other countries choose to opt out from. Table 12.3 sets out the four typical stages in capacity development based on a meta-study of capacity development in 17 countries.

Jänicke and Weidner (1997) rank countries in terms of their timeliness in setting up formal measures aimed toward the institutionalization of environmental policy. Their ranking emphasizes a general convergence to a set of roughly seven measures over a remarkably short period of time, even though there is little evidence that early formal institutionalization necessarily led to higher environmental quality. Formal institutionalization without substantive policy successes is a characteristic of countries with little public involvement in the policy cycle. Environmental policy in Eastern European countries, for example, remained largely ineffective prior to their transformation phase during the late 1980s, whereby participation of civil societies in the policy-making process had been strengthened.

The emerging international consensus is that a minimum set of institutions is required to carry out environmental policy effectively. While some countries deviate from this minimal list and still attain policy effectiveness, they do so by assigning the relevant responsibilities to other institutional players and by maintaining a highly functional policy environment in general.

Table 12.3 Stages in capacity development

Stage	Environmental policy institutions	Green NGOs	Media	"Green" business sector
1	No central ministry/agency for environment	Local organizations	Few, largely official reports on the environmental situation	Environmental interests scarcely articulated in economic sector
2	Weak and isolated national ministry/agency for environment	Weak or non-professional environmental NGOs	Environmental reports in some critical sections of the media	Environmental interests articulated mainly by the producers of clean-up technology
3	Environmental institutions at all levels and sectors of political system	Strong and highly competent green NGOs involved in environmental policy	Environmental problems widely reported in all the media	Environmental interests articulated mainly by particular green business organization
4	Environmental policy integration; long-term environmental planning	Strong and highly competent green NGOs involved in environmental policy and industry	Frequent direct media attacks against polluters	"Green" business sector with strong impact on the whole economy

Source: Weidner and Jänicke (2002).

Country case studies from the United States and other OECD countries document clearly that the legislative and judiciary channels are important for creating an enabling environment for the public's participation and the proper dissemination of information. They also show that it is possible, during transitional periods, to rely exclusively on the executive wing of the government. However, this reliance on the executive branch exposes environmental protection to significant political risks, and is therefore no substitute for a functioning judicial and legislative apparatus.

International experiences in vertical policy integration

Environmental problems are always issues with an explicit spatial dimension: river basins tie together vast stretches of land into inter-related systems. Air pollution affects locations far from the source in predictable fashion. Biodiversity reserves generate their greatest benefits frequently to people living a considerable distance away from the place of conservation.

In general, policy-makers have a choice of whether:

1   to build an institutional structure around the geographical nature of the problem so that the spatial scope of the institutions fits the environmental problem; or alternatively,
2   to attempt to fit the environmental problem into the spatial structure of existing institutions.

The empirical evidence on the spatial implementation of environmental policy shows that the general approach is to take the spatial structure of existing institutions as a given factor, and to make the environmental problem fit into this setup. There are two main reasons for this approach. The first is that, as a principle, fitting institutions around the environmental problem leads to a proliferation of spatially overlapping institutions, each charged with addressing a particular issue, and requiring coordination at a different level all over again. The second is that, even within the spatial scope of an environmental problem, there are sufficient heterogeneities in terms of endowments, incomes, preferences, environmental conditions, etc. to undo the gains from adjusting the institution to the environmental problem alone.

With the exception of a few isolated examples, therefore, countries generally carry out environmental policy using multiple layers of government, involving existing institutions from the national or federal level all the way down to municipalities and communities. This governance at several levels raises a number of issues for the design of the institutional framework for environmental policy that will be answered in the national case studies.

There are at least two reasons why there is a special role for institutions at the national level in such a multi-layered setting.

1   *Vertical implementation objective*: the first reason is that institutions at the national level need to ensure implementation of national legislation and reg-

ulation at state and local levels where preferences, conditions, and costs may differ from the national level.

2   *Coordination objective*: even when there is no legislation at the national level to implement, national institutions will want to ensure that the pursuit of regional or local policies does not result in negative spillovers from one region or locality to another.

As the case studies demonstrate in detail, all countries face some degree of difficulty with the challenges of multi-layered governance. The real and binding trade-offs between a more uniform national set-up that neglects local and/or regional heterogeneities and a more spatially-differentiated system that sacrifices national environmental goals and invites inter-regional policy spillovers lead to some amount of imperfection in even the most advanced systems. For example, the US and German water and air pollution policies strike less than perfect and often inconsistent trade-offs between national and regional objectives. The US policy is characterized by excessively rigid federal rules, while Germany has simultaneously too much and too little decentralization (Rose-Ackerman 1995).

While imperfections persist everywhere, international case studies also demonstrate that there are a number of mechanisms that help institutions operating at the national level align the choices of institutions at lower levels of spatial hierarchy with national objectives. These mechanisms range from simple devices that help decrease transaction costs between different levels of government, to step-in clauses for the national institution, to sophisticated combinations of carrots-and-sticks in the form of conditional grants. The important policy lessons that arise from the international experiences in this area can be summarized in a few points. The first is that a meaningful trade-off between uniformity and heterogeneity can be struck. These trade-offs need to be supported, however, by a carrot-and-stick system between the national government and the regional and local governments to which policy responsibilities are devolved. One particularly useful stick is the presence of threat points in the relationship between the national and the regional or local government; and one particularly productive threat point is the possibility of the federal government taking over the running of environmental policy if the lower-level administration consistently falls short of the required performance. This feature of the US policy landscape has been credited with significant contributions to the implementation of federal environmental policy. The example of the Czech Republic shows that procedural features, such as a requirement for higher spatial levels to sign off on the proper completion and inclusion of environmental impact assessments, can provide additional support.

A distinct point emerging from international experiences is that delegation and monitoring arrangements need to be formalized in order to attain the status of binding commitments on which different agencies can act. Performance Partnership Programs, as pioneered in the United States, are one successful model of how to institutionalize such arrangements. Delegation and monitoring arrangements also need to contain clear incentives. The US system of Performance

Partnership Grants provides a template on how to combine positive incentive payments with the threat of substantive penalties.

Cross-sectoral governance and its coordination

Within the executive branch, responsibility for environmental issues is usually allocated chiefly to a specialized department (usually the Ministry of the Environment), but policy remits of other departments often overlap with that. The presence of such overlaps necessitates the design of mechanisms through which potential synergies (win–win situations) in policy-making can be exploited, and policy conflicts can be resolved.

The feasibility of synergies at the intersection of different government departments is amply demonstrated by evidence from "green" tax reforms in many European countries. Green tax reforms are the result of cross-departmental cooperation, typically involving coordinated regulatory changes by ministries of the environment, finance and social affairs. These ministries coordinate a budget-neutral offset through which revenues raised by new environmentally-related taxes are used to fund a reduction in the tax burden on personal income and corporate profits as well as in social security receipts.

As illustrated by case studies from OECD countries, there are two main avenues through which countries try to manage the cross-sectoral conflict. The first avenue is the creation of dedicated institutions at the interface between departments. One particularly widespread model is the creation of inter-departmental working groups that are either standing committees or are organized around a specific policy measure. The other avenue refers to procedural provisions of a legal nature that offer the Ministry of the Environment a clear mandate to be consulted, to influence, and to veto policy formation for programs or projects that have environmental consequences. These procedural provisions are most effective where ministry approval is required for the release of funds.

Despite the heterogeneity of the institutional choices of individual countries, successful cross-sectoral policy integration is therefore characterized by important common features. All OECD countries that are successful in terms of horizontal policy integration share three forms of coordination mechanisms. One is *institutional* and it involves creating a dedicated mechanism through which different agencies are forced to exchange information and coordinate activities. Germany is a particularly useful example having a Standing Committee of all Ministries with an environmental remit, various thematic Inter-ministerial Working Groups (IMAs), and the establishment of environment departments (EDs) in eight of 13 non-core ministries. The second is *strategic* and it involves the design of overarching policy frameworks (such as Sustainable Development Plans) to which sectoral agencies need to respond to and against which they need to define their policy actions. The third element is *procedural* and it entails requirements in the policy-making process to consult with and, at times, receive approval by environmental policy agencies for policies that directly or even indirectly affect environmental policy objectives. Typical examples are environmental impact assessment requirements at the project and program level. These procedural requirements have a good track record in providing sectoral coordination under two conditions:

1   that they are properly enforced; and
2   that they are combined with conditionality regarding funding, both in environmental and non-environmental areas.

Environmental policy systems are most successful when combining several coordination devices. This is an important lesson since there is little evidence that one individual coordination device is able to perform policy integration without auxiliary mechanisms. The benefits of coordination devices are most easily observed in cases where they are absent. The experience in the United States provides ample evidence for the losses in effectiveness that arise due to a lack of institutional coordination (Rose-Ackerman 1995).

Openness: integrating non-governmental players into environmental policy

Private citizens, companies and NGOs are just three of the many groups of players in the broader context of environmental policy-making that are able to assist policy formation by contributing expertise, information and influence. Openness to these players and an ability to integrate their contributions into environmental policy determine a country's capacity for environmental protection.

Businesses

Typical examples of policy integration of non-governmental players are consultation and agreements with businesses. For example, voluntary agreements are instruments of environmental policy that are based on both formal and informal agreements between firms and regulators. Voluntary agreements can be advantageous since they impose little additional regulatory workload on the public administration, require less direct intervention and can exploit information about cost-effective pollution abatement more efficiently than governments. As a result, there is an argument that voluntary agreements can be more efficient as a means of regulation than traditional form of environmental policy. The key trade-off in the use of voluntary agreements concerns the efficiency gains of more flexible regulation, on the one hand, and the loss of policy control for governments, on the other. Most OECD countries have used the tools of voluntary agreements in order to integrate corporate inputs into environmental policy. As a result, there is now ample evidence that voluntary agreements between government and regulated parties have significant potential for efficient and effective policy implementation, achieving objectives frequently at a low cost. In this area, in particular, however, caution has to be used in drawing conclusions about the replicability of such results in countries with a different enforcement culture than the countries under review in this chapter.

Public

Involving the public is one of the most important factors in driving forward environmental policy. The choice of institutional set-up determines a country's potential for harnessing the public's inputs into environmental policy-making. Private citizens challenging policy decisions individually or in an organized fashion in courts, reporting environmental offences to regulatory agencies, or organizing political movements at the local or national level to push for environmental legislation are signs of openness of a system. Responsive court decisions, changes in regulatory performance, and changes in laws and regulations are evidence of capacity to integrate. However, the relationship between policy-making and the public need not be reactive only. In systems in which the public is regarded as the final arbiter of regulation, this requires political support to be built in order to provide legitimacy to policy changes. Example of successful anticipatory integration of the public in policy-making are environmental tax commissions (see Table 12.4) set up in a number of industrialized countries in order to collect public opinion and enlist public support for extending the use of environmentally-related taxes – e.g. using taxes to reduce, or to offset, through "green" revenues, environmentally-damaging subsidies.

Since 2007, the United Kingdom also has a Green Fiscal Commission, which, in contrast to the commissions listed in Table 12.4, has been established without the initiative of the government.

Openness and integration requires the **exchange of information** between government and the public. To allow for the exchange of information, both measures of information pull and information push are used. **Information pull** gives citizens the right to request information to be released, with the cost of information exchange borne by the citizen. Information pull has been replaced in many instances by **information push**, which obliges regulators and authorities to release information to the public even in the absence of a specific request from the public. As international experiences document, some of the most exciting developments in environmental regulation come from the introduction of information push policies in industrialized countries. A key example of information push strategies are the US Emergency Planning and Community Right-To-Know Act (EPCRA) passed in 1986, which forced companies to make public data on their releases and transfers of toxic chemicals. This led to dramatic decreases in toxic releases because of greater production efficiency and greater public pressure.

Integrating legal instruments into environmental policy

Who should be responsible for enforcement of rights in the environment, and how can those to whom these rights are assigned enforce them? The diversity of

Table 12.4 Environmental tax commissions in Europe

	Date of introduction	Environmentally related taxes	Recycling revenues	Damaging subsidies	Other damaging effects of fiscal reform	Within the context of broader tax reform
Belgium	1993	Yes	Yes	No	No	n/a
Denmark	1993	Yes	Yes	No	No	Yes
Finland	1991	Yes	Yes	Yes	No	No
Ireland	1996/7	Yes	Yes	No	n/a	n/a
Japan	1996/7	Yes	Yes	No	n/a	Yes
Italy	1994	Yes	Yes	Yes	No	n/a
Netherlands	1999	Yes	Yes	No	Yes	Yes
Norway	1994	Yes	Yes	Yes	Yes	Yes
Sweden	1994	Yes	Yes	Yes	Yes	Yes

Source: Based on Schlegelmilch (1997).

Note
The official status of the commissions included in the table vary considerably, so does the approaches to any studies of possible uses of revenues raised (revenue recycling), and the follow-up of the proposals presented.

legal frameworks in different countries shows that policy-makers can choose from a highly diverse set of possible attributions of responsibility. Three basic approaches exist:

1   To invest private citizens with explicit rights in the environment. The corresponding enforcement of these rights is through the pursuit of individual or class claims under tort law in a civil court.
2   To charge regulators with the monitoring and enforcement of public rights in the environment. This case requires a legal framework that grants regulators the powers of both monitoring and enforcement of those rights under an administrative law, sometimes, but not always, involving the adjudication by a separate court.
3   To charge public prosecutors with the prosecution of violations of public rights in the environment. The corresponding enforcement of these rights takes place in courts of law under the provisions of criminal law.

All three approaches are observable in different countries and are not mutually exclusive. However, the relative reliance differs markedly from country to country, with a number of lessons available from the case studies. For example, suits by citizens against polluters violating their operating permits are a fairly recent phenomenon in environmental law. Environmental policy in the United States relies most extensively on this approach, but it is virtually unknown in most European Union countries, where private access to judicial remedies is much more restricted and usually not available unless some harm has already occurred.

Administrative law, and the concomitant processes of monitoring and enforcement by regulators, have traditionally been a mainstay of environmental policy in all OECD countries. The central role of administrative law is justified on account of the overwhelming evidence on its contribution toward ensuring compliance. Evidence from the United States shows that each additional dollar spent on the Environmental Protection Agency's (EPA) enforcement budget leads to between US$2.66 and US$4.20 of investment into protection equipment in the 14 major industrial sectors covered by regulation (Nadeau 1997). Empirical studies on environmental compliance in the US steel industry demonstrate that increases in inspections lead to a more than proportional increase in the relative probability of compliance, and even more so for increases in enforcement actions. Investing in inspection and enforcement therefore generates immediate compliance improvements.

The role of criminal prosecution of environmental offenders is also important. The criminalization of environmental offences has its origins in the 1980s. EPA's criminal enforcement program was established in 1982, with full law enforcement authority granted in 1988. As a result, the EPA initiates between 300 and 650 criminal cases per year. Another leader in criminalization of environmental offences, Germany, included environmental offences in criminal law for the first time in 1980, with amendments expanding the range of offences in

1994. In Germany, between approximately 3,400 and 5,100 environmental crimes were prosecuted between 1995 and 2006. There is evidence that both environmental lawmakers and regulators have been actively reviewing the use of criminal sanctions, both in the United States and in the EU. The Senate Judiciary Committee, for example, held hearings on strengthening criminal enforcement for environmental offences in 2002. After a preparatory period, the European Commission is now aggressively pursuing the introduction and strengthening of criminal sanctions for environmental offences committed within the EU.

It is also evident from the experience of some of the countries, such as the Czech Republic, that administrative law can perform some aspects of the role of the judiciary, potentially at lower cost, but also at the price of decreased effectiveness. Overall, however, a strong judiciary is of paramount importance for building an effective system of sanctions for noncompliance.

Conclusions

This chapter has set out international experiences on the question of which institutional framework countries choose in order to deliver effective environmental protection at acceptable cost. The international experiences used as basis of this chapter were drawn both from large number of industrialized countries such as the OECD as well as from the three countries under particular consideration: the United States, Germany and the Czech Republic.

Key considerations in developing governmental institutions for environmental policy of relevance to the PRC case were identified to lie in the areas of:

1 **Institutionalization and institutional capacity**: here, the chapter discussed the branches of government involved in environmental policy in different countries and the reasons for the different choices witnessed in different countries.

2 **Spatial policy integration**: the chapter considered the different designs pioneered in different countries for ensuring consistent and effective environmental governance at multiple spatial levels both in terms of the choice of institutions and mechanisms for their coordination. This comprises both the spatially-devolved enactment of national environmental policy along vertical lines and the horizontal coordination of environmental policies carried out at lower levels of spatial aggregation.

3 **Horizontal (sectoral) policy integration**: countries commonly face the question on how to design environmental governance across different sectors and different ministerial domains. The chapter studied the institutional, strategic and procedural measures in place in different countries in order to effect the integration of environmental policy objectives into the total of governmental policies.

4 **Openness**: here, the chapter discussed the international experiences in integrating non-governmental players into environmental policy-making in order to establish public acceptance and legitimacy for policy action and in

order to utilize to its best potential information relevant for policy solutions that exists in society, but is not immediately available to policy-makers.

5   **Enforcement**: countries understand that compliance with environmental laws and regulations requires mechanisms for monitoring and enforcement. The chapter discussed various approaches employed by different countries for building monitoring systems and for sanctioning non-compliance.

In the area of institutionalization, the chapter stresses the international consensus that a minimum set of institutions is required to carry out environmental policy effectively. Some countries deviate from this minimal list, but are able to retain policy effectiveness either by assigning the relevant responsibilities to other institutional players or by maintaining a highly functional policy environment in general.

As far as cross-sectoral policy integration is concerned, the heterogeneity of individual country experiences comes with important common features. All countries surveyed in this chapter have three forms of coordination mechanisms – namely:

1   institutional, which involves creating a dedicated mechanism through which different agencies are forced to exchange information and coordinate activities;
2   strategic, which involves the design of overarching policy frameworks where sectoral agencies define their policy actions; and
3   procedural, which entails requirements in the policy-making process to consult with environmental policy agencies for policies that affect environmental policy objectives.

Spatial governance is a universal challenge for environmental policy-makers since policy faces real and binding trade-offs between a more uniform national set-up that neglects local and/or regional heterogeneities and a more spatially differentiated system that sacrifices national environmental goals and invites interregional policy spillovers. Neverthless, meaningful trade-offs can be struck, but these trade-offs should be supported by a system of carrots-and-sticks between the national government and the regional and local governments. A commonly used "stick" for failure of lower-level authorities to perform satisfactorily is the threat of federal government taking over the implementation of environmental policy.

Openness of environmental policy-making requires information and the possibility for non-governmental actors to take an active role in policy-making. In terms of information management, strategies of information pull and information push have proved successful, with information push becoming increasingly widespread. Information push is particularly helpful for allowing non-governmental groups to provide functions of monitoring and oversight that complement government activities. Voluntary agreements between government and regulated parties have also demonstrated significant potential for efficient and effective policy implementation, achieving objectives frequently at a low cost.

Legal instruments and activities of monitoring and enforcement are a mainstay of environmental policy in the countries under consideration in this chapter. This role is justified on account of the convincing evidence regarding the high effectiveness of all legal modes of tort law, administrative law and criminal law. It is also evident from the experience of some of the countries that administrative law can perform some aspects of the role of the judiciary, potentially at lower cost, but also at the price of decreased effectiveness. Overall, however, a strong judiciary is of paramount importance for building an effective system of sanctions for non-compliance.

To conclude, there is solid evidence on what features of the institutional framework of environmental policy deliver effective environmental protection at acceptable cost. Some of these features can be integrated into existing frameworks without substantial procedural difficulty, in particular, with regard to vertical policy integration and openness. Some areas require a more long-term strategy for implementation, such as the development of a functioning environmental judiciary. The international evidence demonstrates that investments in the institutional framework of environmental policy generate significant gains in terms of developing a country's capacity for environmental protection. It also demonstrates that these gains are attainable within the timespan accorded in the PRC's 50-year Macro-Environmental Strategy.

References

Howlett, M. and M. Ramesh (1995) *Studying Public Policy.* New York: Oxford University Press.

Jänicke, M. and H. Weidner (1997) National Environmental Policies. A Comparative Study of Capacity-Building. Berlin: Springer.

Jänicke, Martin, Lutz Mez, Pernille Bechsgaard, and Börge Klemmensen. 1999. "Innovative Effects of Sector Specific Regulation Patterns. The Example of Energy Efficient Refrigerators in Denmark." In Klemmer, P. (ed.) *Innovation and the Environment. Case Studies on the Adaptive Behavior in Society and the Economy,* 49–69. Berlin: Analytica Verlagsgesellschaft.

Müller, E. (2002) "Environmental Policy Integration as a Political Principle: The German Case and the Implications of European Policy." In Lenschow, A. (ed.) *Environmental Policy Integration.* London: Earthscan, pp. 57–77.

Nadeau, L.W. (1997) "EPA Effectiveness at Reducing the Duration of Plant-Level Noncompliance." *Journal of Environmental Economics and Management* 34(1), 54–78.

OECD (1994) *Capacity Development in Environment.* Paris: OECD.

OECD (2007) *OECD Environmental Data Compendium 2006/2007.* Paris: OECD.

Rose-Ackerman, S. (1995) *Controlling Environmental Policy: The Limits of Public Law in Germany and the United States.* New Haven: Yale University Press.

Schlegelmilch, K. (1997) *Green Budget Reform in Europe: Countries at the Forefront.* Heidelberg: Springer.

Weidner, H. and M. Jänicke (2002) *Capacity Building in National Environmental Policy: A Comparative Study of 17 Countries.* New York: Springer.

13 Recurrent issues in environmental governance

James Salzman

Introduction

From one perspective, the environmental challenges facing the People's Republic of China (PRC) are unique. No other country has seriously grappled with environmental protection in the face of such rapid economic growth in such a short period of time. The PRC geography, climate, education and political system are, of course, unique as well. As a result, one must be cautious in drawing overbroad conclusions from the experience of environmental protection in other countries. A policy instrument that works well in Europe or the United States may be a poor fit in the PRC. The same may be true for particular methods of public participation or enforcement strategies.

From another perspective, however, while the PRC situation is undeniably unique, it shares important, indeed fundamental, similarities with the environmental protection challenges faced by other countries. If one reads the sectoral assessments by the international experts in this volume, it quickly becomes apparent that the sectoral reports and analyses share a number of common themes that cut across air pollution, water pollution and nature conservation. This chapter provides a synthesis of the cross-cutting themes, highlighting four of the most important for further analysis.

Because these common themes are fundamental to effective environmental governance, they inevitably overlap with one another. Community groups' monitoring of pollution is discussed under the topic of individual participation. But it could equally have been addressed as an aspect of enforcement, citizen participation or information collection.

This chapter is intended to provide core lessons on how to structure an effective regulatory system for environmental protection in a complex jurisdiction, drawing from experiences in the United States, the European Union and international organizations.

Cross-cutting themes

Coordination between central and local authorities

Any large, populous country faces the challenge of coordinating national and local governmental authorities. This is particularly difficult in the field of environmental protection, where local interests may favor economic development over ecology. The People's Republic of China faces these challenges today and so, too, do the United States and Europe. In fact, they both faced an even more similar situation 40 years ago. This section explores the five strategies they employed in evolving toward strong policy and regulatory control at the central level with effective compliance and implementation at the local level.

Enforcement

Laws on the books are little more than words without effective enforcement. Penalties for non-compliance may be too weak. Conversely, there may be powerful opportunities for greater cooperation between government and polluting parties to facilitate compliance. This section explores the dual concerns that current sanctions are *not strict enough* and that there is *too much emphasis on sanctions* and greater attention should be paid to creating incentives for compliance. These types of concerns reflect a widespread challenge faced by environmental protection authorities in many countries.

Individual participation

Formal participation by individuals can address two different types of issues. The first lies in increasing the effectiveness of current environmental protection efforts, creating mechanisms for citizens to act on behalf of environmental authorities. This leverages the limited resources of both central and local environmental agencies and can be done in the fields of enforcement (through individual rights to bring suits), compliance monitoring and education, among others. The second model for citizen participation lies in providing an avenue for citizens' voices to be heard in a manner that reinforces environmental protection efforts.

Information management

Collecting, using and sharing information are central to environmental protection. Management at the level of river basins, identifying where to focus conservation efforts, and calculating acceptable levels of air pollution from a facility all require information. Because agencies require a great deal of information but have limited resources, a key strategy relies on shifting the burden of information collection and analysis from the government to regulated parties. Key issues in this area turn on how much information is enough for effective governance, who should pay for or provide the information, who should be given access to the information, and how it should be shared.

Coordination between central and local authorities

An issue that comes up in all the case studies is the relationship between local authorities and the central government. The PRC's Ministry of Environmental Protection (MEP) depends critically on local Environmental Protection Bureaus (EPBs) for effective implementation of national laws, meaningful enforcement of legal requirements and information on local problems. Conversely, the local EPBs rely on the MEP for technical expertise and standard-setting. While both local and national authorities need each other, their relationship is complex. Personnel decisions and financing of EPBs occur primarily at the provincial and local level. Enforcement is primarily carried out at the local level with varied degrees of oversight by the MEP. Moreover, EPB officials sometimes face strong local pressures to favor economic development over environmental protection. Enhanced coordination in this evolving relationship is fundamental to strengthening environmental protection over the coming decades.

While the details obviously differ, 40 years ago the EU and the United States also faced the similar problem of a central authority that desired stronger environmental protection in occasional conflict with local authorities more closely committed to development. The evolution of environmental protection in both the EU and the United States has shown a similar transition to the current models of strong central authorities that set strict environmental requirements with generally effective compliance at the local level. As a result, both jurisdictions boast much cleaner environments than three and four decades ago.

Despite their many differences, the US national government and the EU's governing institutions have employed very similar strategies. These strategies rely on pervasive central authority as the leverage to influence local authorities to promote and carry out national environmental policies in the face of local development pressures. The PRC's challenge in developing an effective relationship between national and local environmental authorities is, at its core, quite similar. There is no single "correct" strategy and the PRC's solution will certainly be different than that employed in other jurisdictions. Nonetheless, complex jurisdictions tend to rely on quite similar strategies no matter where they are, and these provide useful models for the MEP to consider as its relationship with local authorities matures.

If one looks broadly across the history of US and European environmental protections over the last 40 years and, in particular, the coordination between national and local authorities, five separate coordination strategies emerge. The first three are jurisdictional strategies, while the last two are financial strategies. It is important to note that the Ministry is relatively weak in two of the most important areas – i.e. secondary enforcement and conditional funding.

Coordination strategies between central and local authorities

Legislation that pre-empts local authority in favor of national authority

- The passage of central laws that supplant state environmental programs in place of a national, uniform program for specific pollutants.

Reliance on shared authority

- Providing flexibility to local authorities to determine how best to meet the national goals.

Secondary enforcement

- Either delegating, monitoring and enforcement authority of national laws to state and local authorities but retaining the authority to bring enforcement actions if the local enforcement is deemed to be inadequate, or creating mechanisms for citizens to challenge non-compliance and inadequate governmental responses at the local level.

Directed funding

- Providing money from the central authority to local authorities in order to improve environmental protection infrastructure, such as grants for construction of local wastewater treatment plants, or environmental protection capacity, such as training and hiring inspection officials.

Conditional funding

- Conditioning grants of central funds on local authorities meeting performance goals.

Legislation that pre-empts local authority in favor of national authority

At a minimum, coordinating environmental protection between national and local authorities requires a clear understanding of respective rights and responsibilities. In most countries, these are set out in general terms in the constitution. In the environmental field, this is often complemented with specific statutes, often media-specific statutes. In both the United States and the EU, consolidation of authority has been preceded by passage of national laws that supplant state environmental authority in place of a national, uniform program. While passage of laws alone is never enough to ensure effective implementation, it is, nevertheless, a necessary precondition.

There are a number of justifications for concentrating environmental protection authority in a central administration. Most important, natural boundaries rarely track political boundaries. Maps of most countries' provinces and states will show straight lines and right angles, with little or no relationship to the region's watersheds, ecosystems or forests. The mismatch of natural and political scales poses difficult challenges for environmental management. Air pollution, water pollution and wildlife certainly pay no heed to state borders, with the result that often the generator of the pollution is politically distinct from those harmed.

Since some environmental harms, particularly air and water pollution, are transboundary, governance can prove difficult because the costs of pollution often fall outside the jurisdictions where the pollution was created. Upwind jurisdictions have little incentive to reduce the costs of their emissions on downwind jurisdictions. And downwind (or downstream) jurisdictions, those with the greatest cause for concern, have no political voice in upwind jurisdictions where the harms originated. As a result of these geographical spillovers across jurisdictions, transboundary environmental problems often pose the challenges of collective action (the high transaction costs to bring differing parties together), equity (ensuring that the parties enjoying the benefits of environmental protection also bear a share of the costs), and enforcement (monitoring compliance at a distance from the source of authority). Central authority overcomes these problems by matching the scale of harm to the same scale of governance.

Centralized authority can stifle potential competition for industry among local authorities by mandating uniform standards. Uniform, centralized standards also can promote commerce, allowing industry to operate more efficiently and not having to worry about manufacturing different products to satisfy different local requirements. It makes sense to concentrate the relevant technical expertise for setting standards and modeling pollution in one central agency rather than reproducing it in every jurisdiction.

These points are illustrated clearly in the experiences of the United States and the EU. For both air and water pollution legislation in the United States, for example, there has been a clear transfer over time from local control over environmental protection to centralized control, a remarkable change when compared to 1970. The same is true, though perhaps to a lesser extent, in Europe. Nonetheless, it has been estimated that more than half of the environmental legislation followed by member states has resulted from EU actions.[1] The percentage is even higher for laws in US states.

Shared authority

As described above, in the transition from decentralized environmental protection to centralized protection, the primary responsibility has shifted from the provincial and state level to central ministries and agencies. Importantly, the transfer of power from local to central authorities is rarely complete. Local authorities still retain significant power.

Sharing authority between central and local agencies provides a number of important benefits. It leverages resources, allowing the central authority to focus its resources and personnel on policy development and local authorities to focus on local implementation. It takes advantage of relative economies of scale. While local authorities clearly may want a voice in policy development, it makes sense to concentrate the relevant technical expertise for setting standards and modeling pollution in one central place, rather than reproducing it in every jurisdiction. It also takes advantage of relative expertise. State and local environmental agencies are better placed to develop local solutions to problems that can take into account local factors, whether geography, housing and income or industry and workforce. Finally, sharing authority provides for greater experimentation. Setting goals centrally and providing flexibility for local agencies to achieve them fosters creative solutions that can provide a natural laboratory for environmental instrument design and application.

The most appropriate means to share authority, however, is a contentious topic. In fact, the EU has developed a special term for this issue, "subsidiarity," and in the United States it is often described as "federalism." In the United States, the US Environmental Protection Agency (EPA) sets national standards but delegates much of its responsibility for permitting, standard-setting, monitoring and enforcement to state authorities. These delegations are established by written agreement, and states must conduct these activities as stringently as the federal authorities would. Under the statute governing waste disposal, for example, 98 percent of the inspections and 95 percent of enforcement actions are conducted by states.[2]

The EU follows a similar model. The primary instrument for environmental law in the EU is the directive. By its very nature, this provides a form of cooperation. Directives set out broad goals or precise numeric standards that are binding on member states, but the method for achieving these goals or standards is left to each member state as it transposes the requirements into national law. This approach allows member states to set their own priorities within the broader goals and restrictions of the central authority's law.

In the PRC, too, significant authority is shared between the MEP and the local EPBs. How this relationship evolves in the coming decades will be a fundamental issue for the course of the PRC's environmental protection.

Secondary enforcement

In delegating responsibilities from a central authority to local environmental authorities, there is a fundamental concern that implementation will not follow. Central authorities may pass a law or regulation, but that is no guarantee it will be carried out at the local level. Local concerns over economic development may result in weak implementation or enforcement. The key question, then, is how central authorities can best ensure local implementation and enforcement. There are two fundamental strategies to address this challenge, described in this section and in the one that follows:

1   secondary enforcement; and
2   conditional funding.

Secondary enforcement is a form of oversight. It can be either *centralized* or *decentralized*. Under direct oversight, the primary responsibility for permitting and enforcement of national laws is placed in the hands of local officials, but the central authority retains the ability to bring enforcement actions if the local enforcement is deemed to be inadequate. In the EU, for example, the European Commission may bring an enforcement action against member states for inadequate implementation of European law. The US EPA relies on a practice known as "overfiling," where the agency can seek to impose penalties in addition to the state's sanctions if the state has not taken "timely" and "appropriate" enforcement action against polluters.

Importantly, environmental enforcement in the EU focuses on member states, not private actors. This is a significant difference from other centralized jurisdictions. The US EPA, for example, can bring actions against agencies and public bodies, but it focuses its enforcement efforts on individuals and companies – the actual polluters.

The other type of secondary enforcement is decentralized. Local officials have primary responsibility for permitting and enforcement of national laws but actions may be brought against polluters or the government agencies by individuals. These types of actions are considered indirect because they are not centrally coordinated. Central agencies consciously decide which state settlements to overfile or which member states to start infringement proceedings against. There is no such deliberate planning with suits brought by individuals. Individual rights to bring suits are most effective when brought against agencies failing to carry out mandatory duties or polluters who are not being prosecuted by local authorities. This mechanism has proven more important in the United States than in Europe or other regions.

Secondary enforcement has proven extremely important in the successful centralization of environmental authority in both the EU and the United States. Local enforcement is much more effective if the authorities know the state is looking over their shoulder and can step in to intervene. By contrast, secondary enforcement is weak in the PRC. The MEP has weak oversight authority, nor does individual enforcement provide strong oversight of local enforcement. Moreover, secondary enforcement only works if there is a strong judiciary. The key question, then, is which institution should the central authority turn to for secondary enforcement when the local authorities are not providing effective enforcement?

Case study: centralized enforcement by the European Commission

As in other centralized jurisdictions, such as the United States and the People's Republic of China, most European environmental laws are adopted at the community level but then implemented and enforced within the member states, among whom there are significant differences in income, commitment to environmental protection and administrative capacity. Enforcement is focused on two types of non-compliance. The first is failure by the member states to adopt the directive appropriately or on time. The second is failure to follow the requirements of the directive or regulation.

If the Commission determines that an enforcement action is necessary, it commences an "infringement" procedure against the member state, setting forth the basis for the action. A period of negotiation follows and, if unsuccessful, the Commission may sue the state before the European Court of Justice. If the Commission's case is successful, the state must correct the non-compliance and can be sanctioned with financial penalties, as well. In July 2000, for example, the Court imposed penalties on Greece of €20,000 per day of delay in implementing several EU waste directives. Interestingly, there have been more infringements proceedings in the environmental area than in any other fields of EU law.

The entire process can be quite long, often three years or longer before the case is resolved by the Court. In practice, however, few cases are ever fully litigated. The vast majority are negotiated during the early stages of the infringement process. In 1999, for example, of the 1,900 cases closed that year, only 5 percent were considered by the Court. In other words, 95 percent of the cases were resolved prior to referral to the European Court of Justice.[3]

While the Commission can take significant action against member states, it remains a relatively weak enforcer compared to environmental ministries and agencies in other jurisdictions. As noted above, the Commission cannot bring actions against regulated parties or issue sanctions against regulated parties within member states. The Commission has neither inspectors in the field nor the ability to monitor specific facilities. As a result, it has far weaker enforcement capacity than many other central environmental institutions.

While there have been some efforts to increase the Commission's enforcement capacity, these have been unsuccessful to date, in large part because of subsidiarity concerns – the principle that enforcement can be better achieved at the level of member states. The European Environment Agency has been created to monitor and collect information, but its role in enforcement has been limited.

Case study: centralized enforcement by the EPA

With delegated enforcement authority, states must notify the Environmental Protection Agency (EPA) officials of local enforcement actions. If EPA officials determine that the state's response to non-compliance was too slow (i.e. not within 90–120 days from the date of discovery of the violation) or too lenient (i.e. an inadequate response given the severity of the violation), it can seek to increase the penalties or impose other appropriate remedies, so long as they are consistent with the substantive law of the state in which the violation took place (since the state program was approved by EPA in lieu of the federal program). Overfiling authority is generally provided both by the statute authorizing delegation and a memorandum of understanding between EPA and the state at the time of delegation. In practice, this has proven controversial.

For example, Harmon Industries was a company that assembles circuit boards for railroad control and safety equipment.[4] A company official found that maintenance workers had been regularly discarding volatile solvent residue behind their plant, a practice that had been going on for 15 years. Following this discovery, Harmon stopped the disposal activities and contacted the Missouri Department of Natural Resources (MDNR). The MDNR conducted an investigation and decided that the past disposal activities did not pose a threat to human health or the environment. Harmon agreed to a settlement with the state agency that would clean up the disposal area but not impose any fines. The EPA decided to overfile, and commenced an administrative enforcement action against Harmon seeking over US$2 million in penalties. An administrative proceeding rejected the EPA's requested fine but levied a penalty of US$586,716 against Harmon (this award was later overturned on appeal).

The *Harmon* cases demonstrates the potential power of overfiling. In *Harmon*, the EPA sought to transforming an agreement with no penalty into a US$2 million fine. While the number of cases where EPA overfiles a state enforcement action is quite small, under 1 percent of all cases, it can be quite effective. EPA must notify the violator and the state prior to overfiling, and this provides them an opportunity to modify their settlement. Second, overfiling sends a clear message not only to the polluter but to the state agency, as well. The federal environmental authority is willing to share authority with a state agency, but it is going to be looking over the shoulder of the state agency and stepping in with its own sanctions, potentially significant sanctions, if the state agency is viewed as too soft on local polluters. This can provide political protection for a state agency against local political pressures – allowing the local regulators to say they would like to impose weaker sanctions but that the federal government is looking over its shoulder so it has no choice but to be strict.

Directed funding

A significant cause of weak performance by local environmental authorities does not stem from bad faith but, rather, simply from inadequate resources. Local authorities may want to enforce environmental laws, but they do not have enough funds to hire inspectors, analyze air samples from monitoring stations, or carry out enforcement activities. As a result, effective environmental protection can be greatly strengthened by financial assistance from the central authority. Such grants can support environmental protection through two means:

1   Central funds can help build infrastructure, such as grants for construction of local wastewater treatment plants and other built-in capital.
2   Grants can strengthen personnel capacity, such as training and hiring inspection officials.

This is a common strategy. For example, in the United States, billions of dollars have been distributed to state and local governments to help pay for construction of wastewater treatment facilities. Similarly, the EU's LIFE financial instrument supports environmental and nature conservation projects throughout the EU, as well as in some neighboring countries. Since 1992, it has co-financed over 2,700 projects with roughly €1.35 billion. Funding can also improve human capacity.

The challenge of directed funding in most countries lies in persuading the central funding authority to give the MEP sufficient funds to disburse to local authorities for specific environmental purposes.

Conditional funding

Funding can be a powerful incentive for effective local environmental protection and, equally, potential *loss* of funding can be a powerful incentive, as well. Thus another key strategy for effective coordination lies in conditioning central funds on meeting specific performance goals. This strategy is even more effective if the central authority is able to withhold funds that are not controlled by it. As the case study below on highway funds illustrates, limiting the ability of *other* agencies to disburse funds raises the potential impact of the sanction considerably. EPA can withhold highway funds from states that fail to comply with the Clean Air Act. Because these funds are very important to the states, EPA holds a powerful hammer to ensure compliance.

This strategy is used at the international level, as well. Under the Montreal Protocol, for example, parties that fail to comply with the treaty's requirements may be denied access to the financial and technology transfer benefits of the Multilateral Fund. Similarly, many international environmental treaties rescind trade benefits for parties that are not in compliance, including the Basel Convention on hazardous wastes, the Montreal Protocol and CITES (the Convention on International Trade in Endangered Species of Wild Fauna and Flora).

As with direct funding, the challenge for this strategy is to provide the central authority greater control over funds to local authorities. In some cases, the central authority is given control over funds from *another* ministry. In the PRC context, one necessary reform would be to increase the MEP's role as a conduit of funding to local EPBs or to condition infrastructure funds from another ministry on environmental compliance.

Case study: state highway funds and state implementation plans

State Implementation Plans (SIPs) are a fundamental part of the Clean Air Act. SIPs set out how states will meet the national ambient air quality standards. If a SIP is inadequate to meet these national goals, the Environmental Protection Agency (EPA) can impose a number of sanctions on the state. The most effective sanction relies on conditional funding.

If a state fails to provide an adequate SIP or has not adequately implemented its SIP, the Clean Air Act prohibits agencies from funding projects that "cause or contribute to any new violation of any standard," "increase the frequency or severity of any existing violation," or "delay timely attainment of any standard." Because new roads lead to greater traffic and mobile source emissions, in practice this provision has meant a ban on federal funds for highway construction and transit projects. Since federal funds pay for most highways, this can result in states potentially losing hundreds of millions of dollars. As such, it provides the EPA with a very powerful threat.

After determining that a state has failed to prepare or implement an adequate SIP, the EPA must provide notice to the states and cannot impose funding sanctions for 18 months. It is hoped, of course, that states will come into compliance and either submit an acceptable plan or meaningfully implement the measures in the SIP within the 18-month period. And this usually is exactly what happens. From 1990 through 1998, for example, the EPA issued 858 formal notifications to states that it intended to impose sanctions. Only 18 sanctions, however, were imposed. In other words, in 98 percent of the cases, states came into compliance, a remarkably high rate of response. When the sanction has been imposed, it has been powerful. The city of Atlanta, for example, was determined to be out of conformity with its SIP in 1998 and federal funding for transportation halted for two years, postponing many projects during a period when the city was experiencing rapid growth. The city ultimately developed a new transportation plan, including the banning of diesel buses, and started receiving federal funds again.

Conditional funding has proven a blunt but effective tool. Without this sanction, states would be more likely to submit inadequate SIPs or lag in implementing the plans. Through the threat of lost highway funds, a more level playing field is created and states are effectively penalized for not enforcing their SIPs. It also provides an obstacle to a potential race-to-the-bottom, where lax standards and enforcement are intended to attract or retain pollution-intensive industries. Conditional funding also provides an example of an effective sanction that need not be used. The simple threat of lost funds has been extraordinarily effective in bringing states into compliance quickly. Such threats, interestingly, are also useful at the state level. As one commentator has written, "state officials anxious to have their state legislature enact laws implementing a State Implementation Plan may argue that failure to act will lead EPA to cut off the state's highway funds."[5]

Environmental enforcement

Environmental enforcement is a critically important topic. The mere fact of a law's existence is no assurance of its implementation. Rules on the books can prove worthless if they are not enforced. At a minimum, an effective system of enforcement should seek to achieve both the *force of law* – to ensure the law is effectively applied – and the *rule of law* – to ensure the law is justly applied. Yet ensuring the force and rule of law is by no means a given. Indeed, this is a very real challenge faced daily in many countries around the world.

It is virtually assumed among regulators and the regulated alike that few parties, if any, are in compliance with all relevant regulations all of the time. A careful inspection will almost certainly uncover instances of non-compliance, some unintentional, and some knowing.

Enforcement speaks to several parties. Most obvious, enforcement efforts seek to punish the offending party such that they do not profit from their non-compliance. This helps ensure a level playing field for those who comply with the law. Enforcement also speaks to parties *outside* the particular action. That is, enforcement not only deters the particular lawbreaker who was punished, but it should also deter potential lawbreakers from violating the law. Punishing a speeding motorist with a heavy fine not only deters that motorist but others who learn of the punishment, as well, who do not want to pay a fine in the future.

One of the themes addressed in every sectoral study, whether air, water, nature conservation or governance has been the importance of enforcement activities. Two different types of concerns have been raised.

1   The problem of *under-enforcement*: the concern that current penalties for pollution are too low to change behavior.
2   The problem of *misdirected enforcement*: the concern that there should be greater cooperation between government and industry in order to create incentives for compliance.

The strategic choice between compliance facilitation and sanction is not unique to the PRC. Indeed, it reflects a widespread challenge faced by environmental protection authorities in many countries.

Remedy choice for non-compliance

Remedies lie at the heart of the enforcement process. Regulated parties need to understand what the potential consequences of non-compliance will be. The challenge for effective enforcement lies in selecting the appropriate type of remedy in each situation. In a setting where most enforcement is carried out by local authorities, this also requires determining how much discretion to give the local authorities.

One can think of environmental penalties in four basic categories:

1   monetary fines;
2   criminal sanctions;
3   injunctions; and
4   supplemental environmental projects.

If one seeks to punish the party, then criminal sanctions may be appropriate. If one seeks to punish the party and also level the playing field to remove the economic benefit of non-compliance, then monetary fines are needed. If one is most concerned with returning the violators to compliance immediately, then a tailored injunction may be appropriate. If one seeks to restore the harmed environment, then supplemental projects may be necessary. Drawing on the earlier discussion of good actor and bad actor theories of enforcement, one may also want to craft a remedy that fosters compliance facilitation.

The following sections highlight key aspects of choosing civil penalties, criminal sanctions and supplemental environmental projects that may be of particular interest to Chinese authorities in crafting enforcement policies. There are two strategies central officials must consider in this context. The first is to rely on uniform, rigid guidelines that determine the type and level of sanction. This approach intentionally *removes discretion*, and is guided by the principle that all violations must be treated equally. The second approach *provides much greater discretion* to enforcement officials, allowing them to craft sanctions that are appropriate for the particular violation, taking into account all the relevant factors. This second approach is much more compatible with a compliance facilitation strategy. Greater discretion, however, also creates the possibility for greater abuse and potential *under*-enforcement.

Civil penalty policies

By far the most common remedy for environmental non-compliance is monetary fines, known generally as civil penalties. When the government decides to seek civil penalties, it must obviously also calculate the appropriate level of monetary penalty. A general concern of authorities not only in the PRC but in many countries, both developed and developing, is that the level of penalty is not high enough to act as a meaningful deterrent. In other words, the fine is too low to change polluters' behavior and is simply regarded as a cost of doing business.

Criminal sanctions

A range of environmental statutes, including the key statutes governing air, water and solid waste, provide for criminal sanctions. Heavy civil fines and injunctions can also provide powerful deterrents to regulated parties. One might therefore ask, when are criminal sanctions appropriate for environmental violations? Criminal sanctions send a very different message both to the regulated community and to the public. Put simply, criminal sanctions are not regarded as just another cost of doing business. Criminal sanctions are the ultimate form of punishment for an individual. When applied to a company or a public agency, they also make a strong public statement that their non-compliance was very serious.

Despite their greater deterrent force and powerful rhetoric, criminal sanctions can be problematic in an environmental context. We discussed earlier the difficulty of achieving full compliance all of the time. In any highly regulated field, if enforcement officials want to find instances of non-compliance at a company, it is likely that they can. The key enforcement question then becomes when criminal charges should be brought instead of, or in addition to, civil charges.

If one looks across the range of criminal cases that have been brought, typical cases include falsifying documents, tampering with monitoring or control equipment, and repeated violations. The common theme in all these situations is *knowing* violation of the law. The key issue, in other words, is intent. This is true more generally in criminal law, where a person or organization has knowingly and willingly committed the illegal act. This simple requirement can be problematic in a technical, highly regulated field such as environmental law, however. Enforcement officials often need to determine whether criminal sanctions for environmental violations require intent only to commit the act, or whether it was necessary to commit an act *and* have knowledge that the act is illegal, as well?

Consider, for example, a case where the manager of a wastewater treatment plant discharges large amounts of effluent into a harbor. He knows he is discharging pollution, but he also believes the amount of discharges is within his permit limit. It turns out he is incorrect and the discharges exceed the effluent limits. Is criminal sanction appropriate in this context?[6]

Supplemental projects and non-traditional remedies

One of the most interesting developments in enforcement strategies over the past ten years has been the significant growth of non-traditional, flexible agreements between environmental enforcement agencies and regulated parties. Known as supplemental environmental projects (SEPs), SEPs are part of negotiated settlements between the government and violators for "beyond compliance" environmental activities either in place of or in addition to monetary penalties. Put simply, SEPs represent a negotiated agreement that trades off a reduced penalty for the violator in exchange for an environmentally beneficial action that is not mandated by law. SEPs have ranged from purchasing lead paint abatement kits for schools and restoring endangered species habitat to installing a closed-loop wastewater recycling system. Indeed, enforcement officials can be very creative with remedies, as the case studies below demonstrate.

Supporters of SEPs argue that supplemental projects lead to greater environmental protection than traditional sanctions. The polluter is still given a deterrent, since it has to pay, but its money is now specifically directed toward environmental projects rather than simply going into the general government treasury.

Some critics respond that SEPs give too much discretion to enforcement authorities, and that companies may end up paying much less than they would have paid in civil fines. Consider, for example, the SEPs performed by the oil company, Citgo, in Port Arthur, Texas, for unauthorized benzene emissions.[7] The SEP agreement entered into with local regulators required the oil company to fund a program that monitors car pollution and donate to a local bird refuge. These might be worthwhile projects, but community groups criticized these actions as completely irrelevant to the people who had been harmed by exposure to the refinery's emissions of air toxics. In addition, they may benefit from positive public relations from their SEPs (though, to guard against this, violators whose SEPs involve public awareness projects often are required to state that the project is part of the settlement of a government lawsuit).

In the PRC context, SEPs raise the same strategic choice as that identified at the introduction of this section. SEPs are only possible if enforcement officials are given the discretionary authority necessary to bargain for particular sanctions. Greater discretion, however, also creates the possibility for greater abuse and potential *under*-enforcement.

Choosing between sanction and compliance facilitation strategies

Ideally, environmental policy should create incentives for compliance. The challenge is how best to do this while still ensuring effective compliance with the law. In jurisdictions that share enforcement power between local and central authorities, one often finds a tension over the proper approach to non-compliance. This grows out of a broader tension over the fundamental causes of non-compliance.

Traditionally, enforcement in the environmental field (as in others) has been based on strategic deterrence. In this model of behavior, the rational actor will comply when it is in his economic self-interest to do so, but will otherwise violate the law. A profit-maximizing company's decision to comply simply comes down to comparing the costs and benefits of non-compliance. This notion of regulated behavior rests on the assumption that most non-compliance is due to "bad actors" and, as a result, the appropriate enforcement strategy is one of sanction. Lawbreakers respond most effectively to punishment. Only when the sanction is painful enough, and the likelihood of detection high enough, will the regulated party comply. In the environmental field, the sufficient pain can take any number of forms, ranging from public notice of violations, ineligibility for government contracts, civil penalties and supplemental environmental projects to injunctions or even jail time. Regardless of the final penalty, though, under this behavioral model it is assumed that non-compliance is intentional.

While the sanction model is based on the assumption of regulating bad actors, the competing approach assumes that most companies are well-intentioned and would comply at higher rates than experienced but for lack of resources or poor understanding of the law.

If the logical consequence of the rational polluter model is the punitive deterrence of enforcement, the obvious response to the well-intentioned model of behavior is compliance facilitation. Helping regulated parties come into compliance, rather than threatening them to do so, not only seems more appropriate if parties truly want to comply, but equitable as well. After all, compliance facilitation simply asks that government help the regulated parties overcome obstacles that government largely created in the first place.

In practice, central authorities often take the enforcement perspective of punishment, while states often take the perspective of compliance facilitation. There is no single answer as to whether enforcement should primarily take a sanction or compliance facilitation approach. The more useful question is how flexible these approaches should be and, more fundamentally, how much discretion should be given to local authorities and how much oversight central authorities should keep. This relates back to the more general discussion of coordination between central and local authorities previously discussed in this section.

Individual participation models

Central to effective environmental protection are the roles played by individuals and environmental groups. Formal participation by individuals in environmental protection can address two different types of issues. The first lies in increasing the effectiveness of current environmental protection efforts. In any country, the Ministry of Environment and the local agencies have limited resources. In an environment where there is pressure to further reduce government expenditures, opportunities to leverage environmental protection activities become particularly important. Thus one model for citizen participation lies in *partnership*, providing citizens and environmental groups opportunities to reinforce government protection efforts. This can be done in the fields of enforcement and compliance monitoring, among others.

The second model for citizen participation lies in providing an avenue for citizens' voices to be heard. While this can also reinforce environmental protection efforts, the goal here is to create structures so citizens' voices can be heard in a constructive fashion. The clearest example of this approach is the use of environmental ombudsmen.

There is currently a limited legal basis for public participation in the PRC's environmental protection than in the OECD countries, hence there is great potential to create structures for participation that reinforce environmental goals and promote a harmonious society. Done wisely, increased participation will both strengthen the credibility of environmental protection efforts and leverage scarce governmental resources.

Individual right to bring suits

This topic has already been addressed in the earlier section on secondary enforcement. The right of individuals to bring suits provides a means for individuals and organizations to challenge a person or any organization, either public or private, alleged to be in violation of an environmental law before a court. Environmental groups have actively used this opportunity both to supplement the government's limited enforcement resources and to pursue violations that the government is ignoring or under-enforcing. The potential to file such suits has provided citizens, environmental groups and industry considerable influence in the field of environmental protection.

Similar to the requirement for Environmental Impact Statements, individual suit provisions have been adopted in many countries around the globe, though in a much more restricted form than citizen suits in the United States, where they have become an integral part of the US environmental protection system. In the EU, for example, individuals cannot file suits against regulated parties that violate EU environmental laws. Individuals can file complaints against member states with the European Commission, but it is the Commission that decides whether or not to pursue the matter. In limited circumstances involving the "direct effect" doctrine, individuals can also sue member states in national courts.

It is important to recognize two points in regard to citizen suits. First, there must be a strong judiciary for this mechanism to be effective. Second, the strong reliance of the United States on citizen suits stems from its particular history. The Anglo-Saxon common law has relied on courts to resolve a broad manner of social conflicts for well over 700 years. In many other countries, including the PRC, courts have played a different role. Thus one must be cautious in holding out the use of environmental citizen suits as a readily-applicable model for countries where neither litigation nor the judiciary have played central roles in conflict resolution.

The key question, then, is determining which aspects of the right to bring individual suits make most sense in an Asian setting. This turns on two related questions:

1 What is the appropriate role for private groups and individuals in enforcing environmental laws?
2 If the government uses its prosecutorial discretion not to sanction a company that has violated an environmental law, should an environmental group or individual be able to sue?

Environmental ombudsmen

Another common method to engage citizens in environmental protection is through the use of so-called ombudsmen. Unlike the individual right to bring suits, this strategy allows citizens to make complaints, but the research and advocacy is carried out by an independent agency on their behalf. This concept was pioneered in Sweden as a general means to provide citizens an office they could take their grievances to and ensure these complaints would be heard. This is not solely, or even primarily, an environmental role. Indeed, in Sweden today there are ombudsmen who investigate complaints about courts, prisons and government agencies. This approach has proven popular and ombudsmen offices are now found in national and local governments around the world, as well as in a number of international organizations.

The basic idea behind ombudsmen is that government officials do not always act in the public interest. Even in the best-governed country, problems exist of bureaucratic self-interest, incompetence and occasional corruption. Asking an aggrieved individual to bring his complaint to the very agency that he feels has acted improperly poses both problems of credibility and effectiveness. It seems very possible, if not likely, that an agency would cover up its misdeeds rather than zealously investigate and punish the guilty official.

By creating an independent authority, whether within or outside the agency, whose salary is not determined by the agency and who does not report to agency officials, independence is more likely and the perception of fairness is much stronger. Environmental ombudsmen are particularly interesting options in countries with a weak judiciary or a tradition of not relying primarily on courts to resolve conflicts. Ombudsmen provide trusted agents that individuals can turn to and have a reasonable hope for their concerns to be heard and acted upon.

In the PRC context, a number of EPBs have created hotlines and receive complaints from individuals. The key difference is that an ombudsman is *not* part of the agency. His salary and evaluations are independent. Ombudsmen may prove an interesting option to consider if the MEP is unable to build up a strong local presence in particular areas with very strong development pressures. They might also be worth considering if a weak judiciary makes citizen suits impractical. In any case, ombudsmen are likely less threatening to a local agency than citizen suits.

Information management

The importance of information in environmental protection cannot be overstated. Managing river basins, for example, requires a large amount of data about the threats in separate watersheds and how these combine downstream. Identifying where to focus conservation efforts requires information, as well, on biodiversity and the threatened status of particular sites. An environmental regulator needs accurate information to understand the nature of a problem and the consequences of potential responses. Likewise, the regulated community needs information to decide how best to comply with adopted rules. And the public needs information in order to feel adequately protected and potentially participate in the regulatory regime. These challenges of information management are posed with special significance in the context of environmental law.

Decision-makers rarely have anything approaching complete knowledge when asked to put in place rules and regulations. To many observers, this inherent need to make decisions under conditions of uncertainty – whether the decisions regard scientific, economic or technological matters – is *the* defining feature of environmental protection. The challenge of environmental protection is made even more difficult by the problem of information asymmetry. Facilities that pollute know more about what, when and how much they release than government officials. A key goal for environmental agencies, therefore, is to create incentives for firms to disclose this information, whether through monitoring and self-reporting or reliance on third parties.

Thus information plays a number of different roles in environmental protection. To make this clearer, the model in Figure 13.1 sets out three distinct – though related – processes or stages through which information flows in environmental protection:

1   collection;
2   use; and
3   access and dissemination.

These processes can be seen as efforts by government regulators to acquire, utilize and share the information needed for environmental decision-making. The processes can also be viewed as structuring a balance of power and responsibility within various relationships, whether between market actors and regulators, government and citizens, or market actors and citizens.

A key consideration of information management is whether, on balance, initiatives to collect information, provide access to information, or disseminate information improve agency actions or hinder them. In theory, more information should improve decision-making. The problem is that government resources are

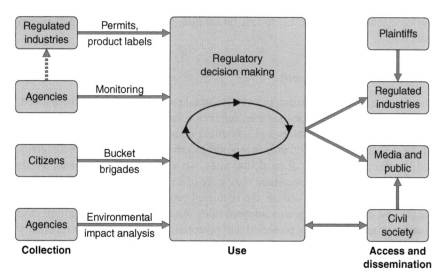

Figure 13.1 The stages of information flows in environmental protection (source: Kysar and Salzman 2008).

limited (as, of course, are private resources) and the time and money spent collecting, generating and sharing information means fewer resources and less time available to dedicate to other worthy needs. As a result, a key strategy for environmental information relies on *shifting the burden* of information collection and analysis from the government to regulated parties. Shifting the burden of information provision from public regulators onto polluters also counterbalances the informational asymmetries described above.

Information collection

Decision-makers need a wealth of information about the present and predicted state of the environment and its inhabitants in order to effectively shape policy. Is the climate changing? How will this affect panda habitats? Assuming that the answers to such questions suggest the need for regulation, decision-makers further require information regarding the anticipated effects of competing policy options. Would a tax on greenhouse-gas emissions curb energy use? Would it risk bankrupting specific industries or slow development?

These various needs for scientific, economic and technical information require decision-makers to collect relevant information from relevant information-holders. The surest way to collect information is for the government to do so, itself. Official monitoring stations can collect data on ambient air quality or river conditions. The PRC, for example, in recent years has greatly increased its air monitoring capacity. This provides a much better understanding of air quality, but it is still incomplete. The challenge is that non-compliance occurs at the smokestack and effluent pipe. Agencies could monitor every source of pollution, but this would be prohibitively expensive

In surveying the range of environmental governance systems in different countries, there are five basic strategies governments employ to collect environmental information from regulated parties. They are briefly described below.

Information collection strategies

Permit requirements

- A common strategy to ensure adequate monitoring in the face of limited resources is to shift the costs and responsibility to the polluting sources. Permit requirements generally require polluters to monitor their emissions and regularly report them to the agency. The key challenge lies in ensuring the accuracy of the information.

Pollutant release reporting requirements

- This strategy requires polluters to provide data on their annual releases of certain compounds above a threshold amount. Known generally as Pollutant Release and Transfer Registries (PRTRs), this mechanism provides a means to track and quantify toxic chemical use, transfer and release from polluting facilities. While these programs do not mandate anything beyond information collection and reporting, they have proven effective in reducing emissions in a variety of settings.

Manufacturer warning labels

- A separate approach to information generation relies on industry providing data not to the government but, rather, directly to consumers. This strategy also puts the burden and expense on the regulated community to report on the environmental and health impacts of its activities. This strategy requires a highly regulated marketplace. A key consideration is whether the information will be understood or acted upon by consumers.

Individual-provided data

- A recent strategy has been the reliance on community groups to monitor pollution in their backyard on behalf of the agency. Given scarce resources and almost limitless number of places one could place pollution monitoring stations, reliance on community groups allows environmental agencies to leverage their resources. Greater reliance on citizen-provided data holds significant potential as an environmental protection strategy for the PRC. "Bucket Brigades," for example, are a fast-growing example of citizen-provided data. Residents living near industrial facilities use inexpensive air monitoring equipment in a bucket to collect samples. These are sent to a lab and, if the samples show high levels of pollutants, the information is sent to the local enforcement agency. This greatly increases the monitoring capacity of environmental agencies. These local individuals and groups are making powerful use of information collection in order to gain the attention of state regulators and polluters and shifting priorities for enforcement activities.

Environmental impact assessment

• This strategy for information gathering relies on government agencies that are engaged in actions with major environmental impacts to assess those impacts. Environmental impact assessment laws exist in over 130 countries, including the PRC. Such information-generating laws do not require that agencies select the most environmentally preferable course of action but, rather, that they consider the environmental impacts of their proposed actions and alternatives. This is a costly means to gather information but also the only information collection strategy directed specifically at government actions.

Information access and dissemination

The preceding sections have focused on how agencies collect relevant information for regulatory decision-making. The flipside of this issue concerns how non-governmental entities, such as community groups, the media, industry or victims of environmental harm gain access to information the government has collected. Much of the work of information dissemination is performed by governmental entities. Obviously, regulated industries themselves will be a primary target of government communications because those industries must have relevant information to guide their conduct and, relatedly, may want to see and evaluate the informational basis on which regulations were premised. But regulators also often package information for broader public use. Given the rise of the Internet, the provision of such information can provide a low-cost way of sharing information with the broader public.[8]

Encapsulated in the powerful phrase, "the public's right to know," and embodied in treaties such as the Aarhus Convention,[9] a right of access to government information is considered by many to be an essential prong of good governance. Public officials and agencies often have mixed feelings about releasing information concerning the hazards they have discovered or the regulations they have chosen to address those hazards. Nevertheless, just as the government's collection of information about impacts on the natural world serves a vital function in ensuring the effectiveness of its regulatory efforts, the broader public's access to and understanding of information about the environment serves the function of ensuring the credibility and, ultimately, the effectiveness of the regulatory regime.

There are two broad strategies to address information access and dissemination. The first might be called a "push" strategy. This involves the government actively sharing information. This can happen through searchable websites from environmental agencies with data on waste, water, toxics, air, land, radiation, compliance and other issues. Agencies may publish various "State of the Environment" reports on specific subjects. Specific dissemination strategies vary from country to country, but this is a very common approach and one followed in the PRC, as well.

A second, more controversial approach, involves what might be described as a "pull" strategy. This involves giving citizens and organizations the right to demand specific information from government agencies. The most developed example of this approach is a US law, the Freedom of Information Act.

No similar law currently exists in the PRC, and this general approach raises a series of important questions. Which strategies for information dissemination are most likely to engage the public in environmental protection, especially in light of new technologies and capabilities for involvement? How should government assess the costs and benefits of information access and dissemination?

Case study: agricultural subsidies and conservation of wetlands

Another example of conditional funding may be found in the so-called "Swampbuster" program. Known formally as the Highly Erodible Land Conservation and Wetland Conservation Compliance provisions of the 1985 US Farm Bill, the Swampbuster program seeks to slow the development of wetlands on farms. Wetlands provide a suite of ecosystem services, including flood control, sediment control, groundwater recharge, water quality and wildlife habitat. Most of the nation's wetlands have been developed, and over three-quarters of this loss since 1950 has been due to agricultural conversion. The Swampbuster provisions do not require farmers to conserve wetlands. Rather, they threaten the loss of benefits. Farms that plant a commodity crop on converted wetlands (or highly erodible lands) are ineligible to receive any farm program benefits. For many farms, government support payments make the difference between profit and loss for a crop, so eligibility to receive these benefits is extremely important.

In order to encourage conservation of ecosystem services, the Farm Bill provides that the Swampbuster provisions will not apply if farmers make up for the loss of services by enhancing existing wetlands, restoring former wetlands, or creating new wetlands. Farmers can also receive benefits if a prior converted cropland is not planted for more than five consecutive years and wetland characteristics return.

Notes

1 Ludwig Kramer, EC Treaty and Environmental Law 5–27 (2nd edn 1995).
2 Gale Norton and Patricia Bangert, "Federal–State Enforcement of Environmental Laws: A Story of Beauty and the Beast," *Natural Resources and the Environment* 8, 21 (1994).
3 Jonas Tallberg, "Paths to Compliance," *International Organization* 56, 609, 619 (2002).
4 *Harmon Industries, Inc.* v. *Carol M. Browner*, 191 F.3d 894 (8th Cir. 1999)
5 Congressional Research Service, Highway Fund Sanctions and Conformity Under the Clean Air Act (1999, RL30131).

6 In the United States, different courts have decided this question differently, so there is no single answer. A minority of courts have determined that simply committing the act is sufficient to justify criminal sanctions. Such a "public welfare" offense should give rise to criminal punishment, the argument goes, because the offending actor *should have known* such an action would endanger the public welfare. Most courts, however, have held that enforcement authorities must show both that the act took place and that the actor knew the act was illegal.
7 Michelle Chen, "Citgo Indictment Hints at Pollution Scourge, Texas Activists Say," *The New Standard*, September 1, 2006.
8 See, for example, EPA Envirofacts Data Warehouse, www.epa.gov/enviro.
9 Convention on Access to Information, Public Participation in Decision-Making and Access to Justice in Environmental Matters, June 25, 1998, 2161 U.N.T.S. 447.

Reference

Kysar, Douglas A. and James Salzman (2008). "Making Sense of Information for Environmental Protection," *Texas Law Review* 86.

14 Conclusion

"The path to a brighter future"

Tun Lin, James Salzman and Timothy Swanson

Overview

This chapter sets out the lessons learned from examining other countries' experiences with environmental regulation across a history of economic growth and expansion, as well as the lessons learned from exploring the People's Republic of China's (PRC) own experience in this light. The international team of experts has worked with the Chinese experts to examine the experience of the PRC across the past 30 years of unprecedented growth, and to learn of the regulatory challenges that they face. The international team has also worked on matters dealing with environmental regulation in many parts of the developed world: the United States, the European Union, the Organization for Economic Co-operation and Development (OECD) and individual countries such as Norway and the United Kingdom. This breadth of experience has been brought to bear on the question of the best way forward for improving the PRC's environmental regulation. In this set of policy recommendations, we set out what we have learned in the briefest format possible.

First, we set out the basic or general principles of environmental regulation in a rapidly developing country. What is the point of environmental regulation in the context of rapid growth? What are the essential components? Why is it important, and when should it be implemented? Hence, we make the case for the basic role and importance of an environmental regulation framework within a rapidly developing country. We state here that a system of environmental regulation is the fundamental means by which a society's competing demands for resources are aggregated, balanced and allocated. This is an essential mechanism for the efficient functioning of any society. We then show that regulation plays a fundamental role in leading the development process in the right direction, especially in regard to technological change. At the outset of any development process, technologies tend to be basic and the choices straightforward. Rapid economic change makes technological choice and transition an important part of the economic transformation, and regulation can play an important part in this in terms of market transformation (elimination of inefficient technologies), technology leadership (identification of leading technologies) and trade harmonization (disallowance of incongruent technologies). All of these are important roles for the regulator to play in guiding industries toward the appropriate direction in terms of future growth opportunities.

Next, we identify the important themes that emerged in the study of the sectors of air, water, ecosystems and institutional governance in the PRC's Macro-Environmental Strategy. These common themes cut across experiences in environmental protection of other countries and international organizations as well. Thus, we also assess the strategies employed in the United States, the EU and international organizations, drawing core lessons on how to structure an effective regulatory system for environmental protection in a complex jurisdiction.

Then, we focus on the recommendations to address the major problems brought about by the rapid economic growth in the PRC in each of the above-mentioned sectors in the country's Macro-Environmental Strategy, with particular emphasis on the regulatory measures to manage these problems. We consider the general problems of regulation – information acquisition, balancing of values and allocation of resources. In light of these considerations, we make very concrete and specific policy recommendations on how to proceed in the management of these problems.

In sum, we outline here our policy recommendations on the importance of environmental regulation in the management of a rapid growth process, and the specific recommendations for the sectors identified in the PRC's Macro-Environmental Review. These recommendations are derived from both the accumulated experiences in developed countries' regulatory processes and our (much less informed) estimation of the PRC's recent economic history.

In the succeeding section, we detail our recommendations in four parts:

1   general relation between economic growth and environmental regulation;
2   cross-cutting issues affecting the development of the PRC's environmental governance;
3   recommendations for institutional and sectoral change in the PRC based on international experiences; and
4   recommendations of the Chinese experts on how to proceed in the development of the long-run environmental strategy for the PRC.

Policy recommendations

The general relationship between economic growth and environmental regulation

Most developed countries have followed the same sort of development path – periods of substantial economic growth combined with significant degrees of environmental deterioration. The path has been followed in different places at different points in time, but the experience has been very much the same. This is because economic activities often make use of basically the same environmental resources (such as air, water, ecosystems) for production or for disposal of wastes. When environmental regulation does not exist to effectively control access to these resources, it encourages economic activities to indiscriminately expand usage of these resources, thereby resulting in predictable declines in their quantities and qualities.

Unregulated access allows environmental resources to be used on a first-come, first-served basis. Likewise, it provides incentives for firms and individuals to quickly access these resources and exploit them completely. This arbitrary approach to resource use hinders the optimum allocation of these resources among competing uses. Economists advocate allocating resources to the uses that value them most highly, providing some resources to various uses in accordance with the value generated. Unregulated use of environmental resources usually results in their unbalanced and excessive use. Access to these resources becomes increasingly costly to society as their other uses are denied by reason of their prior appropriation by few polluters. As frustration of other users with their inability to use environmental resources (e.g. for breathing air or for drinking water) progressively builds up, demands increase for the regulation and more rational, balanced or "efficient" allocation of these resources.

Most developed countries have gone through this economic growth process and created systems for environmental regulation and management. As seen in the usual pathway of the development process, initial stages of growth are often marred by environmental degradation. But with relevant structural adjustments, later phases of development will witness significant environmental improvements. Such a development path is to be expected as demand for an effective environmental regulatory system soars in response to economic growth and environmental degradation – as in the case of the PRC, where an increasing need and demand for environmental regulation is finally seen after 30 years of economic growth.

In order to provide a sound regulatory system for environmental resources, it is important to set up a mechanism whereby public demands for environmental resources are duly recognized and then a rational and balanced allocation of these resources between public and private demands is determined. It is, henceforth, critical to create a system of governance capable of setting, implementing and enforcing environmental standards. We have seen in this volume how this process is occurring in the PRC, first with the creation of environmental standards, and then with the increasing recognition that public participation and environmental governance are crucial to a successful environmental regulatory system.

It is well known that economic growth can be slowed down by the introduction of regulation of environmental resources, but this should not be an issue as growth cannot be the sole objective of any society. There are many other forms of value provided by environmental resources, including health, stability, leisure, tradition and enjoyment. A balanced regulatory approach aims to maximize the total value from the use of environmental resources, where economic growth is but one of those objectives. It also aims to lead economic growth in directions most compatible with environmental objectives. Economic growth and environmental regulation must go hand-in-hand in the long run.

The environmental governance issues facing the PRC: cross-cutting themes

The environmental challenges facing the PRC are unique. No other country has seriously grappled with environmental protection amidst rapid economic growth in such a short period of time. Likewise, the PRC geography, climate, economic and political system are also unique. Despite this, however, the PRC situation shares important, if not fundamental, similarities with the environmental protection challenges faced by other countries. While these challenges are not identical, the strategies employed by the other countries to address them provide useful precedents for relevant authorities in the PRC to consider in drafting the country's Macro-Environmental Strategy.

The sector reports have provided a careful assessment of the PRC's management of air pollution, water pollution, ecosystems and institutional governance. This section provides a synthesis of the assessments, highlighting four of the most important cross-cutting themes.

Theme one: strategies to improve coordination between central and local authorities

A recurrent issue observed in all the case studies is the relationship between the central government and local authorities. As much as the Ministry of Environmental Protection (MEP) depends critically on local Environmental Protection Bureaus (EPBs) for the effective implementation of national laws, meaningful enforcement of legal requirements and information on local problems, the local EPBs equally rely on the MEP for technical expertise and standard setting. Whilst both local and national authorities are reliant on each other to effectively attain the environmental protection objective of the government, theirs is a complicated relationship.

Forty years ago, albeit the details obviously differ, the EU and the United States also faced the similar problem of occasional conflicts between a central authority that wanted stronger environmental protection and local authorities that were more closely committed to development. The evolution of environmental protection in both the EU and the United States has shown a similar transition to the current models of strong central authorities that set strict environmental requirements with generally effective compliance at the local level.

A broad look across the history of the US and European environmental protection over the last 40 years would reveal five strategies for the coordination of national and local authorities – namely:

1   legislation that pre-empts local authority in favor of national authority;
2   reliance on shared authority;
3   secondary enforcement;
4   directed funding; and
5   conditional funding.

It is important to note that the MEP is relatively weak in two of the most important areas – secondary enforcement and conditional funding. Thus clearly, the Macro-Environmental Policy will need to consider these areas.

At a minimum, coordinating environmental protection between national and local authorities requires a clear understanding of their respective rights and responsibilities. In both the United States and the EU, the consolidation of the authorities has been preceded by passage of national laws that put in place a national and uniform program that supplants state environmental authority. And while the passage of laws alone is never enough, it is nevertheless a precondition to ensure effective implementation. The PRC has done well in this regard.

In the transition from decentralized to centralized system of environmental protection, the primary responsibility has shifted from the provincial- and state-level authorities to central ministries and agencies. It is important to note, however, that the transfer of power from local to central authorities is not absolute, as local officials still retain significant authority. This is true as well in the EU and the United States where the most appropriate means of sharing authority remains a contentious topic. In the PRC, too, significant authority is shared between the MEP and the local EPBs. How this relationship evolves in the coming decades will be a fundamental issue for the PRC's Macro-Environmental Strategy.

The role of enforcement, for example, should be delegated to local authorities in order to minimize the costs of enforcement (information, compliance, incentive compatibility). At the same time, for the purpose of coordination among local authorities, the ultimate responsibility for overall enforcement still needs to be vested to central authorities. This highlights the importance of providing some incentive structure between the central and the local authorities that will induce functional performance at the provincial and local levels. It also points to the importance of providing some manner of centralized appellate procedure (such as a judicial mechanism at the central level) to hear complaints on, and then pronounce upon, the need for harmonization of implementation procedures across regional and local authorities.

Secondary enforcement is an important strategy permitting central authorities to ensure adequate local implementation and enforcement of environmental laws. In some cases, the central authority retains the ability to bring enforcement actions against the polluter or the local authority if the local enforcement is deemed to be inadequate. In other cases, local officials have the primary responsibility to permit and enforce national laws, but individuals may bring actions against polluters or the concerned government agencies.

As mentioned above, it is crucial that the central authorities have means to provide incentives for local authorities to enforce environmental laws. It is also the case that weak enforcement efforts by local environmental authorities sometimes stem from inadequate resources. Local authorities may want to enforce environmental laws, but if they do not have enough funds to hire inspectors, analyze samples from monitoring stations, or generally carry out enforcement activities, then poor enforcement ensues. Having the central authorities channel funds for environmental enforcement to the local authorities is an important means to create an effective linkage between the role of local authorities and the ultimate responsibility of central authorities as above-discussed.

A key strategy for effective coordination is setting as a condition for the release of central funds the compliance by local authorities of specific performance goals. This strategy is even more effective if the central authorities are able to withhold funds that are not under their control, thus limiting the ability of *other* agencies to disburse funds, which in effect raises considerably the potential impact of the sanction. In some cases, the central environmental authority is given control over funds of *another* ministry, such as the Ministry of Transportation.

Theme two: environmental enforcement

One of the themes addressed in every sectoral report has been the importance of enforcement activities. Two different types of concerns have been raised:

1   the problem of *under-enforcement* arising from the concern that current penalties for pollution are too low to change behavior; and
2   the problem of *misdirected enforcement* stemming from the concern that there is not enough cooperation between government and industry to create incentives for compliance.

The choice of which between compliance facilitation and sanction is strategic is not only faced by the PRC but also by environmental protection authorities in many countries. In jurisdictions where there is shared power of enforcement between local and central authorities, tension often occurs over the proper approach to non-compliance.

Theme three: individual participation models

Many of the Chinese and international experts emphasized the important roles that can be played by individuals and environmental groups. There is currently a limited legal basis for public participation in environmental protection compared to OECD countries. Both formal and informal participation by individuals and groups in environmental protection can increase the effectiveness of current efforts. Considering that the MEP and the local EPBs have limited resources, one model for citizen participation advocates partnership to provide citizens and environmental groups with opportunities to reinforce government protection efforts in the fields of enforcement and compliance monitoring, among others.

The second model for citizen participation which can also reinforce government environmental protection efforts has as its main goal the provision of avenues and creation of structures for citizens' voices to be heard in a constructive fashion. This could be done through greater use of environmental ombudsmen and increased rights of individuals to bring lawsuits against polluters, among others.

Theme four: information management

In every sector report, both Chinese and international experts have highlighted the importance of information. An environmental regulator needs accurate information to understand the nature of a problem and the consequences of potential responses. Likewise, the regulated community needs information to decide how best to comply with adopted rules. And the public needs information in order to feel adequately protected and potentially participate in the regulatory regime. These challenges in information management pose special significance in the context of environmental law.

A key consideration in information management is whether, on balance, initiatives to collect, provide access to, or disseminate information improve agency actions or hinder them. In theory, more information will improve decision-making. The challenge is that government resources are limited (as are private resources) and the time and money spent collecting, generating and sharing information may well mean fewer resources and less time available to dedicate to other worthy needs.

Suggestions for institutional and sectoral reforms in the PRC based on international experiences

In this section, we review the recommendations derived from the examination of international experiences with regard to the following four sectors:

1   institutional development;
2   air quality management;
3   water management; and
4   ecosystem management.

Here, we list the conclusions to be drawn from the wealth of experiences derived from the other countries which have gone through the same growth process. In the next section, we finish with the conclusions reached by the Chinese experts on which recommendations to adopt.

Institutional development: recommendations from international experiences

Traditionally, the incentive system for local and regional leaders has explicitly rewarded economic growth rather than environmental protection. This lack of incentives has been a major reason for weak implementation of pollution and ecological regulations.

This is changing. In the Eleventh Five-Year Plan (FYP) of the PRC covering the period from 2006 to 2010, for example, explicit goals were set for sulfur-dioxide reduction and energy efficiency. Future plan periods need to include far more environmental and conservation targets, which should be observed throughout the government. Thus, contracts of local government officials should include in their objectives environmental outcomes that influence their promotion and reward appraisals. Just as these officials have "hard" targets for economic growth, industrialization and infrastructure projects, they should also have the task of complying with environmental regulations and meeting environmental goals, subject to accountability assessment.

EPBs which are the primary government bodies for the implementation and enforcement of environmental laws are typically funded by the local governments. The funding is often inadequate to pay for the necessary personnel and boost monitoring and enforcement capacities to ensure effective environmental protection. Moreover, considering that funding is sourced from the local governments, enforcement and monitoring activities by EPBs are made closely aligned with the local governments' priorities which are often focused more on economic development than environmental protection. As a consequence, the intensity of enforcement efforts varies considerably from one region or province to the next and is often weak. International experience shows that effective monitoring and enforcement of environmental policies is usually financially and politically independent of local government, and directly accountable to central government. EPBs must therefore be given greater funding and independence from local authorities in order to ensure meaningful and consistent environmental protection efforts.

Over the last four decades, the EU and the United States have successfully strengthened their environmental protection efforts while maintaining a shared responsibility and authority between local and central authorities. Their experiences are testaments to the effectiveness of having central governments retain authority to take over provincial and local responsibilities during times when provincial and local governments fall short of environmental performance targets.

An effective means to ensure strong local environmental protection is conditional funding which empowers the central authority to withhold funding from local governments for serious non-compliance. Since the MEP does not disburse significant funds to EPBs, this strategy will be more effective if the MEP is given the power to restrict funding from *other* government ministries to provincial governments, similar to US experiences where the Environmental Protection Agency (EPA) can withhold funds for highway construction of states for non-compliance with the Clean Air Act.

Experiences in both the EU and the United States also provide proof of the necessity of empowering the central authority to bring independent actions against either polluters or local governmental authorities in cases of under-enforcement and widespread non-compliance in order to maintain a meaningful deterrent to local industries from not complying with environmental laws.

A critically important strategy for environmental protection is the facilitation of the efforts of groups *outside* of the environmental agencies to challenge instances of non-compliance. The participation of outside stakeholders increase accountability. The identities of these watchdogs vary from country to country, and often include the media, environmental groups, the scientific community and courts. Greater use of citizen suits through which individuals report suspected environmental infractions directly to the judiciary and ombudsmen offices merit special consideration. The primary goal should be the provision of a venue for citizens to turn to upon discovery of lack of implementation and which will ensure a meaningful response.

International experience also clearly shows that an effective judiciary is needed to ensure effective implementation of environmental laws. The judiciary must also be competent. This requires training of prosecutors and judges in the substance and application of the PRC's environmental laws.

Government resources for environmental education and monitoring are limited. Greater reliance on public participation provides a powerful means to leverage scarce public resources, raise the profile of environmental activities and reinforce government protection efforts. The PRC has taken important steps to enlist public participation in environmental decision-making, including most recently the issuance of the Regulations of the People's Republic of China on Open Government Information. The non-governmental organization sector is also growing, with the rise of the Institute of Public and Environmental Affairs (which has a web-based pollution map derived from public data) and the "Green Choice Initiative" (which informs consumers about these issues), to name a few. These measures should be significantly enhanced in the areas of monitoring, education, research and enforcement.

As discussed earlier, Chinese and international experts have highlighted the importance of information in each of the case studies prepared. Indeed, managing river basins, identifying where to focus conservation efforts, or setting air quality standards all require information. Monitoring capacity has greatly increased in the PRC in recent years but much work remains to be done. There should be an increase in the number of monitoring stations and the creation of a national database on pollution levels which should be taken into consideration in the evaluation of local governments. The internet also provides an effective and inexpensive means to share environmental data with minimum delay.

Air pollution management: recommendations from international experiences

Based on international experience, target setting must be as much a scientific as a political process. Scientific institutions need to be given the authority and capacity to monitor and formulate models for the purpose of providing provincial and central governments informed and objective advices on which targets to set.

Although the strong emphasis on the reduction of sulfur dioxide, current air quality and emissions regulation in the PRC is warranted, epidemiological evidence strongly suggests that particulate matter and ground-level ozone constitute greater health risks. Despite this, however, both pollutants do not figure as high priority at present. Thus, a monitoring program for both these pollutants should be started with meaningful reduction targets set.

While respecting the principle of similar but differentiated responsibilities, we believe it is only a matter of time before the PRC must take on significant commitments to reduce greenhouse gas emissions. As the largest source of greenhouse gas emissions in the world, meaningful reductions today will help avoid future damage from climate change. Efforts to address climate change should be coordinated with efforts to reduce local air pollutants, since both greenhouse gas and traditional pollutants can be addressed through source control, process control and end-of-pipe abatement strategies.

Although both outdoor emissions (such as those from open-air biomass burning) and indoor emissions constitute major health risks, there is currently little attention to these problems in the rural areas of the PRC and only few environmental regulations addressing these problems are in place. One obvious reason, which should be changed, is that the MEP's responsibilities do not cover rural areas.

Air quality monitoring in the PRC has improved greatly in recent years, though it remains scant in rural areas. The lack of information on air quality leads to insufficient control over both household and regional air pollution. Improved monitoring capacity outside urban areas is a necessary precondition for tackling these problems.

There are a number of areas where air pollution extends well beyond city limits. In areas such as the northern PRC, regional pollution is brought about by a wide range of causes and comes from a wide range of sources. To address regional pollution in these areas, air quality management institutions need to be established at the regional level to collect regional air quality data, identify and understand the significant sources of pollution in the region through the formulation and employment of models, and coordinate with local authorities for the issuance of multiple pollutant permits to major emitters. Without a coordinating mechanism, strong reduction efforts in one area will be undermined by weak efforts in another area of the same airshed.

The PRC relies primarily on command-and-control regulation. This can be an effective strategy, but greater use should be made of economic regulation that gives regulated parties greater flexibility in meeting performance standards. An emissions trading system in the power industry should be given particular consideration.

Quite a number of energy policies in the PRC are counterproductive to air pollution management. Among these policies which should be stopped are de facto subsidy to coal by virtue of the domestic price of coal which is lower than the world market price, the subsidy on electricity consumption by virtue of the regulation of the price of electricity, and the subsidies in the form of value-added tax (VAT) refunds received by oil refineries which are thus not granted normal return on capital. These subsidies not only stimulate consumption but also encourage the use of low-quality coal and discourage abatement efforts to save on operation and maintenance costs.

While end-of-pipe abatement will remain necessary in many cases, major pollution reductions will be obtained if energy efficiency, renewable energy and mass transit are further encouraged. Reducing fossil-fuel consumption reduces many air pollutants. Thus, economic regulation of energy use and pricing of pollution costs should be regarded as important strategies for the reduction of air pollutants.

Water sector management: recommendations from international experiences

Compliance with water quality standards was the only target in the Tenth FYP (2001–5) that was not met. There is an "implementation gap" and many agree that failures concerning water quality and pollution stem from the overly complicated and overlapping institutional structure which makes coordination of horizontal institutions difficult. For instance, both EPBs and Water Resource Bureaus (WRBs) have responsibilities for water quality measurement and monitoring. This leads to duplication of work and disagreement on measurements when coordination is required.

Another cause for the gap and failures is the ambiguous legal framework. Despite the 1996 Law on Water Pollution Prevention and Control, which called for coordination and consultation between the Ministry of Water Resources and the MEP (then the State Environmental Protection Administration), these organizations remain uncoordinated. For instance, EPBs and WRBs can submit incompatible water management plans to the State Council. Legally speaking, a province has no accountability to another province or to act for the benefit of the river basin as a whole. For this reason, River Basin Commissions (RBCs) have very little power of enforcement on the area of border pollution.

Proceeding from the above discussion, there must be greater coordination among agencies regulating water resources. RBCs could be endowed with more power and a clearer mandate on the areas of water quality enforcement and border pollution regulation. There are poor incentives for implementing agencies, particularly local government officials, which are frequently rewarded for achieving economic growth rather than for environmental protection. As earlier discussed, EPBs typically receive funding from local governmental bodies and are therefore at the mercy of the latter's priorities for the environment, which means that the level and intensity of enforcement varies considerably from one region or province to the next and is often weak.

Fines on water pollution have historically been low and, in many cases, have been lower than the cost of abatement technologies. Application and enforcement of pollution fees are patchy geographically and the structure of the tariffs is weak. Specifically, pollution charges are only applied on emissions in excess of the standards, while emissions below these standards are not charged. Pollution charges are levied on the basis of concentrations, not total emissions. Moreover, charges and fines are frequently negotiated with the polluters and are not set based on broad objective criteria. Also, not all polluters are being subjected to pollution charges and wastewater treatment user fees as enforcement is weak.

In accordance with the polluter-pays principle, pollution charges should be applied to all pollution, not just emissions in excess of standards, and should be levied based on total emissions, not solely on emissions concentration. Charges should be large enough to stimulate adoption of pollution control technologies or process changes. In order to limit the impact on industry, as well as ease the political economy issues associated with tax increases, the Refunded Emissions Payments approach currently employed in the PRC should be reviewed.

Despite the employment of volumetric water pricing in urban areas for residential and industrial users for many years, the low levels of tariffs have encouraged investment in inefficient and water-intensive technologies and inefficient location decisions, and contributed to costly water shortages in many cities. The combination of these factors has caused unsustainable water use (as evidenced by groundwater mining and excessive abstractions from rivers) and a perceived need for water supply augmentation. Furthermore, financing of water supply and sanitation is likely to be unsustainable in the absence of cost recovery. To address distributional issues and the impact on the poor, increasing block tariffs and alternative tariff structures should be considered.

The prospects for enabling wider intra-basin and inter- and intra-sectoral water trades, such as in the water-intensive agricultural sector, should be considered. This will most likely require a redefinition of water rights and careful assessment of potential environmental harms (such as reduced instream flows) that could result. The prospect of having RBCs or Irrigation Districts acting as coordinators should be explored. Tradable permit schemes are more likely to be successful if:

1   the total pollutions or emissions can be easily defined;
2   there is accurate and sufficient data;
3   the abatement costs are heterogeneous; and
4   there is adequate institutional structure for monitoring and enforcement.

The overlapping monitoring responsibilities of the WRBs and the EPBs must be resolved. An independent organization should collect and collate data via agreed processes. An obvious choice for the initial oversight organization would be the RBCs, although a harmonized central data source could also be beneficial. Disclosure provides the public with information about water quality and international experience shows that it makes firms and regulatory bodies more accountable. These schemes are extremely cost effective and easy to implement in areas where expertise in enforcement and monitoring is lacking.

Total Maximum Daily Loads (TMDLs) have received much interest from Chinese policy-makers. TMDLs provide a clear strategy to convert ambient water standards into emissions targets for point and non-point sources. However, the implementation of TMDLs in other countries has been problematic due to legal uncertainties and their information-intensive nature. If implemented, they should apply only to ambient water quality-problematic areas, where the main thrust of pollution control policy would be enforcing current effluent standards.

Eco-system management: recommendations from international experiences

Responsibility for ecosystem protection is shared by numerous agencies, including ministries of environment, forestry, water and agriculture. This leads to multiple programs implemented by the different agencies that can create conflicting incentives. As a result, comprehensive planning at the national level is often frustrated, preventing efficient or consistent policy development and implementation. In order to improve integration of ecological protection, there must be, at a minimum, strengthened cooperation among relevant agencies, as well as strengthened coordination between national and local agencies.

To address the coordination problem, a cross-sectoral body may be needed. This body would be explicitly charged with coordinating multi-agency activities that result in ecosystem harm, protection and restoration. Such a body would not only ensure that different agencies are aware of how their activities are affecting ecosystems but also facilitate the formulation of comprehensive policies.

When conservation is mandated, costs are often incurred by the landowners or land users rather than by the beneficiaries of protected lands. As a result, landowners do not have incentives to increase conservation beyond the minimum required level, and may have incentives for non-compliance if enforcement is weak. Payments to landowners or communities for provision of ecosystem services provide potential to achieve both effective ecosystem management and poverty alleviation. Particular attention should be given to payment schemes for watershed services, biodiversity and landscape restoration, and carbon sequestration and storage. Payment schemes are more effective when designed in conjunction with a larger rural development policy.

In areas where development does occur, the developers should be required not only to minimize but also offset the ecological harm through on-site or off-site restoration activities. This is particularly important for high impact activities, such as those in extractive industries like mining. Policies imposing fees for ecological damages caused by construction and engineering projects are well established in the PRC at both the local and national levels. These should be coupled with requirements for offsets, to ensure that ecological impacts are mitigated in the field. Offset possibilities could also be included in environmental impact assessments. Requiring offsets will better internalize environmental regulation and ensure a more rational and sustainable course of economic growth.

Ecological protection relies on a combination of protected areas enforcement, specific land use restrictions, and forest and river management, among other measures. Evidence suggests restrictions on various land uses are frequently poorly enforced. Adequate funds and oversight must be provided for local enforcement of these measures. Otherwise, there is little reason to expect consistent or meaningful compliance with regulations or offset requirements.

Despite their importance, most ecological benefits and ecosystem services, such as flood control and water quality control, have little or no market value. As a result, the social value of these public goods is generally ignored or given little attention in development decisions. To ensure that the full social costs and benefits of development options are considered, ecological assets should be measured and, if possible, valued when making land use decisions. This is particularly important in environmental impact assessments.

Recommendations by the Chinese experts for the PRC's long-run environmental review

We now turn to the recommendations of the Chinese experts, commencing with the proposals of sectoral experts and then proceeding to the institutional suggestions of Dong *et al.* (Chapter 11) and Xia *et al.* (Chapter 2). These recommendations provide directions that may be taken by the PRC in its long-term strategy for environmental management.

With respect to air sector management, Hao and Wang (Chapter 5) suggest that the national strategic target of atmospheric environmental protection be set toward the compliance by 2050 with the national ambient air quality standard for the entire country and achievement during the same period of the World Health Organization ambient air quality guideline values for most areas of the country. And in order to achieve the strategic target of atmospheric environmental protection, the following four strategies are proposed by Hao and Wang:

1   whole process control strategy through change of economic structure and adoption of clean production technology;
2   multi-pollutant co-control strategy through the establishment of a set of scientific air quality and emission standards;
3   environmental impact based integrated control strategy through the implementation of total emission control of air pollutants in the important sectors and the concurrent institution of measures to control emissions from other coal-burning sources; and
4   regional air quality management strategy through the establishment of regional air quality management coordination systems and institutions in developed city-clusters.

In addition to the following three major policies:

1   implementation of the National Clean Air Action Plan;
2   control of total coal consumption in heavily polluted areas; and
3   enhancement of the vehicle pollution control in megacities

Hao and Wang also recommend the following specific measures:

1   application of clean coal technologies, optimization of energy structure and improvement of energy efficiency;
2   enhancement of vehicle pollution control;
3   reinforcement of sulfur dioxide (SO_2) emission control;

4   immediate control of nitrogen oxide (NO_x) emissions;
5   enhancement of primary particulate emission control;
6   control of volatile organic compounds (VOC) emissions;
7   control of ozone and fine particulate pollutions;
8   improvement of air pollution control law and standard system;
9   use of the power of environmental economic regulation; and
10   enhancement of international cooperation on global problems.

With respect to water sector management, Xi and Meng (Chapter 6) emphasize the need to carry out research on water environment criteria and standards, and build a suitable system of water environmental quality and water pollutants discharge standards in the PRC. Xi and Meng opine that pollution control should be implemented by types, regions, grades and stages to respond appropriately to the different classifications and characteristics of water pollution. There must also be a formulation of technical norms for total amount reduction of pollutants and the establishment of a technical management system of the PRC's environmental pollution control of watersheds. Efforts to further strengthen and promote the supervision and management, and implementation of the Environmental Protection Law and the Water Pollution Prevention Law shall also be necessary. Xi and Meng propose the adoption of the following specific measures to attain total water pollution in the PRC:

1   adoption of financial incentives and contracts;
2   establishment of independent monitoring and enforcement institutions;
3   coordination of independent institutions;
4   enhancement of pollution charges;
5   focus on total emissions; and
6   public disclosure of industries.

Xi and Meng also see the need for the establishment of a macro water environmental protection stratagem, toward the achievement of which experts have presented the following seven strategic transformations:

1   transformation of the conflict between environment and economy to amalgamation of these two issues;
2   transformation from pure point source treatment to integrated disposal of watershed pollutants and coordinated management of upstream and downstream water sources;
3   transformation from end treatment to whole process control and water ecology management;
4   transformation from pure water pollution treatment to optimization and coordination of watershed economy distribution and structure;
5   transformation from parallel to integrated management;
6   transformation from target amount control to capacity amount control; and
7   transformation from the single management to integrated management model with different divisions, classifications and stages.

With respect to ecosystem management, Gao and Han (Chapter 7) suggest that the PRC adopt a systematic approach of ecological protection. Through this, the single-factor control is transformed into a comprehensive ecosystem management with integrated structure, process and function, and simple ecological protection is raised to the level which shall optimize economic growth and coordinate effectively the ecosystem structure, process and function to strengthen state ecological safety and provide potent support to sustainable development of economy and society. In order to achieve this, three strategic directions are suggested by Gao and Han:

1   establishment of a state ecological safety framework system centered on nature reserves and key ecological function zones;
2   pursuit of economic growth with due consideration of the ecological bearing capacity of the area; and
3   establishment of a state ecological supervision and management system and formation of a structure for the harmonious development of ecology and economy.

With respect to institutional development, Dong *et al.* (Chapter 11) see the need to develop the position, authority and capability of the MEP and, to achieve this, they propose that there must be improvement in the aspects of international environmental diplomacy and cooperation, environmental and developmental comprehensive and integrated decision-making, and management of environmental social affairs. Moreover, the environmental protection agency should be further reformed through the reconstruction of the strategic objectives and goals of the environmental management system, reform of the legislative and judicial systems, adoption of reform strategies for the national environmental protection agency and cultivation of environmental protection in civil society.

Finally, Xia *et al.* (Chapter 2) assert that the relationship between economic growth and environmental protection must be transformed from one of conflict to one of coordination and integration through the coordination of economic development and environmental protection which they propose to be achieved through efforts to:

1   promote harmonious development of regional economy and environment;
2   develop circular economy and environmental protection industry;
3   optimize economic growth through environmental protection; and
4   undertake the two major adjustments at the national policy level.

First, adjustment is in the aspect of economic growth which includes policy modification, change of the growth mode that is harmful to the environment, and realization of environment-friendly economic growth. Second, adjustment is in the aspect of environmental protection which includes the implementation of relevant and existing policies, restructuring and upgrading of economic structure, technology advancement in the field of economy, and optimization of the mode of economic growth.

In sum, the Chinese panel of experts recommend substantial changes to the regulatory and institutional structure managing the PRC's economy. These changes must pursue Xia *et al.*'s declared objective of coordinated pursuit of both economic growth and environmental protection. This involves re-structuring the environmental institutions in the PRC in order to better implement the path desired by the Chinese people.

Conclusion

The conclusion of this collaboration is that the PRC must learn from the experience of this phenomenal period of growth and change. It must learn from its own experiences, as well as from those of others. Then it must make a critical choice on the nature of its path into the future.

At this juncture, it is important for the PRC to recognize the role of environmental regulation in the development of its economy. Environmental regulation should move out of the initial phase of reactive or "clean up" regulation, and move toward a more constructive phase of involvement in the industrial and institutional development of the PRC. This implies new levels of public and institutional engagements to provide the means for effective regulation.

First, there should be informed environmental regulation through citizen participation, and an accumulated understanding of the social and economic conflicts inherent in the growth process. This means that regulation must perform the important role of resolving conflicts between competing uses and users of important resources. This also implies openness in information and efficiency in standard making through citizen participation.

After determining well-informed standards, regulation must then establish well-coordinated institutions of governance capable of monitoring for and enforcing these standards. These institutions will be informed through the several criteria tackled in this volume: local–central coordination for implementation, secondary enforcement by central authorities or individual actions, and funding-based incentives for local implementation. The core of effective regulation is a more coordinated and integrated governmental structure, capable of providing incentives and information throughout the entire regulatory institution.

In sum, the path toward a brighter future for the PRC requires that environmental regulation incorporate some new institutions and ideas. Most importantly, environmental regulation must be proactive and future-oriented in order to provide this path. Effective regulation is based on solid governance and well-conceived institutional reform. The objective of this publication has been to shine a little light upon that path.

Index